MALCOLM SWANSTON & ALEXANDER SWANSTON

AIR WARFARE
ILLUSTRATED ATLAS
FROM WORLD WAR I TO THE PRESENT DAY

This edition published in 2025

First published in 2019

Copyright © 2025 Amber Books Ltd.

Published by Amber Books Ltd
United House
North Road
London N7 9DP
United Kingdom
www.amberbooks.co.uk
Instagram: amberbooksltd
Facebook: amberbooks
Twitter: @amberbooks
Pinterest: amberbooksltd

All rights reserved. With the exception of quoting brief passages for the purpose of review no part of this publication may be reproduced without prior written permission from the publisher. The information in this book is true and complete to the best of our knowledge. All recommendations are made without any guarantee on the part of the author or publisher, who also disclaim any liability incurred in connection with the use of this data or specific details.

ISBN: 978-1-83886-494-1

Editorial & design: Amber Books Ltd

Printed in Malaysia

PICTURE & ILLUSTRATION CREDITS:
All maps and illustrations courtesy of Red Lion Media, except pages 217 & 218, courtesy Patrick Mulrey

All photographs courtesy of Art-Tech/Aerospace except:
Air Portraits: 100 bottom
AirSeaLand Images: 159, 170 top
BAE Systems: 92 top
Boeing: 90, 91
British Airways: 77 bottom
Bibliotek fur Zeitgesch: 50 left
Charles Brown: 111, 113, 114
Bundesarchiv: 37, 46, 50 right, 82
Corbis: 119, 141, 143
Creative Commons: 47
Fleet Air Arm Museum: 29, 79 top
Flight International Archives: 16
Getty Images: 219 (Global Images Ukraine)
Imperial War Museum: 36, 40, 41, 44, 50, 51, 66, 140, 146 top, 155, 190
Library of Congress: 11, 12, 14, 68 top, 74
MacClancy Collection: 139
Musee de L'Air: 21
Public Domain: 15, 18, 30, 32, 34, 43, 57, 68, 70, 75, 103, 104, 122, 157
Private Collection: 27, 28, 80 top
RAF Museum: 54
Red Lion Media: 42 top left, 43 top right, 64, 70 bottom
Rolls Royce: 73, 92 bottom, 93 top
Smithsonian Institution: 77 top
US Air Force: 78, 149, 178, 179, 194, 201 bottom
US Department of Defense: 216
US Naval Historical Centre: 132 top
US Navy: 72, 79 bottom, 127
Alfred R. Ward: 10

CONTENTS

INTRODUCTION	6
EARLY AVIATION	10
EARLY AIR FORCES: 1914–18	18
AIRSHIPS: 1914–18	30
FIGHTERS: 1914–18	40
BOMBERS: 1916–18	56
AMERICA MOBILIZES: 1917	64
FINAL BATTLES: 1918	66
THE INTER-WAR YEARS	70
EMPIRE OF THE AIR	76
SEABORNE AVIATION	78
BIRTH OF THE LUFTWAFFE	80
SPANISH CIVIL WAR: 1936–39	84
JAPANESE WAR IN CHINA: 1937–41	88
CLIPPERS: LONG RANGE TRANSPORT 1934–39	90
ANGLO-FRENCH REARMAMENT	92
THE WORLD'S AIR FORCES: 1939	94
INTRODUCTION TO BLITZKREIG: Poland 1939	96
SCANDINAVIA: Finland 1939–40	98
SCANDINAVIA: Denmark and Norway 1940	100
INVASION OF THE WEST: 1940	102
THE BATTLE OF BRITAIN: June–October 1940	106
BOMBING: Britain and Germany 1940–41	110
MARITIME AIR PATROL: 1940–41	112
THE MEDITERRANEAN: 1940–42	114
THE BALKANS: The Fall of Crete	118
BARBAROSSA AND THE BOMBING OF MOSCOW	120
PEARL HARBOR: December 1941	124
FALL OF SOUTHEAST ASIA: 1942	128
THE BATTLE OF THE CORAL SEA: 1942	130
THE BATTLE OF MIDWAY: 1942	132
THE CAUCASUS AND SOUTHERN RUSSIA: 1942	136
STALINGRAD: 1942–43	138
AVIATION INDUSTRIES AT WAR	140
GUADALCANAL: 1943	142
OPERATION CARTWHEEL	144
BOMBING GERMANY: 1942–44	146
TARGET BERLIN: 1944	150
NORTH AFRICA AND THE MEDITERRANEAN	152
SICILY AND SOUTHERN ITALY	154
EASTERN FRONT: 1943 Soviet Initiative	156
KURSK: 1943	158
UKRAINE AND THE CRIMEA	160
CARRIERS IN THE PACIFIC	162
'THE MARIANAS TURKEY SHOOT'	164
THE ISLAND-HOPPING CAMPAIGN	166
CLOSING THE GAP: Patrolling the Atlantic	168
D-DAY: The Assault	170
D-DAY: The Aftermath	172
MARKET GARDEN AND VARSITY: 1944–45	174
SOUTHEAST ASIA: 1944–45	176
CHINA: 1941–45	178
BAGRATION AND THE LIBERATION OF WEST USSR	180
SPECIAL OPERATIONS: Partisan Support	182
THE END OF THE REICH	184
B-29: Development and Deployment	186
NUCLEAR WAR	190
THE POST-WAR WORLD	192
BERLIN AIRLIFT	194
KOREA: 1950–53	196
WORLD REALIGNMENT	198
THE CUBAN MISSILE CRISIS	200
INDOCHINA AND VIETNAM	202
ARAB–ISRAELI WARS	206
THE FALKLANDS WAR	212
CRISIS IN THE GULF	214
AFGHANISTAN	217
RUSSIA–UKRAINE WAR	218
INDEX	221

Introduction

INTRODUCTION

*EARLY BOMBING
Bomb aiming technology at the beginning of World War I was somewhat basic. Improvements were rapid, but bombloads remained relatively small during the conflict.*

Gunpowder may have transformed the battlefield, but the aircraft transformed war itself. The invention and development of the aircraft has had a profound effect on both combatants and civilians. Soon after the first successful flights in the early 20th century, visionaries had predicted the potential of air power to revolutionize warfare. H.G. Wells' novel *The War in the Air* of 1907 saw the great powers deploying vast fleets of aircraft in a global war. In reality the evolution of air power has been even more remarkable.

Lighter-than-air observers
The deployment of simple balloons offered a never-before-seen perspective of the battlefield. These innovative craft were deployed in the French revolutionary wars and during the US Civil War and their use continued through World War I. However, the balloon's inherent lack of control restricted its effectiveness other than the ability to see over the land-bound horizon.

With the development of the airship, a rigid or semi-rigid gas balloon powered by engines, reconnaissance could be carried out behind the enemy's front line. An airship could be steered in whichever direction the commander desired, albeit at a limited speed. It was an airship that made the first use of air-delivered weaponry in Libya during the Italo-Turkish War of 1911.

It was with the development of controllable, heavier-than-air craft that military aviation began to fulfil its promise, as imagined by writers and the more gifted military thinkers of the day. When the Wright Flyer first flew in 1903, it failed to attract military interest in its homeland, the United States of America. However, other great powers, led by France, took a keen interest. Six years later the crossing of the English Channel by Louis Blériot in 1909 clearly demonstrated the dynamic and strategic possibilities offered by aircraft.

Dynamic possibilities
Five years later, in August 1914, the world was at war. At the start of World War I, aircraft were initially only used in a reconnaissance role. Now the deployment and lines of supply, which revealed the intentions of the enemy, could be clearly viewed and mapped. In order to counter this development, pilots began to arm themselves, firstly with revolvers and rifles, then with machine guns, in order to destroy their opposite numbers and deny their enemy the same information. Improved machines that were faster and could fly higher took to the air, some dedicated to the destruction of the enemy. It became clear that the best way to shoot down another aeroplane was to simply point the aggressor aircraft straight at its target and fire a fixed forward-facing machine gun. This was easy with a pusher machine, with the engine behind the pilot, but with a tractor aircraft – with its engine at the front – the

*BIGGER AND BETTER
The Handley Page Type O/400 entered service with the RAF towards the end of World War I. This long-range bomber could carry up to 750kg (1650lb) of bombs.*

Introduction

propeller arc was in the line of fire. This problem was solved most effectively by the Dutch aircraft manufacturer Anthony Fokker, who developed interrupter gear to enable the gun to be synchronized with the propeller, thus allowing it to fire through its arc. The truly effective fighter aircraft was born.

Total war

As aircraft grew larger and more capable, most combatant forces developed some sort of strategic bombing element. The German bomber arm regularly flew heavier-than-air missions alongside their Zeppelin airships. These raids rarely made any real physical impact but the psychological blow was huge. No individual at home now seemed safe from the violence of war. Total war was born.

Within the four terrible years of World War I, the aircraft had developed from a tool of tactical air reconnaissance to the ultimate strategic weapon, soaring far above land armies and armoured fleets to destroy the industrial and emotional heart of the enemy, destroying its means to make war. The theory of the long-range bomber as the most effective weapon of war had taken root.

In the years following World War I, military aviation inevitably slowed its pace of evolution. However, in the civilian sphere aircraft were pushed to the limits in terms of range and altitude. Aircraft could now cover the vast oceans, making the world a smaller place and linking the widespread colonial possessions of Imperial powers.

Terrifying threat

During the 1930s, as long-range aircraft developed, it seemed that nowhere on earth was beyond reach. People viewed the air threat much as they did the nuclear threat decades later. Among the wars fought between 1920 and 1939, the Spanish Civil War was the proving ground in which theories of air power were introduced and tested. The bomber was still seen as important, but many believed it was best used in a tactical role in support of ground troops. The Spanish Civil War was also the first conflict to see the use of all-metal monoplane aircraft, with Republican Polikarpov I-16s taking on Nationalist Messerschmitt Bf 109s in high-speed dogfights. Both aircraft would be further refined in the coming conflict that would consume the world once more.

On 1 September 1939, Germany's new war machine smashed through its border with Poland. The Luftwaffe's medium bombers paved the way, while the fighter wings established air superiority by destroying the opposition in the air and on

RAF TRAINING
A squadron of British Hawker Hurricane pilots are briefed before a training sortie prior to the outbreak of World War II.

the ground. The ubiquitous Junkers Ju 87 'Stuka' would also play a major role as flying artillery. These elements, combined efficiently with ground troops, made for a rapid victory. *Blitzkrieg* (Lightning War) had arrived. This chain of events would be repeated across Norway, the Low Countries and France.

The Battle of Britain in the summer of 1940 proved that a strong fighter defence, radar, and an efficient command and control system, could successfully provide an effective defence against a bomber offensive.

QUICK TURNAROUND
An SC500 bomb is quickly loaded onto a Heinkel He 111 by Luftwaffe ground crew on the Eastern Front.

Introduction

AMERICAN MUSCLE
This P-51D of the 374th Fighter Squadron is pictured on a ground attack mission, carrying a pair of 2,226kg (500lb) bombs.

Britain's RAF might have fought off the medium bombers of the Luftwaffe, but it would take the additional involvement of its US allies to bring the war to the German homeland day and night. Following the Japanese attack on Pearl Harbor in Hawaii, bringing the USA into the war, the USAAF and the RAF bomber forces flew day and night missions to bomb key targets in Nazi-occupied Europe. The accepted theory was that the bombing of German production centres would disrupt the enemy war effort. Although destruction was widespread in German's cities and heartlands, it did not bring about a total collapse or reduce the frontline soldier's will to fight, as many had predicted.

In the Far East, the potential of Naval aviation was proven with the surprise attack on Pearl Harbor. By lucky chance the US Navy's aircraft

RECORD-BREAKING SPYPLANE
The SR-71 Blackbird supersonic reconnaissance aircraft remains the fastest air-breathing aircraft ever, despite being retired from service in 1998.

Introduction

carriers were absent at the time. It would be these same aircraft carriers that provided the core of American resurgence in the Pacific.

Tactical bombing, especially when in conjunction with forward observers on the ground, grew to be particularly successful and proved itself very effective, from the open plains of western Russia to the hedgerows of Normandy in 1944 and the final Allied advances in Europe and Asia.

Speed and devastating power

By the close of World War II, aviation had changed spectacularly. The new jet aircraft could now reach speeds in excess of 800kph (500mph), missiles could be launched at cities hundreds of miles away, and just a single atomic bomb could almost wipe a city off the face of the earth. Air power, particularly the bomber, was back on the agenda, at least until replaced by long-range missiles.

With suspicion and mistrust growing between the two former allies of Soviet Russia and the USA, the world entered into a 'Cold War' from which it would not emerge for decades. Nuclear power deterred the two dominant powers from going into direct conflict, though this did not stop them fighting wars by proxy as America attempted to curb the growth of Communism in Korea and Vietnam. In Vietnam, air power was used both strategically and tactically, with mixed results. The bombing of north Vietnam, however, was not employed consistently enough to have a major effect. Bombing had failed to break the will of the North Vietnamese to fight on or their ability to take the war to their enemies. Without the support of the American population, and with an enemy willing to put up with terrible hardships for its political goals, the US efforts in Vietnam came to nothing.

Air power today

Air power remains at the forefront of modern warfare. In Afghanistan, attack aircraft and bombers are still called upon by ground forces for support, just as in World War II. Ground offensives are supplemented and informed by improved reconnaissance, much as they were during World War I. This time the machines are likely to be unmanned, and are armed with ever-improving, sophisticated weaponry.

Air power, it seems, cannot win a war single-handedly, although it can have an enormous impact. For the foreseeable future, troops will still be called upon to occupy and control the ground in any conflict. In today's wars, commanders can deploy aircraft equipped with an array of sensors that can clearly see over hilly terrain and can deliver precision-guided munitions without risking the life of a live pilot.

This book explores how, in a startlingly short time, the aeroplane came to dominate military events and, to some extent, all of our lives.

BOMBING VIETNAM
Led by a B-66 Destroyer, a flight of F-105 Thunderchiefs releases its bombs over a North Vietnamese target.

SHOW OF DOMINATION
A flight of Israeli F-15 Eagles overflies the ancient fortress at Masada.

9

Early Aviation

EARLY AVIATION

The concept of flight has enthralled the human mind for centuries. From before the time hot-air balloons were first developed in China around the second century AD, humans strove to conquer the air. This goal was eventually realized in the latter part of the nineteenth century, when a new generation of inventors and designers utilized new materials and especially new powerplants based on the internal combustion engine. Before the aeroplane came into its own, however, lighter-than-air craft provided the first means of controllable flight.

Up, up and away …
Serious work began in the late eighteenth century, with a series of hot-air balloon designs. In 1783, the first successful recognized flight by humans took place in Paris. A hot-air balloon piloted by Jean-François Pilâtre de Rozier and François Laurant d'Arlandes flew – or, more correctly, drifted – some eight kilometres (five miles). Designed by the Montgolfier brothers, it was kept aloft by heat from a wood fire and had no means of steering. Work continued on developing a steerable balloon, or airship. Frenchman Henri Giffard designed and built a steam-powered dirigible balloon, which he successfully flew in 1852, flying a distance of 24km (15 miles). In 1884, the electric-powered *La France*, produced under the auspices of the French Army, made the first controlled dirigible flight, travelling a distance of eight kilometres (five miles). Most of the early airships were extremely frail and dramatically underpowered. Regular controlled flight awaited the development of lighter metal alloys and the internal combustion engine.

During this time, heavier-than-air flight was not forgotten. Sir George Cayley, Félix du Temple de la Croix, Francis Wenhan, Otto Lilienthal, Clement Ader, Samuel P. Langley – all made important contributions to aircraft as we know them today. The Wright brothers, Orville and Wilbur, famously brought to fruition their dreams of aviation. By 1903, they had installed an internal combustion engine in one of their series of gliders, and on 14 December they made what is considered by many to be the first successful sustained, controlled and manned flight. They continued to develop their 'Flyers' until confident of achieving sustained controlled flight; their persistence and vision changed the world. But first it was the time of the airships, and it was almost inevitable that they would be put to use in war.

In Revolutionary France, the Council of Public Safety, through one of its scientific commissions, recommended the use of balloons for aerial reconnaissance. In an atmosphere of secrecy, two scientific experts, Charles Coutelle and N.J. Conté, carried out a series of experiments on improved balloon designs on the outskirts of Paris. They developed existing hydrogen balloon technology into a craft that was strong enough for most weather conditions. Operated by a ground crew, it carried two passengers: one pilot and one observer. The observer's task was to report enemy troop positions and movements via a cable on which messages could be passed back and forth.

War from the air
On 29 March 1794, the first aviation group in the world, Compagnie d'Aérostiers, was formed. Its initial equipment was the hydrogen balloon *L'Entreprenant.* In June, the 'aerostiers' were deployed for action at Maubeuge, where the revolutionary army faced its Austrian enemies. At the ensuing Battle of Fleurus, Charles Coutelle and his observer, General Morlot, floated for the entire 10 hours of the engagement, providing accurate information on the disposition of the enemy forces; this gave a clear tactical advantage to the French army. On 26 June 1794, for the first time in history, aerial reconnaissance made a direct contribution to victory on the battlefield. The Austrians were to complain bitterly that the use of a balloon was 'ungentlemanly' and against the rules of warfare.

The French went on to construct three more balloons – *Intrepide*, *Hercule* and *Celeste*. Each of these was deployed with its own set of ground crew on various battle fronts from 1795–96. Napoleon was persuaded to take the Compagnie d'Aérostiers on his Egyptian Campaign in 1797; however, its deployment was mismanaged and the British were able to destroy the French balloons. On his return to France in 1799, Napoleon disbanded the 'aerostiers', effectively ending French interest in balloons and aviation for more than 40 years.

By 1849 the Austrians had changed their view on the use of balloons in warfare. While defending the Austrian empire's interests in northern Italy, they launched 200 pilotless bomb-carrying hot-air

U.S. CIVIL WAR OBSERVATION BALLOON
From November 1861, a converted coal barge, the G.W. Parke Custis, was used to tow the Union Army's balloons along the Potomac River. The balloon Washington, *seen here, was used in support of General George B. McClellan's Peninsula Campaign in May and June 1862, notably at the Battle of Seven Pines.*

10

balloons, each fitted with a bomb released by a time fuse. The deployment went badly wrong, however, when the wind changed direction, sending the balloons over Austrian lines. The idea was abandoned, until revived by the Japanese 95 years later, during World War II. They launched high-altitude balloons from Japan to be carried by the little-understood jet stream to the west coast of the United States; this was also a failure.

At the outbreak of the American Civil War, the country's balloonists and scientists were keen to contribute to the war effort. After considering various proposals, the Federal Government appointed Professor Thaddeus Lowe Chief Aeronaut of the Union Army's Balloon Corps. One of the first assignments was assisting the Army's Topographical Engineers in mapmaking. The extra altitude enabled major improvements in the quality of the army's maps, especially when combined with photography. The Balloon Corps also took part in various engagements, notably at Fair Oaks, Sharpsburg, Vicksburg and Fredericksburg. During one particular engagement, the balloon *Eagle*, under Professor Lowe's direction, ascended from Fort Corcoran, Virginia, and observed the nearby Confederate encampment. Using a series of predetermined flag signals, Lowe directed fire onto the Confederate positions until it landed accurately on target. This was probably the first use of a forward artillery observer and, as such, revolutionized artillery use.

Meanwhile, French interest in air warfare revived. During the Franco-Prussian War of 1870–71, Prussian-led German forces surrounded Paris. During what became a lengthy siege, several French aeronauts suggested the use of balloons to communicate with the rest of unoccupied France. On 23 September Jules Durouf, professional aeronaut, took off from the Place St Pierre in Montmartre in his balloon, *La Neptune*, loaded with 103kg (227lb) of letters. He landed safely some three hours later well behind Prussian siege lines, near Château de Craconville. This balloon, like the others that followed, drifted whichever way the wind was blowing; the objective was simply to cross enemy lines. Its success resulted in a building frenzy. Eventually 66 balloons were built and launched, and 58 landed safely; they carried two million pieces of mail, 102 people, more than 500 pigeons and five dogs. Trained to return to Paris carrying packages of microfilm, none of the canines managed to make it back to its master. The most famous escape was a minister of the new French Government, Leon Gambetta, on 7 October 1870. Landing behind German lines with the aid of his chief assistant Charles Louis de Saulces de Freycinet, he made his way to unoccupied France to establish a provisional capital at the city of Tours.

LZ 1
The LZ 1, seen here during its trials over Lake Constance, was the first of a long series of airships built by Count Zeppelin. It made its third and last flight on 21 October 1900, and was broken up soon afterwards.

After the war, the balloonists' contributions led to a Commission des Communications Aériennes, which in turn recommended the establishment of a permanent military aeronautical branch, set up three years later. Other countries quickly followed suit: Great Britain in 1879, Germany in 1884 and Austria-Hungary in 1893. Russia soon founded an aeronautical training school near St Petersburg.

The rise of the Zeppelin
Count Ferdinand von Zeppelin, as part of his career in the German army, had served as an observer in the Union Army Balloon Corps in 1863. During the Franco-Prussian War, he witnessed the successful French use of balloons. Convinced of the potential of lighter-than-air aviation, Zeppelin founded his own company. Construction of his first airship, *Luftschiff Zeppelin*, or LZ 1, began in 1889. It first flew on 2 July 1900. After modification, LZ 1 flew again in October of the same year, yet despite being faster and more manoeuvrable than *La France*, the craft attracted little support. Zeppelin accumulated sufficient funding to construct LZ 2, but this airship was later destroyed by a storm. Undaunted, Zeppelin recovered every usable part and built LZ 3, which became a truly successful craft. By 1908 it had flown successfully 45 times over a distance of 4400km (2733 miles).

Deutsche Luftschiffahrts-AG, the world's first airline, operated Zeppelin-built airships. Thousands of people and airmail were carried on scheduled flights across Germany before World War I. The German military administration also took an interest in Zeppelin's machines and purchased LZ 3, renumbering it Z 1. Before war's outbreak, Zeppelin had built 21 reliable and competent airships.

Meanwhile, flying machines had been built and tested around the world with varying degrees of success. The age of sustained controllable powered flight was about to arrive.

Early Aviation

THE WRIGHT BROTHERS' SHORT HOP

On 17 December 1903, a cold and windy day, the Wright brothers made their first successful powered flight, with Orville at the controls. After travelling 12m (40ft), with Wilbur running alongside and holding on to a wingtip to steady the machine, the 'Flyer' rose into the air and flew a distance of 37m (120ft) into a wind gusting up to 43kph (27mph); the flight lasted just 12 seconds.

The year 1903 seems to have been a remarkable one for aviation. Richard Pearse, a New Zealand farmer, built a monoplane aircraft that he reputedly flew on 31 March. Preston Watson reputedly flew his machine during the summer, not far from Dundee on the east coast of Scotland. Karl Jatho, from Hanover, Germany, managed a short but unstable flight in August. One name stands out in history, though – that of the Wright brothers. Wilbur and Orville Wright's flight on 17 December was witnessed, recorded and photographed, and is a clear benchmark in aviation history.

Following the success of their flight in 1903 and their later developments up to 1905, the Wright brothers gained their first orders for aeroplanes from the United States – one from the Army Signal Corps and one from a syndicate of French businessmen; both of these customers required an aeroplane capable of carrying a passenger. The 1905 model 'Flyer III' was adapted and a more powerful engine developed. The new developments were tested in an atmosphere of great secrecy at the site of their original success at Kittyhawk, North Carolina. Between 1908 and 1909, Wilbur left the United States for Europe, where he spent a year demonstrating the Wright aircraft to European governments and also to excited crowds.

A European pioneer

Europe had its own aviation experts, including Alberto Santos-Dumont. Born in Brazil, Santos-Dumont lived in France for most of his life. His interest in aviation led him to design a practical dirigible airship. He may not have made the first controlled dirigible flight – that honour having gone to Charles Renard and Arthur Krebs in 1884, when they succesfully flew *La France* – but he did achieve worldwide fame. On 19 October 1901, he confirmed that controlled flight was entirely possible when he piloted his dirigible gracefully around the Eiffel Tower over the heads of amazed Parisians.

As well as his innovative work on lighter-than-air craft, Santos-Dumont also designed and produced aircraft. It was in one of these, which he designated the *14-bis*, that he made the first European public flight of an aircraft, in Paris on 23 October 1906. Unlike the Wright brothers' early aircraft, this unlikely-looking contraption, a box-like canard machine with the mainplanes to the rear and the elevators to the front, was able to take off and land without the use of catapults, launch rails or any other assistance. Many consider his aircraft to be the most important in early aviation. In Brazil, he is still honoured as the 'father of aviation'.

Santos-Dumont pioneered the use of ailerons – surfaces on the trailing edge of the wing used to control the roll of the aircraft, which had previously been used only on gliders. He also urged – and achieved – developments in the power-to-weight ratio of aviation engines. His final designs were the 'Demoiselle' monoplane aircraft, his designation 19, 20, 21 and 22. Moving away from the box-like *14-bis*, the Demoiselle was far more conventional to the modern eye, but still extremely frail. It had a wingspan of 5.1m (16.5ft) and a length of 8m (26ft); the pilot was positioned just under the wing at the conjunction of the fuselage. The controllable tail surfaces were at the rear of the fuselage. The liquid-cooled Duthuil & Charmers engine, mounted above and to the front of the pilot, was originally rated at 20hp. The aircraft possessed outstanding performance for its day, flying at speeds of up to 100kph (62mph). Santos-Dumont continued to tinker with his Demoiselle design for several years.

Sharing knowledge

Eager to see aviation advance, Santos-Dumont released drawings of his design for free, supporting his belief that aviation heralded a new era of peace and prosperity. In 1910 the Demoiselle was flown in the United States by Roland Garros, a famous earliy aviator originally from Reunion in the Indian Ocean. In June of the same year, *Popular Mechanics* magazine published a full set of drawings. In later life, Santos-Dumont grew increasingly depressed by the use of aircraft in warfare.

While Santos-Dumont conducted most of his flying development in public, the Wright brothers

Early Aviation

preferred a degree of secrecy in an attempt to protect their series of patents. It was not until 1909 that Wilbur flew in front of a huge crowd of spectators over New York Harbor, the first public flight in his native land – the brothers had achieved celebrity status. Orders for their aircraft grew, and the brothers established aircraft factories in the United States and Europe; they also founded pilot-training schools.

Once the Wrights' aircraft were open to the public gaze, various attempts were made to copy or adapt their designs. This drew them into a series of costly and time-consuming legal battles to protect their patents. Perhaps the most famous of these was their lengthy and bitter battle with Glenn Curtiss. As part of his defence, Curtiss borrowed Samuel Langley's unsuccessful 'Aerodrome' aircraft from the Smithsonian Institute, intending to prove that the 'Aerodrome' could have successfully flown before the Wright 'Flyer'. He spent so much time and effort getting the doubtful machine airborne that the ploy failed. The court ruled in favour of the Wrights, causing enduring feelings of bitterness between the brothers and the Smithsonian.

Meanwhile, the Wrights' 'Military Flyer' had been developed, and on 14 May 1908 it made what is now accepted as the world's first two-person aircraft flight. The world's first passenger was Charlie Furnas. Later that year, Thomas Selfridge became the first person to be killed in a powered aircraft accident, when Orville crashed his two-person aircraft near Fort Myer in Virginia.

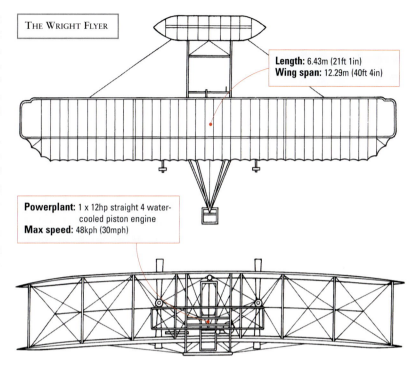

THE WRIGHT FLYER
The Flyer's pilot lay prone on the lower wing, operating the elevator by rocking a small lever with his left hand. He controlled the warping of the wings and the rudder by moving his body from side to side.

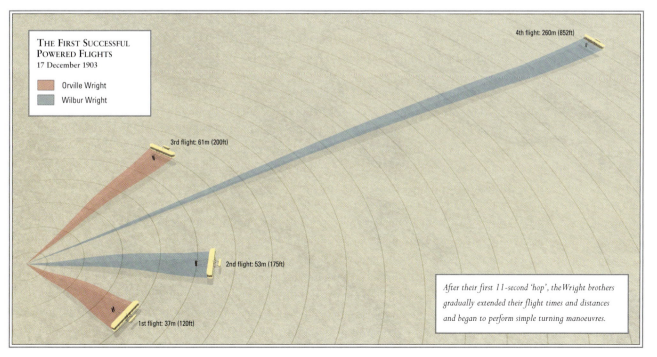

After their first 11-second 'hop', the Wright brothers gradually extended their flight times and distances and began to perform simple turning manoeuvres.

Early Aviation

LOUIS BLÉRIOT
Louis Blériot – who had been building experimental aircraft since 1908 – exhibited three of his designs at the Salon de l'Automobile et de l'Aéronautique, Paris, in December 1908. It was the third machine, the Blériot XI, that was destined to make Blériot's reputation, and his fortune.

In Europe, Louis Blériot had been forging ahead with his plans to fly the English Channel and claim the £1000 offered by the London *Daily Mail*. Blériot had studied engineering at the École Centrale Paris, after which he founded a successful business producing headlights for automobiles. Using some of the money generated by his business, he began to invest in aircraft design and construction. By 1900, he had tested an 'ornithopter' – unfortunately, it failed to take off. Undeterred, he went on to develop several unstable aircraft designs. After experimentation with various forms, he eventually created the world's first successful monoplane: the Blériot V. This particular model was still unstable in flight; however, by 1909, he had developed the Blériot XI, a far more stable and reliable model.

Cross-Channel rivals

The £1000 prize had attracted two other rivals. The first, Hubert Latham, was originally favourite to win. On 19 July, taking off from Sangatte near Calais, France, Latham's aircraft, an Antoinette IV, developed engine trouble just 9.6km (6 miles) short of Dover in England; he was forced to ditch into the sea. He was rescued promptly and, as soon as he dried out, was on his way to Paris to order a replacement Antoinette; however, it was not delivered to his Sangatte site before Blériot was ready for his own attempt.

Blériot's second rival was a Russian aristocrat of French extraction, Charles de Lambert. Badly injured in a preparatory test flight, he was forced to withdraw from the competition. Blériot had also suffered injury on a test flight, when a petrol line ruptured, catching fire and badly burning one of his feet. He decided, as ever, to persevere.

His aircraft, a Blériot XI, weighed in at 300kg (661lb), excluding the pilot, and was powered by a 25-hp Anzani three-cylinder air-cooled semi-radial engine driving two bladed propellers of just over 2m (6ft 2in) in diameter. It had a wingspan of 7.8m (25ft 7in) and a length of 8m (26ft 3in).

As dawn broke on 25 July 1909, the French Navy deployed a destroyer in mid-Channel to observe and assist if necessary. At 4.35 a.m., after running his engine briefly, Blériot took off from Calais and flew out over the sand dunes heading northwestwards. Later the pilot remembered:

> *Ten minutes have gone. I have passed the destroyer, and I turn my head to see whether I am proceeding in the right direction. I am amazed. There is nothing to be seen, neither the destroyer, nor France, nor England. I am alone. I can see nothing at all. For ten minutes I am lost. It is a strange position, to be alone, unguided, without compass, in the air over the middle of the Channel. My hands and feet rest lightly on the levers. I let the aeroplane take its own course. And then, 20 minutes after I have left the French coast, I see the cliffs of Dover, the castle, and a way to the*

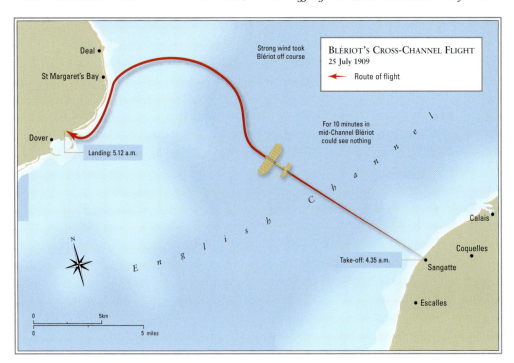

BLÉRIOT'S CROSS-CHANNEL FLIGHT
Louis Blériot completed his cross-Channel flight more by luck rather than expert navigation.

Early Aviation

west the spot where I had intended to land. What can I do? It is evident that the wind has taken me out of my course ... I press the lever with my foot and turn towards the west. Now, indeed, I am in difficulties, for the wind here by the cliffs is much stronger, and my speed is reduced as I fight against it ... I see an opening in the cliff. Although I am confident that I can continue for an hour and a half, that I might indeed return to Calais, I cannot resist the opportunity of making a landing on this green spot ... I enter the opening and find myself again over dry land. Avoiding the red buildings on my right, I attempt a landing, but the wind catches me. I stop my motor and the machine falls.

Blériot had landed on English soil 36 minutes after his departure, smashing the propeller and the undercarriage in the process. The effect was immediate. The author H.G. Wells wrote:

... in spite of our fleet this is no longer from the military point of view an inaccessible island.

The effect on Blériot was less startling. He enjoyed a celebratory lunch with his wife, then returned to France by boat. The *Daily Mail* had different plans. Under the terms of the £1000 prize, Blériot was required to return to England and enjoy a lavish dinner at the Savoy Hotel, a guest of the *Daily Mail*. Barely had he digested his feast when the French newspaper *Le Matin* hauled him back to Paris, where they had displayed his aircraft at their offices before crowds of amazed and very proud citizens. France had confirmed its world lead in aviation.

Those magnificent men ...

Nothing could quite surpass the cross-Channel flight in the popular imagination, but the first aviation event, held near Reims from 22–29 August 1909, was nonetheless a great public testing ground that proved just how far aviation had come in the mere six years from the Wright brothers' flight. For seven days, in front of a crowd 200,000-strong, the Grande Semaine d'Aviation de la Champagne flew nine different types of aircraft piloted by 23 of the best aviators of the day competing for glittering prizes. Two pilots came from abroad – George Cockburn from Britain and Glenn Curtiss from the United States – but it was the French aviators that the huge crowds had flocked to see. Spectators were delivered to the plain of Bétheny by a specially constructed branch line from the main railway station in Reims. This was the big show. Scattered among the throng were VIPs such as the ex-President of the United States Teddy Roosevelt and the British politician David Lloyd George. Among the crowd, ominously perhaps, was a large number of high-ranking military officers, eager to see what could be made of these innovative machines.

Bad weather grounded the aircraft at first, but towards the end of the opening day flights began. Some lucky people were taken aloft to experience the novelty of flight as a passenger. Among them was Englishwoman Gertrude Bacon. She was not the first woman to fly – that feat had gone to Thérèse Peltier in July 1899 – but it certainly caused a stir among the spectators. Gertrude later exclaimed:

The ground was rough and hard, and as we tore along ... I expected to be jerked and jolted. But the motion was wonderfully smooth and then, suddenly, there was a new indescribable quality, a lift! a lightness! a life!

There were plenty of incidents to keep the crowd on edge. The most serious involved the cross-Channel champion, Blériot, when his type XII machine caught fire – a ruptured fuel line again. He managed to land his burning machine, walking away with no more than singed pride. All of the machines on display were frail and fitted with unreliable engines, the curse of powered flight for years to come. But for now they faced three major tests: speed, altitude and distance.

The distance prize, the Grand Prix de la Champagne, was won by Henri Farman, who flew a distance of 180 km (112 miles). The crowd watched, becoming more and more excited as he flew for more than three hours around a fixed circuit. Both Henri Farman's aircraft and the crowd overheated. The police were growing concerned – public order was getting out of control – when he ran out of fuel and landed. The speed prize was put up by the newspaper publisher Gordon Bennett. This test came down to two finalists: the American Glenn Curtiss, in his 'Reims Racer', and Blériot, in one of his own machines. In a very close final, Curtiss won by a narrow six seconds at an average speed of 75kph (47mph). The Stars and Stripes fluttered over the heads of a disappointed French crowd. Finally, in the high-altitude test, Hubert Latham, the same man who had challenged Blériot's cross-Channel ambitions, achieved the dizzy height of 180m (508ft); most aviators flew at around 20 m (60 ft) off the ground.

GLENN CURTISS
On 30 June, 1910, pioneer American aviator Glenn H. Curtiss dropped dummy bombs from a height of 15m (50ft) in an area representing the shape of a battleship marked by buoys on Lake Keuka, New York. It was an early demonstration of the aircraft's potential as a war machine.

Early Aviation

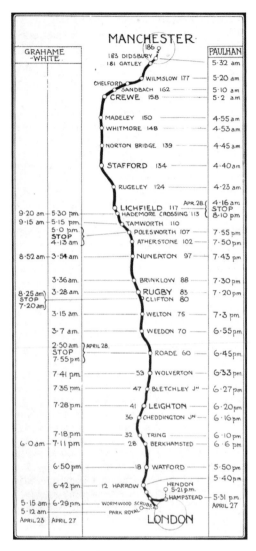

AIR RACE CHART
This graphic from 1910 shows the route and timings of the two air racers, Claude Graham-White and Louis Paulhan, on their London to Manchester race. Despite taking off in the dark to make up lost time after a forced landing due to a mechanical fault, Claude Graham-White was easily beaten by Louis Paulhan.

Interest in aviation was expanding. Aviation meetings and competitions sprang up across Europe. One of the most famous competitions was again sponsored by the *Daily Mail*, the London to Manchester air race, which was flown in April 1910. The two contenders were Louis Paulhan, from France, and Claude Grahame-White, from England; they competed for a massive £10,000 prize. The weather was typical of an English spring: rain and wind. But, on the early evening of the 27th, there was a break in the conditions. The Frenchman got away first, with Grahame-White in hot pursuit. Both were flying Farman-built biplanes. At this time, pilots on cross-country flights generally followed railway lines from town to town. Paulhan and his team had thoughtfully hired a special train, which he followed northwards from London. Grahame-White also followed the railway lines; his support team followed in a squad of automobiles. Crowds flocked around newspaper offices in Manchester, London and Paris eager for news of the race's progress. As night fell, both pilots made a safe landing alongside the railway tracks. In 1910 night flying was unknown. Grahame-White decided to take off by moonlight, his only hope of overtaking the Frenchman. But his bravery counted for nothing. Paulhan took off at first light and, following his special train, reached Manchester at 5.32 a.m. on the 28th, spending 4 hours and 18 minutes in the air. The Parisian crowds were ecstatic. Once again, French aviation had taken a key prize.

Dogged determination

Meanwhile, in the United States, air frenzy was not quite as intense as in Europe. Still, several large meetings were held, including those at Boston; Belmont Park, New York; and Los Angeles. A glittering $50,000 prize was put up by the newspaper publisher William Randolph Hearst for the first successful coast-to-coast flight across the United States. The challenge was eventually taken up in September 1911 by Calbraith Perry Rodgers, a former college football star. Equipped with the Wright 'Flyer', he was supported along the way by a specially hired train. Rodger's flight was a catalogue of disasters. It took him 49 days to reach California, during which time he crashed 19 times. In his last crash, just 14.5km (9 miles) short of California, he broke both legs and a collarbone. From his hospital bed, he announced his determination to 'finish that flight'. While he recovered in hospital, his support team lovingly rebuilt his aircraft – only a rudder and two wing struts remained from the aircraft that had set off from Sheepshead Bay, New York, on 17 September. Leaving hospital, he took off for the final leg of his epic journey, finally reaching Long Beach, California, 84 days after leaving New York. Unfortunately, he had failed to qualify for the prize money, but his backers, the Armour Company of Chicago, producers of the carbonated drink Vin Fiz, after which his aeroplane was named, had enjoyed 84 days of free publicity while the national press followed Rodgers' 'record-breaking' adventure.

Records continued to be made. At the Belmont Park meeting in October 1910, Claude Grahame-White, this time flying a Blériot monoplane powered by a 100hp Gnome rotary engine, flew at an average speed of 98kph (61mph) and took the Gordon Bennett speed prize, now an annual event. In Europe, Jorge Chávez, a French flier of Peruvian extraction, was attracted by a prize offered by the Aero Club of Milan for the first crossing of the Alps.

Early Aviation

In 1911 Chávez flew from the Swiss town of Brig in a Blériot XI, heading for the Simplon Pass, which rises to a height of 2013m (6600ft). Navigating by a special beacon at the top of the pass, he slowly gained altitude and flew over the Simplon with 30m (100ft) or so to spare, while an amazed crowd looked on. Unfortunately, as his tiny machine headed down the mountainside towards the Italian town of Domodossola, it suddenly dived into the ground. Chávez was dragged from the wreck and died four days later in hospital. His heroism was acclaimed across Europe.

Increasing reliabilty

Records continued to be made – crash by crash it seemed – but slowly the aircraft became a more stable and controllable machine. Governments took more interest, as the idea of reconnaissance ahead of the army or fleet took root in many a military high command. Italy's was among these. A new state, unified from 1870, Italy had by 1910 established a small air element within its armed forces. As a counterbalance to growing French power in North Africa, Italy laid claim to the Ottoman possession of Libya. In the ensuing war, Italy's aircraft, 11 in total and all foreign-built, were used in operations in support of the army. They largely carried out reconnaissance, but on 1 November 1911 Lieutenant Guilio Gavotti dropped four grenades from his Blériot onto a Turkish position at the Oasis of Tagiura, the first bombing raid in history.

By 1912–13, European governments had become major customers for aircraft and airships. Germany led in airship production, to some extent at the expense of aircraft. Aircraft manufacturers grew with the strength of government orders. By 1914, the French Gnome Engine Company had more than 1000 employees. A sense of gearing up for war existed in Europe – air forces began to be counted in hundreds of aircraft. Not so in the United States. Without the spectre of political or military rivalry, its aviation 'industry' employed fewer than 200 people; its air force stood at 15 aircraft.

In 1912, the first Balkan War broke out. The Balkan League – Serbia, Montenegro, Greece and Bulgaria – launched a campaign against the crumbling Ottoman Empire, and the Bulgarians utilized their tiny air force against Turkish positions. The League was successful in its ambitions, but left the Balkans a tinderbox of conflicting interests.

THE ITALIAN–TURKISH WAR
Italy's declaration of war on Turkey on 29 September 1911 was followed by a naval bombardment of the Tripoli coast. In addition to raids by heavier-than-air types, on 10 March 1912, two Italian Army airships, the P.2 and P.3, carried out a reconnaissance of Turkish positions. Their crews dropped several grenades. On 13 April, during another reconnaissance mission, they remained airborne for 13 hours, their crews spotting for Italian artillery. The P.2 and P.3 were small non-rigid craft, designed by the engineer Enrico Forlanini.

Early Air Forces: 1914–1918

EARLY AIR FORCES: 1914–1918

In the early summer of 1914, Europe was a hive of military and political rivalries. In an attempt to ensure some form of security, nations and empires built alliances that crisscrossed the continent. The arthritic Austro-Hungarian Empire allied itself with the young and potent 45-year-old German Empire. France, still nursing wounds from its defeat in the

BLÉRIOT XI
In a notable mission on 14 August, 1914, Lieutenant Cesari and Corporal Prudhommeaux of France's Aéronautique Militaire, flying a Blériot XI, bombed the German airship sheds at Metz-Frescaty.

Franco-Prussian War, allied itself to the Russian Empire to the east and, in 1904, the United Kingdom to the west. Russia, for its part, considered itself the more powerful big brother of the Balkan Slavs, and as such their protector. In the early twentieth century, however, the Balkans remained a region riven with ethnic religious and political divisions. In 1878 Austria-Hungary had occupied Bosnia, and in 1908 it formally added the territory to its empire.

The shot heard around the world
On the sunny morning of 28 June 1914, a young southern Slav nationalist, Gavrilo Princip, shot and killed Archduke Franz Ferdinand, the heir presumptive to the Austro–Hungarian throne. Suspicious of Serbian involvement, in a deliberate act, Austria made unacceptable demands on Serbia. Serbia acceded to all but one, but Austria was not interested in negotiation and declared war on 28 July. In accordance with existing alliances, after some hesitancy, Russia mobilized against Austria-Hungary and Germany on 29 July. In turn, Germany declared war on Russia. After demanding the right of passage for its troops, Gemany then assumed a two-front war in accordance with the Schlieffen Plan, declaring war on France on 23 August. The Germans' actions led to the United Kingdom declaring war on Germany for violating Belgian territory. Europe – and by default, Europe's allies and possessions across the world – was at war.

A new role in the air
Armed forces across Europe mobilized for war. While soldiers and sailors could be counted in their millions, aviators were only in their hundreds. Pre-war aviation stars rushed to join their respective air services, but the armies had little use for these stunt flyers. What they wanted were reliable flyers who could cross over into enemy territory and report on deployment – reconnaissance – a role traditionally carried out by the cavalry. Therefore, a young man from a good family who was able to ride a horse was seen as providing the right stuff:

> *There was a very nice young cavalry officer who was interviewing possible candidates for the Royal Flying Corps. He noted my shoulder straps, and he said, 'Ah, you're Gloucester Yeomanry. You ride a horse?' 'Yes,' I said, 'I do.' 'Do you know where the pole star is?' he asked. 'Yes,' I said, 'I think I could find it.' 'You'll do,' he said.*
> **Frederick Winterbotham, 1914**

The aircraft to be used in this 'new' role needed to be sturdy, reliable and capable of being flown and maintained by men called up from all walks of life. Men with trade skills made up the mechanics. In the United Kingdom, for the most part, men from 'decent schools' made up the aircrews.

Almost all of the aircraft available to the warring parties in August 1914 were unarmed, although Germany did have seven airships available for action that were capable of delivering a worthwhile bomb load. Given the small numbers of aircraft and airships, they would play a surprisingly important role on the first weeks of the war. In August most military commanders expected, and planned, for a swift war with rapid movement – it would all be over by Christmas …

Early Air Forces: 1914–1918

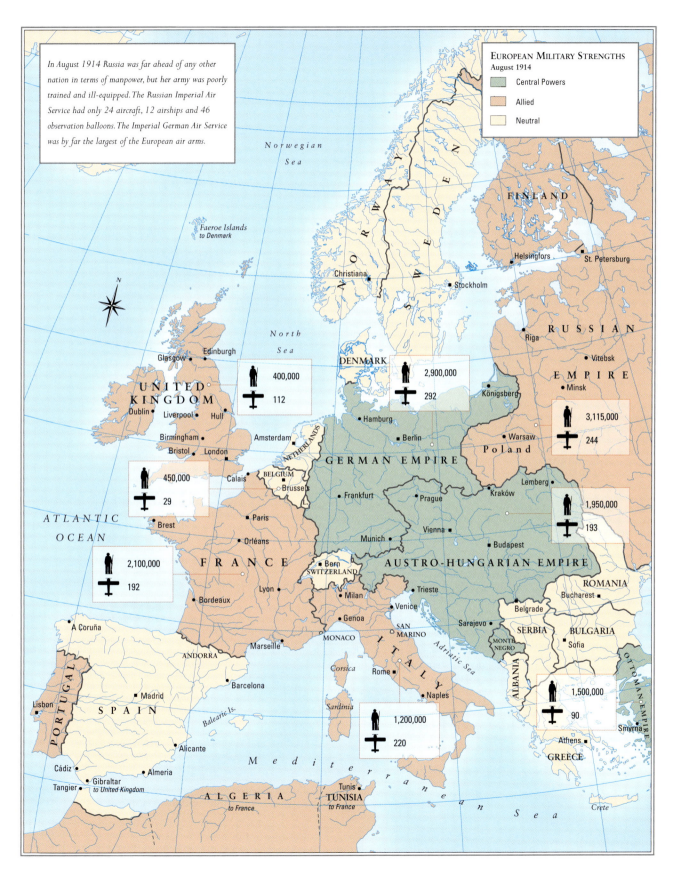

Early Air Forces: 1914–1918

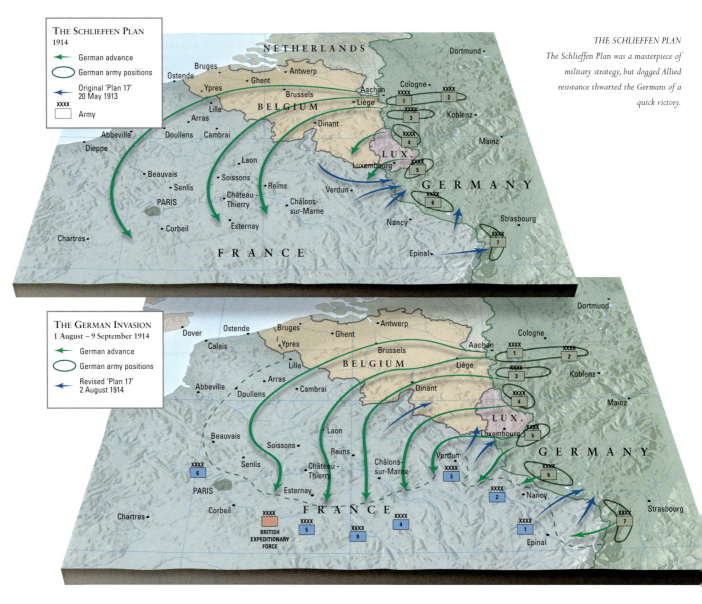

THE SCHLIEFFEN PLAN
The Schlieffen Plan was a masterpiece of military strategy, but dogged Allied resistance thwarted the Germans of a quick victory.

ALFRED VON SCHLIEFFEN
Von Schlieffen's operational plan envisaged a lightning campaign that would knock France out of the war in a matter of weeks.

Indeed the first few weeks of World War I worked out just as imagined. In the west, huge German armies marched across Belgium and into northern France. Following Field Marshal Alfred von Schlieffen's original concept, this called for huge sweep through Belgium, then on to Paris – the might of the German advance was on the right. But the advance would not stop there. It would push on, circumventing the bulk of the French field army and its static defences. If all went according to plan, everything would be over in six weeks. Germany could then turn east and finish off Russia.

The French, meanwhile, had constructed a series of fortresses along their northern and eastern borders By 1914, however, the offensive had taken the primary role in repelling the invader. The main body of the French army would attack towards Alsace-Lorraine, push the Germans back to the Rhine, then turn north, cutting German lines of supply. This was 'Plan 17'.

In accordance with this plan, the French army duly mobilized, deployed and attacked towards Alsace-Lorraine, the provinces lost to Germany in the war of 1870–71. The French field army was not well supplied with basic essentials, its maps were outdated, and reconnaissance was incomplete. The French soldiers went forwards in attack with 'elan'; however, dressed as they were in red trousers and blue tunics, they were easily seen by the grey-clad, well-sited and well-prepared defenders. The French army paid a heavy price, losing 330,000 men and gaining nothing but a toehold in Alsace.

Early Air Forces: 1914–1918

To the north and west, everything was going pretty much according to plan for the Germans. As the main First, Second, Third and Fourth armies swept through Belgium, Zeppelins operating from their base in Cologne bombed the besieged town of Liège. Rumpler Taube reconnaissance aircraft flew ahead of the advance, gathering and feeding information to German High Command. The French and their British allies were falling back all along the line; the Belgium Army was brushed aside. Battles were fought in the Ardennes, along the Sambre and Meuse, and at Mons, La Cateau and Guise. But the German plan had fundamental weaknesses: supplies and communication with High Command.

False confidence

To the Commander in Chief Helmuth von Moltke, the victories along the frontier of Alsace-Lorraine looked convincing and supported the opportunity of a double envelopment of the French army. On the extreme right wing, however, the German armies running well ahead of their slower moving supply columns. Poor communications between his field armies and headquarters served to create a picture far rosier than it actually was. As a result, Moltke ordered his Sixth and Seventh armies to prepare for a new offensive in Alsace-Lorraine, instead of backing up the big sweep to the west as originally planned. The right wing he ordered to continue its march on Paris.

Meanwhile, at the Battle of Guise, the French Fifth Army, under the command of General Charles Lanrezac, attempted to relieve pressure on the British Expeditionary Force (BEF) by attacking the German First Army's flank. The Fifth Army also attacked Germany's Second Army, whose men were fought to a standstill and called on the extreme right flank of the First Army for help. What was left of Schlieffen's original plan was about to be abandoned.

On 29 August the German armies approached Paris and the valley of the Marne. Anticipating victory, a lone German aircraft flew a circuit of the Eiffel Tower. The pilot dropped five small bombs around the Gare de l'Est, three of which failed to explode, although one bomb did kill a woman who was out shopping. A note then fluttered down from on high:

The German Army is at the gates of Paris. You can do nothing but surrender.
Lieutenant von Heldsen

HENRI FARMAN
Henri Farman (front) was the son of an English newspaper correspondent working in Paris. In 1909 Farman set up his own aircraft factory, and the Farman series of biplanes went from strength to strength, becoming the most reliable and widely-used aircraft of the period, not just in Europe but around the world.

FARMAN F.20
The Farman F.20 was used by both the British and the French at the start of World War I as an observer and light bomber aircraft. Its design was swiftly outclassed and it was withdrawn from frontline service by 1915.

Length: 9.45m (31ft)
Wing span: 16.15m (53ft)

Powerplant: 1 x 100hp Renault 8 cylinder inline engine
Max speed: 106kph (66mph)

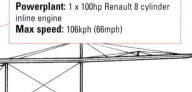

FARMAN F.20

Early Air Forces: 1914–1918

Having delivered its message, the aircraft veered northwards, back to the safety of German lines.

The French expected the Germans to arrive on the outskirts of Paris within a couple of days. Much to the French commanders' surprise, though, the German First Army turned southeastwards, away from the city. On 2 September a French aircraft, flown by Corporal Louis Breguet, reported German columns heading eastwards. More flights were ordered, and they confirmed the reports. The Commander of the Paris Garrison, General Joseph-Simon Galliéni, a strong supporter of aviation, made instant use of this vital intelligence and set into motion plans that would become known as the Battle of the Marne – the 'Miracle of the Marne'.

Turning the tide

Meanwhile, General Joffre, Commander in Chief of the French army, had called a halt to his own offensives, planning to leave just sufficient strength to guard the eastern border. He moved the bulk his of his available forces westwards towards Paris. This movement transformed the situation.

Joffre's newly formed Sixth Army was transported to the front, in part by Paris taxicabs, where it attacked the flank of the German First Army. This caused the First Army to turn westwards, facing its attackers. The French forces now counterattacked the German Second Army. A gap appeared between the two German armies, and into this gap the French and BEF began to advance. In order to save the increasingly exposed position of General Alexander von Kluck's First Army, the German commanders had no choice but to order withdrawal. This forced the German armies to fall back in line to prevent exposure of an open flank. The right wing of the German army duly fell back to the high ground above the river Aisne, and all hopes of a quick victory in the west were gone. Although the German army saw this move as a 'regrouping', after which the advance would resume, German defensive positions created on the high ground above the valley of the river Aisne were an ominous forerunner of things to come.

By late September, a trench line ran from the positions on the Aisne to the Swiss border. The Allies and the Germans glared at each other from their respective 'temporary' trenches. The only open flank was to the northwest. Each side began a series of manouevres in this direction, attempting to outflank the other, in what became rather misleadingly known as the 'race to the sea'. Both the Allies and the Germans were in fact merely trying to maintain a war of movement by outflanking each other. How this might be maintained with each combatant on the edge of its line of supply is open to question.

In the end, there was no open flank. The Belgian coast was reached with amazing speed, and a continuous line of trenches appeared,

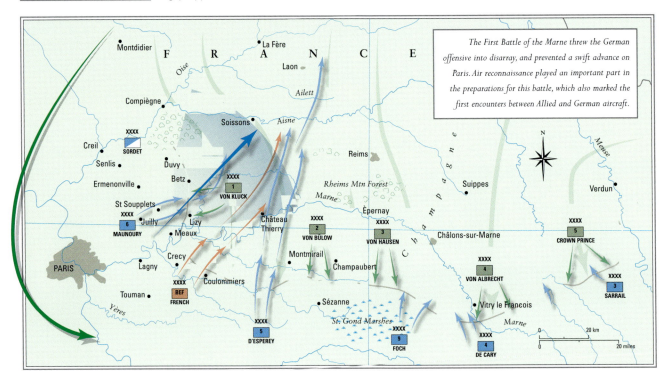

The First Battle of the Marne threw the German offensive into disarray, and prevented a swift advance on Paris. Air reconnaissance played an important part in the preparations for this battle, which also marked the first encounters between Allied and German aircraft.

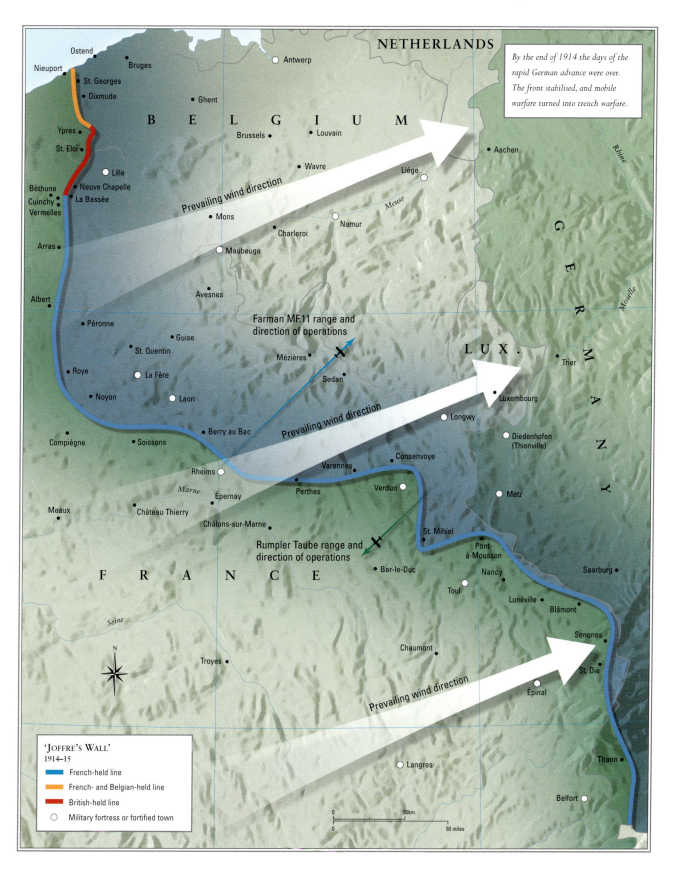

Early Air Forces: 1914–1918

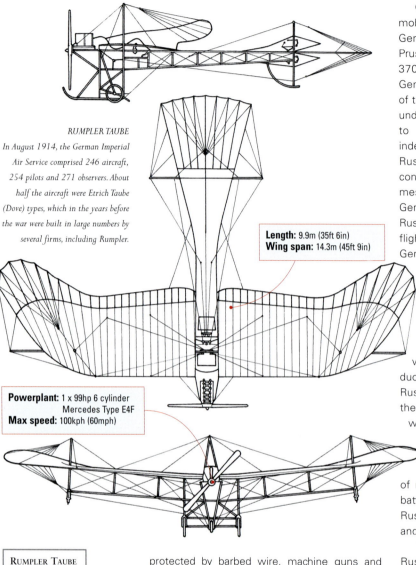

RUMPLER TAUBE
In August 1914, the German Imperial Air Service comprised 246 aircraft, 254 pilots and 271 observers. About half the aircraft were Etrich Taube (Dove) types, which in the years before the war were built in large numbers by several firms, including Rumpler.

Length: 9.9m (35ft 6in)
Wing span: 14.3m (45ft 9in)

Powerplant: 1 x 99hp 6 cylinder Mercedes Type E4F
Max speed: 100kph (60mph)

RUMPLER TAUBE

protected by barbed wire, machine guns and artillery. An unbroken line of earthworks and men was now in place from Belgium to Switzerland. The war was at a stalemate, a situation that both sides would spend the next three years trying to break. The defensive position was now the master of the battlefield; the war of manoeuvre, at least in the west, had disappeared.

Steering towards victory from the air

On both sides, the much-needed 'breakthrough' attack was a subject in all commanders' minds: punch through the enemy line, follow up with the cavalry and restore the war of manoeuvre. Yet the cavalry waited to no avail. Meanwhile, aircraft proved their worth overhead. Within a month of the Battle of the Marne, the French army ordered a doubling of its air force to 65 escadrilles.

On the eastern front, the Russian Empire mobilized its forces with greater speed than the German war plan anticipated. Closing on East Prussia were two Russian armies of some 370,000 men. Russia's First Army, under General Paul von Rennenkampf, advanced north of the Masurian Lakes, while the Second Army, under General Alexander Samsonov, advanced to the south. The armies operated independently with almost no cooperation. The Russian commanders compounded this ill-conceived operation by sending uncoded radio messages, which were eagerly interpreted by German radio operators. With some idea of the Russian plan, Rumpler Taube reconnaissance flights were organized. It was now the turn of German aviators to save the day.

The German eastern front now came under the command of the generals Paul von Hindenburg and Erich Ludendorff. Taubes overflew Russia's armies almost hourly, reporting on the numbers and direction of Russian formations. Possessed with this valuable information, the German duo set a plan in motion to deal with the two Russian armies in separate operations. First, the Russian Second Army would be dealt with, while a cavalry screen and local landstorm troops kept watch on the Russian First Army. Dealing with the invading armies separately reduced the Germans' problem of numerical disadvantage. On 26 August the battle began at Tannenberg, and very quickly Russia's Second Army was outmanoeuvred and surrounded.

The German Eighth Army killed some 30,000 Russian soldiers and captured 100,000, effectively destroying the entire Russian Second Army. Its commander, General Samsonov, unable to face the consequences of his defeat, shot himself. The Germans then changed front and marched on the Russian First Army. Rennenkampf now faced the complete strength of the German Eighth Army and had no option but to fall back into Russian territory. Eastern Germany, against the odds, was cleared of invaders. General Hindenburg simply said:

Without airmen, no Tannenberg!

SUPERIOR TACTICS
The battles of Tannenberg and the Masurian Lakes proved the superiority of German tactics and firepower over Russia's Imperial Army.

Early Air Forces: 1914–1918

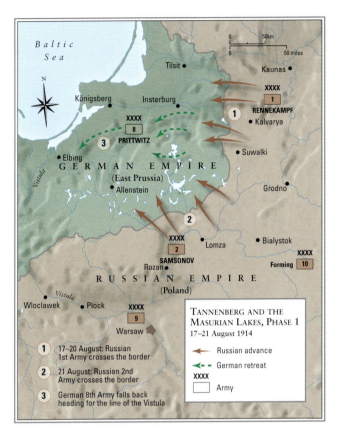
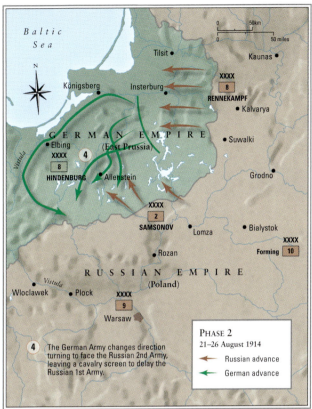
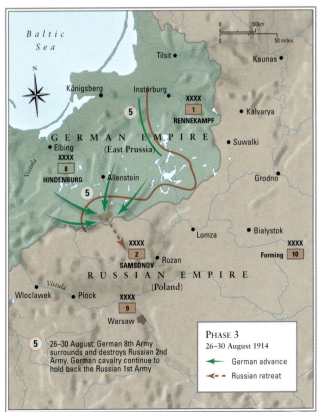
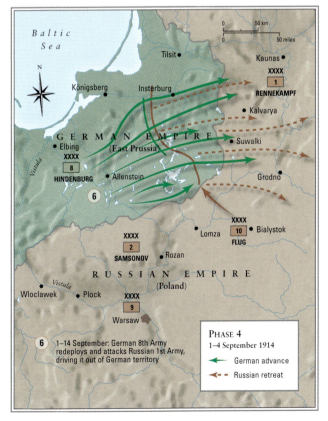

25

Early Air Forces: 1914–1918

As air forces were still in their infancy, roles and tactics were constantly evolving. And that was now the situation on the western front. Although a handful of aviators had begun to arm themselves, the concept of defending air space was a new one. Aviators supplied aerial reconnaissance to their military commanders, but at the same time needed somehow to deny the same advantage to the enemy.

To date, neither equipment nor training had allowed for the development of air-to-air combat. The prevailing view from among most army commanders was that bullets fired from two moving machines in flight was an alarming proposition. The little experimentation that had taken place pre-war did little to foster the idea of effective aerial combat.

Lt William Sholto Douglas, who one day would command the RAF Fighter Command in another world war, was flying as an observer with No. 2 Squadron in August 1914. He spotted a German aircraft, and he closed the gap between that aircraft and his own. Since both aircraft were unarmed, the respective pilots decided to wave to each other and fly on. It was clear to Douglas, however, that aircraft must be defended and the enemy denied the ability to fly over British territory. Very quickly the Royal Flying Corps (RFC) and Royal Naval Air Service (RNAS) flyers armed themselves with whatever the individual crew could get their hands on:

> *In the observer's cockpit, you had a rifle, which stood up in a little catch, so you could get it out easily. If you saw an enemy aircraft, you took this rifle out, waited for an opportunity and, if he came to within 50 to 100 yards, you let him have it as best you could. Beyond 100 yards, it was a waste of ammunition. Even close up, you seldom got him. You needed a hell of a lot of luck to hit him. If the enemy aircraft was behind you, you undid your belt, stood up and knelt on your set and watched to see where he was. You had to be very careful not to shoot any of the controls away.*
>
> **Archibald James**

On 2 October, the French Army intercepted an order to German aviators instructing them to avoid wasting time indulging in aerial combat. Some individual French aviators took a different view. A few days later, a Voisin Pusher equipped with a machine gun shot down a German two-seater. In the final months of 1914, however, the main mission of the air forces was still reconnaissance. As the battle front settled down into what would become familiar siege warfare, accurate maps were essential.

Mapping from the air

The French Government had not surveyed much of its territory since the fall of the Second Empire in 1870. Surveying the German-occupied zone meant matching up 40- or 50-year-old maps with good aerial photographs. This massive project began with observers hanging over the side, holding the camera and hanging onto the aircraft. The subsequent photographs suffered from various distortions, depending on the angle of the camera, but solutions were eventually found.

The British developed the 'A'-type camera. Initially this mahogany-encased instrument was hand-held, but was later strapped to the side of the aircraft. Six 'plates' could be exposed, each plate loaded and changed by hand while the pilot flew a straight and level course.

Artillery spotting

Meanwhile, the tethered balloon remained the major method of spotting for the artillery. These balloons were tied to the ground with cables and had telephone lines connecting them to their ground crews. They floated up to altitudes of around 900m (3000ft) and provided artillery batteries with means to control their fall of shot and indirect fire on enemy positions, out of sight of the gun crews. The hydrogen-filled balloons were highly susceptible to ground fire and later fire from aircraft. The crew were issued with parachutes from September 1914 onwards and given orders to jump on sight of enemy aircraft.

The use of radios in observation aircraft had been the object of experiment before 1914. Until early 1915, however, there were no aircraft equipped with radio or aircrew trained its use. With new maps being issued to Allied aircrews, an observer could place a clear celluloid disc on his map, on which were marked 12 slices (the 'clock code'), with slice number 12 indicating north. From the centre, a number of rings marked out 100yd (91m) intervals. The centre ring A was at 100 yards, and the rings worked sequentially through to the letter F, or 600 yards. Therefore, if a shell fell 300 yards due south of the designated target, the airborne observer sent the simple message of 'C6' to the artillery commander, who would then adjust the aim of his guns accordingly. The infantry, pushing forwards through mud and smoke, operated a prearranged series of signals in the form of panels laid out on the ground. These signals showed the infantry's exact position to the aircraft flying overhead. The observers could then inform friendly artillery of the exact position of their own infantry, thus avoiding the horrific spectre of 'friendly fire' and emphasizing the importance of these contact patrols.

Casting a forbidding shadow

The menace of the airship, the Zeppelin, loomed large, particularly in the British imagination. The German army had ordered its first airships in 1909; the German navy ordered two in 1912, both of which were lost in accidents in 1913. Despite this, replacements were ordered in an attempt to increase German fleet reconnaissance capability. The new German High Seas Fleet needed some way to assert a heavy advantage so that it could meet and surpass the challenge

WATCHER IN THE SKY
French cavalrymen look up with interest as a Breguet Br 14 reconnaissance aircraft cruises overhead. The aircraft soon replaced cavalry in the reconnaissance role.

Early Air Forces: 1914–1918

of the superior British Fleet. From the British perspective, it was the ability of airships to cruise high above the fleet and attack the British homeland that caused most concern. Popular works of fiction, such as H.G. Wells' *War in the Air*, painted lurid pictures of fleets of airships and aircraft reducing cities to ruins.

In 1911, Winston Churchill took over as First Lord of the Admiralty and had a keen interest in aviation and its potential uses. In an attempt to lessen the perceived threat of bombing by airships, a series of limited measures was taken. It was not until 3 September 1914 that Lord Kitchener, Secretary of State for War, requested of Churchill that the Admiralty take over responsibility for the United Kingdom's air defence. This handover would take time and organization, as little material was immediately available. Churchill therefore decided that the best defence was offence; striking at the sheds where the Zeppelins were housed would be the best way to prevent the enemy from bombing Britain.

Raiding the raiders

The vulnerability of airships to attack was not quite so obvious then as it is today. For some time, it was believed that the Zeppelin's inflammable hydrogen cells were surrounded by an outer cell of inert gas that would deaden the effects of incendiary bullets. As a result, the British felt that the best form of attack would be to drop bombs on the Zeppelin's home bases and their large, vulnerable sheds. The RNAS was already in position, as its Eastchurch Squadron (later No. 3 Squadron) was then based at Ostend, Belgium, assisting advance elements of the Royal Naval Division. The Squadron moved to Antwerp and, after a setback caused by bad weather, the first mission was flown on 22 September 1914. It was made up of two raids of two aircraft each, one aimed at the Germans' airship sheds at Cologne and one at Düsseldorf. Of the four British aircraft involved, only one dropped its bomb – at Düsseldorf – but missed. On 8 October, two more aircraft tried again, this time with more success: one hit its target at Düsseldorf, destroying the Zeppelin Z9.

Almost immediately after this Antwerp fell to the advancing Germans. The following month a special group of four RNAS aircraft was sent to Belfort on France's eastern border. Their objective was the heartland of the Zeppelin menace: the Luftschiffbau Works at Friedrichshafen, on the shores of Lake Constance, a round trip of some 402km (250 miles). The raid was flown on 21 November. At first it was believed that heavy damage had been inflicted, but in fact the raids achieved almost nothing – although the deep penetration of German territory did not go unnoticed. This attempt was the to be last by the RNAS on the European mainland in 1914. Its colleagues back in the United Kingdom had been hard at work on a plan to attack the German Naval Airship Division at what intelligence reports indicated to be its main base, in what would become known as the Cuxhaven Raid.

Striking from the sea

Before the war, the Royal Navy experimented with a cruiser, the *Hermes*, converting her to a seaplane carrier. She was tested thoroughly during the fleet manoeuvres of 1913, and as a result the Royal Navy ordered an uncompleted merchant ship to be converted into the world's first specialized aviation ship. Unfortunately, this work was not finished when war broke out. Quickly, however, two cross-Channel steamers – *Riviera* and *Engadine* – were acquired and underwent rudimentary conversion to seaplane carriers. They were shortly joined by another converted ship, the *Empress*.

In August 1914, the German cruiser *Magdeburg* had run aground in the Baltic Sea, and the Russians seized its three surviving code

SIGNALS CHART
Ground-to-air communication using the symbols below was laborious and inefficient, and was soon replaced by wireless telegraphy. Some of the first practical experiments with airborne wireless telegraphy were carried out during the British Army manoeuvres of 1912, when the non-rigid airships Gamma *and* Delta *transmitted signals that were received up to 56km (35 miles) away.*

Early Air Forces: 1914–1918

books, one copy of which was handed over to the British. This made planning for the Cuxhaven Raid much easier, as the code used in German navy radio signals could now be deciphered.

The attack on the airship base at Cuxhaven – the base was actually at Nordholz, 13km (8 miles) to the south – called for three seaplane carriers with three aircraft each, to be covered by carriers and destroyers of the 'Harwich Force'. Heavy units of the Grand Fleet would offer distant support. The next operation put into effect was on 23 December. The following day, more than 100 ships sailed from their bases in support – a massive effort to back the operation of just nine flimsy floatplanes. For the first time shipboard aircraft were the striking force of the fleet. At 6.59 a.m. the first seaplanes took off. Two suffered complete engine failure and were hoisted back on board. Then, between 7.10 and 8.12 a.m., British pilots reported seeing a German airship, L6, heading for Heligoland.

While British flyers were patrolling over a mist-bound German coast, German floatplanes were attacking the *Empress*, dropping eight or nine small bombs – all missed. The L6 now engaged the embattled *Empress*, dropping four 50kg (110lb) bombs; again all missed. The *Empress* returned fire, her crew armed with rifles, and the carriers HMS *Undaunted* and *Arethusa* charged to the rescue, firing shrapnel shells at the airship. The L6's commander broke off the action.

The British force resumed formation and had begun recovering its seaplanes when more German floatplanes attacked. All bombs missed their targets, some narrowly. The airship L5, from Nordholz, then appeared in the vicinity of the British force and spotted the British submarine E11 with three seaplanes surrounding her. She was taking on the crews of the three aircraft that had run short of fuel and were unable to reach the seaplane carriers. The crew of the British submarine machine-gunned the floats of the German planes, then crash-dived to escape the Zeppelin's bombs. With four seaplanes still missing, presumed lost, and the U-boats closing in and the L5 overhead, the British commander ordered withdrawal to begin. The tangible results of the operation were in the end negligible, but for the first time the major elements of offence and defence were provided by airpower.

SHORT SEAPLANE

Short Seaplane No 74, first flown in January 1914, was one of a batch of seven delivered to the Royal Naval Air Service and shared between the air stations at Grain, Kent, and Dundee.

DARING RAID

On Christmas Day 1914, the Royal Navy carried out its first combined sea and air attacks on German soil, using Short Seaplanes. The crews of all seven aircraft survived the raid.

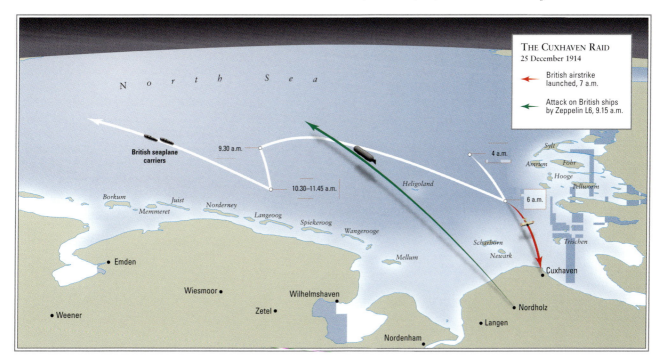

29

AIRSHIPS: 1914–1918

COUNT FERDINAND VON ZEPPELIN
When his military career was over, Zeppelin, then 52, turned his whole attention to airship design. In 1893, in collaboration with an engineer named Theodore Kober, he submitted a design for a rigid airship to the German War Ministry.

In popular memory, it is the Zeppelin – the 'monster of the purple twilight' – that dominated the skies during World War I. It began its path to fame at the hand of its creator, Count Ferdinand Adolf August Heinrich Graf von Zeppelin. As a young Oberleutnant serving in the Royal Army of the Kingdom of Württemberg before Germany was unified in 1871, Zeppelin was a sanctioned military observer during the American Civil War. Here, he admired the work of the Union Army Balloon Corps. He carried his experiences with him, and after 11 years began to put his deliberations on the use of airships on paper. Over the next decade and a half, Zeppelin championed the cause of his native Württemberg as Prussia gradually dominated the Imperial German Army. When he was forced to leave the army in 1892, his real work began.

Zeppelin had tinkered with various designs, and by 1898 had acquired the design patents for an airship designed by David Schwartz. Adding these to his own plans, he had a new airship, which he named LZ 1, ready for flight in June 1900. Months of testing and various problems followed, but in the early part of 1906 Zeppelin's second airship, LZ 2, made its first flight. It incorporated many improvements gained from the first Zeppelin, but was lost on its second flight due to a mixture of bad weather and engine imbalance. Undaunted, Zeppelin went ahead to produce a third airship, the LZ 3. This proved the best to date, and the German army was now taking an interest. Alas, the latest craft did not measure up to the army's exacting requirements. But Zeppelin was undeterred, and he began working on a fourth airship, LZ 4, designed to meet army requirements. This was ready by June 1908; in a heartbreaking rerun of the past, it was destroyed in a storm after suffering engine failure.

Building a fearsome beast
Zeppelin's efforts should have been finished at the crash site, but his perseverance had made him a German national hero. He was seen as a symbol of scientific progress, and the German public began to send him donations to rebuild his company and continue his work. Zeppelin set up the Zeppelin Foundation for the Promotion of Aerial Navigation, which in turn financed Luftschiffbau Zeppelin and Deutsche Luftschiffahrt AG, quickly known as DELAG – the world's first airline. Then, in 1909, the German army placed an order for two Zeppelins, adding the airship to growing German air assets.

In 1910–11 a rival firm, Schütte-Lanz, produced its first airship; unlike the aluminium-framed Zeppelin, its internal framework was made of laminated plywood. Schütte-Lanz airships also introduced newer technical ideas and improved aerodynamic forms. By 1912, the German army was proclaiming the airship as a bomber:

> … in the newest Z ships we possess a weapon that is far superior to all similar ones of our opponents and that cannot be imitated in the foreseeable future if we work energetically to perfect it. Its speediest development as a weapon is required to enable us at the beginning of a war to strike a first and telling blow whose practical and moral effect could be quite extraordinary.
> **Helmuth von Moltke,**
> **Chief of the General Staff,**
> **December 1912**

Airships can be classified into three types, depending on their construction: non-rigid, semi-rigid and rigid. The non-rigid airship relies on gas pressure to maintain its form, and can be deflated, packed and transported to the nearest air station. The semi-rigid type relies partly on its framework and partly on its gas-filled envelope for its form. The rigid airship, as its name suggests, depends on its framework to keep it in form and hence in the air.

It was not just the German army that was showing interest in airships. The growing German navy, the High Seas Fleet, was being built up to challenge British sea power. In its haste to construct a battle fleet, it had neglected the role of the cruiser for reconnaissance. The airship, flying out ahead of the fleet, was seen as a quick fix, and in 1914 a hasty programme for new airships and bases was ordered.

Challenging the Germans

Although the Germans seemed to hold a clear lead in airship design, Italy had also produced a series of airships, mostly non-rigid and semi-rigid designs. One of the latter, a Crocco-Ricaldi N1, was first flown in 1910, powered by a Clément-Bayard 110hp motor driving two propellers. The 66m (217ft) airship attained an airspeed of 52kph (32mph) and was among the first of its kind to go to war. In 1911 Italy sent three of this type to Libya, as part of a small aviation group, in its short war with Turkey. They mostly performed in the reconnaissance role, but also dropped the occasional small bomb.

Italian airships were designed for army cooperation, which would include bombing raids. The ability to operate at high altitude for relatively short flights was therefore a primary consideration, in order to evade possible interception and gunfire. The long duration needed for maritime patrols, built into German and British airships, was a much lower priority to the Italians.

The semi-rigid design was also popular in France. Between 1898 and 1905, Alberto Santos-Dumont, aviation innovator extraordinaire, designed, built and tested no fewer than 14 airships. Each new craft was built on the expertise garnered during the last, and in many ways his experiments defined the airship of the early twentieth century. In 1902 he flew from the aerodrome of the Paris Aero Club around the Eiffel Tower and back to the starting point in one of his airships – a feat that won him the Deutsch de la Meurthe Prize.

Later the same year the Lebaudy brothers, in conjunction with M. Julliot, an engineer, and M. Surcouf, an aviator, built and flew a new design, again semi-rigid. The airship was rebuilt in 1904 and again in 1905. M. Lebaudy offered his much-modified airship to the French Minister of War, who accepted it on behalf of the French nation. The French Government ordered a new airship of the same type, proudly called *La Patrie*. Good fortune did not follow these two airships – both were lost in bad weather. A replacement, *La République*, was ordered in 1908 and proved to have exceptional qualities. It was so influential that the readers of the British newspaper the *Morning Post* purchased an example of the type and presented it to the British Government, which to date had done very little to equip Britain with these novel machines.

SANTOS-DUMONT AIRSHIP
On 19 October 1901, Alberto Santos-Dumont claimed a 50,000 franc prize offered to any aeronaut who successfully flew from Saint-Cloud, the headquarters of the Paris Aero Club, and returned to the starting point after making a circuit of the Eiffel Tower. The distance involved was 11km (7 miles), and the course had to be completed within 30 minutes. Santos-Dumont did it in 29½.

Airships: 1914–1918

French companies Maison Clément-Bayard and the Société Astra des Constructions Aéronautiques both produced a series of large and efficient craft known as the Clément-Bayard and Astra-Torres, respectively. Numbers of the latter design were purchased by Britain in 1912–13.

A reluctant latecomer

British airship technology badly lagged behind that of its continental neighbours. Enthusiastic individuals produced a few smaller designs, but the government view was to spend as little as possible and gain from other country's developments – and disasters.

Watching progress in France and Germany was the head of the British army's Balloon Section, Colonel James Templer. In 1902 he managed to persuade the British Government to allow a small amount of money for experimental purposes. Two small airships were built, but money ran out after only a few tests. Nothing more was done until 1907, when the first complete military airship was built, reusing one of Colonel Templer's original envelopes. This cigar-shaped craft was grandly christened *Nulli Secundus*. The airship proved strong and successful, and after several tests it flew over London, landing at Crystal Palace, in October 1907. The flight lasted 3 hours 25 minutes – a world record at the time. In addition to two airships acquired from France, the army went on to acquire the British-designed *Baby*, *Beta*, *Gamma*, *Delta* and *Eta*. Of these, *Delta*, built and flown in 1912, was the largest and most capable. In that year the airship took part in the annual military manoeuvres.

On 1 January 1914, the British army disbanded its airship section and the surviving craft – *Beta*, *Gamma*, *Delta* and *Eta* – were handed over to the Royal Navy, together with their trained crews, which then assumed responsibility for all British airships. The Royal Navy had experimented with a rigid airship, popularly named the *Mayfly* and completed in 1911; however, the craft was unsuccessful, and work on further rigid airships was discontinued in 1912.

Stepping up the pace

August 1914 saw rivalry turn into all-out war. In Britain, fear of Germany's mighty air fleet loomed large in both public and government minds. The idea of the United Kingdom as a safe haven, with its all-powerful Royal Navy patrolling the seas protecting the nation from invasion, was no more. The British military estimated that Germany had about 20 airships capable of reaching the United Kingdom with some kind of bombload. German army airships had already bombed Liège and Antwerp in support of advancing army units. This had prompted three strikes by British aircraft, two raids launched from bases in Europe and one launch from seaplane carriers operating off the coast of Germany, known as the Cuxhaven Raid. More by luck than planning, just one German airship had been confirmed destroyed – the Z 9 at Düsseldorf.

In the wake of the Cuxhaven Raid, if anything, British apprehension concerning attack by airships increased. In a presentation to the War Council on 1 January 1915, Winston Churchill warned that the air defence, or lack of it, could do nothing to stop the Zeppelins once they were in the air. Spoiling attacks on their home bases was Britain's only hope. Before this could be attempted, the dreaded and much-feared event occurred – Zeppelins bombed England. Korvettenkapitan Peter Strasser, Commander of the Naval Airship Division, was given permission to proceed by Admiral Hugo von Pohl, Chief of the Naval Staff, on report of favourable weather conditions. The German army had already sent its airships to targets in France; now the navy would share the glory. Strasser lost little time. The first raid set out on 13 January, the L 5 and L 6 from Nordholze and the L 3 and L 4 from Fuhlsbüttel, but deteriorating weather forced them back. Another raid was attempted on 19

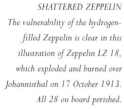

SHATTERED ZEPPELIN
The vulnerability of the hydrogen-filled Zeppelin is clear in this illustration of Zeppelin LZ 18, which exploded and burned over Johannisthal on 17 October 1913. All 28 on board perished.

Airships: 1914–1918

January, with the L 3, L 4 and L 6. Strasser himself flew aboard L 6, but the craft never reached the United Kingdom. Suffering from engine problems, it was forced to return to base. The L 3 reached England's Norfolk coastline at 7.50 p.m., just north of Great Yarmouth. This port and naval base was on the approved German target list, and the airship soon located the town, delivering a total of 11 bombs. The L 4, originally bound for the Humber estuary, arrived over northern Norfolk at 8.30 p.m. – many miles to the south of its target. It bombed the villages of Thornham, Brancaster, Henchem, Snettisham, and Sheringham, and the town of King's Lynn. Although no military targets were hit, four people were killed and 18 more wounded. The humble cottages of old England bore the brunt of the country's first air raid. L 3 and L 4 returned safely to base at Fuhlsbüttel. The raid was not as described in pre-war novels, but the myth of the mighty airship was not dead yet. The unfortunate crews of L 3 and L 4, however, would soon be so. Both airships were lost in February while on a scouting mission over the North Sea, again hit by bad weather. Still, a popular song was born, reinforcing the cult of myth and expectation built around the airship:

Zeppelin, flieg,
Hilf uns im Krieg,
Flieg nach England,
England wird abgebrannt …

(Zeppelin, fly,
Help us in the war,
Fly to England,
England shall be destroyed by fire …)

EARLY RAIDS
As far as possible, Zeppelin commanders tried to make landfall on the British coast near river estuaries, which were easily recognisable.

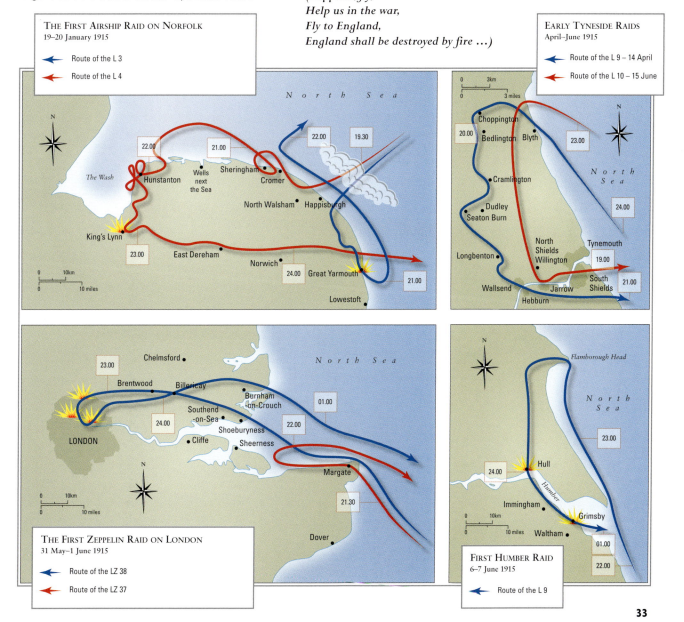

Airships: 1914–1918

ZEPPELIN KILL
On 7 June 1915, Flight Sub-Lt R.A.J. Warneford of No. 1 Squadron RNAS, flying a Morane-Saulnier L from Dunkirk made a single pass over Zeppelin LZ.37 and dropped six 9kg (20lb) bombs. The airship exploded in flames and fell on a convent, killing a nun and two children. Warneford was awarded the Victoria Cross, only to be killed in a crash a few days later.

Meanwhile, at the base of No. 1 Squadron RFC, its commander Spencer Grey was determined to fight back and had decided to hit the beasts in their bases. On the night of 6–7 June, three aircraft, under the command of Lieutentant J.P. Wilson, took off. Each aircraft carried six small bombs, and each pilot had a rifle and a few rounds. A newcomer, Sub-Lieutenant Reginald Warneford, lost sight of his two companions in the night. The flight commander and his companion, Mills, headed east towards Brussels. They managed to find the Evere airship shed and executed a perfect attack. They delivered nine of their 12 bombs on the shed, and a large fire was seen by the pilots as they quickly withdrew. Intelligence reports later confirmed that LZ 38, the first airship to bomb London, had gone up in flames.

Remarkable success ... and safe return

Warneford was in the meantime circling the night sky, looking for his comrades. He was unable to find them, but he did happen upon LZ 37 on a routine patrol. On board were a number of specialists from the Zeppelin factory, intent on gaining experience of the problems faced on everyday active service. Warneford could hardly believe the size of the 158.5m (520ft) giant he had encountered. He saw the flash of machine-gun fire from the airship's gondolas, and bullets peppered his small aircraft. He wisely moved out of range to consider the situation. He carefully stalked the airship and opened fire with his rifle – nothing happened. The airship's commander, Oberleutnant von der Haegan, dumped water ballast and quickly gained altitude, leaving Warneford puttering away at 2130m (7000ft).

Warneford did not give up the pursuit, but urged his aircraft up to 3350m (11,000ft), hoping to gain some tactical position on the Zeppelin. The airship suddenly put its nose down, heading for cloud cover and safety. Warneford seized his opportunity. With the airship now below him, he dived into a bombing attack on the Zeppelin's undefended upper side. Hurtling down in his tiny Morane-Saulnier, he released six small bombs, which penetrated the envelope. For a moment there was nothing – then a gigantic explosion. It turned Warneford's small aircraft upside down, but he could not take his eyes off the blazing wreck, as it floated to earth visible for miles around. The Zeppelin fell on a suburb of Ghent, killing a nun and badly burning several other people. Only one member of the crew survived, the helmsman, who jumped clear at 61m (200ft) and fell through a roof, landing in an unoccupied bed.

Warneford wrestled his singed aeroplane back under control. After a spluttering sound from the Le Rhone engine, it cut out. He was some 60km (35 miles) inside German-held territory, with not a hope of reaching Allied lines. Undaunted, he managed to land his battered aircraft near a farmhouse. All was quiet. His first instinct was to destroy his machine, but on closer inspection he discovered a severed

RECRUITMENT POSTER
The British government lost no time in making capital out of the terror generated by Zeppelin raids on Britain, which was very real. This recruiting poster was a by-product.

Airships: 1914–1918

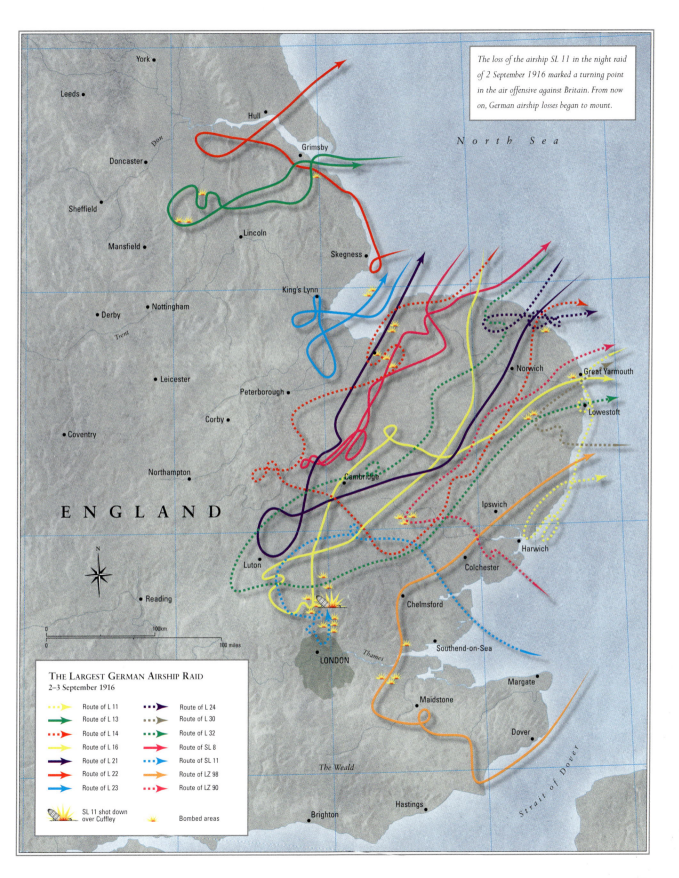

Airships: 1914–1918

In all, there were 20 German airship raids in 1915, and 37 tons of bombs had been scattered across Britain, killing 181 people and injuring 455. Despite the newspaper headlines and popular outrage, the damage inflicted was slight for the effort expended.

Undeterred determination

Italy joined the war in May 1915, on the side of the Allies. Its airships and Caproni bombers flew against the Austro-Hungarian enemies, while French airships flew on a few raids over Germany and occupied France. Germany's prime strategic target for 1916 was still Britain. By now the Kaiser had put aside any concerns about bombing London or any other city deemed a worthwhile target. An obscenely brutal war was going to get nastier – death and destruction would reach the streets of many towns and cities if the airships had their way.

There were 23 German airship raids on the United Kingdom in 1916, most of which proved uneventful. But the raid on 2 September was to be the largest of the entire war, involving 16 airships. By 1916 there were two generations of airship in service. Strasser pinned high hopes on the newer, larger L 30s, of which five had been built. Of the 12 German navy airships that set off on 2 September, two were Super Zeppelins; the army contributed four airships to the raid. Altogether, they carried some 32 tons of bombs, and 14 of the original 16 airships arrived over

SKELETAL REMAINS
On the night of 22–23 September 1916, Zeppelin L 33, severely damaged by AA fire and air attack, crash-landed in a field at Little Wigborough, Essex, and was set on fire by its crew, all 22 of whom were taken prisoner. Its commander was Kapitänleutnant Alois Böcker.

fuel line, but ample fuel left in the tank. With remarkable presence of mind, he effected a repair and swung the propellers; the engine, still warm, started easily. He climbed aboard and took off. He finally landed at Cap Griz-Nez 16km (10 miles) down the coast from Calais. There he collected more fuel and telephoned his commander at Dunkirk. By the time he arrived back at his base, his name had been flashed across the Empire. George V acknowledged Warneford's victory by presenting him with the Victoria Cross. The French followed with the Grand Cross of the Legion of Honour. At last, the myth of the airship had been punctured.

Airships: 1914–1918

LAST RAID
In the last raid of the war on Britain, on the night of 5–6 August 1918, Zeppelin L70 (Kapitänleutnant von Lossnitzer) was shot down in flames by Major Egbert Cadbury and Captain Robert Leckie in a DH.4 and fell into the sea off King's Lynn, Norfolk. Among the 22 dead was Peter Strasser, commander of the Airship Division.

eastern and southern England (the navy's airship L 17 and the army's LZ 97 turned back with mechanical problems). Alarms sounded; searchlights probed the night sky; aircraft formed defence squadrons that took to the air. During the summer of 1916, new machine-gun ammunition had begun to reach the squadrons. Two types of explosive bullets, named 'Brock' and 'Pomeroy', were mixed with a third, 'Buckingham', a phosphorus incendiary bullet. These were a lethal combination when fired at hydrogen-filled airships.

Among the 14 airships floating over England was the army craft SL 11, commanded by Wilhelm Schramm. The SL 11 arrived over the northern suburbs of London at around 2.00 a.m. As it dropped its bombload, the airship was picked out by searchlights. As it turned north, the SL 11 was spotted by Lieutenant Leefe Robinson, flying a much-maligned BE.2c of No. 39 Squadron RFC. His report to his commanding officer read:

Remembering my last failure, I sacrificed height – I was at about 12,900ft [3,930m] – for speed and nosed down in the direction of the Zeppelin. I saw shells bursting and night tracers flying around it. When I drew closer I noticed that the anti-aircraft aim was too high or too low; also a good many shells burst about 800ft [243m] behind – a few tracers went right over. I could hear the bursts when about 3000ft [914m] from the Zeppelin. I flew about 800ft [243m] below it from bow to stem and distributed one drum among it (alternate new Brock and Pomeroy). It seemed to have no effect; I therefore moved to one side and gave them another drum along the side – also without effect. I then got behind it and by this time I was very close – 500ft [152m] or less below, and concentrated one drum on one part (underneath rear). I was then at a height of 11,500ft [3,500m] when attacking the Zeppelin. I was hardly finished the drum before I saw the part fired at, glow. In a few seconds the whole rear part was blazing. When the third drum was fired, there were no searchlights on the Zeppelin, and no anti-aircraft was firing. I quickly got out of the way of the falling, blazing Zeppelin and, being very excited, fired off a few red Very lights and dropped a parachute flare.

Robinson was the hero of the hour. More importantly, millions of British citizens learned of the end of SL 11, and thousands managed to visit the crash site. It was a major boost to civilian morale, and once again the myth of the indestructible airship took a beating.

In a further boon to British hopes, in the early morning of 23 September a combination of fighter aircraft and anti-aircraft guns forced naval airship L 33, commanded by Kapitänleutnant Böcker, to crash-land at Little Wigborough near Colchester, Essex. This was a brand-new state-of-the-art airship on its first mission. British experts examined the wreck intently, gaining insight for their own design approach. Indeed, one of the L 33's 250hp engines was retrieved and fitted to the old, underpowered British airship R9.

During the 1916 raids, 125 tons of bombs were dropped, killing 293 people and wounding 691. But the tables were turning. Effective, well-armed fighters were beginning to end the airship threat.

By the end of 1916 and early 1917, most German commanders had concluded that the airship, with its high costs and maintenance, and relative fragility, was not the way to execute a strategic air offensive. Nevertheless, airship development continued. They grew bigger and were capable of flying higher, beyond the reach of fighters and anti-aircraft guns. The efficiency of airship crews at higher altitudes declined severely,

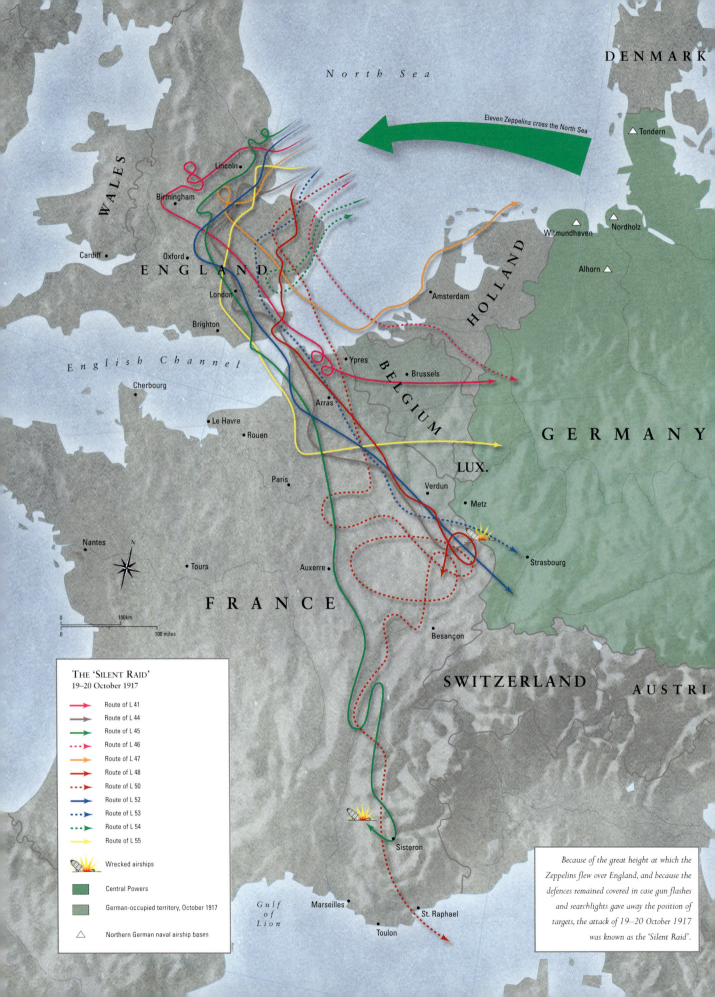

and bombing accuracy was consequently reduced. Airships still had their dedicated followers, though, including Peter Strasser, Commander of Naval Airships. He felt that the British response to the threat and the actuality of airship raids clearly showed their worth. Indeed, by 1917, the United Kingdom's air defence was made up of 10 squadrons of fighters and hundreds of guns and searchlights, manned by 10,000 or more personnel.

Diminishing support, declining role

There were only 11 airship raids against Britain in 1917 and 1918. On 24 September 1917, Peter Strasser led a ten-airship raid on northern England, with the city of Hull as its primary target. In October, Strasser returned. Eleven airships arrived over eastern England intent on bombing the industrial towns and cities of the Midlands. The fleet cruised in at a height of around 4600–6100m (15,000–20,000ft). As it approached the Midlands, it was hit by 100kph (60mph) winds blowing in a southeasterly direction. At least four airships passed over or near London defences.

Down at ground level, mist shrouded the London area, and the order was given for the guns to remain silent and searchlights to be switched off. The raiders passed over the silent capital, giving the operation its nickname of the 'Silent Raid'. The raid delivered 273 bombs on scattered targets, killing 236 people and wounding 55. The Germans lost five airships, four during operations and one on landing back in Germany. The raids continued into 1918, and Peter Strasser continued to agitate for a war-winning Zeppelin offensive. He died on 5 August 1918, leading the last airship raid of the war in the latest in airship construction, L 70. But from 1917 onwards, the airship had a rival for glory – the bomber.

In one curious episode, the airship's immense range capability was to be used to supply an isolated German force fighting in its colony in eastern Africa. The specially enlarged L 59 was selected and flew to Jamboli in Bulgaria, the most southerly German airship base available. After two attempts, the airship finally set off on 21 November 1917. She had reached the area of Khartoum, in Anglo-Egyptian Sudan, when recalled by radio. It was believed that German forces had surrendered. The airship turned north and made it back to base on the morning of 25 November.

In total, 88 German airships were built, 74 for the naval airship division. Sixty were lost, but 34 of these losses were attributed to accidents caused mostly by bad weather. Of the remaining 26, 17 were destroyed in attacks on the British Isles, some by French anti-aircraft fire as they returned home. The others were shot down over the Russian Front or in operations over France. Between 1914 and 1918, German airships dropped 5806 bombs, killing 557 people and wounding 1358. On the bloody balance sheet of World War I, however, this was little more than a pinprick – the equivalent of an average day's loss on the Western Front.

The flight of the Zeppelin L59 was an epic of endurance that paved the way for the global airship flights of the 1920s and 1930s.

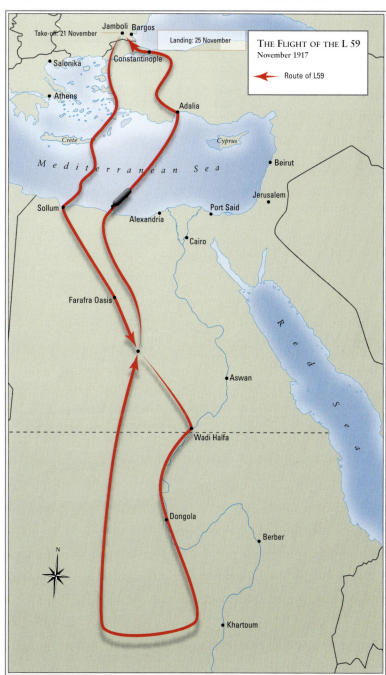

FIGHTERS: 1914–1918

'Fighter' is perhaps the most evocative word in military aviation. This is a machine dedicated to destroying enemy aircraft and dominating the airspace in which it operates – a concept almost unknown in 1914.

Overcoming stalemate

As the weeks of manoeuvre gave way to a frenzy of entrenchment, the war in the west took on the form of a gigantic siege. All sides attempted to create a breakthrough in the almost static line so that they could restore a war of manoeuvre and, by doing so, bring about a decisive victory. But this did not happen and, no matter how expensive the attempts in terms of human life, the position of the armies changed little. For now, the defensive battle far outweighed the offensive one – artillery and machine-gun fire could destroy even the most determined attack on barbed-wire-defended entrenchments.

Above the blood-soaked battlefields, small, frail aircraft puttered about their daily routine of reconnaissance, but it had occurred to some that preventing the enemy enjoying the same visual benefit of their own defensive line was an increasingly critical matter. By late 1914, the first aerial attacks on enemy aircraft were recorded. The crew of single-seater and two-seater aircraft took pistol or rifle shots at each other, almost always without effect. One British pilot took off armed with a sawn-off shotgun:

> *I spotted a strange aircraft, which I thought didn't look like any I knew, so I sidled up to him and saw that he was a Hun, so I got my shotgun out, and I fired it all away. Then I got my revolver, and we had a revolver battle up there. We were very close to each other, and I could see him quite well, and he could see me quite well. I finished my six shots and he had finished his. We both waved each other goodbye and set off.*
>
> **Kenneth van der Spuy, RFC**

The chances of a fatal hit resulting from a bullet fired from an aircraft travelling at around 110kph (70mph) was virtually nil, even with the best shot.

The first person to solve the problem of air-to-air combat was Roland Garros, a pre-war aviator and a test pilot for the Morane-Saulnier Company. It was Raymond Saulnier who had experimented, before World War I, with a device that would allow a machine gun to fire through the blades of a turning propeller. He took out a patent for his design, but had no time to perfect it before the outbreak of war.

Garros took things into his own hands. Instead of attempting a deflection shot – not easy even when firing a machine gun – he decided to fire a machine gun forwards through the propeller arc. As no effective interrupter gear had been proved so far, he fitted his propellers with metal deflector plates. On a ground test he discovered that only one bullet in 10 hit the propeller blade.

Garros set off with his newly adapted aircraft. His method was to approach an enemy aircraft from behind; with both aircraft travelling in the same direction there was no need to allow for deflection. This would allow a far greater number of hits – that is, if the bullets did not bounce off his propeller and hit Garros himself or some vital part of his machine instead. Despite his system's inherent risk, Garros downed three German aircraft in 18 days, a remarkable score given that most encounters ended without loss on either side.

PIONEER AIR FIGHTER
Roland Garros, seen here in the cockpit of his Morane-Saulnier Type 'N', had already achieved fame as one of France's pioneer aviators before the outbreak of World War I. He shot down six enemy aircraft in three weeks before being forced down with engine trouble and taken prisoner.

Fighters: 1914–1918

On 18 April Garros's fuel line clogged, and he was forced to make a glide landing behind enemy lines. He and his Morane-Saulnier Type N were quickly captured. The captured aircraft was hurriedly sent to Berlin, where Anthony Fokker was given the job of finding an answer to this new French threat. In common with technicians in other countries, German engineers had been working on the idea of interrupter gear for forward-firing guns. Fokker perfected a design and fitted it to his 'Eindekker', the Fokker E.I, powered by an 80hp engine.

German high-fliers

Fokker's newly equipped machine was hurried to the front, where it would be flown by two outstanding pilots. The first of these was Max Immelmann, born in Dresden in 1890. Immelmann entered the Dresden Cadet Corps at the age of 14. He was a gifted engineer, but his bad behaviour led to his departure from military service. With the outbreak of war, he rejoined the army and requested service in aviation, attracted by its engineering and mechanical innovation, as well as the skill involved in flying. After training, his first assignment was to fly post and supplies to forward airfields.

On 3 June 1915, while flying a reconnaissance mission, Immelmann was shot down by a French aircraft. He survived the experience, collecting the Iron Cross Second Class in the process. Still an unknown pilot, Immelmann was introduced to the aircraft that would make him famous:

> *We have just got two small one-seater fighters from the Fokker factory. The Crown Prince of Bavaria visited our aerodrome to see these new fighting machines and inspected us and Section 20. Direktor Fokker, the constructor of this fighter, was presented to him. Fokker and a Leutnant Parschau gave demonstration flights for him and fired at ground targets from the air. Fokker amazed us with his ability.*
>
> **Max Immelmann**

Soon afterwards, Immelmann flew one of the first examples of the new Fokker E.I, together with Oswald Boelcke. The two pilots returned to the front, and on 1 August they took off in pursuit of ten British BE.2c aircraft that had bombed their airfield. Boelcke attacked, but after firing just a few rounds his gun jammed, so he turned for home. Immelmann pressed on, attacking several aircraft until picking on one, chasing it, and eventually wounding the pilot and forcing the aircraft to land in German-held territory. For this he was awarded the Iron Cross First Class.

Immelmann continued to score against the enemy. He was shot down by a French pilot on 23 September, but his luck held – he survived and was back in the air to shoot down his fourth victim, a BE.2c of the Royal Flying Corps. By now his

AIRCO DH.2
The DH.2 was a single-seat 'pusher' type powered by a 100hp Monosoupape engine, armed with a single Lewis gun installed on a pivot at the port side of the cockpit.

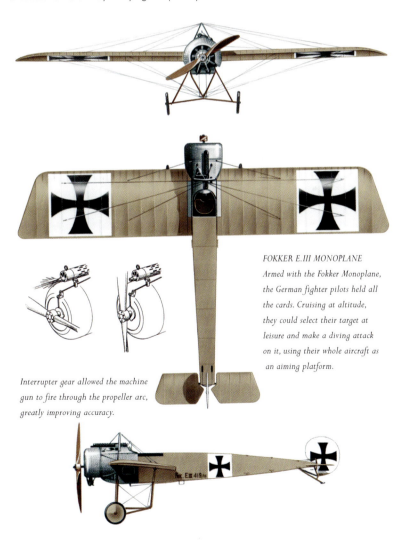

FOKKER E.III MONOPLANE
Armed with the Fokker Monoplane, the German fighter pilots held all the cards. Cruising at altitude, they could select their target at leisure and make a diving attack on it, using their whole aircraft as an aiming platform.

Interrupter gear allowed the machine gun to fire through the propeller arc, greatly improving accuracy.

41

Fighters: 1914–1918

Rolling out of the climb, the pilot can then repeat the attack

The pilot dives his aircraft at the target, usually out of the sun

Pulling out of the dive into a zoom climb, the pilot re-establishes his height advantage

The Immelmann turn involved building up speed in a dive towards the enemy, then pulling up from below and opening fire. After firing, the Fokker pilot continued to climb until he was in the near-vertical position, at which point he applied hard rudder, stall-turned and dived on his adversary to repeat the attack.

Fighters: 1914–1918

exploits had been lionized in the German press, he was now 'Der Adler von Lille' (the Eagle of Lille). His flying skills made him a deadly enemy. He is credited with developing various manoeuvres, including the 'Immelmann turn'. There is some doubt as to whether the light, underpowered Eindekker, which used wing warping instead of ailerons, was able to perform this feat. If anyone were capable of making it do so, however, it would be Immelmann, with his engineering knowledge and superb flying skills. An alternative manoeuvre also associated with Immelmann is the 'stall turn', which involved a sharp rudder turn, off a vertical zoom climb, then kicking the rudder over just before airspeed was lost, so that the aircraft turned into a steep dive and returned to attack the enemy once again.

By the time of his death on 18 June 1916, he was credited with 15 victories and had been presented with the coveted *Pour le Mérite*, later known as the 'Blue Max' in his honour, as well as many other decorations.

Oswald Boelcke was another exponent of the Fokker Eindekker in all its versions. He went on to form Jagdstaffel 2, where he carefully passed on his air combat experience, coaching his new recruits with extreme care and producing practical notes for his fighting squadron, known as his 'Dicta':

1. *Try to secure advantages before attacking. If possible, try to keep the sun behind you.*
2. *Always carry through an attack when you have started it.*
3. *Fire only at close range and only when your opponent is properly in your sights.*
4. *Always keep your eye on your opponent, and never let yourself be deceived by ruses.*
5. *In any form of attack it is essential to assail your opponent from behind.*

MAX IMMELMANN (above)
The autumn of 1915 marked the ascendancy of the first German air aces, Max Immelmann and Oswald Boelcke, whose scores mounted steadily towards the end of the year. The word 'ace' was coined by the French to describe fighter pilots of prowess, and was adopted by the Germans amid much publicity.

FOKKER E.1 (above left)
The Fokker E.1 monoplane was the first to be armed with a single Spandau machine gun firing through the propeller disc. This was a development that still eluded the Allies, whose only aircraft fitted with forward-firing machine guns were slow 'pusher' types.

BRISTOL F2B FIGHTER
When flown offensively, in the same way as a single-seat fighter, the Bristol F2B Fighter proved to be a superb weapon and went on to log a formidable record of success in action. The F2B equipped six RFC squadrons on the Western Front, four in the UK and one in Italy.

43

Fighters: 1914–1918

FOKKER DR.1 TRIPLANE
Made famous as the red-painted mount of Baron Manfred von Richthofen at the time of his death, the rotary-engined Dr.1 triplane was introduced into service in October 1917. Although it was a supremely manoeuvrable fighter, it was already being outclassed by a new generation of fighting scouts.

FE.2D REAR FIRING
An officer demonstrates the technique required to defend this FE.2D from attack from the rear. The defending gunner had no seat belt and in a pitching, rolling dogfight had to use brute strength to operate his gun and cling on to the aircraft.

6. If your opponent dives on you, do not try to evade his onslaught, but fly to meet it.
7. When over the enemy's lines, never forget your own line of retreat.
8. Attack on principle in groups of four or six. When the fight breaks up into a series of single combats, take care that several do not go for one opponent.

Boelcke's Dicta

These rules proved so useful that they were still in use during World War II.

Boelcke's last flight with Jasta 2 took place on the afternoon of 28 October 1916. He was flying to intercept a DH.2 of No. 24 Squadron RFC, led by Major Lanoe Hawker – a legendary crack shot and one of Britain's greatest flyers – in a dogfight. Boelcke only just collided with the undercarriage of his wingman, Erwin Böhme, tearing the fabric of the upper wing of his Albatros D.II. Fighting all the way down to control his damaged aircraft, Boelcke managed a relatively good crash landing, but in his haste he had not strapped himself in – an oversight that proved fatal. Exhausted by many combats, even this legendary flyer could make a simple mistake. Boelcke had scored 40 victories, and even his enemies acknowledged his loss – a lone British aircraft dropped a wreath with the inscription:

To the memory of Captain Boelcke, our brave and chivalrous opponent. From the English Royal Flying Corps.

Answering the scourge of the Fokker

Britain's answer to the 'Fokker scourge' was the Airco DH.2. This 'pusher' type, with its engine behind the pilot, was designed from the outset as a 'fighter', or scout, under the guiding hand of Geoffrey de Havilland. The beauty of the pusher design was that it gave a clear field of fire forwards. Powered by a 100hp Monosoupape Gnome engine and designed with generous control surfaces. the aircraft handled well and first flew in July 1915. By November, production machines were leaving the factory.

By February 1916, the first DH.2-equipped RFC No. 24 Squadron arrived in France. This squadron holds the distinction of being the first 'fighter' squadron in the RFC, although the two-seater pusher Vickers FB5 had been operating with No. 11 Squadron since 25 July 1915 in what was essentially a fighter role. The French air force, meanwhile, began to equip its new fighting escadrilles with the capable Nieuport II 'Bébé', the first aircraft designed as a fighter. A single-seater tractor biplane, it was equipped with a Lewis gun mounted above the upper wing, firing forward over the radius of the propeller. Both these aircraft were some 16–24kph (10–15mph) faster than the Fokker E.III.

The Germans forbade their Fokker pilots to fly over Allied territory, desperate to keep their interrupter gear technology a secret; however, the British managed to capture an aircraft in April 1916. The French procured another one intact when a German pilot, lost in fog, landed on a French airfield by mistake. The Allies quickly reverse-engineered the Germans' interrupter gear for use on their own aircraft, but they also discovered the Fokker's flight characteristics, which were as good as the Fokker myth suggested. The Fokker's dominance was almost over.

Long-awaited acknowledgement

The respective high commands of the combatants' forces at last began to understand that speed was not just a 'fad' and that manoeuvrability was not mere 'stunting', but rather they were essential skills required by the combat pilot – something the pilots themselves had long understood. Fighting a three-dimensional battle forced the flyer not only to practise loops and dives, but also quickly to develop any new move that would throw a pursuer off his tail or, equally, give some advantage.

Training became the key to supplying the fighting squadrons with pilots and aircrew that at least stood a chance in the aerial battlefield. The British, in particular, had a casual approach to training. They had estimated that it cost £1000 to build a scout aircraft and £5000 to train a pilot to fly it, and British trainee pilots still had to go through two months of military studies before they were

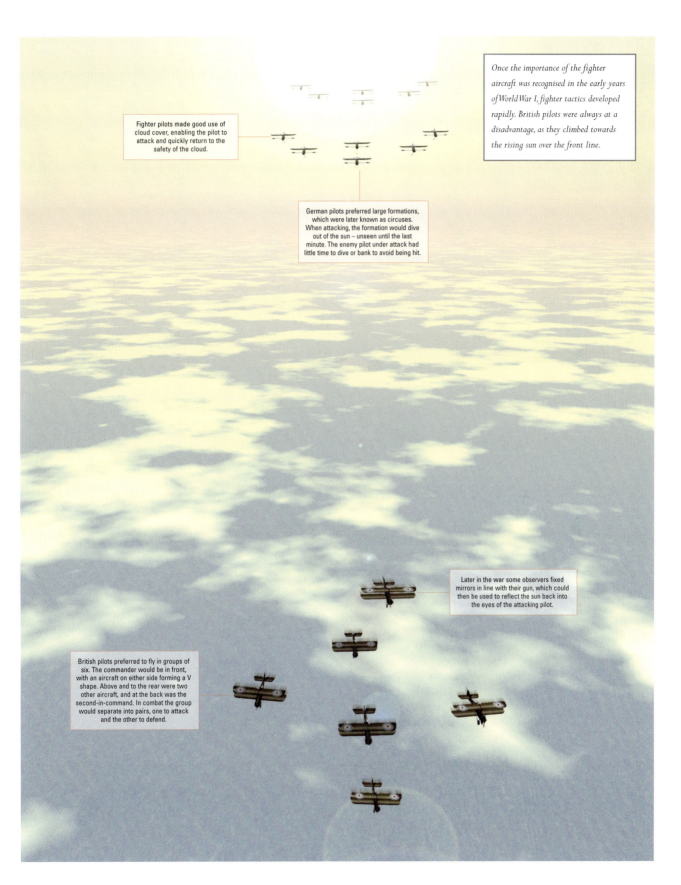

Fighter pilots made good use of cloud cover, enabling the pilot to attack and quickly return to the safety of the cloud.

Once the importance of the fighter aircraft was recognised in the early years of World War I, fighter tactics developed rapidly. British pilots were always at a disadvantage, as they climbed towards the rising sun over the front line.

German pilots preferred large formations, which were later known as circuses. When attacking, the formation would dive out of the sun – unseen until the last minute. The enemy pilot under attack had little time to dive or bank to avoid being hit.

Later in the war some observers fixed mirrors in line with their gun, which could then be used to reflect the sun back into the eyes of the attacking pilot.

British pilots preferred to fly in groups of six. The commander would be in front, with an aircraft on either side forming a V shape. Above and to the rear were two other aircraft, and at the back was the second-in-command. In combat the group would separate into pairs, one to attack and the other to defend.

Fighters: 1914–1918

GENERAL ERICH VON FALKENHAYN
Von Falkenhayn was forced to adopt a strategy that envisaged a battle of attrition at Verdun, in the hope that slaughter on a massive scale would compel Europe's leaders to end the war and negotiate.

given any aviation training at all. The French model was more methodical; however, just to remind future flyers that they were still soldiers of the Republic, they were given a few weeks of square bashing and close-order drill. They could then study the theory of flight. The trainee would then be given a clipped-wing aircraft, incapable of flight, in which they would learn to control the aircraft's direction by use of the rudder. Little by little, as they passed each test, they were allowed more powerful aircraft for their ground training until the first flight. The entire training process up to a pilot receiving his wings took about 50 hours.

A difficult, dangerous job

When pilots finally reached their squadrons, they faced a death rate of occasionally around 16 per cent in certain parts of the front and around 100 per cent during times of major offensive combat. On average, a World War I pilot faced a 50 per cent chance of death, wounding or capture. The mere art of keeping an aircraft under control when exposed to the slipstream in an open cockpit, and at altitudes where frostbite was a regular experience, required continuous concentration and physical strength.

As air-to-air combat developed, formation flying for offence and defence became part of daily operations, demanding the development of new skills. Keeping station in formation took practice; when a formation changes direction, the aircraft on the inside of the manoeuvre slow down, while those on the outside edge speed up. During World War I, all this had to be achieved in aircraft with no throttle or carburettor, in which speed was regulated simply by adjusting the fuel–air mixture.

Just as the winter frosts began to fade in February 1916, General Erich von Falkenhayn launched a massive attack on the French line around Verdun. His plan was not to break through, although this would have been useful, but to bleed the French army white in a gigantic battle of attrition. A million men, backed by 850 guns, attacked. Overhead flew the 'Luftsperre', an aerial blockade designed to prevent French aircraft reporting German movements or interfering with the attack's progress in any way.

Fighting for air superiority

The French were caught by surprise, but, with this war now being one of defence, managed to hold on. With just two escadrilles to face the mass of German aircraft, Joffre called the local air

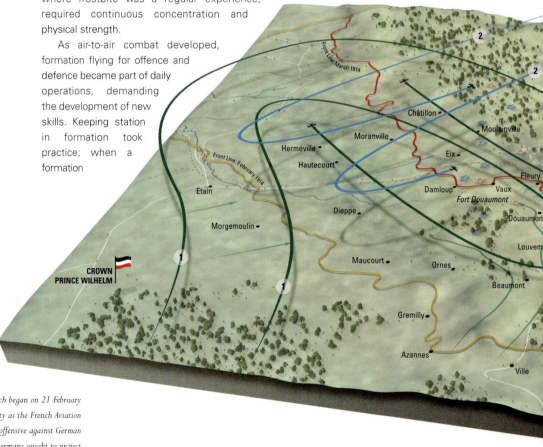

The battle for Verdun, which began on 21 February 1916, saw intense air activity as the French Aviation Militaire went on the offensive against German observation aircraft, and the Germans sought to protect the latter by increasing their fighting patrols.

Fighters: 1914–1918

commander, Major Trincornot de Rose, to his headquarters and gave him complete authority in the air over the battlefield of Verdun. De Rose acted quickly, concentrating 15 escadrilles of Morane-Saulniers and the newer Nieuport XIs. His instructions to the pilots were simple and succint:

The mission of the escadrilles is to seek out the enemy, fight him and destroy him!

While the Germans were locked into their barrage patrols over the heads of their soldiers, the French were able to attack from any angle and from any direction. They were not protecting or patrolling – just attacking where the best advantage presented itself. The Germans were driven from the skies, brought down more by faulty tactics than anything else. General Joffre and his air commander de Rose had launched the first air superiority campaign in history: dedicated fighter aircraft with no other mission than to destroy the enemy.

NIEUPORT 10
From the spring of 1916 the task of overcoming the Fokker menace was shared, alongside the FE.2b and the DH.2, by the Nieuport Scout single-seat fighter biplane. The Nieuport was armed with a single Lewis gun mounted on the top wing and firing over the propeller arc.

BATTLE OF VERDUN
February–June 1916
⇨ Field works
⇨ Major fort

1. The German air force mount permanent patrols in huge numbers, forcing French aircraft out of the area.

2. The French air force only had two Escadrilles for the whole area. This was increased to 15 Escadrilles with just one instruction: to hunt down and destroy enemy aircraft. They become 'Fighters'.

47

Fighters: 1914–1918

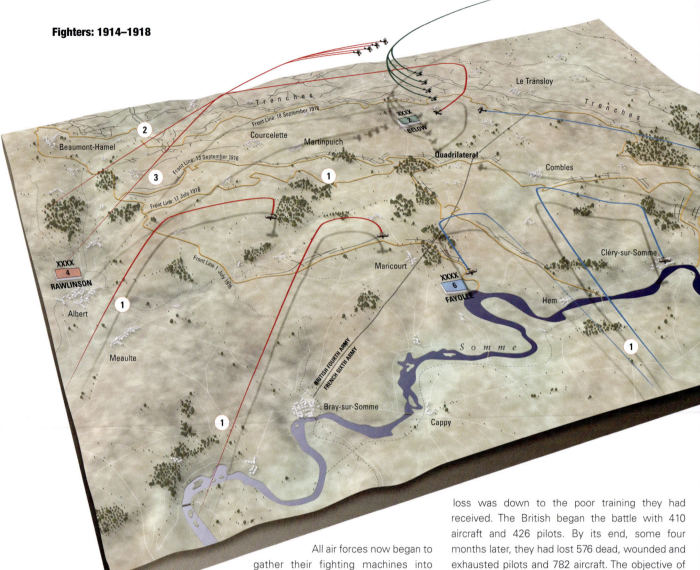

THE BATTLE OF THE SOMME
July–November 1916

- xxxx ☐ Army
- ─── British flights
- ─── French flights
- ─── German flights

(1) From 1 July, Allied aircraft fly contact patrols, reporting on the exact position of advancing Allied troops.

(2) Allied aircraft operate fighter patrols suppressing German attempts to intercept allied reconnaissance and bomber operations. Allied air superiority is maintained throughout the battle, losing well over 1000 aircraft in the process.

(3) Allied air reconnaissance continues throughout the five months of the battle.

All air forces now began to gather their fighting machines into specialized units – *groupes des chasses*, *Jagdstaffeln*, pursuit squadrons – and the fighter squadron was born.

On 1 July 1916, the largest attack by the British army so far was launched on the Western Front. This massive offensive was designed to break the German line, ending the seemingly interminable deadlock. Offensive air action and a week-long artillery barrage preceded the general attack. Offensive air action against the German air force was surprisingly successful. The British and French were able to operate reconnaissance and artillery-spotting missions without interference from the enemy. Allied fighters dominated the air over the battlefield, and almost no German aircraft entered Allied airspace.

On the fateful day, 1 July, the guns fell silent, and 100,000 British troops went 'over the top'. By the end of that bloody day, 19,240 were dead. More than 50 per cent were either wounded, killed or captured. Overhead on the same day the RFC lost 20 per cent of its flying strength. Part of this loss was down to the poor training they had received. The British began the battle with 410 aircraft and 426 pilots. By its end, some four months later, they had lost 576 dead, wounded and exhausted pilots and 782 aircraft. The objective of the offensive – not only to dominate the air, but also to assert moral ascendancy over the enemy – had been bought at an extraordinarily high cost.

Wresting back the offensive

Towards the end of 1916, the struggle for air superiority swung further in Germany's favour. A new fighter, the sleek Albatros D.I, began to reach the *Jagdstaffeln*. The sole aim was to reclaim the skies over the battlefield. It was not only new aircraft that made the difference, but also the manner of their deployment. They fought in larger formations, concentrated where needed to overwhelm the old DH.2s and Sopwith 1½ Strutters. As the Battle of the Somme reached its conclusion, RFC losses began to climb. By November the life expectancy of RFC aircrews over the Somme Sector had fallen to just under four weeks.

During the last few months of 1916 and the spring of 1917, the Germans reorganized their entire defence system along the Western Front. They created a defence in depth: their best troops

Fighters: 1914–1918

The Allies succeeded in establishing air superiority over the Somme battleground with new aircraft types, and to counter it the Germans ordered the formation of Jagdstaffeln *– fighter squadrons – which were to be stationed on the most active areas of the front.*

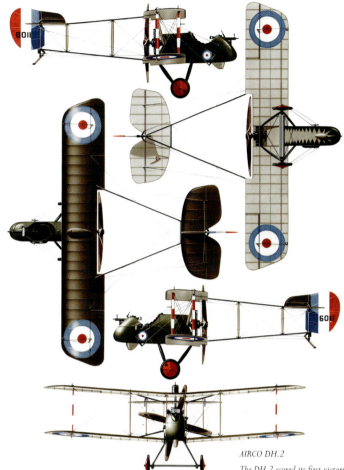

manned strong points and machine-gun posts elaborately defended by miles of barbed wire, while the bulk of the army's infantry and artillery manned reserve lines, some of which were beyond the range of Allied artillery. The first lines would break up Allied attacks, while the reserves chose their moment to counterattack.

Overhead the Albatros provided air superiority, suppressing Allied reconnaissance aircraft and balloon observation. The Germans could now see – but the Allies were blind.

Fighter squadrons practised various supporting formations that would allow the leader, or leaders, to concentrate on the offensive, searching the sky for the enemy and deciding on the best tactic. The wingmen, or supporting aircraft, concentrated on the defensive at the rear or extremes of the formation. Their sole job was to scan the sky for potential threat. The stepped 'V' formation was favoured by many squadrons: number one would lead, two and three would be 45m (150ft) behind and 45m (150ft) higher. Then came four and five at the same remove – their role was defensive, to protect numbers one, two and three. The formation could break into pairs, attacker and defensive wingman, or into a circle formation, with each aircraft defending the tail of the one ahead. In the turmoil of aerial battle, formations could fracture very quickly. In battle, even trained, self-supporting formations could break up. The distraction of fighting for survival among the clouds meant that an individual could one moment be in the thick of the battle, twisting and turning – then, almost instantly, he could find himself alone, the battle dispersed. The lone aircraft was the most vulnerable in the sky, except perhaps in the hands of a superb flyer. The best chance was to head home at the best speed possible. Among the mass of pilots, there emerged a few experts.

The stuff of legend

On 27 February 1916, Britain's first dedicated fighter squadron was deployed on the Western Front with its commander, Major Lanoe G. Hawker, whose flying ability was legendary. Hawker was experienced and had complete mastery of his machine, the DH.2. He was a magnificent shot with his preferred weapon, the beautifully made Wesley Richards 300 single-shot stalking rifle, at least in the early months. His aim was such that one single deflection shot would kill an enemy pilot or hit some vital part of the machine. Enemy squadrons were deeply puzzled to see machines fall out of the sky without the usual associated clatter of machine-gun fire. With the introduction of the Albatros D.I, however, the DH.2s became increasingly outclassed. Hawker continued to

AIRCO DH.2
The DH.2 scored its first victory on 2 April 1916, and from then on its tally rose steadily. In June 1916 its pilots destroyed 17 enemy aircraft, followed by 23 in July, 15 in August, 15 in September and 10 in November. On 23 November, Major Lanoe G. Hawker (below) was shot down by an German pilot after a 35-minute duel over Bapaume. The pilot's name was Manfred von Richthofen.

Fighters: 1914–1918

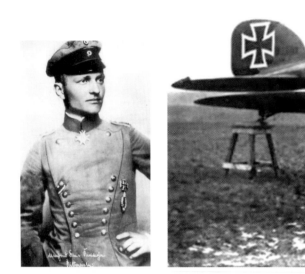

ALBATROS D.III
The first of the Albatros 'V-strutters', the Albatros D.III was the most effective of all the Albatros fighter designs produced during World War I.

MANFRED VON RICHTHOFEN
Rittmeister Freiherr Manfred von Richthofen was the top-scoring air ace of World War I, with 80 victories. He was shot down and killed on 21 April 1918. It is now generally accepted that an Australian machine gunner was responsible, rather than Captain Roy Brown of No. 209 Squadron RFC, who received the credit at the time.

SOPWITH CAMEL
Although it had a number of vicious tendencies, the Sopwith Camel – first issued to No. 4 Squadron RNAS and No. 70 Squadron RFC on the Western Front in July 1917 – was a superb fighting machine in the hands of a skilled pilot, and by November 1918 the many squadrons operating it had claimed the destruction of at least 3000 enemy aircraft, more than any other type.

survive based solely on his flying and shooting skills. Twice he was shot down and once wounded.

New aircraft were now arriving from British factories: the Sopwith Pup from the autumn of 1916 and the excellent, manoeuvreable Sopwith Triplane to the pilots of RNAS squadrons (but which was not issued to the RFC). This aircraft struck fear into German flyers' hearts, and they went out of their way to avoid it. Major Hawker's No. 24 Squadron battled on with their old DH.2s. His fame, almost like that of a Western gunslinger, attracted new German pilots to test their skill; all failed. That is, until his nemesis appeared in the form of Rittmeister Freiherr Manfred von Richthofen, the Red Baron, a student of Boelcke and a practised hunter who would never allow the few seconds Hawker would need to line up his target. On 23 November 1916, there would be no escape. Time and again, Hawker's skill took his aircraft out of the line of Richthofen's fire. Twisting and turning, the two pilots fought for survival on the one part and the final kill on the other. Hawker sought every

chance at low level, weaving between buildings and around tall trees, but the powerful Albatros continued to close. In a last final effort, Hawker, characteristically, gave his DH.2 full left rudder in an attempt to face his enemy. Richthofen used his margin of power to cut off the turn, firing a long burst into Hawker's body and his aircraft. The DH.2 hit the ground and burst into flames.

The losses suffered by No. 24 Squadron, including that of its leader, were the result of the policy of 'offensive patrol' enforced by Major-General Hugh Trenchard, Commander of the RFC. As a direct result of this policy, the demand for pilots meant that they were still being rushed to frontline squadrons with less hours spent in training than their German opponents. Most arrived with around 20 hours' flying time. Only the best would survive the first few days on the fighting front. Some squadron members did what they could to add to the new mens' flying skills; others shunned their company, almost ashamed to look the new men in the face.

Capitalizing on mistaken policy
Slaughtering these newcomers was Manfred von Richthofen's Jagdstaffel 11, now reaching the height of its fame led by its legendary commander. The German flyers, with their superior aircraft, could choose when and where to fight. The British policy of offensive flying condemned its crews to seek the enemy at all times, with consequential and yet avoidable loss.

The lesson that it was a mistake to distribute fighting aircraft in small numbers, each assigned to defend part of the front line and under the command of a local army commander, was drawn from the battles of the Somme and Verdun. French Air Commander Jean du Peuty reported:

> *Fighting machines which are taking the offensive should be grouped together under a single command.*

By the end of 1916, the Germans had learned this lesson, and were now committed to creating a large autonomous fighter force. In mid-1916, Germany deployed some 60 fighters on the Western Front; by the year's end some 33 *Jagdstaffeln* of 18 aircraft each were operating under a single commander. This organization was given a new title – 'Luftstreitkraft', or air force.

The Germans still preferred to let the enemy come to them, a tactic interpreted by Lord Trenchard as lacking in moral fibre. He had failed to grasp the simple principle of fighting your enemy on the best possible terms. The German air force welcomed Allied forays into its airspace. The enemy could then be attacked at a time and place of the Germans' choosing. The French and British, but more the British, were entering a phase of increasing losses.

Richthofen, the most successful ace of World War I, was originally a cavalry officer. He served on the Western and Eastern fronts, but, when barbed wire and machine guns seemed to end the traditional role of the cavalry, he volunteered for the air service. Initially he was an observer, operating with Fliegerabteilung 69 on the Eastern Front from June–August 1915, carrying on the traditional cavalry role of reconnaissance. He transferred to the Western Front, operating over the Champagne area of the front. There, with his observer's

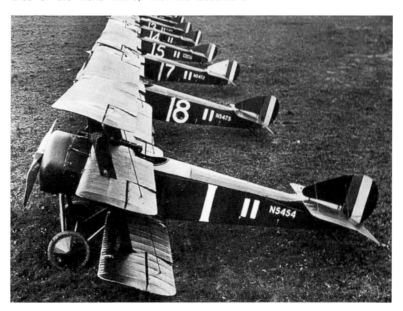

machine gun, he shot down a Farman of the French air force. His claim was disallowed, as the aircraft fell to earth in Allied territory. He began training as a pilot in October 1915. In March 1916, he flew as a pilot operationally for the first time with Kampfgeschwader 2 in an Albatros C.III two-seater. A short time was spent flying the Fokker E.I, with which he attacked a French Nieuport over Verdun, which again crashed in Allied territory – and again he was not credited with the victory.

He returned to the Eastern Front once more, flying two-seaters. While there he met Boelcke, who was on a tour of frontline squadrons recruiting pilots for his new fighter unit Jagdstaffel 2; Richthofen was selected. Now back on the Western Front, flying the single-seat Albatros D.II,

SOPWITH TRIPLANE
The Sopwith Triplane was a successful attempt by Sopwith's talented designer, Herbert Smith, to produce yet more manoeuvrability from the basic design that had produced the Pup. The Triplane had superlative agility and rate of climb, so much so that it had still not been outclassed when the Sopwith Camel began to replace it in the summer of 1917.

Fighters: 1914–1918

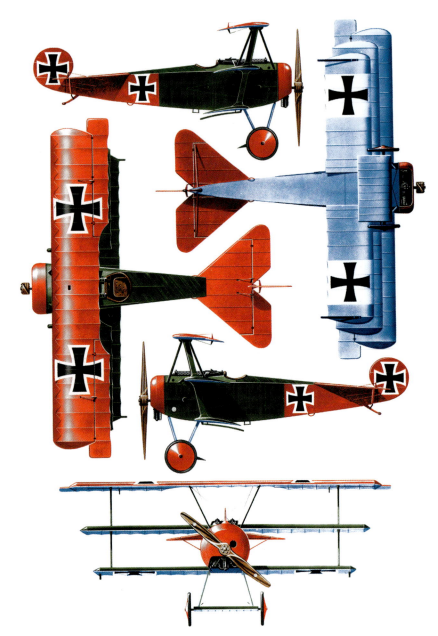

FOKKER DR.I
The Fokker Triplane's early career was marred by a series of fatal crashes. The fact that it received many accolades – at which Anthony Fokker himself expressed surprise – was due in the main to the skilled men who flew it, such as Richthofen and Werner Voss. It was never used in very large numbers.

managed to hold the line, but failed to create the desired breakthrough. The new man Nivelle had the answer: a carefully planned bombardment of enemy rear areas involving around 7000 guns, then a rolling barrage, which would be followed by 700,000 troops, with many more held in reserve for the inevitable breakthrough. As a preliminary to this attack, British and Dominion forces of the 1st, 3rd and 5th armies would attack at Arras and Vimy Ridge. This system, or something very similar, had been tried before. It failed, and it would fail again. The resulting horrific losses reduced large part of the French army to a state of mutiny.

In the clouds above, Allied aircraft were as committed as ever to reconnaissance. As the big push was imminent, this was more important than ever. But this was the high point of German airpower, and Allied aircraft were shot out of the sky in their hundreds – 'Bloody April' earned its name.

The only aircraft to hold its own against the Albatros was the Sopwith Triplane. Only 140 were built and issued to RNAS squadrons operating along the Belgian coast. The 'Tripehound' – the pilots' preferred name – was still underarmed by German standards, but at least it offered hope of a better machine to come.

Mounting losses

Trenchard's policy of taking the offensive over enemy lines continued unabated – not dissimilar to Allied tactics on the ground. Again, casualties began to mount. Inferior machines and inferior tactics meant that, in mid-April 1917, the life expectancy of a new pilot was just 17 days.

Richthofen won his first confirmed victory on 17 September 1916, while operating over Cambrai. Richthofen was an ardent admirer of Boelcke and followed his 'Dicta' in combat, choosing not to engage in risky tactics, but planning and executing carefully orchestrated attacks, in which he and his wingman held all the advantages. This, together with superior aircraft, gave the enemy little chance of escape. The German air force had reached the height of its killing efficiency.

That same month France's new Army Commander, Robert Georges Nivelle, had taken over from the taciturn Joseph Joffre. Joffre had

I looked back, and saw a wicked looking little scout spitting fire and coming down on us at a frightful speed. My observer fired like stink while he was manoeuvring to get behind us again (he was firing through his prop). Just as he was about to make another dive on us, I turned and we kept on firing. By the time he was ready to dive again, he was up to 30 yards [27m] from us so I went into a split-arse spiral, which hid him altogether, so he made off, and flattening out, we sent another shower of bullets after him, eventually regaining out own lines with 16 holes in our biplane. Even then they wouldn't let us alone but sprinkled us well with shrapnel from field guns.
Bernard Rice

The ground offensive that promised so much delivered little but marginal gains here and there, at

Fighters: 1914–1918

horrendous cost. The French armies were mutinous; the British exhausted. Nivelle was sacked.

On 29 April, towards the end of the battle, Richthofen shot down four aircraft, all over German territory. During April 1917 he scored a total of 21 victories.

Light on the horizon

New aircraft were at last entering service with the Allies, which began to restore the balance. The demand for more powerful engines was in part answered by a Swiss engineer, Birkigt, resident in Spain, who offered his services to the French Government. His revolutionary engine – the Hispano-Suiza, was a monobloc design. The cylinders were arranged in V8 form, the bloc was made of aluminium alloy, the moving parts were contained within the engine casing – all providing an excellent, well-balanced design. The first models produced 150hp, with later variants increasing this to 220hp. Early 1917 saw the appearance of the Royal Aircraft Factory S.E.5a, powered by the Birkigt engine. It was capable of more than 210kph (130mph). After some initial hiccups, this aircraft became one of the mainstays of the RFC.

At about the same time, the hard-pressed French fighter escadrilles began to receive the SPAD XIII, powered by the same engine. French industry manufactured 20,000 Hispano-Suiza engines between January 1917 and the end of the war. More were licence-built in the United Kingdom and the United States.

At last the Allies had fighters that matched, and even surpassed, the Germans in performance and fire power. But the German aviation industry was not defeated yet. In 1917 the trim little Fokker Dr.I Triplane was introduced. Its rate of climb and manoeuvrability were phenomenal and, although

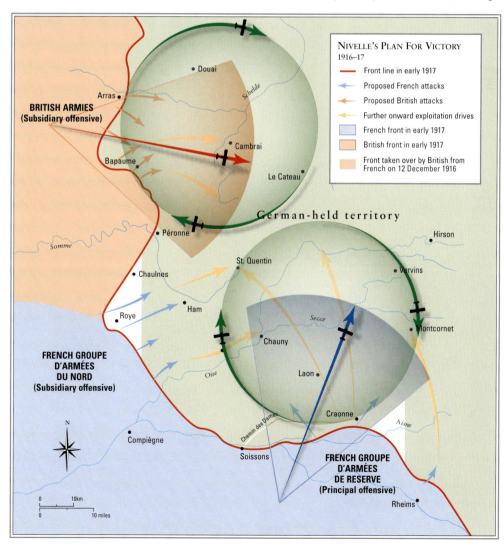

From 1917 onwards, bomber aircraft played an increasing part in supporting Allied ground offensives. The French pioneered both tactical and strategic bombing, using the excellent Breguet Br XIV.

Fighters: 1914–1918

*MESSINES RIDGE
The importance of aerial photography was such that the need to protect reconnaissance aircraft brought about a requirement for fighter escorts, which in turn gave enormous impetus to the development of air-to-air fighting as a whole.*

only 420 were built, it gave a good account of itself. Richthofen became closely associated with a red Dr.I, although most of his victories were won with the Albatros D.III. Fighter tactics continued to evolve; fighter squadrons began to be 'grouped'. Richthofen himself formed and commanded Jagdgeschwader 1. This was made up of Jastas 4, 6, 10 and 11. A mobile force on the ground as well as in the air, it was provided with ample vehicles, enabling it to move its base to any threatened part of the front. With its tented quarters always on the move, it was likened to a circus – a flying circus.

Trying to grab the initiative

After the catastrophe of Nivelle's failed attack, it fell to the British army to maintain what was seen as the 'initiative' and launch a new offensive. This would be no massive breakthrough, but rather a measured attack aimed at specific gains that would not take the army to breaking point. It would be along the lines of Vimy Ridge and the French counterattacks at Verdun.

On 7 June, mines placed under the German lines exploded. So began the Third Battle of Ypres. When the one million pounds of TNT went up, the sound was heard in London. The battles, known to most as Passchendaele, struggled on with limited success until November 1917.

That might have been the end of British efforts for 1917, but High Command, under Field Marshal Haig, had other ideas. A quiet sector was chosen where a new weapon could be tested en masse: the tank. The Cambrai sector was relatively thinly manned by the Germans, the ground had not been pounded by artillery and, importantly, a relatively new technique could be used. By now aviation had provided millions of photographs, which in turn were made into extremely accurate target maps. Guns could now be fired on map coordinates so accurate that individual enemy positions could be destroyed. There was no need to register guns onto targets. The element of surprise would be restored. After a brief artillery bombardment, followed by tanks and then infantry, all supported by ground-attack aircraft and fighters, the Cambrai attack gained as much ground in one day as Passchendaele had gained in three-and-a-half bloody months.

The air battles on the Western Front had a material effect on the Eastern and Italian fronts. The most technically advanced of the Central Powers, Germany was under continuous pressure to match and, if possible, surpass the British and French developments. Both the Russians and the Austro-Hungarians were unable to create comparable air forces to those deployed in the west. The Russians, however, had produced the giant, four-engined Sikorsky Ilya Muromets, of which small numbers were operational by 1914. The general incompetence of the Imperial regime however, together with the relative backwardness of its aviation industry, meant that Russia's ability to develop, produce and deliver aircraft to its forming squadrons was seriously impaired. The creaking Empire of Austria-Hungary was not much better. Despite this serious state of affairs, Imperial Russia had the largest number of aircraft available for war duties in 1914. Again, it was organization that let the country down. Most were inefficient single-engine designs, preferred by many generals because they could be manufactured quickly. This was in a country where large numbers mattered. Still, on the Eastern Front, the force-to-space ratio was completely different to the experience of the Western Front.

Armies manoeuvred in vast spaces, and threats could develop so quickly that the few aircraft available could play little role. The Germans had defeated the Russians at Tannenberg in 1914, but through the autumn of 1914 and the spring of 1915 the Russians had given the Austro-Hungarians a severe beating, almost knocking them out of the war. Only German intervention brought a halt to the Russian advance.

Rumblings to the east and south

By the spring of 1915, the Germans and Austrians were ready to attack at Gorlice-Tarnow. The Russians were in bad shape, disorganized and exhausted, and this applied especially to the state of their aviation. The German–Austrian forces could 'see' their enemy's positions; the Russians could not. There were those in the German High Command who wanted to follow up this success with a massive invasion of Russia, but Falkenhayn disagreed. He closed down offensive operations, transferring troops to the West for the battles at Verdun. Without consultation with their allies, the Austrians moved troops to the Italian Front. Given this unexpected breather, Russian forces underwent a miraculous recovery.

As part of what became known as the 'Brusilov Offensive', the Russians used their small number of 250 aircraft to the best effect. They carefully photographed Austro-Hungarian positions. One of the few Russian aviation aces of the war, Aleksandr Kazakov, won a number of victories. He opened his score in May 1915 flying a Morane-Saulnier, and commanded the 1st Combat Air Group in mid-1916.

Fighters: 1914–1918

He scored his final victories over Romania in 1917, when he was wounded, ending his career. His final score stood at 20 victories.

The last great battle of Imperial Russia was launched. The Germans and Austrians, under renewed pressure, hurried troops eastwards, weakening their positions in France and Italy. But the Russians had fired their last imperial shots. Their exhausted armies, riven with revolutionary sentiment, began to melt away. A few loyal divisions held the front – just.

The Austrians faced not only Russia, but also, from May 1915, Italy, along its alpine frontier. Italy was the first country to deploy an 'air force' aggressively, in 1911–12 during its war with the Ottoman Empire. By 1915 the Corpo Aeronautico Militare had around 100 aircraft. Included among these was a number of Caproni Ca.3 bombers. These remarkably efficient aircraft went into action for the first time on 20 August 1915. Italy spent much of its energy attacking well-fortified Austrian positions. Overhead flew the faithful Caproni bombers, mostly attacking important railway junctions and other infrastructure behind Austrian lines. With the backing of their German partners, the Austrians built up a reasonably efficient fighter force, led by flyers such as Godwin Brumowski. He followed the teachings of Richthofen, painting his Albatros D.III red to match his hero's. Brumowski eventually scored 35 victories. This record persuaded the Italian bomber pilots to operate by night, with a consequent reduction in accuracy. Even before World War I, Italy's General Giulio Douhet had been a prophet of air power. He was also an advocate of the bomber's ability to destroy the enemy's morale. Unfortunately, the available technology and alpine mountains proved too much of a barrier in 1915–18.

The Treaty of Brest-Litovsk, concluded in March 1918 between the Central Powers and the Bolshevik Government in Russia, made it possible for the Germans to switch many divisions to the Western Front in readiness for the spring offensive.

BOMBERS: 1916–18

On 1 November 1911, the first aerial bombing mission ever was carried out against Turkish positions in Libya. This action was taken under the command of Giulio Douhet, who was then the officer commanding a small Italian air group fighting in the Italo-Turkish War. He went on to become a leading air power theorist and staunch advocate of strategic bombing.

Fighting for better strategies in the air

Born in May 1869, Giulio Douhet attended Modena Military Academy and was later commissioned into the infantry of the Italian army's famous Bersagliari corps. While in the army, he studied science and engineering at the Polytechnic Institute in Turin, and by the early 1900s he had been assigned to the German Staff. He was an eyewitness to the development of first airships, then aircraft, and to their first effective use in war.

As a result of his role in the war between Italy and Turkey, Douhet was commissioned by the Italian General Staff to write a full report on the lessons gleaned from the conflict. Among the suggestions he made was that bombing should be the primary role of military aviation. Douhet was the most influential military theorist of his time, drawing dedicated followers – usually those out of step with the contemporary High Command – and the admiration of like-minded military officers.

As war clouds loomed over Europe, Douhet became increasingly impatient with Italy's lack of preparedness. He ordered a number of three-engined long-range bombers from his friend Gianni Caproni, without official authorization. For Italian High Command, this 'affront' was the last straw. Already considered a radical for his ideas on air power and the need for a separate air arm, he was promptly relieved of his post as commander of the aviation battalion and sent to an infantry division. Yet the Caproni Ca.3 aircraft that he unofficially ordered turned out to be highly successful. This remarkable three-engined bomber was way ahead of its time; some 269 were built for the Corpo Aeronautico Militare, and a few were supplied to the French air force.

Despite his banishment to the infantry, Douhet continued to write and agitate to improve Italy's fighting potential, particularly in the air:

*To us who have until now been inexorably bound to the surface of the earth, it must seem that the sky, too, is to become another battlefield no less important than the battlefields on land and at sea. For if there are nations that exist that are untouched by the sea, there are **none** that exist without the breath of air.*

Giulio Douhet

Around the same time, hundreds of miles to the east, another revolutionary aircraft was taking to the air: the four-engined Ilya Muromets, brainchild of the Russian aircraft designer Igor Sikorsky. The aircraft had formidable performance for its day, with a range of up to 400km (250 miles) and capable of carrying a considerable war load. Fortunately for Germany and Austria-Hungary, the Russian High Command failed to recognize its value, and it was produced and deployed in very small numbers. Its appearance did not go unnoticed in Germany, however.

When war came to Italy in May 1915, shocked by the Italian army's poor performance, Douhet redoubled his efforts to convince his superiors and the government that the answer to Italy's dismal lack of success lay in the power of war from the air. He did not hold back his views on what he saw as incompetence and lack of preparedness, resulting in his court martial for spreading false news and agitation; his punishment was a year in jail.

Douhet continued to write on air power even while incarcerated, proposing a massive inter-Allied air fleet to bomb the Central Powers into

CAPRONI Ca.3
Caproni bombers like the Ca.3 carried out many strategic operations against targets on the Adriatic coast, including the city and seaport of Trieste. Strategic operations virtually ceased early in November 1917, when the Austrians overran the Capronis' main base at Pordenone following the Italian defeat at Caporetto.

Bombers: 1916–18

submission. He was released and returned to service in 1917, becoming Director of Aviation at the General Air Commissariat. After resigning in 1918, he went on to complete his great work *The Command of the Air* in 1921, in which he argued, as he had always done, that air power could be much more powerful against the enemy than any surface forces. The limitless sky made defence against attacks from the sky almost impossible, in essence making air power's role an offensive one. Bomb the enemy's sources of power, its cities, factories and populations, and you could bring it into submission. The offensive-minded British Air Commander Hugh Trenchard agreed. So, too, did some in Germany ...

Germany's growing air power

Airships had initially been seen by many among the German High Command as the mechanism of long-range bombardment. In 1914–15, their range and load-carrying capacity far outclassed that of any available aircraft. Both the German navy and army deployed their airships in attacks on the United Kingdom, and there was considerable rivalry between the two services. On 31 May 1915, it was an army airship that carried out the first bombing of London. Airship raids continued until the end of World War I, but the huge cost of airships and their increasing vulnerability led the German High Command to begin formulating plans to attack mainland Britain with aircraft.

Major Wilhelm Siegert had approached High Command – the *Oberste Heeresleitung*, or OHL – in October 1914. He was eventually given command of a small group of aircraft based near Ostend in Belgium. The German army's advance stalled, and the French Channel ports remained in Allied hands. Siegert's small force lacked the

SIKORSKY ILYA MUROMETS
Imperial Russia, with its giant Ilya Muromets series of aircraft, was the first of the belligerents to recognize the potential of the heavy bomber. Heavily armed with up to eight defensive machine guns, the four-engined IMs flew 450 missions and dropped 65 tons of bombs for the loss of only three aircraft in three years of operational flying before the October Revolution of 1917 brought an end to their activities.

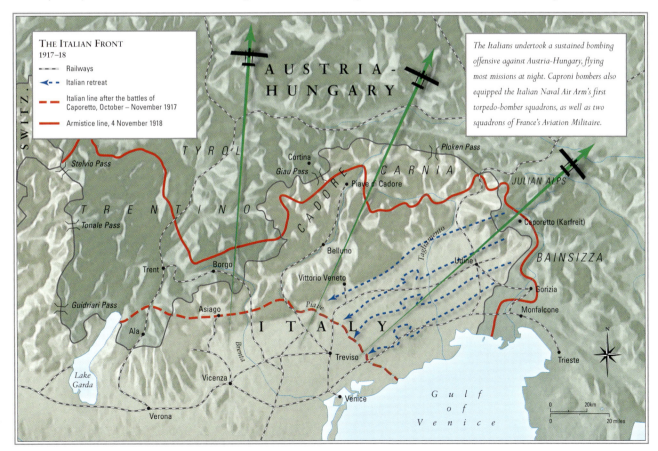

The Italians undertook a sustained bombing offensive against Austria-Hungary, flying most missions at night. Caproni bombers also equipped the Italian Naval Air Arm's first torpedo-bomber squadrons, as well as two squadrons of France's Aviation Militaire.

Bombers: 1916–18

range for any major target in England, so he contented himself with bombing Calais and Boulogne. It was this inability to reach British shores, coupled with the influence of the Russian Ilya Muromets and the success of Italy's Caproni bomber, that stimulated the request sent out for a number of German manufacturers to design new *Grosskampfflugzeug* ('giant battle machines'); the first aircraft began to appear in 1915. German High Command had by now realized the importance of air power and appointed General Ernst von Hoeppner to command the air arm now known as the *Luftstreitkraft*. Now that new long-range machines were available, Siegert's plans were dusted off and re-examined.

Operational air power

By the spring of 1917, the first squadron of bombers was available for operations. Equipped with Gotha G.IV bombers, this first squadron would be joined by a second squadron equipped with even larger aircraft, Zeppelin-Staaken R-Type bombers. The old base commanded by Siegert was now known as Kagohl 1 (*Kampfgeschwader der Obersten Heeresleitung* 1). The original base, near Ostend, was joined by new airfields at Gontrode, St Denis-Westrem and Mariakerke. Hauptmann Ernst Brandenburg was chosen to lead the new force and, after intense training, his carefully recruited bomber crews were ready for operations.

On 25 May 1917, 23 Gothas took off for their first major raid on England. The aircraft landed at Nieuwmunster to refuel before pressing on to their intended target – London. Two aircraft turned back with technical problems; the rest continued on their way. Twenty-one Gotha bombers crossed the Essex coast at Burnham-on-Crouch at around 3660m (12,000 feet), where they faced towering clouds and poor visibility. Realizing that it would be impossible to bomb London under such conditions, the formation turned south, heading for Kent. Targets of opportunity were now the order of the day. The greatest of these was the port of Folkestone. Brandenburg gave the signal, and this small Channel port received the load of bombs intended for London. The aircraft dropped just over five tons of bombs and caused the highest number of air-raid casualties to date – 95 dead and 195 injured. British anti-aircraft guns fired on the raiders, but their shells burst too low. Seventy-four fighters were sent up, but failed to damage the enemy formation. Just one Gotha was lost – it came down in the sea, probably because of engine failure.

A second raid, on 5 June, consisted of 22 aircraft and was directed against the naval dockyards at Sheerness and Sheppey on the Thames estuary. British fighters intercepted them this time, and brought down one Gotha bomber.

Bombers: 1916–18

GERMAN STRIKING FORCE
In 1917 the Germans had several heavy bombers at their disposal, notably the Gotha G.IV and G.V (pictured).

On 13 June, Brandenburg led his Gotha bombers to England once again. Twenty aircraft set out; three turned back with various technical problems, while three more bombed naval targets along the Thames estuary. The rest of the formation pressed on, arriving over East London around 11.32 a.m. A few bombs fell around the docks, but the formation's intended aim was Liverpool Street railway station. Here, almost two tons of bombs fell. The most devastating bomb, however, was one that fell on a school in the eastern suburb of Poplar, killing 16 children. In all, 162 people were killed and 432 wounded. The outcome was British outrage and a sense of solidarity among the populace. The few looters and rioters were soon put in their place – it was not the collapse of morale predicted by Douhet and others.

Calls for better defence resulted in two crack squadrons being recalled to the United Kingdom from the Western Front, much to the annoyance of Major General Hugh Trenchard, whose forces there were at full stretch defending and maintaining an

DAYLIGHT GOTHA RAIDS
Principal attacks by Kagohl 3

- ← 25 May 1917, 5.1 tons of bombs: 95 killed, 195 injured
- ← 13 June 1917, 4.3 tons of bombs: 162 killed, 432 injured
- ← 7 July 1917, 4.3 tons of bombs: 57 killed, 193 injured
- ← 12 August 1917, 2.1 tons of bombs: 32 killed, 46 injured
- • German airfield

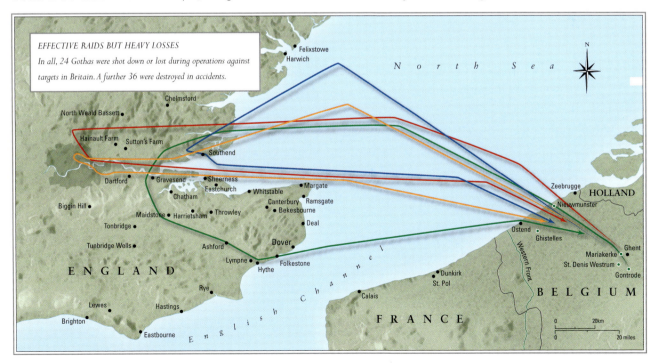

EFFECTIVE RAIDS BUT HEAVY LOSSES
In all, 24 Gothas were shot down or lost during operations against targets in Britain. A further 36 were destroyed in accidents.

Bombers: 1916–18

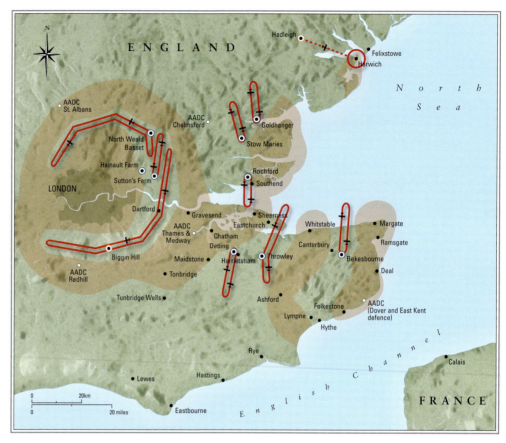

AIR DEFENCES OF THE UK
The Home Defence Group fighter squadrons of the RFC and RNAS developed new tactics to counter the raiders in 1917. 'Readiness' was signalled by three short klaxon bursts, at which pilots and mechanics ran to their aircraft and wheeled them from their sheds. The engines were started up and the pilots sat in their cockpits, awaiting further orders. On the 'patrol' order, defending aircraft climbed in formation to their allotted areas, to be controlled by ground signals.

offensive policy. British defence was at last becoming increasingly capable, and fighters were able to intercept bombers or at least drive them off their primary targets.

Upping the ante

British leaders were forced to take the air war to a new level. Chief of the Imperial General Staff Sir William Robertson saw the need to create a united single air force. With the help of Prime Minister Lloyd George, General Jan Smuts chaired a new committee on air organization. Very quickly, it was realized that a dispersed command split between the navy and army had to end. New coordinated command structures were set in place, and London was given a more comprehensive defence so that it was no longer a relatively easy target for the bomber or airship. German bomber squadrons reacted by bombing at night. In turn, the British set up specific areas of anti-aircraft guns and lines of balloon barrages. The guns were arranged to allow the fighters defined areas for fighter patrols.

Meanwhile, Germany's air force had developed a gigantic aircraft: the Zeppelin-Staaken R-Type, originally designed for use on the Eastern Front. One squadron, No. 501, was sent to Belgium to reinforce the air offensive against the United Kingdom. The R-Type bombers would fly at night with the Gothas; one of these, in the company of two Gothas, reached London on the night of 29 September 1917. The British continued to strengthen their defences and to attack the German bomber airfields in western Belgium. They also began to plan for the bombing of Germany.

The French were quick to recognize the importance of strategic bombing, and from 1916 implemented daylight attacks on German targets in the Rhineland using the excellent Breguet Br XIV, under strong fighter escort. The British, however, were keen to develop longer range bombers from the outset of hostilities. The result was the Handley Page O/100, which owed its origins to a requirement issued in December 1914 for a 'bloody paralyser of an aeroplane' for the bombing of Germany. The O/100 entered service with No. 3 Wing RNAS on the Western Front in November 1916, and from the spring of the following year its two squadrons, Nos. 14 and 16, concentrated on the night bombing of major German installations such as U-boat bases, railway stations and industrial centres.

Bombers: 1916–18

ZEPPELIN–STAAKEN R.VI

Length: 23.1m (76 ft 1in)
Wing span: 42.2m (138 ft 5in)

Powerplant: 4 x Mercedes D. IVa engines
Max speed: 135kph (84mph)
Combat range: 800km (500 miles)

Crew: 7
Armament: 5 x machine guns
Bombload: 2,000kg (4,400lb)

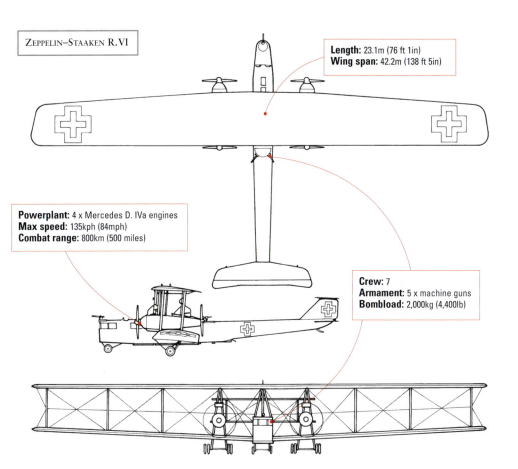

ZEPPELIN-STAAKEN R.VI
The massive R.VI was the first military aircraft to have an enclosed cockpit and was the largest wooden aircraft built until the construction of Howard Hughes' H-4 Hercules 'Spruce Goose' in 1947.

Bombers: 1916–18

Although Trenchard was against taking forces away from the daily battle of the Western Front, he reluctantly agreed to the formation of a dedicated bomber force. This was to be equipped with a new aircraft, the Handley Page O/400, and would hopefully be ready by late 1917. The new bomber force made its first attack on Germany with readily available aircraft, eight DH.4 light bombers, setting off on the night of 17 October 1917 to attack the ironworks at Saarbrücken. Smuts' recommendations for an independent British air force capable of taking the war to the German homeland became a reality in April 1918. The 41st Wing that had begun attacks in October 1917 with three squadrons, only one of which was equipped with the O/400 twin-engined bomber, was expanded to five squadrons that, by May, were part of the newly formed Royal Air Force, combining the RFC and the RNAS.

The new force came under Trenchard's command, as Chief of the Air Staff. He actively promoted a policy of bombing. In fact, most operations were tactical, in support of the British army; however, new aircraft designed for long-range bombing, the de Havilland DH.17 and the Handley Page V/1500 'Berlin Bomber', were in production. Had these aircraft reached service before the war's end, Germany would have suffered concentrated bombing of her larger cities.

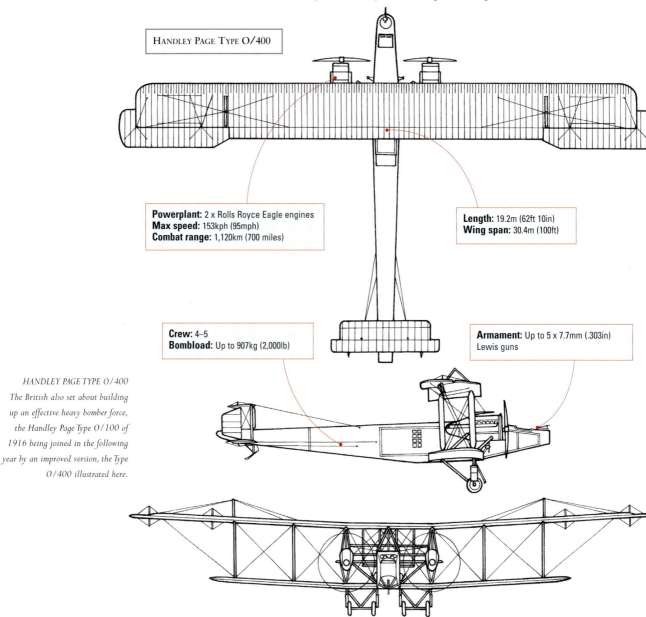

HANDLEY PAGE TYPE O/400

Powerplant: 2 x Rolls Royce Eagle engines
Max speed: 153kph (95mph)
Combat range: 1,120km (700 miles)

Length: 19.2m (62ft 10in)
Wing span: 30.4m (100ft)

Crew: 4–5
Bombload: Up to 907kg (2,000lb)

Armament: Up to 5 x 7.7mm (.303in) Lewis guns

*HANDLEY PAGE TYPE O/400
The British also set about building up an effective heavy bomber force, the Handley Page Type O/100 of 1916 being joined in the following year by an improved version, the Type O/400 illustrated here.*

Bombers: 1916–18

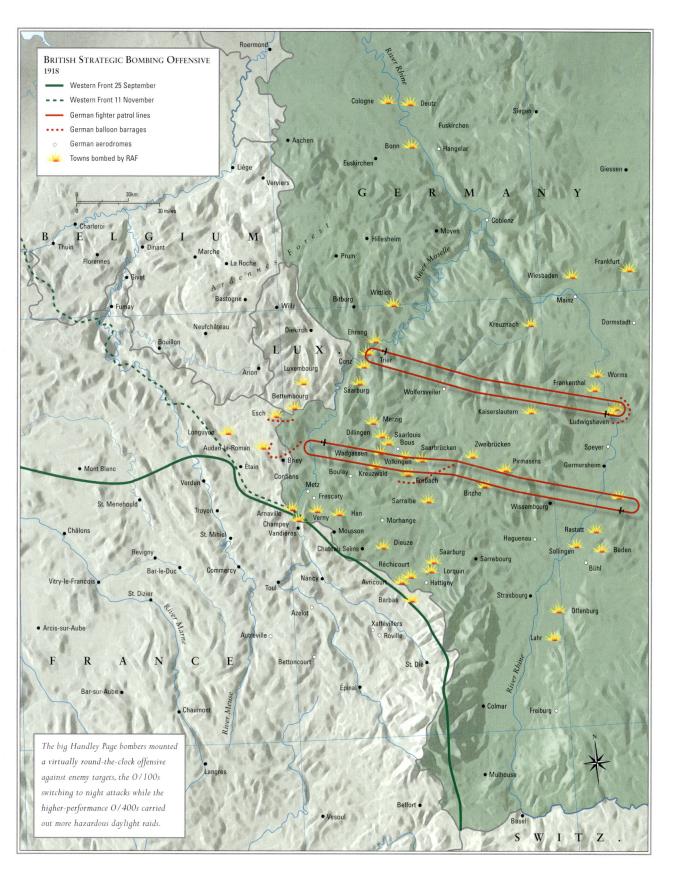

AMERICA MOBILIZES: 1917

OVER THERE!
When the United States declared a state of war with Germany on 6 April 1917, the US Army Aviation Section had fewer than 300 aircraft, none of them combat types, and only 35 qualified pilots among a total of 1100 personnel. The Aviation Act of July 1917 provided for a huge increase in funding and a vigorous recruitment campaign.

The German U-boat campaign was designed to strangle supply lines to the United Kingdom from its vast overseas empire and particularly from its neighbour across the Atlantic, the United States. While the campaign did bring some short-term success, ultimately it backfired on Germany. US President Woodrow Wilson had made it quite clear that German attacks on US merchant ships would be seen as a justification for declaring war. After significant merchant losses, especially the loss of the *Lusitania*, taking with it 168 US citizens to their deaths, the United States entered the war on the Allied side in April 1917.

Measured in purely military terms, the US forces, except for the navy, were insignificant. The United States was in no position to participate on the European mainland in any meaningful way – and so began a massive mobilization.

Volunteer commitment

Official US entry into the conflict may not have come until 1917, but the Americans had been active in the war since almost the beginning, with the American Ambulance Field Service. Later, led by an adventurous New Englander, Norman Prince, American volunteers formed an escadrille in the French air force and began operations on 16 April 1916. In all, 209 US nationals volunteered for the French air force. Most went through regular training at Buc in France, flying Blériots, of which just 31 found their way into Escadrille Layfayette; the rest served with other French squadrons:

> *French training schools were no bed of roses. We were up every morning before dawn, with only a cup of lukewarm chicory, masquerading as coffee, to sustain us till the first meal at eleven o'clock. Daylight found us shivering at our various fields, awaiting our turns on that fearful and wonderful contraption known as the Blériot Monoplane.*

The US Air Service, under the command of Major General Mason Patrick, was created as part of the American Expeditionary Forces. General John J. Pershing, overall commander of the AEF, originally called for the creation of 260 combat squadrons. This was later reduced to 202. The force was divided into 101 observation, 27 night-bomber, 14 day-bomber and 60 pursuit (fighter) squadrons. These would cooperate with the planned three armies of 16 Corps forming in France. At the outbreak of war, the United States had a negligible air force and not much of an aviation industry to supply it. As a result, the US Government placed large orders for French and British machines. These included the DH.4 and Salmson 2 for observation and bombing, and the Nieuport 28, Spad XIII and S.E.5 as fighters. Licence production was also planned to be shared among as many suitable companies as possible. The process was less than successful.

European production techniques required large numbers of craftsmen to hand-finish and fit, but this did not translate well to US methods of mass production, where the production line was king. Also, industrial manufacturers were given little time to switch over from civilian to military mode. Despite all the difficulties, some 4000 DH.4s were produced, powered by a solely US-designed 180hp engine, the Liberty. A massive appropriation of US $640,000,000, dedicated to expanding aviation, was passed by Congress in 1917 – the largest single appropriation dedicated to one objective to date.

In Europe at last

It was August 1917 before the first US combat squadron – the 1st Aero Squadron, operating in an observation role – arrived in France. By February 1918, the US Air Service had entered combat; on the fifth, it scored its first victory. During American ground operations, US squadrons gave vital support at the battles of the Third Aisne and Saint-Mihiel, as well as the Meuse–Argonne Offensive.

Those Americans flying with France's Escadrille Lafayette were absorbed into the US Air Service as the 103rd Aero Squadron. By 11 November 1918, 7 bomber, 18 observation and 20 fighter squadrons operated on the Western Front. Operations included bomber raids up to 257km (120 miles) behind German lines. They were to claim 756 enemy aircraft and 76 balloons destroyed. These actions created 31 air aces, including pilots such Captain Eddie Rickenbacker, with 26 victories. The US Air Service lost 289 aircraft, 48 balloons and 237 aircrew killed in action. By the end of the war, the total number of US squadrons worldwide reached 185, with a full construction, supply, engineering and training infrastructure to support them.

America Mobilises: 1917

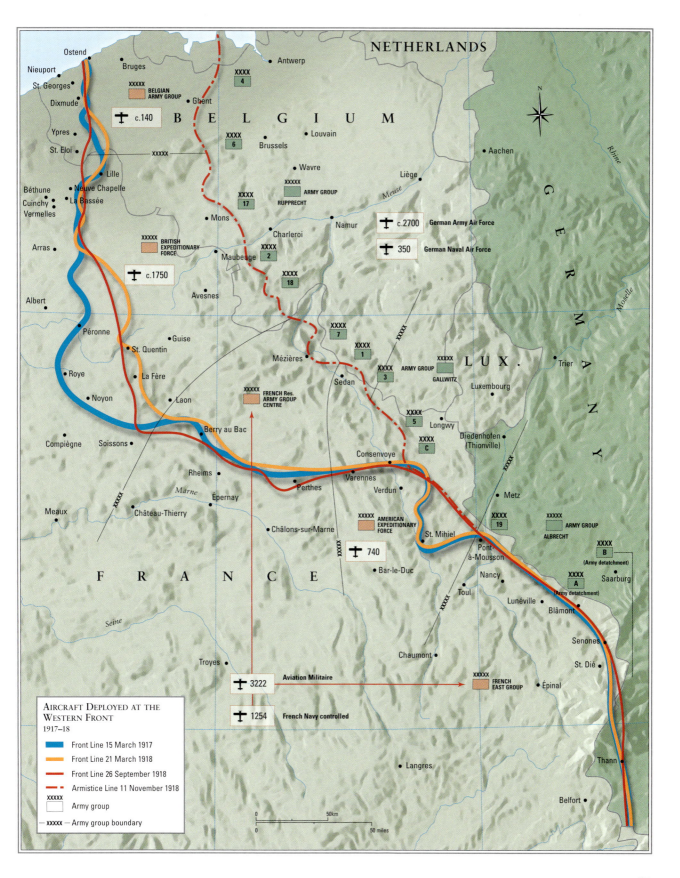

FINAL BATTLES: 1918

As 1917 drew to a close, Russia's exhausted and discredited Tsarist regime had fallen to revolution. The new democratic Provisional Government at first attempted to uphold its obligations to its Western Allies. Launching the Brusilov Offensive in June, the Kerensky-led regime felt that only a major victory on the battlefield could establish its right to rule the new Russia. The offensive briefly prospered but soon began to falter, then fade. Russia was falling apart. Power passed into the hands of the Bolsheviks. Their original plan was to spread revolution into Europe, ending the war from within. They failed in this, but did at least hold power in Russia's cities. For them to consolidate their precarious hold on Russia, peace with Germany was essential – at any price. The Treaty of Brest-Litovsk was the result, granting vast territories to Germany and Austria-Hungary. To some extent, this eased the pressure caused by the Allied blockade. With relative peace in the east, the Central Powers could look to other fronts.

Having held the British attacks in Flanders, the Germans attacked on the Italian Front in October 1917. Troops were transferred to reinforce the Austro-Hungarians, and the offensive was launched at Caporetto, inflicting a comprehensive defeat on the Italian army. The Germans advanced some 129km (80 miles) but, with British and French help, the Italians held along the river Piave.

In France, the attacks by the British at Cambrai, with many of their new tanks in place, alarmed the German High Command enough for it to call a halt on the Italian Front. The Italians would be in no shape to take the offensive until conditions improved considerably. France was still shaken by the costly Nivelle offensives of the spring, and the Americans were still training and shipping troops to Europe, and were as yet only a token force on the battlefield. In German eyes, that left the British as the major opponent for 1918.

Urgent need for increased production

The Americans may have only just begun to make their impact felt in the war, but the German High Command nonetheless recognized the vast industrial potential of the United States. In mid-1917, Germany had launched the aptly named *Amerikaprogramm*. This called for the production of 2000 aircraft and 2500 engines per month and was meant to meet rising production from French, British and now American factories. The added strain of this industrial effort increased the price of aircraft. It also put further stress on morale among Germany's industrial workers. Enthusiasm for the war had waned; strikes broke out, and workmanship declined. During 1917, German industry produced 13,977 aircraft, but only 12,029 engines. During this same period, the French and British together produced 28,781 aircraft and 34,755 engines, and, ominously, aircraft were beginning to emerge from factories in the United States.

During the first few months of 1918, German industry did not produce more than 1100 aircraft per month. The writing was on the wall for the German Air Service. It could either rob the training and reserve establishments to maintain frontline strength, or it could let that strength gradually erode to a point where any attempt at control of the air would be impossible. A policy of long-term defence was becoming necessary. Although Germany and Austria-Hungary controlled large areas of Eastern Europe, these were largely poor agricultural areas, adding little or no industry to the Central Powers' war effort. The Italians may have been given a beating, but the situation on the

FORWARD AIRSTRIP
The Royal Aircraft Factory RE.8, seen here at an improvised forward airstrip, took over the observation task from the BE.2 and was was subsequently very widely used, equipping 33 RFC squadrons. Like the BE.2, it was far too stable to be agile in combat and suffered serious losses, usually having to operate under heavy escort.

Final Battles: 1918

Western Front could only deteriorate, as the American military build-up began to give the Allies a numerical advantage. For the Germans, it was spring 1918 or never in terms of victory. At this time, the Central Powers held a brief advantage. Although they had to police large areas of Eastern Europe after the Treaty of Brest-Litovsk, they could still send troops westwards. This would give a superiority of 192 divisions against 169 Allied ones.

On 21 March, Operation Michael exploded on the Western Front. Its thrust was aimed at the British 3rd and 5th Armies, in the area of Arras and St Quentin. The German army developed new tactics. To maintain surprise, specialist storm troops armed with automatic weapons rushed forwards, bypassing strongpoints; these would be mopped up later by supporting units. Overhead operated the newly organized *Schlachtstaffeln* ('battle flights'), now being grouped into *Schlachtgeschwader* ('battle wings'), with ground-attack aircraft designed to harass enemy supplies, machine-gun posts and any points of resistance, and to report back to army commanders on progress. A *Schlachtgruppe* covered a section of the front, with a constant supply of replacements as ammunition and fuel ran low. Army commanders had highly mobile airborne light artillery and a constant supply of updated information at their disposal. The Allies were to employ similar tactics.

Drive towards the Somme

German air combat strength had grown from 2270 in late 1917 to 3670 by March 1918. Entering service in the early months of 1918 was the new Fokker D.VII. In the hands of the average German pilot, this aircraft was a dangerous opponent; with an experienced pilot at the controls, it was frequently the last thing an Allied pilot saw on this earth. The German offensive was designed to drive southwest towards the Somme. The turn northwest rolling up the British and the Belgian lines went well at first. A huge salient was driven into the Allied line. By 4 April, however, German logistics could not keep the offensive supplied – it simply ran out of steam. The Allies reorganized their High Command and the deployment of its divisions, and held the line. On 9 April Ludendorff launched a second offensive, Georgette, with some initial gains, but by 17 April the British were counterattacking with some success.

During this period, the German Air Service was losing some 14 per cent of its pilots per month, a loss rate that the training establishments could not make up. Also, among the casualties for April was

AIRCRAFT LOSSES
August 1918

- German (green)
- Allied (red)

This graphic shows the losses for Allied and German aircraft on operations in August 1918. Note the heavy losses incurred by the Allied air forces on 8 and 9 August at the beginning of the final offensive of the war.

Final Battles: 1918

BREGUET BR.XIV
Louis Breguet's most effective product of World War I was without doubt the Br.XIV two-seat reconnaissance/bomber. The first production aircraft entered service with the Aeronautique Militaire in the spring of 1917, and the Br.XIV quickly established a reputation for toughness and reliability.

DEADLY FALL
Before parachutes were issued, pilots would jump to their deaths rather than be burned alive. The Germans were the first to issue parachutes; German aircraft generally had more powerful engines, which were better placed to cope with the extra weight.

Manfred von Richthofen, killed flying over Morlan Court Ridge not far from the river Somme. The death of Richthofen, whom modern research suggests was shot down by an Australian machine-gunner, and not by Captain Roy Brown of No. 209 Squadron, as was originally believed, came as a profound shock to the German people. Field Marshal Ludendorff stated that the effect on morale was equivalent to the annihilation of 10 German divisions.

On 27 May it was the French army's turn to be attacked. The Germans advanced 21km (13 miles) in the first 24 hours, the longest advance in one day on the Western Front since 1914. By 3 June they reached the river Marne, scene of heavy fighting in August–September 1914. As with the earlier attacks on the British, Germany's ability to keep the offensive supplied withered; the attack was called off.

In a taste of what was to come, two American divisions were among Allied formations that counter-attacked, the 1st Division at Catigny on 28 May and the 2nd Division at Belleau Wood on 2 June. Two more attacks were launched by the Germans, between 9 June and 15 July; both petered out. By now the Germans were exhausted. The offensives had cost 1,000,000 casualties, including many of Germany's best pilots, and around 2900 aircraft.

Turning the tables

Now it was the Allies' turn to go on the offensive. From 18 July the French army began counterattacks across the river Marne. The French advance reached Soissons on 2 August. On 8 August the British 4th Army and the French 1st Army attacked south of Albert. It was a great success, particularly the British–Australian attack. Aerial photography had carefully identified the main defences: a short bombardment, well sited, followed by tanks and infantry with close air support – an early form of *blitzkrieg*. For once the troops made it across the killing zone of 'no-man's land' and through German defences. Ludendorff called it the 'blackest day of the war for the German army'.

The depleted *Jagdgeschwader* fought to keep Allied bombers at bay as German troops fell back. They succeeded in defending the Somme bridges from Allied air assault, particularly those equipped with the new Fokker D.VII, inflicting heavy casualties on the attackers. Along the 40km (25 mile) front, just 365 German aircraft fought hard to hold back 1900-plus Allied aircraft.

On 12 September, just as Ludendorff organized a withdrawal, the newly formed US 1st Army attacked the St Mihiel salient. The Germans were still fighting hard in the air throughout August and September, inflicting heavy casualties; the US 1st Day Bombardment Group lost 31 aircrew over the St Mihiel salient. Aggressive flying, however, virtually shut down German reconnaissance. American ace Frank Luke, a specialist balloon-buster of the 27th Aero Squadron, destroyed 17 balloons during an 18-day period. German High Command was denied a clear picture of unfolding events.

The Allied offensives continued, forcing the German armies back along most of the line. With each withdrawal, German air units fell back onto less prepared and equipped airfields, and their fighting power decreased accordingly. Between March and November, German air strength fell from around 3700 aircraft to 2700. Production figures underlined the worsening situation Germany faced: up to November, Germany produced 8055 aircraft and just over 9000 engines; over the same period, the United Kingdom and France had produced 56,378 aircraft and a massive 66,651 engines, enough to supply their own forces and the US Air Services. And while the ambitious US programme had not proven a great success, it was expected to produce significant results by 1919.

The world of aviation had changed beyond recognition. In 1914 the aircraft was regarded by most as a sort of flying observation post, but by 1918 and the cessation of hostilities, the waging of war was inconceivable without the deployment of aircraft. Even the Treaty of Versailles mentioned aircraft in general, and the Fokker D.VII in particular, such was the impact that this aircraft made in the late summer of 1918. The major powers had entered World War I with air forces of a couple of hundred aircraft and crews; they ended the conflict with air forces numbering in the thousands. There was no turning back from air warfare.

Final Battles: 1918

By 1920 the map of Europe had changed substantially, with the new states of Poland, Czechoslovakia and Yugoslavia created out of the wreckage of the Central Powers and the Ottoman Empire.

The Inter-War Years

THE INTER-WAR YEARS

CHARLES KINGSFORD SMITH
The first complete crossing of the Pacific was made in 1928 in a Fokker F.VIIB-3m named Southern Cross *captained by Charles Kingsford Smith. After an adventurous flight through electrical storms, with several stops en route, landfall was made at Eagle Farm, Brisbane, the* Southern Cross *having covered a distance of 11,890km (7389 miles) in an elapsed time of 83 hours 38 minutes.*

CONVERTED BOMBER
Some of Handley Page's big O/400 bombers were converted into transports in the years after World War I. The example seen here made its first commercial flight from Cricklewood on 30 April 1919, carrying newspapers and 11 passengers, and reached Manchester three hours later.

Signed on 28 June 1919, the Treaty of Versailles was the peace agreement between Germany and the Allied forces that officially ended the 'war to end all wars', some six months after the end of actual fighting on 11 November 1918. The treaty imposed severe penalties on Germany, including a ban on military aviation. It did not ban civilian aviation, however, and nor did it anchor Germany into a new status quo. Marshal of France Ferdinand Foch, who was Supreme Commander of the Allied armies by the war's end, simply suggested that the treaty was nothing more than a 'twenty-year truce'.

On the scrapheap

With the coming of peace, thousands of aircraft were surplus to requirement, and were scrapped, sold off or mothballed. It was possible to buy a brand-new Royal Aircraft Factory SE5a fighter (minus its guns) for £5. A Curtiss Jenny, just off the production line, was yours for US$300. What's more, while a few years before a pilot was a rare creature indeed, now there were thousands of these, too, as well as a multitude of aviation experts of all kinds. After the experience of war, many former military pilots found it hard to fit back into civilian life. In the United States, the 'barnstormers' became the mainstay of touring fairground shows. They introduced small towns across North America to the wonders of aviation. Adventurous and creative minds turned to new concepts in aviation – if an aircraft could fly hundreds of miles with a cargo of bombs, why not post and, perhaps, people?

Before World War I, airships in Germany had safely carried thousands of passengers, flown by the airline DELAG. In 1913, Florida saw the first attempted scheduled air service. But it was on 25 August 1919 that the first sustained air service began, between London and Paris, launched by the British company Aircraft Transport and Travel Limited. Routes between other European capitals very quickly sprang up. Although most European countries subsidized air services from the beginning, Britain took a little longer. After several private companies failed, the four surviving companies were merged into a subsidized national airline, grandly named Imperial Airways, on 13 March 1924. The main objective was a strategic air connection between Britain and its far-flung empire. Just one month after the end of hostilities, a specially equipped Handley Page V/1500 Bomber, originally designed to bomb Berlin, had taken off from England and made the first flight to India. It was the first of many pioneering flights that would be made by the Royal Air Force.

Routes would be pioneered to South Africa via Malta, Cairo and East and West Africa. French pilots flew to the hub of their African empire, Dakar, with connections to most colonial outposts. The Dutch flew via the Middle East and India to East Asia. Germany, its overseas empire dismantled by the Treaty of Versailles, developed routes into the Soviet Union and on to China. Germany's relationship with the Soviet Union prospered throughout the 1920s and early 1930s, a way of circumventing the hated Versailles peace treaty. As European nations planned to connect with their empires, American eyes turned towards the challenge of the Atlantic.

The lure of the Atlantic

Previously, Lord Northcliffe, owner of the air-minded British newspaper the *Daily Mail*, had offered a prize of £10,000 for the first crossing of the Atlantic between North America and the British Isles, or vice versa. Ireland, the favoured landing place, was then part of the United Kingdom. Two attempts were actively being worked on in 1914, one British and one American, but both had been halted by the outbreak of war. Glenn Curtiss, who had been part of the original American plan, had already produced viable flying-boat designs and set to work in 1918 on newer, better ones. The first Curtiss NC-1 was powered by three tractor 400hp Liberty engines. Subsequent testing produced NC-2, NC-3 and NC-4 models, all powered by four of the same type engines. The biplane design spanned 38m (126ft), and the boat-shaped fuselage was 13.7m (45ft) long and a roomy 3m (10ft) wide. The aircraft were

The Inter-War Years

intended to support US naval operations in European waters. Before the aircraft could be deployed to their stations, however, the war ended.

Interest in long-range deployments did not diminish. The US Navy Bureau of Aeronautics formed a special transatlantic section devoted to study of all the problems inherent in a transatlantic flight, and organizing the expedition. This would be a lavishly supported attempt during 1919.

The maximum range of the flying boats, some 2366km (1470 miles), meant that a nonstop flight was out of the question. Therefore a route via the Azores was chosen. Each flying boat would have a crew of six: two pilots, a navigator, a wireless operator and a reserve pilot who would also act as engineer. Each of the four aircraft had a fuel supply of 6094 litres (1610 gallons), carried amidships. A line of no fewer than 50 warships dotted the route between Trepassey Bay, Newfoundland, and the Azores. Shortly before the planned departure, NC-2 had to be withdrawn because of mechanical problems.

Transatlantic success

On 16 May, Curtiss NC-1, NC-3 and NC-4 set off for the Azores. During the hours of darkness, the line of ships attempted to guide the way with searchlights and by firing starshells. On the morning of 17 May, the navigator of NC-4 spotted the most westerly Azores island, Flores. He then plotted a course for the largest island of São Miguel, but fog forced the aircraft to land at Horta on Faial, after a flight of some 2229km (1380 miles). After three days NC-4 flew

PIONEERING FLIGHTS
Brothers Ross and Keith Smith became the first to fly from England to Australia in 1919, completing the journey in 28 days in a Vickers Vimy and collecting a reward of £10,000 from the Australian Prime Minister. Also flying a Vimy, Lt Col Pierre van Ryneveld and Flt Lt Quintin Brand received a similar amount for their record-breaking flight from London to Cape Town. All four airmen were knighted for their achievement.

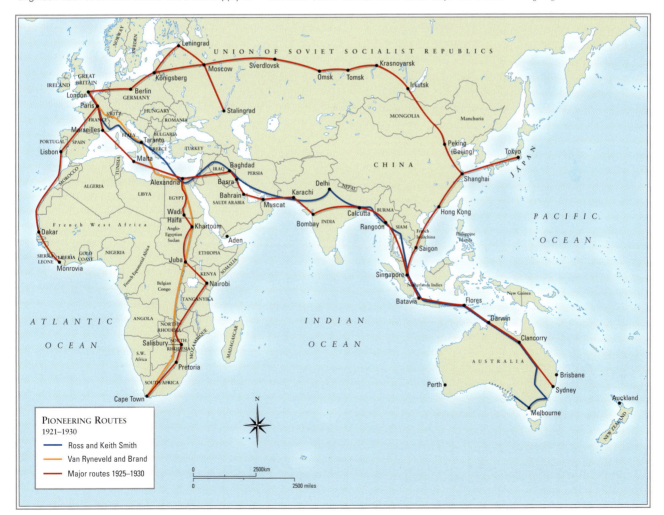

The Inter-War Years

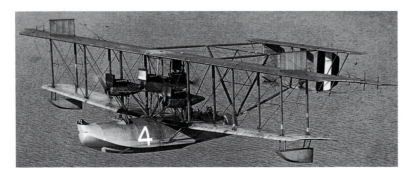

CURTISS NC-4
On 27 May 1919, a Curtiss NC-4 flying boat of the US Navy's Seaplane Division One, commanded by Lt Cdr A.C. Read, became the first to make a transatlantic flight, arriving in Lisbon, Portugal after flying from Newfoundland via the Azores. Its two accompanying aircraft, NC-1 and NC-3, both landed short of their goal. The successful machine spent ten days in Lisbon before flying on to Plymouth, England.

into São Miguel, where the aircraft was held up for a further seven days. On 27 May, NC-4 left the Azores heading for Lisbon, a flight of 1489km (925 miles). This last leg was flown in 9 hours 43 minutes, completing the first crossing of the Atlantic by air. With the aircraft's commander, Lieutenant Commander A.C. Read, were Lieutenant W. Hinton, Lieutenant J.W. Breese, Lieutenant E. Stone, Ensign H.C. Rodd and Chief Machinist's Mate E.S. Rhoads. Of the other two aircraft, NC-1 landed en route, fearful of a collision with the mountainous Azores in fog. The NC-1, damaged in heavy seas, sank shortly after the crew was rescued by the merchant ship *Ionia*. The NC-3 landed to determine its position, but was then unable to take off. Eventually, damaged by heavy seas and in a ragged state, with its wing fabric hanging in shreds, the flying boat taxied safely into the islands' capital, Ponta Delgada, to a rapturous welcome.

The NC-4 left Lisbon heading north, after relatively minor mishaps, and the seaplane arrived in the United Kingdom on the afternoon of 31 May 1919, after a flying time of 53 hours 58 minutes, covering a distance of 6952km (4320 miles) from Trepassey Bay to Cattewater in England.

ATLANTIC ADVENTURES
Crossing the Atlantic Ocean by air was achieved in the 'golden age' between the two world wars. After Read's US Navy crossing, and Alcock and Brown and Lindbergh's pioneering non-stop flights, other adventurers took to the air. Clarence Chamberlin was the first to carry a passenger, von Hünefeld the first to achieve an east–west non-stop flight, and Assolant was the first Frenchman to cross the Atlantic, in the bright yellow Oiseau Canari. Kingsford Smith, as well as pioneering routes to Australia, saw the Atlantic as his one remaining challenge. Transatlantic firsts culminated with the crossing by Wilcockson, Bennett and Coster, making the first of many commercial flights on 20–21 July 1938.

The Inter-War Years

Flying nonstop

The first successful nonstop Atlantic flight was undertaken by British duo Captain John Alcock and Lieutenant Arthur Whitten Brown, only two weeks later. Their aircraft was the Vickers Vimy, a bomber produced towards the end of the war. Powered by two Rolls-Royce Eagle VIII engines, it could fly at a speed of 160kph (100mph). All military equipment was removed, and extra fuel tanks were added to make a total of 3274 litres (865 gallons), enough to fly for up to 3936km (2440 miles).

Just after 4.13 p.m. on 14 June 1919, Alcock and Brown took off from a suitable airfield in Newfoundland. With flasks of coffee, sandwiches and chocolate safely packed, they headed eastwards over the Atlantic. They passed over St John's, urged on by ships' sirens. Not long after leaving sight of land, they ran into fog banks. The dynamo for their wireless transmitter failed, and their newfangled heated flying suits did not work – but at least they had a following wind, and average speed increased. They pressed on through horrific conditions; the airspeed indicator froze, and ice formed on the radiator shutters and the hinges for the ailerons. With Alcock gripping the controls,

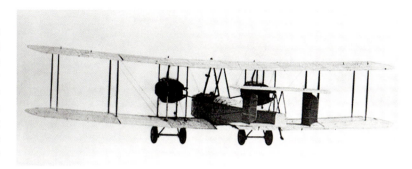

VICKERS VIMY
The first nonstop crossing of the Atlantic, from Lester's Field, Newfoundland, to Clifden in Galway was made on 15 June 1919 by a converted Vickers Vimy flown by Captain John Alcock and navigated by Lieutenant Arthur Whitten Brown. To them went a Daily Mail prize of £10,000, knighthoods, the acclaim of the world and a coveted place in aviation history.

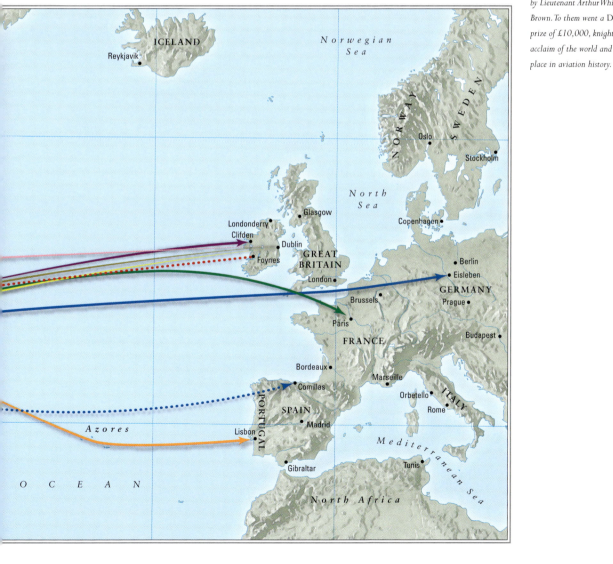

73

The Inter-War Years

Brown was forced to climb out onto the wings no fewer than six times to clear ice from the fuel-intake gauges on each of the engine nacelles.

As dawn arrived, the aircraft was flying at 3353m (11,000ft). Brown was able to get a sextant fix – their position was just to the west of Ireland. Alcock flew down through the cloud layer and came into clear visibility just 61m (200ft) above the sea. Eventually, the tall masts of Clifden radio station appeared. The men chose what looked a likely field to make a landing, but unfortunately it was marshy ground and the aircraft ploughed in, ending up on its nose. Alcock and Brown, well strapped in, were safe, much to the relief and cheers of the radio station staff. They duly received their £10,000 prize from Lord Northcliffe, £2000 of which they gave to the mechanics who helped to make their flight possible.

All-American hero

Perhaps the most famous transatlantic flight was that of Charles A. Lindbergh – nonstop and solo from New York City to Paris. Lindbergh was an experienced flyer of the first air-mail routes; he was also a fully qualified Army Reserve pilot. He persuaded several businesses in St Louis to contribute US$15,000 towards his long-held dream of flying the Atlantic. He then set out to find a suitable aircraft, eventually approaching the small company of Ryan Airlines of San Diego, which agreed to design and build an aircraft for him in just 60 days. A simple, clean high-winged design was produced, powered by a proven Wright Whirlwind, the J-5. Lindbergh named his new aircraft Spirit of St Louis, in recognition of his backers. The aircraft was now set to go through a thorough test flight from San Diego to New York – via St Louis, of course.

Lindbergh took off from Rockwell Field, San Diego, on 10 May 1927 at 3.55 p.m. Pacific Time. He cleared the 3810m (12,500ft) peaks of the Rocky Mountains with 152m (500ft) to spare. Lindbergh stayed one day at Lambert Field, St Louis, then took off heading for New York, landing at 5.33 p.m. local time on 12 May. After its transcontinental crossing, the aircraft was given a complete overhaul. Tests and improvements were made, then, in just one week, reports of good weather arrived. The aircraft was moved to the longer strip at Roosevelt Field for final preparations. The aircraft's tanks were filled to capacity – 1703 litres (450 gallons) of fuel. Conscious of the extreme risk he was taking, Lindbergh opened the throttle of his small aircraft and rolled down the runway. It was 7.52 a.m. on 20 May – just 12 weeks after he had inspected the first design sketches back in San Diego. He cleared a line of telephone wires by just 6m (20ft), and coaxed his aircraft northeastwards towards Newfoundland, then out across the Atlantic.

Lindbergh flew through cloud banks and the night, heading steadily eastwards and following the dawn. He caught a glimpse of small fishing vessels, and circled hoping to find his position, but communication was impossible. He flew on and one hour later crossed Ireland's southwestern tip. He passed over England, then crossed the English Channel, flying over the French port of Cherbourg. In the gathering dusk, the lights of Paris were visible on the horizon. He flew around Le Bourget Airfield, confirming the identity of his landing ground, and touched down at 10.24 a.m. on 21 May 1927. After a flight of 33.5 hours and a journey of 5809km (3610 miles), Lindbergh became an instant hero and a national icon in the United States.

Travelling in the opposite direction

Although the British airship R34 had crossed the Atlantic east to west in July 1919, the first aircraft to complete the journey in this direction was a Junkers W.33 'Bremen', on 13 April 1928. Two Germans – Gunther von Hünefeld and Hermann Köhl – and Irishman James Fitzmaurice flew from Baldonnel Airfield, near Dublin, to tiny Greenly Island, off the coast of Labrador. Other great flyers of their day, including Amy Johnson and Jim Mollison, also crossed the Atlantic. One particular series of flights stand out. In the 1920s and 1930s, Italy, which had been pioneering the development of long-range flying boats, ambitiously decided

CHARLES LINDBERGH
On 21 May, 1927, a Ryan Monoplane named Spirit of St Louis *landed in darkness at Le Bourget, Paris. It had flown from New York to Paris at an average speed of 163kph (108mph), and its shy and serious-looking young pilot, Charles Lindbergh, had flown into the pages of history. For Lindbergh, the first solo transatlantic crossing was only the beginning of an eventful career that encompassed fame and tragedy alike.*

The Inter-War Years

to send an entire formation of 24 Savoia-Marchetti S-55s on a round trip, commanded by General Italo Balbo, the Italian Minister for Air.

The possibility of making such a flight had already been tested by an Italian flying boat, the *Santa Maria*, in 1927 – captained by Francesco de Pinedo. With a crew of three, the Savoia-Marchetti flying boat flew from Orbetello, Italy, crossing the south Atlantic via Dakar and the Cape Verde Islands, to the South American coast and down to Rio de Janeiro. The aircraft then flew northwards to the United States. It was lost, destroyed by fire in Arizona. A new *Santa Maria II* replaced it. The same crew took their new aircraft on to Chicago, Montreal and Quebec. They then flew the same route as the first American crossing of 1919, via the Azores to Lisbon, arriving in Rome to a rapturous welcome. On 17 December 1930, General Balbo took a formation of 14 flying boats on the same route to Rio de Janeiro; 10 arrived safely. Only one aircraft was a complete write-off, with the crew killed.

There was worldwide interest in the latest Italian attempt on the North Atlantic. After several false starts, the fleet took off on 1 July 1933. On the overland leg of the route, the aircraft passed over lakes and rivers wherever possible in case the need for an emergency landing arose. They finally reached the Zuider Zee, and landed near Amsterdam. One of the aircraft had been damaged, and a replacement was sent immediately. From Amsterdam, they flew on to Londonderry in Northern Ireland, and after a few day's delay reached Reykjavik, Iceland. From there it was on to Cartwright in Labrador, then to Montreal, via Shediac Bay, New Brunswick. The fleet finally arrived in Chicago on 16 July, in time for the World's Fair. The flying boats had completed a journey of 9799km (6095 miles).

The return journey took the fleet via New York, where General Balbo lunched with President Franklin D. Roosevelt – the Italian crews were feted wherever they went. On their return route, bad weather forced them to fly further south via the Azores, which they reached on 8 August. Unfortunately one aircraft capsized on takeoff, but the other 23 flew on to Lisbon. Rome was reached, in perfect formation, on 12 August. The world had witnessed an amazing achievement, and Italian national pride was at bursting point.

SAVOIA-MARCHETTI S.55
No fewer than 14 world records were set up by the Savoia-Marchetti S.55 in 1926 for altitude, speed and distance, in addition to the type's trans-oceanic flights.

ITALIAN TRANS-OCEANIC FLIGHTS 1927–1933
- Circular route 1927
- Formation flight December 1930
- World's Fair formation flight 1933

Empire of the Air

EMPIRE OF THE AIR

EMPIRE OF THE AIR
- British territory
- Strategic air route
- ○ Air base

Britain, possessing the largest empire in the world, had more incentive than other nations to open up trans-continental air routes. It was the need to deliver mail to the far corners of the empire that provided the impetus for long-range air exploration.

Empire of the Air

World War I's high cost was felt not only in terms of devastating loss of life, but also economically and financially – and these effects were to be long term. In the United Kingdom, the Royal Air Force suffered severe funding constraints between the wars, and development continued on a shoestring. The politically shrewd Sir Hugh Trenchard remained commander of the RAF after the war's end, and fought off threats to its future and funding from both army and navy. He argued that the major role of the force was strategic bombing, which would protect interests at home and abroad, and help in the policing of the Empire. The use of aircraft to patrol and dominate large areas was an economic use of limited financial resources. As a result of the peace treaties formulated at the end of World War I, the United Kingdom had assumed the long-term control of Iraq. The RAF put a swift end to a major Iraqi tribal uprising, at considerably less cost than would have been the case had ground forces been deployed. During the 1920s, the RAF was also actively deployed along India's Northwest Frontier, a relatively lawless tribal region. Punishment raids by light bombers were usually enough to restore order, at least for a time.

Under Trenchard's rule, a large part of the RAF budget was devoted to infrastructure and air bases, at home and in the colonies. This proved a wise investment when, in the late 1930s, expansion at last began. From 1933–35 the United Kingdom faced a growing threat: Germany in continental Europe, Italy in the vital Mediterranean and Red Sea, and Japan in East Asia. With the home country in the grip of economic depression, the vulnerability of Britain and its sprawling empire was obvious.

Meanwhile, the day-to-day business of Imperial Airways carried on. It was charged with developing air routes within Europe and, more importantly, connecting the empire. In its first year of operation, the airline introduced a new aircraft, the Handley Page W8F, which helped to bolster the year's total of passengers and mail to 11,395 and 212,380 respectively. Over the next 10 years, routes were established connecting almost all parts of the empire. One aircraft of great character stands out – the Handley Page HP.42, a four-engined biplane. It offered passengers a smooth, comfortable flight, and stewards served full-course meals in its opulent interior. Each of the eight aircraft built flew more than 1.6 million km (1 million miles) in service without the loss of a single passenger.

Cementing other interests

Across Europe, the new Soviet Union was also forming an airline – Dobrolet, founded in 1923. Its first service was between Moscow, the new capital, and Nizhni Norgorod, a city where new industries were being created. Here, airlines would serve as an instrument of state policy and philosophy, especially on international routes. In 1921, the two pariah states of Europe – Germany and the Soviet Union – formed a joint venture specializing in flights from Russia to the West. On 1 May 1927, regular services began from Königsberg in East Prussia to Moscow. This was all part of the close relationship forged between the two states as a result of their 'outsider' status. Germany developed and tested new aircraft in complete secrecy at Lipetsk, near Moscow, in return for rendering this service; the Soviets. benefited from German technical expertise.

France also expanded its air routes, connecting its colonial possessions. New airlines sprang up in the United States, with services stretching throughout North, Central and South America. Back in Europe, Italian ambitions focused on the Mediterranean and North Africa, a direct challenge to the interests of the United Kingdom and other less influential states.

SIR HUGH TRENCHARD
Air Chief Marshal Sir Hugh Trenchard, Chief of the Air Staff in 1919, was determined that the RAF should retain its separate identity. He fought to save the RAF from extinction after World War I and to forge the embryo Service into a formidable weapon, advocating the use of air power to police the British Empire.

HANDLEY PAGE HP.42
The Handley Page HP.42 airliner was used on both European services and on the empire routes overseas from 1931. Prior to this Imperial Airways' European services had been maintained by its fleet of Armstrong Whitworth Argosy and Handley Page W.8 aircraft.

SEABORNE AVIATION

W.L. 'BILLY' MITCHELL
General W.L. 'Billy' Mitchell was an enthusiastic advocate of air power, and set out to prove that bombers could be effective against warships. Realising that Japan was likely to be the principal enemy of the United States in a future war, he produced a lengthy report on how a Japanese offensive might develop in the Pacific, predicting an attack on Pearl Harbor.

BOMBING THE OSTFRIESLAND
The United States tested its air power against the captured German battleship Ostfriesland. US Army, Navy and Marine Corps aircraft dropped a total of 63 bombs over two days, eventually sinking her.

Air power at sea had made its debut in 1914, when the Japanese navy deployed its seaplane carrier *Wakamiya*, attacking the German Far East base of Tsingtao (Qingdao). The British also deployed similar ships to attack German airship bases at Nordholz and Cuxhaven. By April 1918, the world's premier naval power, the United Kingdom, had almost 3000 aircraft and 103 airships spread over 130 plus coastal and airfields on the Western Front. In that month the world's first independent air force was formed – the Royal Air Force. Strictly speaking, the Finnish Air Force, with one aircraft and one pilot, came into being a few days earlier.

The first aircraft carriers

Aircraft originally went to sea in support of fleet operations in the form of a seaplane carried, of course, by seaplane carriers. The seaplanes were winched over the side into the sea, from which they took off in good weather to perform any assigned operation. The British fleet also needed fighter protection, and from 1917 Sopwith fighters were able to take off from platforms fitted above the main gun turrets of battleships and cruisers. Indeed, a separate fighter launched from a cruiser in August 1918 destroyed a Zeppelin.

One problem the fighter pilot faced when taking off at sea was finding a friendly ship to ditch near or flying to a nearby airfield at the end of the mission. A sort of mobile airfield was developed when a flat-topped lighter was towed by a fast destroyer. By July 1917, the cruiser HMS *Furious* had been converted into a makeshift aircraft carrier. In August, Commander E.H. Dunning RN successfully landed his Sopwith Pup on the foredeck of HMS *Furious*, the first ever landing on an aircraft carrier. The aftward superstructure on the *Furious* was deleted completely on the following ship, and the logistics of landing and takeoff were made considerably easier. HMS *Argus*, converted from an ocean liner, had the first full-length (almost) deck.

The next conversion was based on the hull of an incomplete battleship and became HMS *Eagle*, launched in June 1918. Following this ship was the first purpose-built carrier HMS *Hermes*, launched in September 1919. By this time, the Royal Navy had lost control of its aviation to the new Royal Air Force. With this went a wealth of experience and innovation, and the Royal Navy lost its early lead in seaborne aviation. (The navies of both the United States and Japan retained control of their aviation.)

In the struggle for financial resources, the RAF saw its main function as bombing the potential, or real, enemy, and any other claim came way down the list of priorities. As a consequence, the Royal Navy was forced to make do with old, antiquated aircraft. It did, however, manage to build (or convert) two more carriers in 1928 and 1930. Its first purpose-built 'modern' carrier, the *Ark Royal*, was laid down in 1935. When completed, in 1938, it was a ship of 27,700 tons fully loaded, with an air group of 60 (still) largely antiquated aircraft.

Building and improving carrier fleets

The United States used two battle-cruiser hulls as the basis for its first large fleet carriers: USS *Saratoga*, launched in April 1925, and USS *Lexington*, launched the following October. Although announced as ships of 33,000 tons (without war load), they were up to 37,600 tons, then 43,000 tons, fully loaded. These large, fast ships carried an air group of around 65 aircraft, plus a main armament equivalent to a heavy cruiser, of eight 8in (203mm) guns. The precise role of the carrier was still being defined, but, with these two large ships in service by the late 1920s, the US Navy was well placed to practise operations with large air groups of purpose-designed aircraft.

Despite restricted funding, significant technical progress, better instrumentation, oleo struts and

Seaborne Aviation

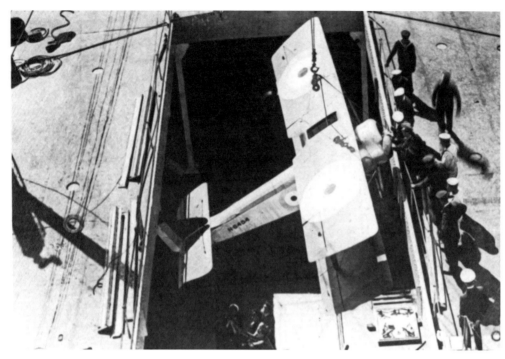

BRITISH AIRCRAFT CARRIER
A Sopwith Pup being hoisted from the hangar of the aircraft carrier HMS Furious. *On 2 August 1917, Squadron Commander Edwin Dunning successfully landed a Pup on this ship.*

folding wings all worked together to increase the carrier's capacity. New tactics developed, including what became known as 'dive bombing'; torpedo attacks on shipping were practised and improved. Cooperating with major fleet units in manoeuvres proved the worth of taking aviation to sea.

The Japanese navy was not far behind. Its first carrier *Hosho*, converted from a merchant ship hull, was in service by 1922, followed by *Akagi* in 1927, converted from a battle cruiser, and *Kaga* in 1928, from a battleship hull. The latter two were large, heavily armoured ships, weighing in at 40,000-plus tons, with air groups of 90-plus aircraft. After its role on the Allied side in World War I, Japan had gained inland possessions across the central Pacific from Germany. To defend its now far-flung dominions, air power was deemed essential to support its large battle fleet. Japan's aircraft designers also spent time designing dedicated aircraft carriers with built-in long range.

In the 1920s and 1930s, fleet manoeuvres began to demonstrate that aircraft could destroy even heavily armoured warships. US bomber pilot Brigadier General William Mitchell proved this in 1921, sinking the old German battleship *Ostfriesland*. Now future fleet engagements at sea could be air attack on ships, rather than traditional ship-to-ship engagements.

USS SARATOGA
The aircraft carrier USS Saratoga *was a converted battlecruiser. Designated CV-3, she was launched on 7 April 1925 and was followed in October by a sister ship, USS* Lexington. *Both took part for the first time in US Pacific Fleet exercises in January 1929. At the time of their completion, they were the biggest aircraft carriers in the world.*

BIRTH OF THE LUFTWAFFE

HANS VON SEECKT
Although Germany's armed forces had been emasculated by the Treaty of Versailles, a small defence ministry remained in Berlin under the command of General Hans von Seeckt.

STUKA PROTOTYPE
Ju 87V-3, the third prototype 'Stuka', made its first flight in 1936, the year in which the type made its combat debut.

The Treaty of Versailles, the peace agreement signed by Germany at the end of World War I, imposed crippling industrial and economic measures designed to punish and cleanse Germany of its Prussian militarism. They were also designed to reduce the state's ability to make war. The economic impositions and loss of territory instead nurtured a determination among many Germans that their country, no longer an empire, must somehow regain its position among the great nations of the world.

Creating an 'air force' by proxy

In 1918 Germany's air service was a force of some 20,000 aircraft. Under the terms of the treaty, these would be handed over to the Allies, along with the vast bulk of the German battle fleet; her army was reduced to just 100,000 men. The Germans were henceforth forbidden to create a military air force or to manufacture or import military aircraft or components. The Allies, however, had largely overlooked civilian aviation. This barely existed before the war, and the treaty was almost devoid of reference to it. Restrictions placed on civil aircraft construction covered a period of just six months.

Germany had been permitted to keep a defence ministry, the *Reichswehrministerium*, wherein the services of key military officers were carefully retained. Behind this legitimate façade, a forbidden General Staff was assembled under the name *Truppenamt*, or Troop Office. This was under the command of the capable and wily General Hans von Seeckt. He was careful to foster Germany's armed forces by every means, always in secret. Seeckt orchestrated the appointment of Hauptmann Ernst Brandenburg, who had been commander of Kagohl 3 during World War I and led the Gotha raids on Britain in 1917, as head of the new Civil Aviation Department in the Ministry of Transport. Civil aviation and its development were now safe in the guiding hands of the Reichswehr. To aid this process, German companies set up factories in 'friendly' states to avoid the strictures and scrutiny placed upon activities at home. Heinkel had a factory in Sweden; Junkers had factories in both Turkey and Sweden. By 1924–26 they were beginning to

Birth of the Luftwaffe

increase their legitimate activities in Germany. In 1924, Willi Messerschmitt was welcomed into the Bavarian Aircraft Company to design 'sporting aircraft'. This move brought him another step closer to designing what was to become one of Germany's most potent and important aircraft in World War II, the Messerschmitt Bf 109.

Bigger and better

The treaty also prevented Germany from building large commercial aircraft. When the restriction lapsed in 1926, design and industrial capacity immediately swung into action to overcome this deficit. That same year Germany established a new state airline, Deutsche Luft Hansa, largely driven by the efforts of an ex-wartime pilot Erhard Milch. Milch set about a large crew-training programme, and built and equipped extensive ground facilities. Within its first year of operation, the airline had opened a route from Berlin to Moscow, and further route-proving flights reached South America. By 1928 Deutsche Luft Hansa was Europe's most efficient airline by a wide margin. The route to Moscow proved very useful, as in 1923–24, in great secrecy, Seeckt completed a deal with the Soviet government. A base was created at Lipetsk some 438km (232 miles) southeast of Moscow, where new German aircraft and weapons could be tested and new tactical ideas could be developed, well away from the prying eyes of the Western powers. Here, in great secrecy, the 'Black Reichswehr' operated.

Meanwhile, Germany encouraged a policy of 'air-mindedness' among its citizens. The *Deutscher Luftsportverband* (German Air Sports Association), formed in 1920, grew to a membership of 50,000 by 1929, using gliders to introduce flying to the populace. When powered aircraft became available, at least Germany would not be short of pilots.

In 1929–30, with economies around the world in the grip of depression, subsidies to the aircraft industry and airlines were cut by 50 per cent. Enter Hermann Göring. In 1923, Göring had supported Adolf Hitler's ill-fated Munich putsch. He was regarded as a member of the Nazi party faithful and nominated as a Reichstag deputy. He was also given the portfolio of Air Minister when Hitler became Chancellor in 1933. Göring was a popular choice, or so the propaganda went, given his victories as a flyer in World War I. It was to Göring that Milch appealed for continued government support. Eager to build his new ministry's power and influence, Göring acquiesced. German training and research went ahead almost unaffected, unlike the situation

BF 109V-4 PROTOTYPE
The Bf 109V-4 prototype was the first to feature a third MG 17 machine gun mounted behind the engine, firing through the propeller boss.

81

Birth of the Luftwaffe

HERMANN GÖRING
A World War I fighter ace with 22 victories, Hermann Göring was the last commander of the Richthofen Geschwader. In 1933, following the establishment of the National Socialist government, he was appointed State Minister for Air, in which capacity he created the Luftwaffe.

with the Western powers, who had to make deeper and deeper cuts in their defence budgets.

In February 1932, the Geneva Disarmament Conference opened, guided by the League of Nations. It soon became obvious to the German delegation that the Western powers were keen to prevent any kind of German rearmament. When, in March 1933, Japan walked out over the League of Nation's failure to recognize Japan's overlordship of the puppet state of Manchukuo (Manchuria), the Conference was doomed.

Nazi rise to power and a new air force

On 31 July 1932, the *Nationalsozialistische Deutsche Arbeiterpartei*, or Nazi party, under their messianic leader, Adolf Hitler, was elected to power in Germany. Hitler became Chancellor on 30 January 1933. By 1934, Germany was out of the League of Nations, and conscription was introduced. The existing Defence Ministry was abolished and a new combined post of the Ministry of War and Commander in Chief of the Armed Forces created. In the same year, Hitler's predecessor Chancellor Paul von Hindenburg died – the last of the old Germany went with him. The new radical Nazi leader assumed total control of the state. Adolf Hitler and his revolutionary comrade Göring inherited the secret rearmament work of previous military organizations.

Despite Seeckt recommending, via a secret memorandum in 1925, that Germany's air force be independent of either army or navy, it was army officers such as Milch who ended up influencing the Luftwaffe's early development. General Wever, first

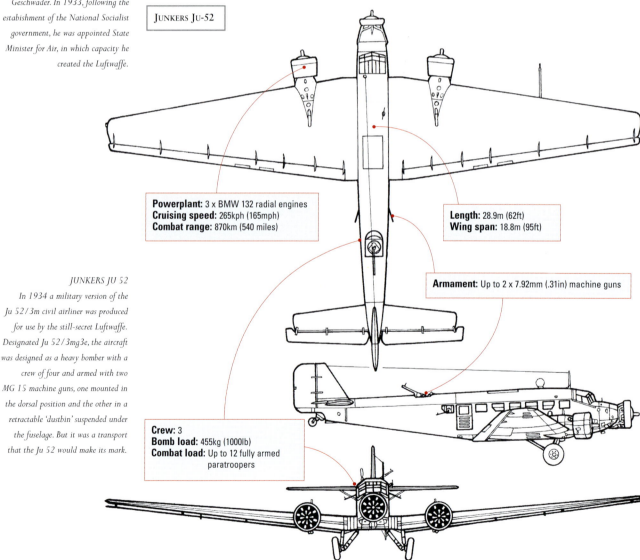

JUNKERS JU-52

Powerplant: 3 x BMW 132 radial engines
Cruising speed: 265kph (165mph)
Combat range: 870km (540 miles)

Length: 28.9m (62ft)
Wing span: 18.8m (95ft)

Armament: Up to 2 x 7.92mm (.31in) machine guns

Crew: 3
Bomb load: 455kg (1000lb)
Combat load: Up to 12 fully armed paratroopers

JUNKERS JU 52
In 1934 a military version of the Ju 52/3m civil airliner was produced for use by the still-secret Luftwaffe. Designated Ju 52/3mg3e, the aircraft was designed as a heavy bomber with a crew of four and armed with two MG 15 machine guns, one mounted in the dorsal position and the other in a retractable 'dustbin' suspended under the fuselage. But it was a transport that the Ju 52 would make its mark.

Birth of the Luftwaffe

Chief of Air Staff, had envisioned a long-range bomber force. In 1936, two large four-engined monoplane aircraft flew for the first time, the Dornier Do 19 and the Junkers Ju 89. The latter had a top speed of around 390kph (242mph), a range of 1609km (1000 miles) and a bombload of 4000kg (8800lb) – performance that the British Royal Air Force's bombers would not match until late 1941. General Wever died in a flying accident in June 1936. His replacement was Albert Kesselring, an ex-army officer with just three years' aviation service. After a survey of aviation projects, Kesselring deleted the two bombers from the programme. As a result, the Luftwaffe developed as a tactical support force, rather than a strategic striking one. Had the strategic bomber programme developed into full squadrons of aircraft, the outcome during the Battle of Britain in 1940 may have been very different.

Under way and in the air

New aircraft rolled off the production lines, and newly trained aircrew arrived from the German Air Training School. When the new Luftwaffe was formed in March 1935, Göring was appointed its Commander in Chief. At its birth, the Luftwaffe had 20,000 men and 1888 aircraft, with 40 factories producing another 184 aircraft per month; this figure grew to more than 300 per month by December. Aircraft such as the Heinkel He 111, Dornier Do 17, Messerschmitt Bf 109, Junkers Ju 87 and Junkers

STUKAS IN ACTION
Although the word Stuka – an abbreviation of Sturzkampfflugzeug, *which literally translates as 'diving combat aircraft' – was applied to all German bomber aircraft with a dive-bombing capability during World War II, it will forever be associated with the Junkers Ju 87, with its ugly lines, inverted gull wing and, above all, the banshee howl of its wing-mounted sirens as it plummeted towards its target.*

Ju 52 left the factories at an ever-increasing rate. These types all drew their first blood in the Spanish Civil War, which broke out in 1936. Both Hitler and Italy's Fascist leader Benito Mussolini supported General Francisco Franco's Nationalist forces. Luftwaffe volunteers served in an independent air unit known as the Condor Legion, under the command of General Major Hugo Sperrle (who was earlier associated with the secret Lipetsk training school near Moscow). The Legion played a role out of proportion to its size. The front line's fluidity created a force that perfected flexibility and mobility.

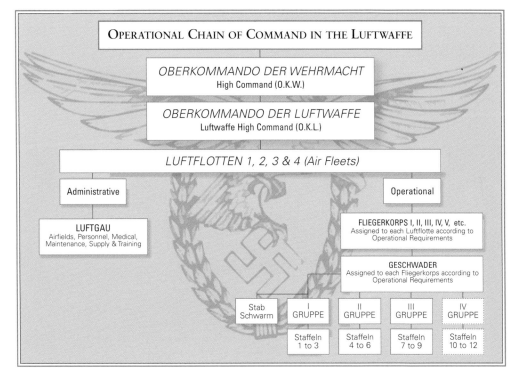

SPANISH CIVIL WAR: 1936–39

In 1936 an unreliable and ineffective socialist government took over Spain following a marginal political victory at the polls. Keen to institute sweeping reforms to redistribute wealth and land, its goal was a popular and prosperous future for the nation; however, it also wanted to make massive cutbacks to the army, thus lowering its political sway. This prompted right-wing leader General Franco to launch a civil war. The international community took sides in the battle of ideals, with the Soviets backing the communist–socialist Republicans and the Fascist states of Italy and Germany backing Franco's Nationalist forces. Both factions began to receive military aid, especially aircraft, almost immediately. The Germans seized the opportunity to use the conflict as a testing ground for their new aircraft.

Visible support for the Nationalists

Within days of the war commencing on 17 July 1936, following an impromptu meeting between a Republican spokesman and Hitler himself, Franco was supplied with 20 Junkers Ju 52 transport planes, along with experienced pilots. In one day alone, more than 3000 Nationalist troops were ferried from Tetuan in northern Morocco to the Spanish mainland. The sea route was barred to the Nationalists by the bulk of the Spanish navy, which remained loyal to the Republicans at the time. Between August and September, more than 12,000 men were ferried over the straits in this way. This was to be the first example of mass air-transported troops into the combat zone – but would not be the last.

By the end of 1936, Germany had provided three fighter groups, deploying the Heinkel He 51 biplane. A rapidly outdated aircraft, it enjoyed some success against similar aircraft, but would soon be outmoded by the more modern designs supplied to the Republicans by the Soviet Union. Four squadrons of Junkers Ju 52 transports, adapted to the role of bombers, were also supplied, but lacked efficient and accurate bomb-aiming equipment.

Invaluable experience

The aircraft supplied to the Nationalists by both Italy and Germany came with 'volunteer' pilots. The Luftwaffe, especially, grabbed the opportunity to give its pilots valuable combat experience. A rotation of service personnel was organized so that as many as possible served in the war zone. By doing this, the Luftwaffe effectively trained 19,000 men,

POLIKARPOV I-15
Large numbers of Polikarpov I-15 biplane fighters were supplied to the Spanish Republican Air Force by the USSR. An improved version, the I-153, dubbed Chaika *(Seagull) because of its distinctive wing shape, was a first-rate combat aircraft and was subsequently to prove its worth in air fighting, being able to out-turn almost every aircraft that opposed it in action.*

Spanish Civil War: 1936–39

SAVOIA-MARCHETTI SM.81
The SM.81 Pipistrello *(Bat) represented a considerable advance over the Regia Aeronautica's existing bomber types when it made its service debut in 1935. Fast, well armed and with a good range, it was used effectively during the Italian campaign in Abyssinia, which began in October 1935, and from August 1936 it was also used operationally during the Spanish Civil War.*

who passed on their experience to thousands of pilots and aircrews. This proved crucial to German success in Poland in 1939, at the start of World War II, and during the invasion of the west in 1940.

German aces started to emerge, Adolf Galland being one. A colourful character who often went on patrol smoking a cigar, Galland was a proponent of new and innovative fighter tactics. He introduced the 'Rotte', a system of utilizing a leader with a wingman guarding his tail. This allowed the leader to concentrate on identifying targets, while his wingman, flying behind, to one side and slightly above, protected his leader. This type of formation is still in use with many air forces today.

When Galland's tour ended, he was replaced by Werner Mölders, another natural talent. Mölders went on to expand Galland's tactics, using two or more Rottes to create a 'Schwarm'. These Schwarms would be seen guarding the vast bomber fleets flying over southern England during the Battle of Britain throughout the summer of 1940.

In 1937, Fascist Italy began to supply Franco with men and machines through the formation of the Casa Legionara, including three-engined

ACROSS THE STRAITS
Once the Nationalist uprising began, it was imperative for General Franco to establish a firm base at the Nationalist stronghold of Seville, from where future operations could be conducted. It was now that his small force of Ju 52 transports proved invaluable, carrying the bulk of the Army of Africa across the Strait of Gibraltar.

AIR TRANSPORT IN THE
SPANISH CIVIL WAR
Summer 1936

Spanish Civil War: 1936–39

*SPANISH CIVIL WAR
The Spanish Civil War, which ended in March 1939 with the surrender of Madrid to Franco's forces, brought Germany immeasurable experience in air combat tactics – experience which their allies, the Italians, failed to assimilate. The Italians, like the Russians fighting for the Republicans, continued to operate in large, unwieldy formations that left little room for individual action, and paid the price.*

Savoia-Marchetti SM.81 bombers and the Fiat CR.32, an excellent biplane fighter. The Republicans, in the meantime, accumulated aircraft for their cause from wherever they could, but especially from Soviet Russia. These had to be paid for in gold before delivery. Among them was the Polikarpov I-16 'Rata'. A short, tubby little monoplane fighter with good speed and armament, it soon had the advantage over Nationalist biplanes. In 1939, however, the Messerschmitt Bf 109B came on the scene. Far and away the most advanced fighter aircraft in the air over Spain, it quickly began to dominate the battle zone.

Many tactics were tried out during the brutal three-year civil war. German commanders noted that the most successful were when the air force worked in close collaboration with ground troops, supporting attacks and, when called upon, bombing or strafing obstacles blocking the army's advances. This would be further adapted into a nascent form of blitzkrieg. Formations for fighters were tested, with the two-man Rotte formation being adopted as the standard formation for the Nationalists.

A new type of war
The opportunity to carry out strategic bombing on troop concentrations as well as cities was also seized upon with great relish by the air commanders, climaxing with the infamous raid on Guernica, a Basque town in the north of Spain.

Spanish Civil War: 1936–39

Originally this raid was meant only to be an attack on a bridge outside of the town. During the first wave, 43 aircraft of the Condor Legion – Heinkel He 111 medium bombers and Junkers Ju 52 transports acting as bombers, escorted by Heinkel He 51 fighters – unleashed hell upon the market town. Bombs were dropped on the busy market square, resulting in the deaths of many civilians. With dust still rising from the first wave's attack, the second wave dropped its bombs into the cloud without identifying targets, resulting in even more destruction. More than 1,500 people were killed.

Chilling forerunner

The bombing of Guernica caused international outrage and was also an ominous portent of things to come: an era in which civilians would be as much of a target as military personnel, and cities would be set alight as a result of terror bombing. For a time, the Nationalists and their German supporters denied the bombing raid. They later admitted the attack, claiming that the town housed reserve Republican troops and was an important crossroads. But the truth was out, witnessed the following day by foreign journalists, who did not hold back in their graphic descriptions. Spanish artist Pablo Picasso created an iconic image of the event, representing the horror of that day and the days of pain to come.

By early 1939, following a rapid series of victories, Franco's Nationalists took control of Spain. Soviet Russia had supplied more than 1000 aircraft, along with their crews, to the Republican cause. Germany supplied 600 and Italy 660 aircraft to the Nationalist forces, along with many thousands of crew and ground staff. The experience gained would prove vital in the coming conflict that engulfed the whole of Europe. It was the Luftwaffe that most successfully took home many of the lessons learned from fighting the Spanish Civil War. British, French and Soviet air commanders clearly lagged behind, and it would be some years before they caught up with Germany's war machine.

TERROR BOMBER OF THE CIVIL WAR
Around 50 Ju 52/3mg4e bombers were included in the equipment of the German Condor Legion, deployed to Spain in support of Franco's Nationalist forces.

FIAT CR.32
Total production of the Fiat CR.32 amounted to 1212 aircraft, making it numerically the most important biplane of its era.

87

JAPANESE WAR IN CHINA: 1937–41

Japanese aviation made considerable progress between 1918 and 1930. Three major companies developed their aviation interests – Mitsubishi, Kawasaki and Nakajima – and essentially built Japan's aviation industry. Most of their early output consisted of building foreign types under licence, notably Douglas and Fokker aircraft. By the mid-1920s, aircraft of indigenous design began to reach the squadrons of the Imperial Japanese Navy and Imperial Japanese Army, aided by new radial engine technology from the United States.

The Japanese Government grew increasingly under the control of right-wing elements. The greater unity demonstrated by neighbouring China under the Nationalist Kuomintang was seen as contrary to Japanese interests. Japan decided to strengthen its position on mainland Asia. In 1931 a short but brutal five-month campaign gave the Japanese control of the region of Manchuria in northeast China. Japan's air force largely flew army support missions, but did see some air-to-air combat. The small but growing Japanese air force gained valuable expertise.

Increasing aggression

Japan and China fought intermittent minor conflicts from 1931 onwards, but full-scale war broke out in July 1937. Japan's aim was to dominate China and to control its valuable assets of raw materials. Air combat began in earnest in August and, by the end of the following year, the Chinese air force was all but wiped out. China lacked the necessary industrial infrastructure to repair or produce new aircraft. The small number of imported machines did not last long in combat. Japan ruled the air above its armies, despite bitter resistance by Chinese troops.

Flying high above the combatant armies and bombing centres of industry and supply, Japan set about destroying China's major cities; Chongking and Wuhan were particularly badly hit. The navy joined in, launching its new carrier-borne aircraft and attacking cities such as Shanghai and Guangzhou. In the first massive continuous air raids on civilian targets, millions were killed, injured or left homeless:

> *Words cannot express the feelings of profound horror with which the news of these raids had been received by the whole civilized world. ... The military objective, where it exists, seems to take a completely second place. The main object seems to be to inspire terror by the indiscriminate slaughter of civilians ...*
> **Lord Cranborne,
> British Under-Secretary of
> State for Foreign Affairs**

China fought on alone until 1941, when Japan's attack on Pearl Harbor brought the Sino-Japanese war into the wider sphere of World War II.

*MITSUBISHI A5M
The Mitsubishi A5M was Japan's first carrier-borne monoplane fighter and marked the end of Japanese dependence on foreign designs. The A5M was widely used in China, but with the exception of one attack on Davao in the Philippines the type did not see combat against the Allies during World War II.*

Japanese War in China: 1937–41

CLIPPERS: LONG-RANGE TRANSPORT 1934–39

BUILT FOR COMFORT
The Douglas DC-2 brought a new dimension to air travel, not least in terms of comfort. Here, passengers enjoy a meal in the DC-2's spacious cabin.

In the nineteenth century, it was the railroads that crisscrossed the North American continent to form the backbone of travel and commerce. During the twentieth century, the railroads still carried goods and raw materials, but it was now air transport that took the cream of passenger traffic.

A sleek new means of transport

The modern passenger aircraft, with lines familiar to today's eye, first flew on 8 February 1933 – the Boeing 247. A low-wing cantilever monoplane powered by two 550hp Pratt & Whitney radial engines, with all-metal construction and retractable undercarriage, the 247 was capable of carrying ten passengers and cruised at more than 240kph (150mph). The sleek 247 immediately outdated the trimotor fixed-undercarriage aircraft produced by Junkers, Fokker and Ford. Early deliveries of the Boeing 247 went to United Airlines, which deployed them on transcontinental routes. With five or six stops, coast-to-coast across the United States could now be flown in just 20 hours, a saving of seven hours over the old trimotors.

Transcontinental and Western Air Inc (TWA) was keen to buy the 247, but Boeing was unable to deliver in the time requested. TWA then issued a specification that led the Douglas Aircraft Company to produce the DC-1 (Douglas Commercial 1). This aircraft flew in July 1933, and was delivered to TWA.

THE DC-2
Transcontinental and Western Air Inc (TWA) was the first customer for the DC-2, and eventually received 32. This example is pictured over Kansas City.

Soon after, the Douglas DC-1 made a record flight from Los Angeles to New York in just 13 hours 4 minutes, and TWA ordered 28 aircraft. The upgraded versions became known as the Douglas DC-2. With uprated engines and variable-pitched propellers, these aircraft could carry 14 passengers. A DC-2 operated by KLM, the Dutch national airline, took part in the 1934 England to Australia Air Race; it won its section, taking just a few hours longer than the specially designed de Havilland Comet racer.

The DC-2 was followed by perhaps one of the mid-twentieth century's most iconic aircraft: the Douglas DC-3. This aeroplane created reliable air route connections around the world, which in time led to the introduction of larger, four-engined aircraft. More than 14,000 examples of the DC-3 – and its military cousin, the C-47 – were produced.

Building international commercial routes

While the US domestic airline market developed, aided by the US Postal Department, a similar process was taking place with international connections. In 1927 the Aviation Corporation of America was founded by a group of wealthy friends headed by entrepreneur and commercial aviation visionary Juan Trippe, a former US Navy pilot. Trippe's group gained control of Pan Am, which at the time held the US mail delivery contract to Cuba. Under Trippe's management, the new airline began developing routes across the Caribbean and on to South America. The airline's first passenger flight was on 9 January 1929, from Miami, Florida, to San Juan, Puerto Rico, via Belize, British Honduras, and Managua, Nicaragua. The 3200km (2000 mile) flight lasted 56 hours, including two overnight stops.

Gradually Pan Am built up its routes and overcame competing airlines, usually by acquiring them. Almost all of Pan Am's routes were serviced by flying boats, romantically named 'clippers'. In a smart marketing move, Trippe appointed the famous transatlantic flyer Charles Lindbergh as technical adviser. Amid a flurry of publicity, Lindbergh, accompanied by his wife, made a spectacular island-hopping flight around the Caribbean and Central America. Using his astute business and marketing skills, Juan Trippe gained US Government approval on practically all postal contracts, and Pan Am became almost the 'chosen instrument' of US Government foreign policy.

Clippers: Long-Range Transport 1934–39

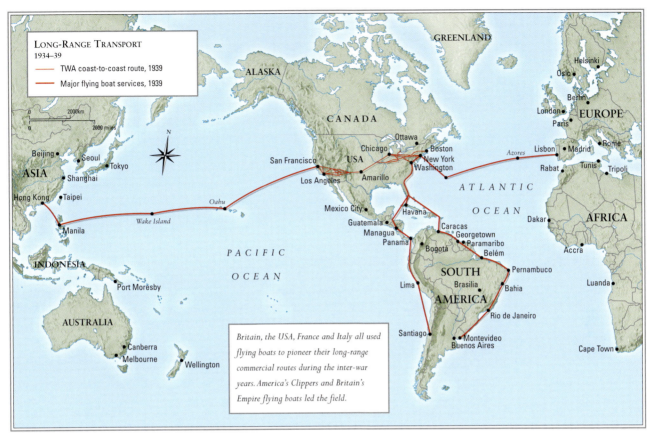

LONG-RANGE TRANSPORT 1934–39
— TWA coast-to-coast route, 1939
— Major flying boat services, 1939

Britain, the USA, France and Italy all used flying boats to pioneer their long-range commercial routes during the inter-war years. America's Clippers and Britain's Empire flying boats led the field.

Pan Am also harboured transoceanic ambitions. New routes demanded new aircraft to span the vast distances of the Pacific Ocean. In 1934 Trippe took delivery of two new flying boats, the Sikorsky S-42 and the Martin M-130, which would pioneer and establish the viability of the new routes. New radio direction was developed, as finding islands in the vast Pacific was a major technical feat in itself.

On 22 November 1935, the Martin M-130 *China Clipper* took off from San Francisco, carrying mail for Manila. Vast crowds were on hand to see the aircraft depart and arrive safely. On 21 October 1936, the first 15 fare-paying passengers flew trans-Pacific, each paying around US$799 for the privilege.

Difficulties in negotiating reciprocal landing rights with European countries, all eager to promote and develop their own share of this new market, delayed transatlantic flights until May 1939.

BOEING 314

The Boeing 314 represented a major stride in flying boat technology. Pan American Airways ordered six, and on 20 May 1939 one of them, named Yankee Clipper *(which was to become Pan American's celebrated callsign), inaugurated a mail service between New York and Marseilles.*

91

ANGLO-FRENCH REARMAMENT

REGINALD MITCHELL
Supermarine's racing seaplanes, designed by Reginald Mitchell, made a contribution to the development of high-speed aerodynamics and high-powered engines that, within a decade, would help the nation to survive her hour of greatest peril.

HAWKER HURRICANE
The Hawker Hurricane was the first of Britain's new monoplane fighters, powered by the Rolls-Royce Merlin engine and given an armament of eight 0.303in Colt-Browning machine guns. Seen here is the prototype, K5083, which first flew on 6 November 1935.

The high losses sustained during World War I, particularly in France, and the equally huge debt created by fighting and winning that war, left France and the United Kingdom straining under huge economic burdens. With demobilization came massive cuts and cancellations for the aircraft industry. In 1918 it had employed tens of thousands of people in both the United Kingdom and France; by 1920 numbers were down to a few thousand in each country. Some companies abandoned aviation altogether; Hispano-Suiza stopped producing aero engines and went into the luxury motor car business instead.

Rebuilding after the Great War

Both France and Britain had colonial commitments, so their defence budgets were spread thinly. The French army and the Royal Navy held the greatest clout when arguing for their share of defence funds. The French Air Arm was still controlled by the army, becoming independent only in 1934. In the United Kingdom, the Royal Air Force had been independent since 1918, but with cost-cutting in place both the British army and Royal Navy argued that the air force should be taken under their respective control. Sir Hugh Trenchard did his utmost to defend and develop his depleted RAF, but there was a moment in 1920 that the United Kingdom's air defence rested on just one squadron of Sopwith Snipes of 1918 vintage.

Most aviation companies survived by producing small numbers of commercial aircraft. From 1920–22, however, limited contracts were placed to develop new military aircraft, albeit on a small scale. For the next decade, both the United Kingdom and France struggled along, buying just enough aircraft to meet perceived commitments and keep the aircraft industry ticking over. By 1935, Germany's rearmament plans were clear, and the new Luftwaffe was flexing its wings. Factory production lines across Germany rolled out new aircraft in a steady flow. Having ignored early signs, British politicians now reluctantly realized that preparations needed to be made to deal with the growing threat from Germany.

In 1935 both British and French air forces were still flying biplane designs dating from the mid-1920s, armed with a maximum of four machine guns. Britain promptly placed orders for the best available new designs. By 1936 the Hawker Company had orders for 3012 aircraft, of which 1582 were subcontracted to other aircraft constructors. These contracts saved the industry, allowing companies to take on and train extra staff, purchase new machinery and build new plants.

In France, production orders had been issued to the enfeebled French aircraft industry. After 16 years of neglect, the industry could not deliver the aircraft required in the time stipulated. Pierre Cot, the Secretary of the new Armée de l'Air, announced that national security was too important for the production of military aircraft to be left in the hands of private enterprises. By July 1936 the French Government began a process of nationalizing aviation businesses, eventually creating six large state-owned companies. It would be this new organization that would deliver France's new aircraft, the Morane-Saulnier 406 fighter, the Bloch 210 bomber and many others.

The RAF's fighter force relied on traditional biplane fighters, the latest of which, the Gloster Gladiator, went into production in 1935. Following discussions with the Air Ministry, Sydney Camm of Hawker Aircraft proposed a new monoplane design powered by the new Rolls-Royce P.V. 12 engine (later named the Merlin) built in Derby. It was also possible to fit eight reliable licence-built Colt machine guns into the wings. The design was based on the earlier biplane, the Fury, and would still be, in large part, metal framework and canvas-covered. This was to become the Hawker Hurricane. The Supermarine Company was also working on a

monoplane design, powered by the same engine and equipped with the same armament configuration. Designed by Reginald Mitchell, its construction was more advanced and included an all-metal finish. This strong, elegant design, with its elliptical wings, was perhaps the most beautiful and iconic fighter ever built – the Supermarine Spitfire.

The Hawker Hurricane first flew on 6 November 1935; the Supermarine Spitfire on 5 March 1936. After successful demonstrations, initial orders were forthcoming for 500 Hurricanes and 310 Spitfires – many more orders would follow. The Hurricane first entered service in December 1937; the Spitfire followed one year later in December 1938.

A new bomber force

New bomber designs were also forthcoming. The Vickers Wellington first flew on 15 June 1936, and six days later the Handley Page Hampden took to the air. The largest of the new bombers going into production was the Armstrong Whitworth Whitley, a twin-engined design that had good range and bomb-carrying capacity for its time. The Whitley made its first flight a little earlier, in March 1936. The RAF desperately needed new bombers. By year's end, 520 of these aircraft – Whitleys, Hampdens and Wellingtons – were on order. They began to reach operational squadrons from March 1937.

The RAF's bomber lobby pressed its demands for the largest slice of the cake in various air force expansion schemes. In yearly war games, however, the fighter squadrons of the Air Defence of Great Britain (ADGB) successfully intercepted attacking bomber formations. In exercises held in 1932, long before radar and a clear command and control system, they intercepted 50 per cent of all daylight attacks and 25 per cent of night attacks. The system of defence used at the time went back to 1918.

By 1937 a handful of modern bomber designs were in production in the United Kingdom and would reach the squadrons in reasonable numbers by 1938–39. It was the same story in France, but about one year behind; better aircraft would arrive for the Armée de l'Air in 1939–40. Unfortunately for both forces, obsolete aircraft were still in production, typified by the Fairey Battle light bomber, which in combat conditions was shot out of the sky wherever it appeared.

By September 1939, fast monoplane fighters had almost entirely replaced the last of the older biplane designs and, particularly in Britain, had been filtered into an equally well-developed air defence system. Bombers were also arriving in fairly large numbers, although their system of getting through to the target was less organized, a mixture of proficiency and blind faith.

ARMSTRONG WHITWORTH WHITLEY
The prototype Whitley flew on 17 March 1936 and was followed by a production batch of 34 Whitley Mk Is, first deliveries being made to No. 10 Squadron in March 1937. The RAF had 207 Whitleys on strength at the outbreak of war.

SPITFIRE PRODUCTION LINE
Thousands of Spitfires were produced by the factory at Castle Bromwich, near Birmingham, where production test flying was carried out by a team under the leadership of the record-breaking aviator Alex Henshaw.

THE WORLD'S AIR FORCES: 1939

In 1939 the world's largest air force was that of the Soviet Union, with approximately 20,000 aircraft in all, of which some 7000 plus were based in the westernmost districts of the Soviet Union. Still, like all other military organizations, air forces were caught up in the politics of the period. The Soviets had begun preparations long before to ensure the new state's survival, determined to avoid Imperial Russia's fate in World War I.

Soviet industry developed through the late 1920s, but always with military emergency in mind; factories that produced typewriters and tractors could, if needed, produce aircraft and tanks. Germany and the Soviet Union cooperated for many years at the secret base at Lipetsk, but ultimately these two increasingly powerful states were from opposite branches of totalitarianism.

Growing divide

The Spanish Civil War had provided an arena where Soviet and German aircraft and tactics could be tested against the other, where 'volunteers' numbered in their thousands, and both countries gained first-hand combat experience. Soviet air forces had also fought against the Japanese on the Manchurian border and against Finland in 1939. Both of these operations provided further practical experience, but the political atmosphere inside Soviet Russia in the late 1930s affected the efficient training of the state's armed forces. Stalin's purges were in hand, and experienced officers could be, and were, denounced and arrested on some pretext or other.

On 11 August 1939, the Soviets conducted a series of talks with the United Kingdom and France regarding mutual defensive arrangements consisting of 140 divisions, in the event of war with Germany. The British claimed that they were able to field 16 divisions immediately (they had just six at the time). The French, digging in behind the Maginot Line, could raise 90 to 100 divisions. At the same time, Germany suggested an entirely new kind of relationship with the Soviets.

On 14 August, the idea of a non-aggression pact between Germany and the Soviet Union was raised. Hitler needed to know that his planned invasion of Poland (which was scheduled for 1 September 1939) would not provoke war with the Soviets. Eventually, after political and diplomatic manoeuvring, the pact was signed on 23 August 1939. Poland's fate was sealed – western Poland would be German, while the east would go to the Soviet Union, along with the Baltic states. Germany could now turn westwards without fear of attack.

In September, Germany's air forces comprised of 3750 frontline combat aircraft, constituting the most advanced and experienced force in the world. Aircraft were pouring out of the factories at the rate of 300–400 per month, and pilots were being trained at more than 1100 per month. In the same month, 70 per cent of this formidable force faced east towards Poland.

Elsewhere in Europe

In the west, France's aircraft industry had produced large numbers of modern combat aircraft. Unfortunately the air force was not ready. The Armée de l'Air had only 119 of its 210 squadrons ready for battle, and even this was achieved only by using reservists in their 40s to fly combat aircraft. Scattered all over France on remote airfields were brand-new aircraft; others delivered from US production lines remained in their crates. Institutional rivalry between army and air force had critically weakened France's defensive capabilities.

The United Kingdom had grudgingly expanded the Royal Air Force. Under the 'shadow factory'

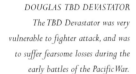

DOUGLAS TBD DEVASTATOR
The TBD Devastator was very vulnerable to fighter attack, and was to suffer fearsome losses during the early battles of the Pacific War.

scheme, leading motor manufacturers created new capacity for airframe and aero-engine production. The RAF had just sufficient aircrew, but maintaining a continuous flow of trained pilots and aircrew remained a problem. To support this and continued expansion, around 700 plus aircraft per month were flowing from British production lines, and imports from the United States added more.

Italy's Regia Aeronautica had been expanded to a force of some 3000 aircraft by 1939. The aircrews had also experienced operations in Ethiopia in 1935 and significant combat in the Spanish Civil War with the large 'volunteer' force that supported Franco's Nationalist forces. The role of the air force was to dominate air space in the central Mediterranean, thus supporting supply lines to Italian territories in North Africa and denying the same area to potential enemies. Italy's fighter force was fairly obsolete, but a few newer designs were entering service. Its bomber force presented the most immediate asset.

East and beyond

In the Far East, Japan had been conducting a war of expansion in China since 1933 and established domination in the skies over China well before 1939. In May to September 1939, Japan fought a hard campaign in the border region of Manchuria and Mongolia. An innocuous incident involving nomadic herdsmen grew into a major armed clash with Soviet forces. Japan's Nakajima Ki-27 fighter defeated the Soviet Polikarpov I-15 and held its own against the monoplane Polikarpov I-16. The standard of Japanese discipline and training went unreported in the West. By the end of 1939, the Japanese Naval Air Service and the Japanese Army Air Service numbered some 2500 capable aircraft with excellent and efficient crew.

By 1939, the United States was benefiting from orders for new designs and new aircraft not only from its own government, but also from Britain and France. The US aviation industry had expanded, laying down new plant and production lines vital for the years to come. By 1937 important new aircraft such as the Boeing B-17 long-range bomber were being introduced into service, and the Curtiss P.40 Warhawk was coming off the production lines in 1939. The air force had some 5000 aircraft, of which about 1500 could be regarded as fit for service. Industry was equipping itself with new tools, and on the drawing board were initial plans that would emerge as the Boeing B-29 Superfortress that, six years later, would end World War II.

EUROPEAN AIR FORCES: ORDERS OF BATTLE, 1 SEPTEMBER 1939

GERMANY

Luftflotten 2 and 3 (Western Frontier)
26 Jagdstaffeln: 336 Messerschmitt Bf 109Ds and 109Es
5 Zerstörergruppe: 180 Messerschmitt Bf 109Cs, 109Ds and 110s
9 Kampfgruppen: 280 Heinkel He 111s, Dornier Do 17s and Junkers Ju 88s
3 Stukagruppen: 100 Junkers Ju 87s
In reserve: 26 Jagdgeschwader, some newly formed and under training

FRANCE

4 Escadres de Chasse: 225 Morane-Saulnier MS.406
2 Escadres de Chasse: 100 Curtiss Hawk 75A
13 Escadres de Bombardement: 155 Bloch MB.210
Of the remaining 240 bombers in service, most were obsolete types such as the Bloch 200 and Amiot 143. Only five – Lioré et Olivier 451s – could be classed as really modern. There were also 59 reconnaissance and observation escadres equipped with the Potez 63 and ANF les Mureaux 115/7.

GREAT BRITAIN

RAF Fighter Command
16 Squadrons: 347 Hawker Hurricane Mk I*
10 Squadrons: 187 Supermarine Spitfire Mk I*
2 Squadrons: 24 Gloster Gladiator Mk II
7 Squadrons: 63 Blenheim Mk IF
* Includes reserves

RAF Bomber Command
15 Squadrons: 158 Vickers Wellington
5 Squadrons: 73 Armstrong Whitworth Whitley
10 Squadrons: 169 Handley Page Hampden
12 Squadrons: 168 Bristol Blenheim Mks I and IV
16 Squadrons: 340 Fairey Battle

RAF Army Co-operation Command
5 Squadrons: 60 Westland Lysander

RAF Coastal Command
10 Squadrons: 120 Avro Anson
3 Squadrons: 36 Lockheed Hudson
4 Squadrons: 40 Short Sunderland Mk I

POLAND

Pursuit Brigade (Warsaw Air Defence)
4 Squadrons: 48 PZL P.11c
1 Squadron: 8 PZL P.7A

Army Air Force
8 Squadrons: 100 PZL P.11c
2 Squadrons: 24 PZL P.7A

Bomber Brigade
4 Squadrons: 36 PZL P.37 Los
5 Squadrons: 45 PZL P.23 Karas

BELGIUM

3 Regiments d'Aeronautique
9 Escadrilles: 150 Fairey Fox
2 Escadrilles: 20 Renard R.31
1 Escadrille: 15 Gloster Gladiator
2 Escadrilles: 23 Fiat CR.42
1 Escadrille: 11 Hawker Hurricane
1 Escadrille: 14 Fairey Battle

NETHERLANDS

Army Aviation Brigade
36 Fokker D.XXI
9 Fokker TV
25 Fokker G.I
55 observation aircraft (various)

POLIKARPOV I-16
The Soviet Polikarpov I-16 was the first cantilever monoplane fighter with retractable undercarriage to enter service anywhere in the world.

INTRODUCTION TO BLITZKREIG: Poland 1939

BLITZKRIEG BOMBER
The Ju 87 Stuka saw early action during the Polish campaign, attacking communications with great precision before flying ground support missions.

Germany's invasion of Poland introduced the world to modern, swift attack, achieving rapid victory with relatively few casualties. It became known, thanks to an American journalist working for *Time* magazine and reporting on events as they unfolded, as *blitzkrieg* – 'lightning war'. For this tactic of short, sharp operations, air power would be a deciding factor. Although the Luftwaffe was short on munitions and did not have all of its squadrons operating the latest machines, it was nonetheless ready to play its part.

Hemmed in by enemies

Poland was in an unenviable position, surrounded as it was by Germany on three sides and with the unsympathetic Soviet Union on its eastern border. It decided to defend its western borders if attacked, as the majority of its heavy industry was based in the west of the country. It was also thought that this would buy time for France and the United Kingdom, which had guaranteed to aid Poland if war should come, to mobilize. This help ultimately did not arrive. Defence of the borders resulted in a front of nearly 1600km (1000 miles), spreading the army extremely thinly. In any case, the Luftwaffe merely flew over this, destroying transport and communications links with the front, bleeding the defenders dry of ammunition and replacements, and disrupting the chain of command.

The Luftwaffe's first task, however, was to achieve total air supremacy. The Poles, alarmed by

MASSED FORCES
On 31 August 1939, the Luftwaffe Order of Battle against Poland included 648 bombers, 219 dive-bombers, 30 ground-attack aircraft and 210 fighters, together with 474 reconnaissance, transport and miscellaneous types, divided between Luftflotten 1 and 4.

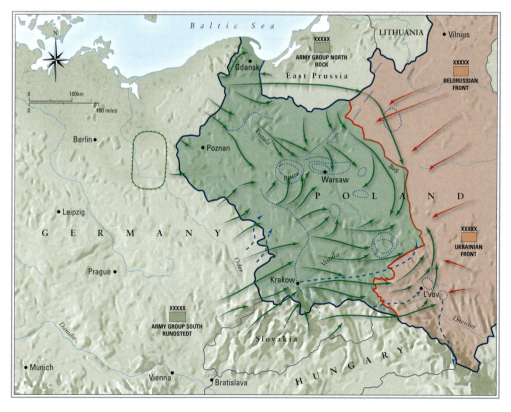

Introduction to Blitzkrieg: Poland 1939

the German build-up on the border, ordered their fighters to hastily constructed, dispersed airfields. When Germany invaded on 1 September 1939, the Luftwaffe swooped down on Polish airfields, only to find very few fighters. The majority of aircraft destroyed on the ground would be training or transport aircraft, leaving the fighters to take on the German air force. When they did meet in combat, the obsolete Polish aircraft fared badly, but still surprised the Germans.

On the opening morning of the invasion, Captain Mieczyslaw Medwecki and his wingman Wladyslaw Gnys took off in their PZL P.11s following an attack on Krakow. Almost immediately after takeoff they were attacked by a pair of Junkers Ju 87s; Medwecki was shot down and killed. This would be the first air-to-air victory for the Luftwaffe of the war. Gnys gave chase to the two Stukas, but they evaded his fire. He continued his patrol alone, coming across a pair of returning Dornier Do 17s. Using his advantage of height, he dove on the unsuspecting bombers and shot both down – the first Allied victory of World War II. Gnys achieved one more victory before escaping through Romania to eventually join the RAF. The majority of casualties inflicted on the Polish aircraft occurred during landing on the hastily constructed satellite fields. With the transport system in total disarray, spare parts and replacement aircraft were impossible to get hold of. The fighters that did manage to get into the air to face the Luftwaffe's Do 17s and Stukas soon clashed with the escorting Messerschmitt 109s and 110s. The Poles, flying obsolete P.11s, were outclassed and outnumbered. Those few flyers that survived these preliminary skirmishes flew to still-neutral Romania, and many Polish pilots went on to get their revenge and become some of the best-scoring flyers in the Battle of Britain.

Changing emphasis

The emphasis within the Luftwaffe now changed, and it moved into the role of ground support for which it had been created in the first place. Junkers Ju 87s and the soon-to-be-outdated Henschel Hs 123s were used in support of the rapid advance. They bombed strongpoints and pockets of resistance with anti-personnel and incendiary bombs, taking a terrible toll on the defending troops of the Polish army. The addition of the Stuka's sirens, nicknamed the 'Trumpets of Jericho', as they were heard on the aircraft's dives, only added to the grief felt by Polish ground troops, severely draining morale.

The Stukas also carried out attacks on naval targets. With their precision dives, they were able to drop armour-piercing bombs very accurately. This led to the sinking of the Polish destroyer *Wicker*, along with a minelayer. Both were ominous portents for the battles that would be waged over the English Channel and particularly the Mediterranean.

The rapid advance of the Wehrmacht on the ground lent its flanks to being overexposed. The Polish army took advantage of this at Bzura, attacking the German lines of communication in force and causing the advance to stall. This problem was also handed to the Luftwaffe, which sent in bombers. They blew all bridges and escape paths, effectively trapping the Poles, who were then ruthlessly finished off by incessant dive-bombers.

On 17 September the Russians invaded from the east, essentially sealing Poland's fate. There was no chance of holding off the German and Russian juggernauts, and eastern Poland was occupied relatively quickly, as there were no troops or aircraft available to beat back the invasion.

By late September the Wehrmacht was on the outskirts of Warsaw. Hitler gave specific orders for the historic city to be bombed and razed to the ground. Wave after wave of Dorniers and Heinkels dropped their loads on the city, destroying many buildings. Eventually, 50 per cent of the city would be damaged and many thousands killed.

By 6 October, all Polish resistance ceased. The Luftwaffe had made it look all too easy, but had still taken heavy casualties, especially in trained and experienced crews that could not be easily replaced. It had also expended almost 30 per cent of its stocks of munitions for a month-long campaign, a factor that came as a shock to commanders.

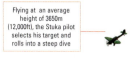

Flying at an average height of 3650m (12,000ft), the Stuka pilot selects his target and rolls into a steep dive

With dive brakes activated, the Stuka dives on the target at an angle of between 60° and 90°

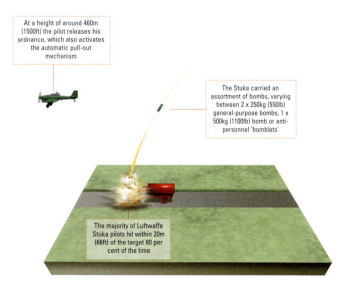

At a height of around 460m (1500ft) the pilot releases his ordnance, which also activates the automatic pull-out mechanism

The Stuka carried an assortment of bombs, varying between 2 x 250kg (550lb) general-purpose bombs, 1 x 500kg (1100lb) bomb or anti-personnel 'bomblets'

The majority of Luftwaffe Stuka pilots hit within 20m (66ft) of the target 80 per cent of the time

SCANDINAVIA: Finland 1939–40

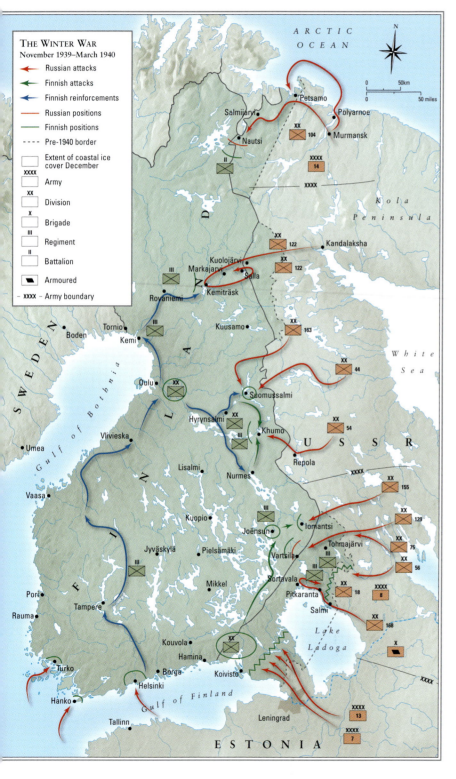

Soviet interest in Finland in 1939 was due to Josef Stalin's desire to strengthen the Soviet Union's northern border. He also wanted to lease the port of Henko for a 30-year period, but talks between Finland and Soviet Russia did not go to plan, even when the Soviets offered territorial compensation in Soviet Karelia. The Finns were wary that, after gaining independence only in 1917, any leeway shown towards the Soviets would lead to Stalin wanting more. After the bargaining failed, Stalin fell back on military intervention.

Dogged defence

Defending Finland was an army of 10 divisions supplemented with a few specialist units. These divisions were poorly equipped and lacked automatic weapons, artillery and, most importantly, anti-tank weapons. Each division had only 30-odd pieces of pre-1918 artillery, with low stocks of ammunition. But what they lacked in equipment they made up for in training and commitment. They were particularly skilled in manoeuvring in the heavily forested and snow-covered countryside, using ski troops to mount surprise attacks, then quickly melt back into the forest. These troops were also highly motivated to fight for the independence of Finland and were led by educated officers and NCOs.

The commander of the defence of Finland was Marshal Carl Gustaf von Mannerheim. He had begun constructing a defensive line earlier in the 1930s, based on a 65km (40 mile) front between the huge expanse of Lake Ladoga and the Gulf of Finland, blocking the main route for an attacking army protecting Finland's most populous region. This defensive line was made up of modern pillboxes and anti-tank ditches along the Karelian Isthmus. It was a strong position to defend, but could by no means hold out indefinitely against the sheer numbers the Soviets could throw at it; the line was designed to give time for outside assistance to arrive.

THE WINTER WAR
The losses inflicted by the greatly outnumbered Finns on the Red Army during the Winter War of 1939–40 came as a profound shock to the Soviet High Command, revealing serious deficiencies in leadership and equipment. Neither had been rectified at the time of the German invasion of the USSR in June 1941.

Scandinavia: Finland 1939–40

Facing these defences were 1.2 million men of the Soviet army, comprising 26 divisions, supported by 1500 tanks and around 750 aircraft of all types, including 230 Polikarpov I-15 biplanes and, later, the more modern Polikarpov I-16. These were deployed along the whole length of the Soviet–Finnish border. The bomber force consisted of twin-engined Ilyushin DB-3F and Tupolev SB-2s. These aircraft were concentrated around the Leningrad area, with some in Estonia. Their target was the Finnish defensive line and population centres in the southern part of the country. Facing the Russian onslaught was the Finnish Air Force of just 145 aircraft. The fighter defence rested on two squadrons of Fokker D.XXIs and one squadron of obsolete Bristol Bulldogs. Two squadrons of Bristol Blenheim Mk.1s formed the bomber force. On the eve of invasion, Finland's front line force consisted of around 55 aircraft.

Lack of experienced officers

Even with their superior numbers, the Soviets soon ran into problems, largely created by bad communication between aircraft, armour and infantry, as well as the problem of supply. The Soviet plan was to advance on all fronts and occupy Finland completely. Mannerheim managed to check the advance of the Soviets on the Karelian Isthmus with relative ease and did not even have to deploy his strategic reserve. This was partly due to the lack of experienced leadership on the Soviet side, thanks to Stalin's earlier bloody purges of the officer class.

The advantage of having so many aircraft did not assist the Soviets either; the short winter days offered few daylight hours to fly, resulting in heavy operating losses and little useful gain. The number of tanks facing the Finns could have created a huge problem: they had little or no anti-armour weapons and scant knowledge of armoured warfare. This deficit was soon realized in the harsh conditions, and the Finns employed many improvised weapons such as the Molotov cocktail, a bottle filled with petrol with a simple fuse, lit before throwing. As the Soviets employed their tanks independently of their infantry, this allowed the Finns to sneak up on them at night and attack with relative ease. In the north, Russian troops had taken the port of Petsamo and began moving south towards Nautsi, cutting Finland off from the Arctic Ocean.

Finnish counterattack

On 6 January, the Finnish army counterattacked all along the Eastern Front, using ski troops to

CURTISS HAWK 75A
Twenty-eight Curtiss Hawk 75As were supplied to Finland by Germany, which captured them when France was overrun in 1940. Finnish pilots claimed 190 victories against the Russians while flying the type.

penetrate around and behind the Russians, who were having to use the road network. These attacks created isolated pockets of resistance that were slowly destroyed one by one. The Soviets suffered heavy losses – almost four divisions – with the Finns using captured equipment, including aircraft, against their former owners. In the air, the Finns continued to hold their own – just. On the same day, eight Ilyushin DB-3 bombers raided the Utti area. All of them were shot down – six by one pilot, Lieutenant Jorma Sarvanto.

At the start of February, after intensive training in tank infantry cooperation, the Soviets launched a fresh attack against the Mannerheim Line, breaking through on 11 February. The Finns fell back to a second line of defence, but this was again broken by the massive attacking force. The Soviets then launched an attack into the rear positions of the Finnish lines across the frozen sea west of Viipuri. The Finns had received some reinforcements from Britain – 24 Gloster Gauntlets, 30 Gloster Gladiator fighters and 11 Blenheim IV bombers. France had sent 30 Morane-Saulnier MS.406 fighters and Italy had sent a few Fiat G.50s. A small Swedish volunteer force arrived with largely obsolete aircraft, but it was too little, too late. Facing bleak prospects, Mannerheim urged his government to make peace.

The Soviet terms were for the port of Hanko and the whole of the Karelian Isthmus, including Viipuri and the northern portion of Lake Ladoga. The Finns hoped for Anglo-French intervention, but when this was found lacking they eventually signed the Treaty of Moscow on 12 March 1940. The Russians lost more than 126,000 men; almost 300,000 more were evacuated through injury and frostbite. Much materiel was lost, but more important was the lack of military competence shown in beating the tiny Finnish army, and serious reorganization of the Soviet army ensued. The lessons of this campaign were not lost on German observers.

Scandinavia: Denmark and Norway 1940

SCANDINAVIA: Denmark and Norway 1940

MESSERSCHMITT BF 110
With its long range, the Messerschmitt Bf 110 Zerstörer was ideal for operations over Norway, where minimal Allied fighter oppositon was encountered.

GLOSTER GLADIATOR
Both Norwegian and RAF Gladiators fought in the campaign. Although obsolete, they still managed to account for a handful of invaders.

In order to sustain Hitler's planned expansion of the Reich, Germany required the raw materials to fuel its growing industries. Most pressing was the need for the iron ore that Germany imported from the neutral country of Sweden. The supply route was to the Norwegian port of Narvik, then by ship to north German ports. The French and the British were well aware of the importance of this material, and it became a race to see who could control its supply first. The German plan would mean the invasion of Norway. In order for Germany to do this, it first had to deal with Denmark.

Denmark was a neutral state, with a tiny army and even smaller air force and navy. This was not going to be the Wehrmacht's toughest assignment. In the early hours of 9 April 1940, Germany invaded. It faced brief resistance in North Schleswig, but this was soon overpowered. The Danish navy, in charge of defending the numerous ports of Denmark, allowed German troop ships simply to enter Copenhagen at will. The very first airborne attacks occurred during this fleeting campaign, with the fort at Madneso and the airport of Aalborg, north of Jutland, being swiftly taken by the elite *Fallschirmjäger* ('parachute troops'). With the capital of Copenhagen occupied by morning, the Danish government ordered a ceasefire. The invasion of Denmark was successfully at an end.

The fight for Norway
France and Britain had been planning to send an expeditionary force to the northern port of Narvik since the beginning of hostilities between Finland and Soviet Russia. This was really a cover for securing the port and controlling the all-important flow of iron ore from Sweden.

The Nazis beat them to it. While German forces were taking Denmark with relative ease, another German combined force was on its way to Norway. Surprise was total, with troops coming in by air and sea. The airborne troops, transported by the tried-and-tested Junkers Ju 52, took the airports of Stavanger and Oslo, which were vital for follow-up air transports landing more troops and materiel. The Norwegian coastal cities were also taken, stretching from Kristiansand in the south to Narvik in the far north. Long-range Messerschmitt Bf 110 twin-engined fighters provided air support, dispatching with relative ease the small number of Gloster Gladiators flown by the Norwegian air force. The Norwegians defending these ports were soon overwhelmed, but did manage to sink the German cruiser *Blücher* with torpedoes and artillery fire from the Oscarsborg fortress in the Oslofjord.

After these setbacks, the Norwegian government retreated into the interior of the country, and King Haakon VII gave command of the army to Major General Otto Ruge, who quickly set up plans for a fighting retreat to slow the German advance long enough for outside assistance to arrive. This came in the form of a British Expeditionary Force from

Scandinavia: Denmark and Norway 1940

south of the port of Trondheim. The BEF was sent to reinforce Norwegian troops in that sector, but was soon evacuated after a poorly attempted attack on the port. After this, all Allied resistance was based in the north of the country.

In the north the Allies were trying desperately to eject German forces from the Narvik area. The Royal Navy had done its part well by driving off the German navy in the area. The Royal Navy flew 18 RAF Gloster Gladiators of No. 263 Squadron from the carrier HMS *Courageous*; they would operate from a frozen lake near Andalsnes. Their operations proved unsuccessful, and most were destroyed on the ice by the Luftwaffe. By 25 April, the few surviving aircraft were destroyed and the crews withdrew to re-equip. The Fleet Air Arm achieved a significant victory when Blackburn Skuas of 803 Fleet Air Arm Squadron sank the German cruiser *Königsberg* near Bergen.

The Allies still concentrated their efforts in the Narvik area. As ground forces secured their hold, No. 263 Squadron returned with a fresh batch of Gladiators and No. 46 Squadron, equipped with Hawker Hurricanes, operated in the Bodö area. Having consolidated its hold in south and central Norway, Germany intensified its air attacks and increasingly isolated Allied forces in the far north.

Declining attentions

The port of Narvik was eventually retaken on 28 May by French and Norwegian troops. But the invasion of Belgium, the Netherlands and France now had the Allies looking elsewhere, and suddenly Norway was not as important as originally thought. The Royal Navy began to evacuate troops at the beginning of June, along with Norway's government and its king, who sat out the rest of the war in exile in London.

Germany suffered the heaviest casualties, losing 5500 men and 260 aircraft. Crucially it also lost two major modern warships, from which losses the German surface fleet would never quite recover. The British lost about 4000 men, including 1500 men lost with the sinking of the aircraft carrier *Glorious* by the battlecruisers *Gneisenau* and *Scharnhorst*. The Norwegians lost 1800 men and the French about 500.

LOST CAUSE

For the Allies, the campaign in Norway was a lost cause from the very beginning. Germany enjoyed complete air superiority, which made it difficult for the Royal Navy to operate effectively in Norwegian waters, while the Allied command, control and supply network was ill-coordinated.

101

INVASION OF THE WEST: 1940

The day Poland capitulated, 27 September 1939, Hitler announced his intention to attack the Western powers. A blueprint for the attack – Plan Yellow – was submitted by *Oberkommando des Heeres* (OKH) on 19 October. This called for a drive to Dutch and Belgian coastlines, creating a secure base for further operations against British and French forces in northern France. Hitler thought the plan inadequate. Bad weather forced a series of postponements, and Plan Yellow was cancelled when a small group of German officers, carrying copies of the plan, force-landed in Belgium on 9 January 1940.

A new plan was drawn up – Sickle Stroke – produced by a critic of OKH, General Erich von Manstein. Somewhat more in line with Hitler's ideas, it became the master plan to encircle the French and British armies. The detailed plan was drawn up by OKH and was ready by 24 February 1940.

Defending the Maginot Line

The Allies depended on the Maginot Line to defend the Franco–German frontier. France had poured an enormous amount of its wealth into construction of this defensive line.

Both sides were about equal in number: 94 French, 12 British, 9 Dutch and 22 Belgian divisions opposed 136 German divisions. The Allies, however, had few dedicated tank formations. Germany concentrated its tank force into ten dedicated divisions, so its 2500 tanks were far more effectively controlled than the 3000 dispersed Allied ones. Germany could also deploy more than 3200 modern aircraft in support of its armies. The Allies had around 2000 aircraft, but many were of doubtful quality. Perhaps the most decisive factor of the operation was the German doctrine of blitzkrieg. Allied forces practised only defensive war, and their High Command lacked a firm, clear structure of command and control.

In September 1939, the United Kingdom and France had mobilized their armies, approximately 3,000,000 for France and almost 450,000 for the United Kingdom, of which some 300,000 were sent to France as the BEF. This was almost all of the British mobile army and all of its tank force. During September, October and the following months, British forces took their places at the 'front' that stretched from Switzerland along the Maginot Line, the Belgian border and to the Channel coast.

After many months of the Phoney War, Hitler was now ready to strike in the west. Predicting that the Allies would expect the main offensive through Belgium and northern France, Manstein drew up a plan that would entail a diversionary thrust through the Netherlands and Belgium, drawing Allied strength and reserves north, while the main Panzer attack would drive through the forests of the Ardennes and head for the coast, catching the main body of the Allied armies in an enormous pocket.

General Fedor von Bock was to lead Army Group B, consisting of 29 divisions of regular infantry, into Belgium and the Netherlands,

DEWOITINE D.520
The Dewoitine D.520 was without doubt France's finest fighter in 1940, but deliveries were slow and it came too late to have an impact on the outcome of the Battle of France. Later, in service with Vichy France, it fought against the Allies over Syria.

Invasion of the West: 1940

drawing the main Allied defence force towards him. General Gerd von Rundstedt's Army Group A was made up of 44 divisions, including almost all of the Panzer divisions: enough to strike through the Ardennes. General Wilhelm Ritter von Leeb controlled Army Group C, consisting of 17 divisions between Switzerland and Luxembourg, and holding the French forces on the Maginot Line.

The French army was similar in size to the German force, if not stronger. This advantage was to become void, as the command structure, under General Maurice Gamelin, was slow to respond to changing situations. France also had great confidence in the truly giant defences of the Maginot Line, never expecting them to be merely bypassed. The United Kingdom had sent over an expeditionary force consisting of ten divisions to bolster the French defence and under French command. The Allies thought that the main German advance would come through Belgium, just as it had in 1914, and based defensive manoeuvres on this. Together, the British and French came up with the Dyle Plan, which entailed the main forces of the Allies advancing to a line drawn by the river Dyle to Wavre, just east of Brussels. In 1940 this line was extended to the river Maas in the Netherlands, to create one long line from the Channel coast to the Franco–Belgian border.

On the morning of 10 May, the Belgian underground fortress of Eben-Emael was attacked by a German airborne force that landed on the roof of the fortress in gliders. Specialist engineers used shaped charges to destroy the gun cupolas that commanded the approaches to the strategic bridges where the river Meuse met the Albert Canal. While the engineers dealt with the fort, *Fallschirmjäger* troops landed next to the bridges and captured them quickly. Within 24 hours the 4th Armoured Division arrived to consolidate the bridgehead. Meanwhile, the remaining Belgian forces still trying to defend the fort capitulated. Germany lost just six soldiers in the manoeuvre, the most successful airborne attack of the entire war.

Ardennes attack

Manstein's plan to lure the Allied armies into a defensive line in northern Belgium achieved great success. Rundstedt advanced through the Ardennes, with the bridge crossing the Meuse at Sedan his target. Panzers rolled through the heavily forested area and met only cursory opposition. German air superiority meant that the French and British had no chance of seeing the enormous traffic jam before them. By the evening of the 12 May, seven Panzer divisions stretched from Dinant in the north to Sedan in the south, ready to forge ahead. On 13 May General Heinz Guderian was ordered to force a crossing of the Meuse, under a massive aerial umbrella, with Stukas dive-bombing any defences

GENERAL HEINZ GUDERIAN
A brilliant tactician, General Heinz Guderian led XIX Corps in the assault on the west in May 1940. His legacy to military history was that he created the Panzerwaffe, the armoured force that is still the nucleus of modern armies.

DEADLY STRIKE
On 13–14 May 1940, German forces broke through the French front at Sedan. The RAF Advanced Air Striking Force despatched all available Battle and Blenheim bombers to attack pontoon bridges and troop columns in this sector. Of 71 aircraft involved, 39 were shot down by flak and fighters.

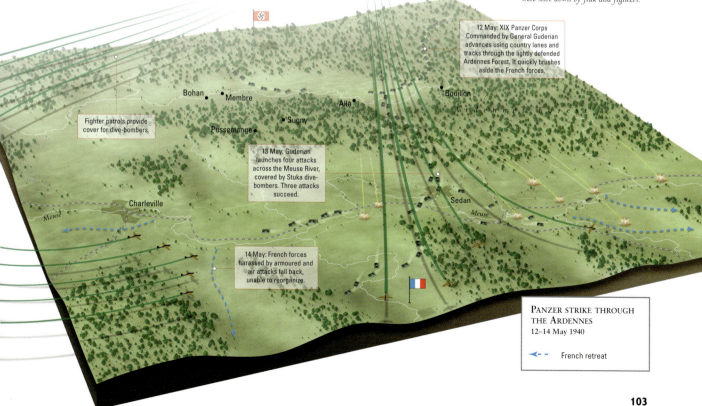

PANZER STRIKE THROUGH THE ARDENNES
12–14 May 1940

◄ - - French retreat

103

Invasion of the West: 1940

and terrifying the French Second Army under the command of General Charles Huntziger. By day's end the 1st Panzer Division held a bridgehead 5km (3 miles) wide and 7km (4 miles) deep. The French were slow to counterattack. The 3rd Armoured Division was keen to strike the weak flank of the German advance, but was held back and spread out along a thin defensive line. With the Allies now aware of the German bridgehead, they attempted to destroy the pontoon that the 1st Panzer Division had used to force a crossing, sending a force of obsolete Fairey Battles. Losses were catastrophic, and the bridge remained intact.

German commanders wasted no time exploiting the French failure to contain the Panzers on the Meuse, turning westwards towards the Channel. The French commanders were in disarray, unsure of the enemy's main objective: Paris or the Channel. No major counterattacks were mounted, except for a local offensive action near the town of Montcornet, led by brilliant young tactician Colonel Charles de Gaulle. This was soon beaten back by a superior German force. Guderian's Panzers arrived at the Channel on 19 May, ending an advance of nearly 330km (200 miles) in 10 days. The majority of the Allies' best fighting units were now caught in a pocket in northern France and Belgium, with little chance of escape and almost assured destruction.

Counterattack and evacuation

The Allies attempted a counterattack on 24 May into the flank of 2nd Panzer, but the Germans eventually beat them back to the start line by the end of the day. Shocking news then came through to the Panzer commanders from the Führer himself for all armoured advances to cease; he wanted to let the supply line catch up to the tanks and save them for the rest of France. Hitler preferred to leave the destruction of the BEF to Göring's Luftwaffe, which would simply flatten the army from the air.

Evacuating an army was a massive undertaking, and the Allies needed to evacuate urgently. General Lord Gort, VC, leading the BEF, set up a perimeter to prevent any infantry penetrating to the beach along the Aa, Scarpe and Yser canals. Churchill placed Vice Admiral Bertram Ramsay in charge of the naval evacuation and duly sent an order to beg, borrow and steal any vessels between 3 and 10m (9 and 30ft) long on England's south coast. These boats, mostly piloted by their owners, braved the bombing and strafing to go right into the beach to pick up the beleaguered troops. Over the next eight days, with the RAF vigorously trying to stave off the Luftwaffe despite being vastly outnumbered, the navy and its assorted craft evacuated 338,226 men.

After the evacuation and Belgium's surrender on 28 May, France was on its own. The Wehrmacht turned its attentions towards the rest of France, with the French digging in along the line of the Somme and the Aisne. The French fought heroically, but the Germans soon broke through and, on 14 June, entered Paris. France was forced to agree to an armistice, signed on 22 June.

The lack of a coherent air operations plan was a major contributory factor in the Allies' defeat. In the first crucial days of the battle, in May 1940, the reluctance of the French High Command to commit its bomber forces for fear of retaliation meant that the RAF, with its limited resources in France, was forced to bear the brunt of offensive operations.

Yet France's contribution to the air battle was significant. The British Air Forces in France lost 578 aircraft up to 24 June 1940, but France's Armée de l'Air and Aéronavale lost 892, about a third of which were destroyed on the ground. The Allied air forces claimed the destruction of 1735 enemy aircraft, a figure that was greatly exaggerated. Combat losses admitted by the Luftwaffe totalled 543 aircraft, but did not include aircraft written off accidentally or as a result of severe battle damage.

FAIREY BATTLE

The Fairey Battle squadrons of the Advanced Air Striking force suffered appalling casualties during the Battle of France. Seen here is a Battle of No. 218 Squadron and its three-man crew. This squadron lost 10 out of 11 aircraft in a single attack on the Meuse bridges on 14 May 1940.

FALL OF FRANCE

The six weeks between 10 May and 22 June 1940 witnessed one of the fastest and most devastating campaigns in the history of warfare. The Germans took the new concept of armoured warfare, based on the lightning thrust by tanks with massive air support, and employed it intelligently and flexibly. Yet it had been a gamble which, had they encountered sterner French resistance coupled with higher qualities of leadership and morale, might not have succeeded.

Invasion of the West: 1940

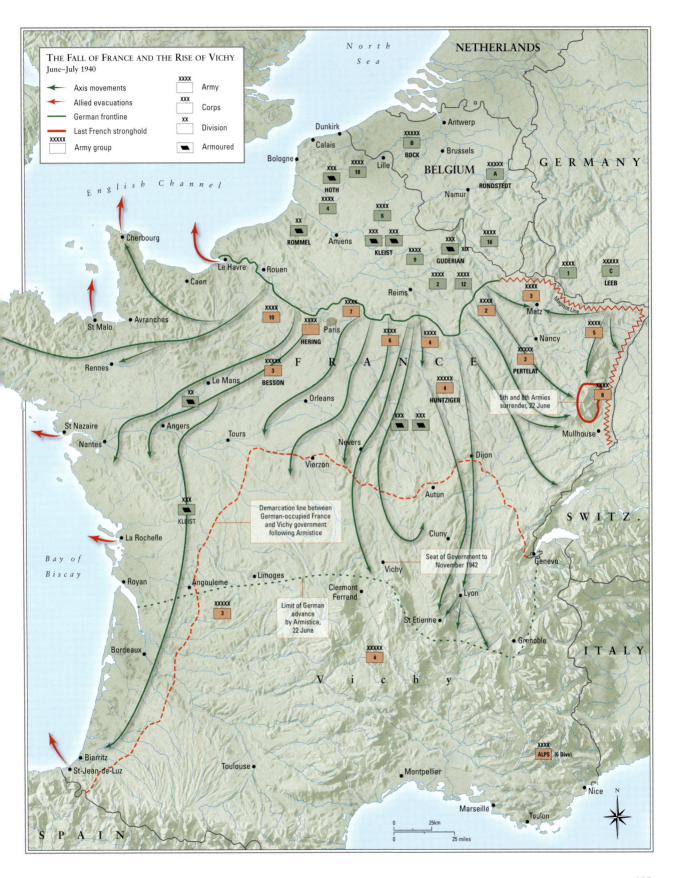

THE BATTLE OF BRITAIN: June–October 1940

Following Hitler's rapid victories in mainland Europe, the only enemy now facing his Reich was the United Kingdom. Hitler did not want to have to invade Britain, owing mainly to the size of its navy. The only way to defeat the United Kingdom would be to keep Royal Navy out of the way and the RAF cleared from the skies, allowing the Luftwaffe and the relatively small Kriegsmarine to protect the invasion fleet. British Prime Minister Winston Churchill prepared the country for the upcoming clash, dependent on a youthful Fighter Command and the as yet untested radio early warning system put into place around the southern coast of the British Isles just in time for the battle.

The Luftwaffe, commanded by Hermann Göring, was confident, but still recovering from almost constant operations since the start of hostilities and the major losses inflicted in the battles for the Low Countries and France. Its weapons were tried, its flyers experienced and tactics sound.

A new weapon: radar

RAF Fighter Command had a strength of 800 aircraft on the eve of battle. Of these 640 were first-rate fighters in the form of the Supermarine Spitfire and the Hawker Hurricane, both armed with eight machine guns, a fearsome amount of firepower. Also in their armoury was a system of command and control conceived and instigated by the exceptional Air Chief Marshal Sir Hugh Dowding. This system utilized the relatively new Radio Direction Finding, later to be renamed RADAR (RAdio Direction And Ranging) and eventually to be know simply as radar. This was a series of towers dotted around the southern coast of England sending out radio beams that, when reflected back by objects such as aircraft, could be translated into the location, height and direction of the attackers. This, supplemented by the eyes and binoculars of the Observer Corps, relayed information back to Command headquarters, which in turn passed it down to Sector Command, where the orders would again be passed on, this time to an appropriate squadron. This system allowed aircraft enough time to take off, achieve an advantageous altitude and meet the oncoming enemy, and not have to fly constant standing patrols, which overfatigued pilots and the aircraft

DOWDING SYSTEM
At the outbreak of World War II, Britain had the finest and most advanced air defence system in the world. The so-called 'Dowding System' was based on the air defence network that had been set up in 1917–18, but now included the priceless advantage of radar.

FIGHTER COMMAND AND CONTROL 1940
← Information
← Information and orders
← Information and interception orders
← Interception of oncoming enemy

BATTLE OF BRITAIN
In June 1940, while the Battle of France was still being fought, the Luftwaffe began to launch small-scale attacks on 'fringe' targets on the east and southeast coasts of the United Kingdom. These attacks lasted for about eight weeks and caused little significant damage, their purpose being to provide Luftwaffe crews with operational and navigational experience in readiness for the main air onslaught.

The Battle of Britain: June–October 1940

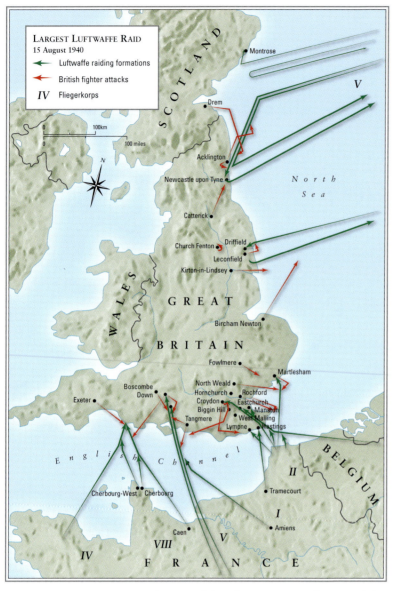

HEAVY ATTACKS
The heaviest fighting of the Battle of Britain took place on 15 August 1940, with heavy attacks on targets in both north and south. In the north, General Jürgen Stumpff's Luftflotte V suffered severe losses when it encountered unexpected fighter opposition. The total German loss was 71 aircraft, the highest of any single day in the battle, while the RAF lost 28.

they were flying. Germany was well aware of the radar system, but had little regard for it, so attacks on these targets were never rammed home. They were also difficult to hit in the first place, with the towers looking similar to a contemporary electrical cable tower. If anything other than a direct hit was landed, the shock wave of the explosion tended to dissipate through the structure.

The opening moves of the battle during the first weeks of July had the Luftwaffe probing the British defences by attacking coastal targets, including the radar stations, but especially naval targets in the Channel. This phase was used to test the defences, but also to draw out the RAF into open battle and completely destroy it. This is where radar came into its own, allowing the RAF to husband its forces.

During these opening skirmishes much was learned by both sides, especially the need to create a dedicated air-sea rescue service for downed airmen, something that the Luftwaffe had recognized and instigated before the start of hostilities. The deficiencies of the Boulton-Paul Defiant and, for the first time, the Stuka, became apparent. Both types were susceptible to the manoeuvrable and fast fighters now in service. The Defiant had no forward-firing armament and was easily picked off with a frontal attack by the Messerschmitt Bf 109, while the Stuka's lack of speed and agility made it easy prey for the Hurricanes and Spitfires.

Launching the next phase

For the next phase of the battle at the start of August, the Luftwaffe launched an all-out offensive against the RAF's airfields, control centres and Britain's aircraft industry. This was also the first time Luftflotte V, flying from its bases in Norway, attempted to attack eastern England. The mission was out of range for the single-engined Bf 109, so the Bf 110 was utilized as the escort for the mission. Resistance was surprisingly strong. The Bf 110s were unable to contend with the British fighters, and German aircraft of all types were cut from the sky. Luftflotte V would not attempt a raid in daylight with as many massed bombers again, preferring to creep in under the cover of darkness.

The attacks on the airfields of No. 11 Group had more dire consequences, with Germany particularly targeting sector control airfields. This bore fruit when Biggin Hill was bombed, severely crippling this sector. But radar still allowed the RAF to be in the right place at the right time, and losses were always in the favour of the defending force. The Luftwaffe's Messerschmitt Bf 109s, with their short available flying time over England, were forced closer and closer to the bombers they were escorting. This took away all the advantages of height and surprise, and Luftwaffe losses started to rise – fighters as well as bombers. The RAF was also starting to direct the more manoeuvrable Spitfires to take on the escorts, while the solid gun platforms of the Hurricanes took down the bombers in droves.

Had the Luftwaffe really pressed home its attacks on the RAF's airfields, the battle may have been theirs. Following an RAF raid on Berlin, however, itself prompted by an accidental attack by the Luftwaffe on London, at the beginning of September Göring ordered the thrust of the attack to be moved to the bombing of British cities. London was to receive the bulk of the offensive.

The Battle of Britain: June–October 1940

Battle withdrawn

The change of objectives gave the RAF a chance to heal its wounds. Now having the relative safety of undamaged airfields, it could concentrate on knocking the Luftwaffe from the sky. This was a chance for the Commander of No. 12 Group, Air Vice Marshal Trafford Leigh-Mallory, to question the tactics of Keith Park, his opposite number in command of 11 Group. Leigh-Mallory suggested that the forming of two or three squadrons into a 'Big Wing' would allow the RAF to attack the bomber streams en masse. This forming up took a long time to achieve, and when it was tried it had limited or similar results to Park's tactic of sending up small groups to constantly harass the bomber streams all the way to their targets and back. The Big Wing was only able to attack once formed, which meant that the bombers had already dropped ther loads on target and were on their way home.

Battles over London led to unacceptable German losses, prompting Hitler to postpone the invasion of the United Kingdom indefinitely on the 17 September. By the end of the month, the Luftwaffe had resorted to purely night-time raids. The Battle of Britain was won, prompting the immortal lines:

Never in the field of human conflict, has so much been owed, by so many, to so few.
Winston Churchill

The invasion of Britain would never again be attempted, meaning that throughout the war there remained a base for further attacks on the heart of the Third Reich and a reassurance to the rest of the world that the United Kingdom had the resolve to defeat Hitler's Germany. Hitler's attention now turned to the invasion of the east and the *Lebensraum* (living space) that it provided.

FIGHTER ATTACK
Almost always outnumbered, RAF fighters relied on the 'eyes' of radar to give them an advantage, placing them in the correct position to set up an attack.

THE BATTLE OF BRITAIN: 10 JULY–31 OCTOBER 1940	
UNITED KINGDOM	**GERMANY / ITALY**
COMMANDERS	
Hugh Dowding	Hermann Göring
STRENGTH	
754 single-seat fighters 149 two-seat fighters 560 bombers 500 coastal **Total: 1963**	1107 single-seat fighters 357 two-seat fighters 1380 bombers 569 reconnaissance 233 coastal **Total: 4074**
CASUALTIES AND LOSSES	
RAF: Pilots and aircrew killed (Fighter Command): 544 **Aircraft losses:** Fighters: 1023 Bombers: 376 Maritime: 148 (Coastal Command) **Total:** 1547 aircraft destroyed	**Luftwaffe:** Pilots and aircrew killed: 2,500 **Aircraft losses:** Fighters: 873 Bombers: 1014 **Total:** 1887 aircraft destroyed

The Battle of Britain: June–October 1940

BOMBING: Britain and Germany 1940–41

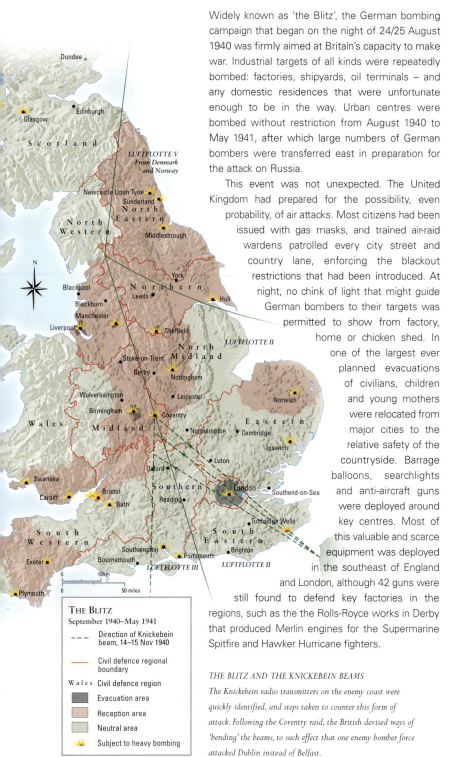

Widely known as 'the Blitz', the German bombing campaign that began on the night of 24/25 August 1940 was firmly aimed at Britain's capacity to make war. Industrial targets of all kinds were repeatedly bombed: factories, shipyards, oil terminals – and any domestic residences that were unfortunate enough to be in the way. Urban centres were bombed without restriction from August 1940 to May 1941, after which large numbers of German bombers were transferred east in preparation for the attack on Russia.

This event was not unexpected. The United Kingdom had prepared for the possibility, even probability, of air attacks. Most citizens had been issued with gas masks, and trained air-raid wardens patrolled every city street and country lane, enforcing the blackout restrictions that had been introduced. At night, no chink of light that might guide German bombers to their targets was permitted to show from factory, home or chicken shed. In one of the largest ever planned evacuations of civilians, children and young mothers were relocated from major cities to the relative safety of the countryside. Barrage balloons, searchlights and anti-aircraft guns were deployed around key centres. Most of this valuable and scarce equipment was deployed in the southeast of England and London, although 42 guns were still found to defend key factories in the regions, such as the the Rolls-Royce works in Derby that produced Merlin engines for the Supermarine Spitfire and Hawker Hurricane fighters.

THE BLITZ AND THE KNICKEBEIN BEAMS

The Knickebein radio transmitters on the enemy coast were quickly identified, and steps taken to counter this form of attack. Following the Coventry raid, the British devised ways of 'bending' the beams, to such effect that one enemy bomber force attacked Dublin instead of Belfast.

During August the Luftwaffe concentrated its efforts on London, flying daylight raids. These proved so costly on aircraft that, by mid-September, night raids were the norm. Night-time attacks were less precise, and bombs aimed in the darkness fell on a much wider area, hitting homes as often as factories. Despite all the preparations, the weight of attacks shocked Britain's civilian population. Residents of provincial cities such as Plymouth camped out in the nearby countryside each night to avoid the bombs. London's Underground system became a haven at night, with people sleeping on the platforms deep beneath the street, seeking shelter from the nightly raiders. Nevertheless, by the end of September, almost 7000 civilians were dead, thousands had been wounded and tens of thousands were left homeless.

Germany's campaign intensifies

On the night of 14/15 November 1940, German 'pathfinder' bombers flying along radio direction beams hit Coventry, an industrial city heavily involved in Britain's war effort. Following the pathfinders were more than 400 bombers. Aiming at the fires already created, they dropped 503 tons of high-explosive bombs and some 30,000 incendiary bombs. The result was hundreds killed, more than 1200 badly wounded and thousands bombed out of their homes. Thousands of buildings were destroyed or badly damaged. Yet, despite the decimation, within a few days factories were back in production, and morale had recovered quickly. It seemed that bombing could not destroy the will to fight and survive. National pride and determination were galvanized against a common enemy.

By Christmas 1940, the raids covered most of the United Kingdom. Glasgow, Belfast, Liverpool and Sheffield had all been badly hit, and London had not been spared. Just after Christmas, on the night of 29/30 December, more than 130 bombers attacked the heart of London. The area between the Guildhall and St Paul's Cathedral was ablaze. The cathedral itself was saved, but homes, offices and historic churches in the surrounding area were turned to ashes; hundreds of years of building and history were lost. Despite this bleak time, the country survived. New equipment came out of battered factories, including radar-directed guns that could predict the height and direction of bombers. Night

110

Bombing: Britain and Germany 1940–41

fighters were now equipped with radar and began to intercept the night raiders with increasing success. Fire and rescue teams became more expert. Bomb disposal units worked diligently at the dangerous task of disposing of unexploded bombs. It was now clear to all that Britain would not succumb under the relentless bombing.

Britain's reply

At the beginning of World War II, there were four types of bomber in service with the RAF: the Bristol Blenheim, Handley Page Hampden, Vickers Wellington and Armstrong Whitworth Whitley. All were reasonable designs with no major mechanical drawbacks. Their maximum bombloads varied from 454kg (1000lb) for the Blenheim to 3630kg (8000lb) for the Whitley. The Blenheim had a restricted range, but the other three types could reach any part of Germany, except the extreme east. RAF Bomber Command had always intended that main bombing operations be carried out by tight, self-defending daylight formations; only the Whitley squadrons of 4 Group were trained in night bombing.

On 1 September 1939, US President Franklin D. Roosevelt called for restraint from bombing operations where civilians might be hit. France and Britain agreed at once. On 18 September, Germany also agreed, but only as the Polish campaign drew to a close. Meanwhile, the RAF was cleared to attack German shipping, as long as it was not alongside a wharf or dock. Bombers could also fly over enemy territory for the purpose of dropping propaganda leaflets. Many RAF commanders felt that this was a waste of time, but it did build up experience in operating over enemy territory before actually being committed to an all-out bombing campaign. It also bought time to build up aircraft numbers and train aircrews beyond the number immediately available at the outbreak of war.

After the fall of France, Germany controlled the Atlantic coast from the Spanish border to the north of Norway. During the Battle of Britain, RAF Bomber Command's main task was to bomb barge concentrations along the occupied Channel coast. Its planned attack on German industry was secondary to the needs of the moment. Despite this, a small number of bombers were sent to Germany night after night; oil-related targets were their priority. Virtually all night raids were carried

COSTLY RETALIATION
Early RAF night bombing operations against German targets were carried out by single aircraft. Formation bombing attacks in the early months of the war had proved prohibitively costly.

out by small groups of aircraft directed to various targets, with each crew responsible for navigating its own way. Navigation equipment and skills were lacking, but on moonlit nights visual sightings of rivers or other identifiable landmarks helped the bomber crews to locate their targets.

As German anti-aircraft artillery and searchlights became more effective, however, the bombers were forced to fly at higher altitudes, making identification of the target even more difficult. Small numbers of RAF aircraft were fitted with bombing cameras, and these were allocated to the best crews. Within RAF Bomber Command, optimism prevailed.

VICKERS WELLINGTON
Designed by Barnes Wallis, the Vickers Wellington featured geodetic construction, giving it great strength and enabling it to absorb an enormous amount of battle damage. It was the most important bomber on the RAF's inventory in 1940.

BOMBING OF NAZI EUROPE
1940–42
✺ 25–1000 tons of bombs
✺ 1000–3000 tons of bombs

111

MARITIME AIR PATROL: 1940–41

At the outbreak of the war in Europe, the German navy began to apply the same tactics of attrition that had failed it in World War I. This was based on the calculation that, if 750,000 tons of Allied shipping, mostly British, could be sunk every month for a year, the United Kingdom would be forced into surrender by starvation. As an island nation, Britain did little to provide for maritime patrols. RAF High Command gave maximum priority for large long-range aircraft to Bomber Command.

Enemies below the surface

Germany began the war with 57 U-boats. German naval planners felt that 350 U-boats were required to reach the proposed goal of sunk Allied shipping, but with the help of mines, aircraft, warships and surface raiders the necessary total might be met. Against this force, Britain could deploy 12 battleships and battlecruisers, 6 aircraft carriers, 58 cruisers and more than 200 destroyers and escorts with anti-submarine capabilities, as well as some 69 submarines. The French navy was also able to provide assistance, but its main task was facing the Italian Fleet in the Mediterranean.

In September 1939, with the exception of two surface raiders out in the Atlantic, the German navy could not operate much further west than a few hundred miles off the British coast, an area known as the 'Western Approaches'. The North Sea and English Channel were about the limits of U-boat operations. The bulk of Allied ships targeted were therefore in these areas. From September 1939 to June 1940, 702 merchant ships were lost.

At the beginning of World War II, Britain had a small number of the excellent Short Sunderland flying boats available for maritime patrol operations. Developed from 'Empire'-class flying boats designed to fly routes connecting the British Empire, the Sunderland could patrol for up to 13 hours. Equipped with radar from 1941, its reputation grew. It also undertook several air-sea rescue operations.

With the German conquest of Norway and later France in July 1940, the nature of the U-boat war in the Atlantic changed. In July 1940, the first U-boat base came into operation at Lorient in western France. The U-boats' route to their patrol area was immediately reduced by some 750km (450 miles). More of the available U-boats could be on patrol for

MID-ATLANTIC GAP
The mid-Atlantic gap provided an ideal killing ground for enemy submarines, as there were not enough surface escorts to counter them. Only after long-range patrol aircraft became available was the gap closed, and merchant ship losses reduced.

BATTLE OF THE ATLANTIC
September 1939–May 1940

- - - Border of Pan-American Neutrality Zone (1939)
- - - Extent of air escort cover
▫ Major convoy routes
× Allied merchant ships sunk by U-boats
↙ U-boats sunk
▪ Territory under Allied control
▪ Territory under Axis control
▪ Neutral territory

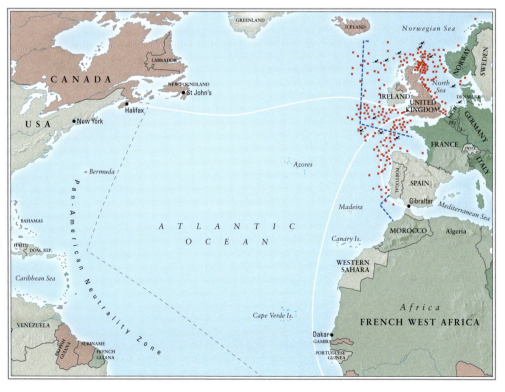

112

Maritime Air Patrol: 1940–41

longer periods, and a greater number of them could be kept in action. Although 25 U-boats had been lost since the start of the war, production had increased. Despite losses, there were now 51 in service.

In addition to U-boats, the Germans had Dornier Do 18 flying boats and Heinkel He 115 seaplanes, adequate for operations along Europe's western coasts, the North Sea and the Bay of Biscay. Any flights further into the Atlantic were the realm of the four-engined Focke-Wulf Fw 200 Condor, a sleek, modern-looking aircraft first flown in 1936 as a long-range airliner. In August 1940, under the command of Oberstleutnant Hans Geisse, KG 40 began operations from an airfield near Bordeaux. Ranging far out into the Atlantic, its role was primarily reconnaissance, reporting positions and directions of Allied convoys. The task completed, the aircraft's bombs were unloaded on any target of opportunity. Between August and September, KG 40's 15 aircraft accounted for 90,000 tons of Allied shipping.

Countering attacks from the air

At this time, most convoys had one or two escorts; these were primarily anti-submarine and could not perform any meaningful anti-aircraft role. In the sky and below the waves, Germany seemed to hold the key to victory. Thousands of Allied merchant seamen lost their lives, and cargoes that meant survival to the United Kingdom ended up on the seabed.

No aircraft carriers were available at this point in the war. One quick expedient was to fit a catapult-launched fighter to merchant ships. The aircraft chosen was the Hawker Sea Hurricane. Once the aircraft was launched, the pilot was forced to ditch his aircraft near Allied ships and hope to be picked up or, if it had the range, head for the nearest landfall. The first success came on 3 August 1941. A Sea Hurricane flown by FAA pilot Lieutenant R.W.H. Everett RNVR was catapulted from the naval auxiliary vessel *Maplin*. It shot down a Focke-Wulf Fw 200 shadowing a convoy bound for the United Kingdom from Sierra Leone. Everett ditched his Hurricane after the combat, was picked up safely and was awarded the Distinguished Service Cross. A more reliable solution appeared with development of merchant ships with operable flight decks – merchant aircraft carriers, or MACs. Fighter pilots could now launch and return to their ship to fly again.

German sinkings of Allied merchant ships reached a peak in April 1941; as the convoy system became more widespread, sinkings began to decline. The German plan to sink 750,000 tons of shipping per month was never fullly realized. Britain instituted careful rationing at home and strict control

of shipping space, reducing import requirements by half during the course of the war, and larger numbers of maritime patrol aircraft began to reach operational squadrons. Among these was the Consolidated PBY Catalina. Slower and less well armed than the Sunderland, it was still a reliable long-range aircraft; more Catalinas were produced than any other flying boat. British escorts became more effective and were joined by the growing Canadian Navy, forcing U-boats further out into the Atlantic, beyond the range of patrol aircraft. As the U-boats moved west, the danger of meeting more US merchant ships and warships increased. US warships were already patrolling towards Britain – it was obvious that the United States was determined to aid Britain's survival. With his armies gathering on the Soviet Union's borders, Hitler wanted to avoid problems with the United States and was happy for the U-boats to do their duty in the Atlantic. The 'gap' in the middle Atlantic remained beyond patrol range until late 1942, when a maritime version of the Consolidated Liberator bomber was introduced.

SHORT SUNDERLAND
The first production Sunderland Mk Is were delivered to No. 230 Squadron in Singapore early in June 1938, and from the outbreak of war the Sunderland made a useful contribution to British anti-submarine efforts. On 21 September 1939, two Sunderlands rescued the entire crew of the torpedoed merchantman Kensington Court, *bringing 34 men to safety.*

FOCKE-WULF FW 200
The Focke-Wulf Fw 200 Condor long-range maritime reconnaissance aircraft presented a major threat to Allied shipping in the Atlantic and North Sea during 1940–41, sinking a greater tonnage of shipping than did the U-boats.

THE MEDITERRANEAN: 1940–42

Control of the Mediterranean was vital to both the Allies and the Axis nations. Both sides needed to keep open supply routes required to support their respective efforts in the North African campaigns. For the United Kingdom, keeping the Suez Canal open was also a major concern, as this was its fastest route to and from colonies in the east.

Negotiations for the French fleet

When France capitulated in the summer of 1940, Britain was aware that France's formidable naval forces could be taken over by Germany and used to seize the balance of naval power. This could not be allowed to happen. Two modern battleships, *Dunkerque* and *Strasbourg*, along with two older battleships, were stationed in the port of Mers-el-Kébir on the coast of Algeria. Negotiations were

FAIREY SWORDFISH
The Fairey Swordfish, known universally as the 'Stringbag', appeared to be an anachronism, yet the design of the Swordfish was exactly right for the principal tasks it had to perform, and its rugged structure made it ideal for aircraft carrier operations. It was to serve with great distinction throughout World War II, from the North Atlantic to the Indian Ocean.

BATTLE OF TARANTO
The attack on Taranto was the first real demonstration of the aircraft carrier as a means of exercising flexible, mobile sea power rather than as a mere adjunct to the fleet, and it was to have a profound effect on the conduct of future naval air operations.

The Mediterranean: 1940–42

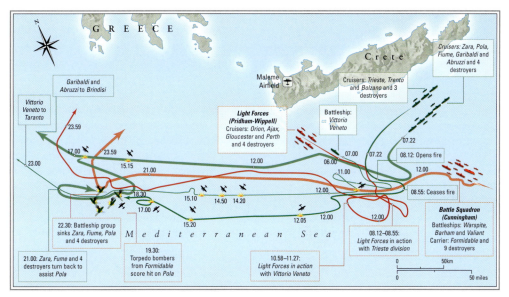

CAPE MATAPAN

The Battle of Cape Matapan was an overwhelming victory for the British Mediterranean Fleet. It was made possible by ULTRA, which alerted the Admiralty to the movements and disposition of the Italian fleet, and by naval air power.

attempted to persuade the French fleet to surrender its ships to the Royal Navy, which would then sail them either to British bases or bases in the French Caribbean, where they would be out of reach of the German navy. Alternatively, they could face destruction. Negotiations were drawn out and muddled. Out of options, the British fleet opened fire on French ships on 3 July 1940. The heavy shells hit the magazine of the battleship *Bretagne*, and she blew up; *Dunkerque* and *Provence* were badly damaged, and two destroyers were sunk. The battleship *Strasbourg* managed to escape to the French base at Toulon. Two days later an air attack using Fairey Swordfish biplanes was launched to finish off the stricken French ships, so severely damaging the *Dunkerque* that she ran aground. The attacks resulted in 1297 French sailors losing their lives, and extremely poor relations between France and Britain, but impressed upon the United States Britain's determination.

Attacking Taranto harbour

On the night of 11/12 November, the Royal Navy, using aircraft of the Fleet Air Arm, launched an attack, considered impossible by many tacticians, against a large part of the Italian fleet at Taranto harbour. A reconnaissance mission flown from Malta confirmed the presence of five battleships (a sixth battleship entered the harbour later, confirmed by an RAF flying boat), seven heavy cruisers, two light cruisers and eight destroyers, a formidable force that could strike a blow at any time against vulnerable British transports struggling to get supplies to Malta and the army in Egypt. A total of 21 aircraft took off from HMS *Illustrious*. Flying in two waves, torpedo- and bomb-armed Fairey Swordfish attacked the ships at anchor, using specially adapted torpedoes that could run in shallow water. They successfully hit the battleship *Littorio* three times, and two more battleships with one hit apiece, for the loss of two aircraft and their crew. The raid's success so alarmed the Italians that they moved the remainder of the fleet to safer ports in northern Italy, and the damaged *Littorio* remained out of action for four months. This attack, carried out by just 21 seemingly obsolete aircraft, shifted the balance of sea power in the Mediterranean back in favour of the British, at least temporarily. Japan also took great interest; the attack on Taranto was influential in its developing plan to strike the US Pacific Fleet at Pearl Harbor.

The Battle of Cape Matapan

Between 27 and 29 March 1941, a large force of Italian warships and the Royal Navy fought a major engagement off the Peloponnese in what became known as the Battle of Cape Matapan. Admiral Sir Henry Pridham-Wippell's force, based off Crete's southern coast, was made up of three Royal Navy cruisers, the Royal Australian Navy cruiser HMAS *Perth*, and a covering force of destroyers. In Alexandria, Egypt, was Admiral Sir Andrew Browne Cunningham's force of the carrier HMS *Formidable* and three battleships, including his flagship, HMS *Warspite*. Cunningham received information, via ULTRA intercepts, that an Italian force, commanded by Admiral Angelo Iachino with the modern battleship *Vittorio Veneto*, was on its way east to intercept troopships taking Allied soldiers to Greece. Pridham-Wippell's force spotted the Italians' approach south of Crete. The Italians gave chase,

115

The Mediterranean: 1940–42

opening fire from extreme range in the belief that the British force was attempting to escape. The chasing Italian cruisers gave up the pursuit, returning to the *Vittorio*, with the British ships shadowing them. Cunningham's force, which had been steaming into the area, then launched an air strike from HMS *Furious* and using land-based RAF medium bombers stationed on Crete. The *Vittorio* turned back to the safety of Italian and German land-based air cover.

A second air attack was launched, this time damaging the *Vittorio*, but she was able to proceed after some repairs. A third strike, however, crippled the cruiser *Pola*. After leaving a force of cruisers and destroyers as protection for her, *Vittorio* continued on her route back to Taranto. The British approached the stricken ship and its escorts during the night, opened fire at short range, and quickly sank the cruisers *Fiume* and *Zara*. The Italian destroyers tried to counterattack, but two of these were also sunk. The British decided to torpedo the damaged cruiser *Pola*, rather than tow her to Alexandria. The Italians never sailed into the eastern Mediterranean again.

The siege of Malta

Malta was an important strategic position between Italy and North Africa, and aircraft and ships based there had the potential to disrupt the enemy's supply lines. Italy therefore began a campaign of bombing the island as soon as it declared war on Britain. The island's original defence consisted of outmoded

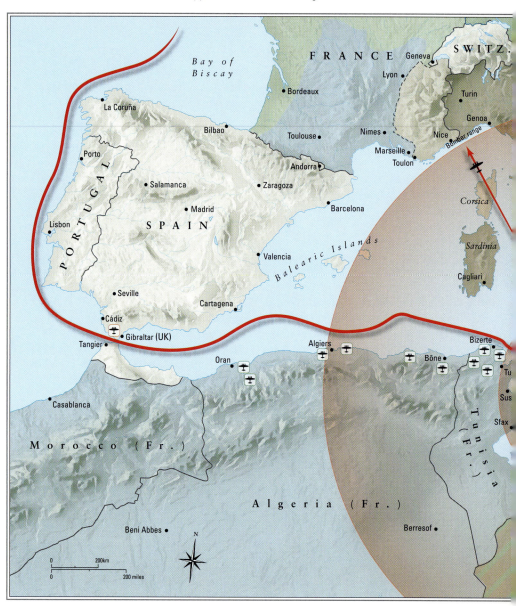

STRATEGIC TARGET
The island of Malta was the key to victory in the Mediterranean, and it might have been captured with relative ease by Axis forces in the early weeks of the Mediterranean war. Instead, Hitler focused his attention on Crete, intent on securing his southern flank.

The Mediterranean: 1940–42

Gloster Sea Gladiator biplane fighters and anti-aircraft guns. Britain decided that Malta must be defended at all costs, and every effort was made to reinforce it. Hawker Hurricanes arrived in August, alongside a few Martin Maryland reconnaissance aircraft and Vickers Wellington medium bombers. From Malta, raids were conducted on Axis forces in North Africa, as well as targets in Italy.

In June 1941, the Luftwaffe arrived in the form of Fliegerkorps X, covering the Afrika Korps sailing to Tunisia. Wellington bomber raids on Luftwaffe and Regia Aeronautica bases provoked a massive response, with Fliegerkorps X attacking Malta's airfields and other installations. What was left of the small British bomber force withdrew to bases in north Africa. Convoys continued to reach Malta, but suffered terrible losses. The island's population was surviving on limited rations. During a respite, HMS *Furious* flew in 61 Supermarine Spitfires to aid in defence, but food, oil and medicine were also urgently required. During August 1942, Operation Pedestal was carried out: 14 merchantmen were escorted by a massive naval force including three carriers, two battleships and 32 destroyers. Just five transports survived. One carrier, two cruisers and a destroyer were lost in the defence of the convoy. As the war moved in the Allies' favour, the siege of Malta eased. In acknowledgement of their bravery, the island's inhabitants received the George Cross, Britain's highest civilian decoration.

THE BALKANS: The Fall of Crete

THE BALKANS
6–21 April 1941
→ German movements

Now that Hitler had conquered most of Europe, his attentions were turning eastwards. He desperately wanted to conquer Soviet Russia, to attain the all-important Lebensraum (living space) for his people. He was also driven by the need to capture the vast fields of Ukraine to feed those people and the oilfields of the Caucasus to fuel his growing empire and keep his armed forces mobile. Before any of this could go ahead, he was forestalled by Mussolini's failed invasion of Greece, in which the Italian army was pushed back into Albania after some initial success. Hitler would have to secure this southern flank for fear of any Allied landings in Greece which might threaten his supply lines into Russia and, more vitally, the oilfields of Romania.

First, control of Yugoslavia was required. Hitler had this goal in his grasp through intimidation of the weak Yugoslav government, until this was overthrown by an anti-fascist coup. German intervention came in the form of a massive air raid on Belgrade on 6 April 1941, at the same time as German troops swept across the Greek border. These raids continued until Yugoslavia's capitulation on 14 April.

Allied evacuation to Crete

By the time of Germany's attack on Greece, Britain had sent three Bristol Blenheim and two Gloster Gladiator squadrons to bolster the Greek air force, equipped with mostly outdated aircraft

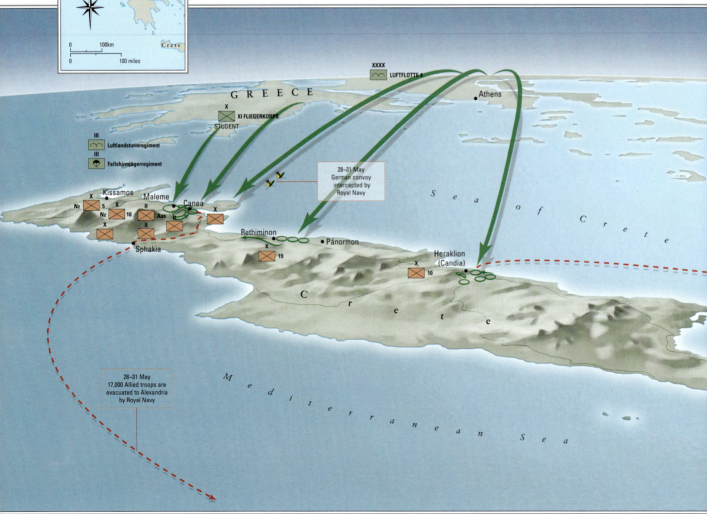

The Balkans: The Fall of Crete

types. A further three squadrons of Hawker Hurricanes flew from Egypt to supplement this force. Facing this motley collection was Luftflotte IV, with 1200 aircraft of all types at its disposal. The RAF and Greek air force put up a stiff resistance, along with the troops fighting in the mountainous terrain of northern Greece, but it soon became obvious that the Allied troops would have to fall back onto the island of Crete. Some flyers stayed behind to cover the evacuation until the last possible moment.

With the Greek mainland now under Axis control, the next target was Crete, which offered whomever controlled it dominance of the eastern Mediterranean. Hitler wanted this secured. On the island was a garrison mostly made up of ANZAC troops with a brigade of British troops and evacuated Greek units. Although these units were poorly equipped, they put up a spirited defence. There were no longer any fighter aircraft on the island, as these had all been left behind in Greece during the retreat or had been evacuated to Egypt. On 20 May, protected by Messerschmitt Bf 109s and Bf 110s, hordes of DFS 230 gliders towed by 700 Junkers Ju 52s flew to the island of Crete and started disgorging their *Fallschirmjäger* cargo. The German paratroops' objective was to land near or on the numerous airfields dotting the northwestern part of Crete. With these secure, further troops from the 10th Mountain Division could be flown in.

A bloody victory

The initial landings were a massacre because the *Fallschirmjäger* drifted slowly down into the sights of the waiting Allied machine guns and rifles. The German paratroops jumped without their personnel weapons, and upon landing they had to scramble to the containers holding their means of protection. Only skill, tenacity and sheer weight of the attack allowed them to make inroads. Airfields were soon in German hands, and Ju 52s swooped down to unload more and more troops. Had Allied High Command allowed a few Hurricanes to stay behind in the defence of Crete, Germany may have rethought the attack. But this was not to be. As the Germans expanded their airhead, so the Allies fell back. Another rearguard action was called for, and the Royal Navy successfully evacuated much of the Cretan force. The Greeks stayed behind to fight an insurgency war, holding down German troops that could have been used on other fronts. Still, Hitler's southern flank was secure, and Operation Barbarossa could proceed.

CRETE, 1941

German airborne forces took tremendous punishment during the battle for Crete, suffering 25 per cent killed and wounded, and they never mounted another major operation, a fact that probably saved Malta. Here, a Junkers Ju 52 goes down in flames near Heraklion.

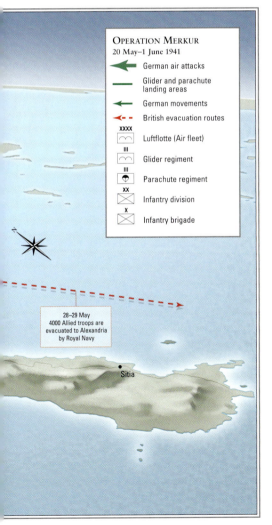

OPERATION MERKUR

The battle for Crete was a tragic demonstration of the vulnerability of naval forces, deprived of air protection, to air attack. The Royal Navy lost three cruisers and six destroyers; two battleships, an aircraft carrier, six cruisers and seven destroyers suffered varying degrees of damage.

119

BARBAROSSA AND THE BOMBING OF MOSCOW

As Hitler's attention towards defeating Britain waned, and his eyes were drawn increasingly east to the vast open areas of Ukraine and western Russia, and to the south Russian steppe with its oil reserves to fuel his thirsty war machine, he made a fundamental mistake. Committing his forces to attacking Russia was an ambitious and daunting undertaking, especially while his troops were still fighting elsewhere. The display of might shown in North Africa would become a sideshow compared to the truly massive force he was about to unleash on the Soviet Union. Hitler urged his generals to conduct yet another quick, decisive campaign. This was essential to success, before the attackers became bogged down and completely frozen in the long Russian winter. Operation Barabarossa would have ideally started in May, but the need to stabilize the southern flank in the Balkans, thanks to Italy's inefficiency and mounting supply problems, meant that Hitler had to wait until late June 1941.

In order to gain a complete victory in the open expanses of Soviet Russia, German military planners favoured rapid advances of the type that had paid dividends in earlier campaigns, engulfing Soviet units guarding the borders, and followed by a massive drive for Moscow. Hitler also wanted to secure the industrial spoils of the Russian economy, however, and ordered that the capture of Leningrad had to be ensured before any advance on the capital. This burden of interference proved the downfall of the invasion, the campaign and the war.

The Luftwaffe's Soviet mission

The Luftwaffe's first directive was to destroy the Soviet air force and attain total air superiority. It would then move to support of the ground offensive – the same proven formula of previous campaigns. Interestingly, no directives were drawn up for the strategic bombing of Russian industrial centres, probably because it was thought that the ground offensive would be so quick that their armaments factories would soon be in German hands. These optimistic assumptions were made from the poor performance of the Soviet forces in the Winter War against Finland and partly in the knowledge that the Soviet forces had few capable commanders, thanks to Stalin's purges of the 1930s.

The Luftwaffe's build-up was kept under a strict veil of secrecy, with airstrips being prepared in East Prussia, but aircraft not actually arriving until a few days before the invasion. On the evening of 21 June 1941, 1000 bombers and dive-bombers with the protection of 600 fighters were going through their last-minute checks before being deployed against the sleeping giant of Soviet Union.

As dawn broke, troops swarmed over the fields of eastern Poland, taking its Soviet defenders by surprise, as the Luftwaffe strived to destroy the Soviet Air Force. Many of the Soviet squadrons were found to be neatly parked in rows, facilitating the ease with which the German flyers destroyed them. Few Soviet aircraft got off the ground, and those that did were soon sent hurtling back down in flames. By day's end Soviet losses amounted to 1200 aircraft of all types. This pattern continued over the next few days, when losses dropped sharply. There were no more aircraft on the front line for the Luftwaffe to destroy. Claims of more than 4000 destroyed enemy aircraft were logged by the Luftwaffe for

SOVIET AIR CREW
Soviet pilots relax and play dominoes, while a Polikarpov I-16 stands ready in the background. The I-16 formed the bulk of the Soviet Air Force in the opening days of Operation Barbarossa.

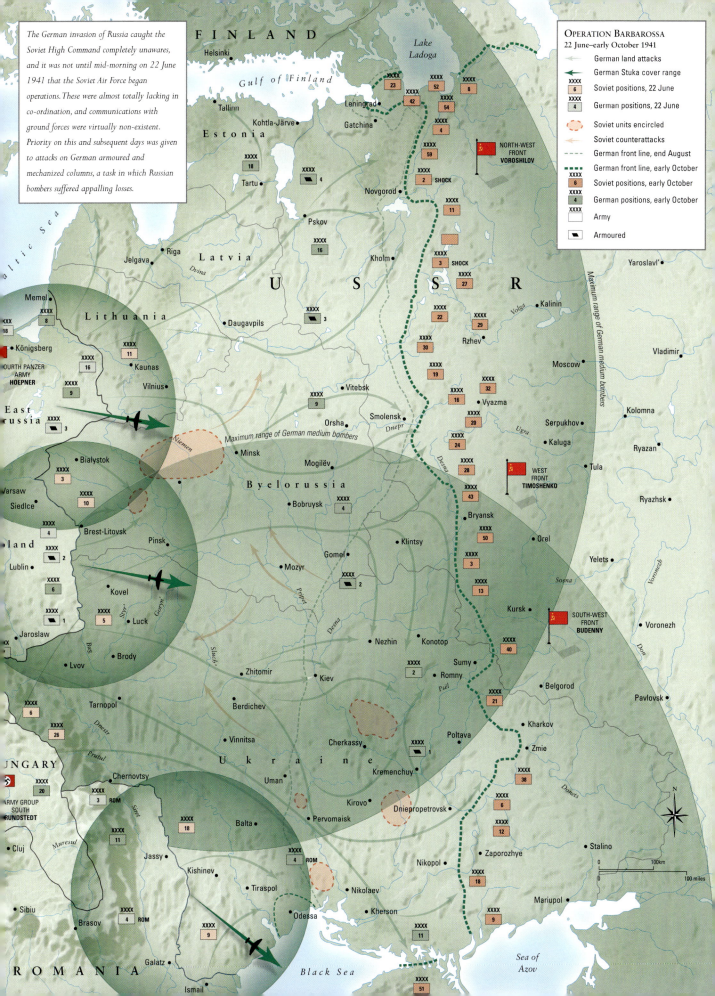

Barbarossa and the Bombing of Moscow

SOVIET ANTI-AIRCRAFT GUNS
Anti-aircraft artillery was in plentiful supply to units of the Red Army from the beginning of the Great Patriotic War. Artillery units were amongst the best trained and equipped elements of the Red Army and continued to improve both in quality and quantity until the war's end.

comparatively few losses of its own. It seemed that all was going according to plan.

On the ground, vast pincer movements by the Wehrmacht's panzers trapped hundreds of thousands of Soviet troops. More than 250,000 alone were captured when Minsk was enveloped. It is thought that the same number of troops died in the fighting around this area. In the north, Leningrad was within sight of the vanguard of the German advance by the beginning of August, while in the southern sector Kiev had been surrounded, yielding an astonishing 650,000 captured troops, according to German reports.

But these massive victories strained Germany's ability to deal with them. Accommodating hundreds of thousands of prisoners while maintaining logistical supply stretched German resources to their limits. As the German forces punctured further into Russia, the distances the supplies had to travel increased. The front also widened, meaning that the Luftwaffe had to fly further, burning even more precious fuel. Russia's vast size was at last beginning to dawn on German commanders. Accustomed to fighting on a far smaller front in western Europe, they were now fighting on a continental scale. The problem of working on ill-prepared forward airstrips was also taking its toll on man and machine, and frontline strength was depleted more by landing accidents than action with the enemy.

Slowing German advance

The advance slowed right down at the end of July, purely on logistical grounds – the Soviets were still not able to put up a solid defence. Once supplies filtered down to German forward units, the advance commenced. Supply to the northern and southern fronts took priority. Leningrad would be placed under siege conditions as the Finns moved down the Karelian Isthmus, surrounding the city for many months. Ukraine was secured, along with its precious grain supplies, and more than half a million Soviet troops were captured.

76.2mm M1938
Muzzle velocity: 815m (2673ft) per second
Range: 9.5km (5.9 miles)

85mm M1939
Muzzle velocity: 800m (2624ft) per second
Range: 8.2km (5.1 miles)

37mm M39
Muzzle velocity: 960m (3149ft) per second
Range: 6km (3.7 miles)

Maxim M1910
Muzzle velocity: 740m (2472ft) per second
Range: 1km (3280ft)

FORMIDABLE WEAPONS
The Russians quickly set up a formidable array of air defences around Moscow, so that in the 31 raids carried out by groups of between 10 and 50 aircraft in October 1941, only 72 bombers actually broke through to the capital. Of the 76 raids on Moscow in 1941, 59 were carried out by groups of between three and ten aircraft.

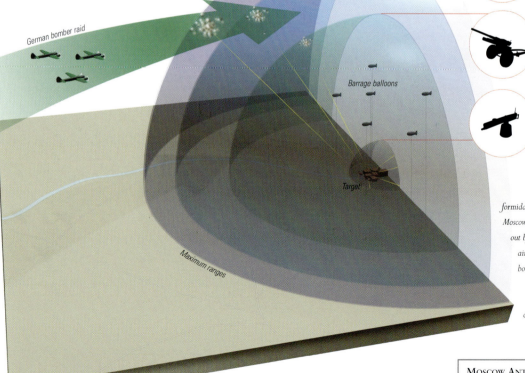

MOSCOW ANTI-AIRCRAFT DEFENCES
September–December 1941

Barbarossa and the Bombing of Moscow

MIKOYAN-GUREVICH MIG-3
A group of MiG-3 fighters of the 12th IAP stand ready for action in the defence of Moscow. Aleksandr Pokryshkin, the second highest-scoring Soviet fighter ace, gained 20 of his 59 victories while flying the MiG-3.

At the start of July, missions were flown to bomb Moscow. More than 100 aircraft flew on the first mission. They dropped high-explosive bombs and incendiaries, hoping to start massive conflagrations in Moscow's suburbs, where buildings were still mostly of wooden construction.

Moscow's anti-aircraft defences were formidable. An outer ring of searchlights and fighters was the first obstacle to fight through, followed by 800 anti-aircraft artillery pieces in and around the city itself. Many important buildings such as the Kremlin were heavily camouflaged from the air. The city's vast underground system, built in the late 1930s, had shelters incorporated into its original design.

After the initial large raids, bombing of the city became a nightly event, although not on the scale of the Blitz over London. Soviet emergency services worked with great skill and speed, quickly repairing or clearing damage so that daily life could continue.

The beginning of the end

By the start of November, German forces were closing in on Moscow. The Luftwaffe's fighters were within range to escort the bombers to the city, but the problems of supply and flying from poor landing strips were still a severe handicap to the flyers. Russian pilots had the advantage of quality concrete runways and warm billets. Civilian casualties did start to rise, though, with the daylight raids, as people tended to be further from shelter when working.

BOMBING MOSCOW
The air defence of Moscow was entrusted to the 6th Fighter Air Corps, which was equipped entirely with day fighters. Soviet pilots took great risks in their attempts to repel enemy night attacks, but their claims of German bombers destroyed were exaggerated.

By January, after a huge Soviet counterattack, the German advance started to slow, after reaching within 45km (27 miles) of the city limits. The German troops fell back, along with their bomber force. On the frozen plains of Russia, its attentions were split. It had to provide tactical ground support as well fulfill its bombing role, flying from unsuitable airfields and with an incomplete line of supply and support. The mission was doomed to failure.

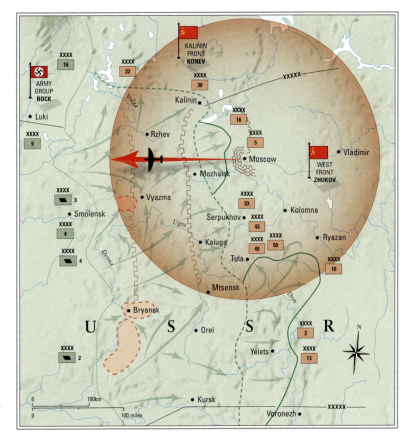

PEARL HARBOR: December 1941

Japan's desired expansion in the Pacific was reliant upon the capture and control of natural resources that the Japanese islands lacked. Without these resources, particularly oil in the Dutch East Indies and British-controlled Malaya, Japanese industry would stall. France and the Netherlands were effectively out of the war after their capitulation to Germany, while Britain's focus was very much on fighting in North Africa. Their colonial outposts in the Far East were open to exploitation. The only impediment to Japanese expansion was the United States and its powerful Pacific fleet.

Similar in size to the Imperial Japanese Navy, the US Pacific fleet presented a serious threat to the Japanese flank if and when Japan made its grab for Southeast Asia's resources. The solution: a surprise attack on the fleet, anchored at Pearl Harbor, Oahu, in the Hawaiian Islands. This would neutralize the threat and provide Japan with much-needed time to capture assets and consolidate its position on the Pacific Rim before the United States could recover.

Neutralizing the US Pacific fleet

In charge of planning this operation was Admiral Isoroku Yamamoto. He had worked with the United States in the 1930s and was initially against an attack, knowing that the United States' industrial might easily outweighed Japan's. After studying the British success at Taranto, Yamamoto realized that, if it could destroy the US carriers and battleships in the harbour, Japan had a realistic chance of victory. He ordered that the standard torpedo be fitted with wooden fins to allow them to run shallower and not dig into the harbour mud of Pearl's shallow waters.

SURPRISE ATTACK
In planning the devastating attack on Pearl Harbor, the Japanese Navy Commander-in-Chief, Admiral Isoroku Yamamoto, was heavily influenced by the British attack on Taranto just over a year earlier. But the Japanese attack failed to neutralize the American aircraft carriers, which would form the nucleus of future naval task forces.

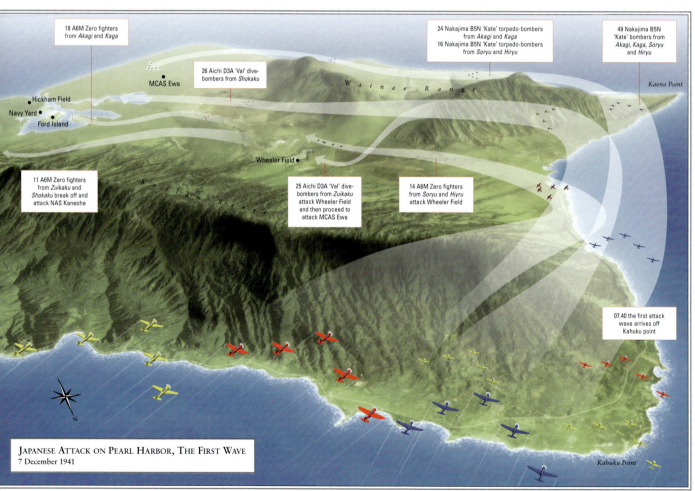

JAPANESE ATTACK ON PEARL HARBOR, THE FIRST WAVE
7 December 1941

Pearl Harbor: December 1941

The men involved in the attack were trained in the utmost secrecy in the isolated Kurile Islands to Japan's north, before setting sail on a northerly route to the Hawaiian Islands. The Japanese fleet was made up of six carriers – *Akagi*, *Hiryu*, *Kaga*, *Shokaku*, *Soryu* and *Zuikaku* – supported by two battleships and two heavy cruisers, plus destroyers and support ships. The attack force carried a total of 430 attack and reconnaissance aircraft.

The United States was well aware of Japanese intentions and had put commanders of all overseas territories on full alert. Unfortunately, the US Army commander of Pearl Harbor thought that, if any attack were to come, it would be launched on the Philippines, Wake or Midway islands. The only attacks he was expecting were small-scale sabotage raids. The anti-aircraft defences of Pearl Harbor were not even issued ammunition for their guns.

By the early hours of 7 December 1941, the Japanese attack fleet was sailing from the northwest towards Oahu, readying to launch. At 0600 hours, 51 Aichi D3A 'Val' dive-bombers, 49 Nakajima B5N

'Kate' bombers and 40 'Kate' torpedo-bombers escorted by 43 Mitsubishi A6M 'Zero' fighters took to the air as the first wave to attack Pearl Harbor. They formed up initially in hazy and cloudy conditions, but as they neared Oahu the cloud broke to reveal a perfect morning. The formation approach was noticed by a radar operator. He reported the contact to the duty officer, but was told to take no

ZERO FIGHTER
A Mitsubishi A6M2 Reisen (Zero Fighter) of the 12th Air Group, seen over China shortly after the type's entry into service with the Imperial Japanese Navy in 1940.

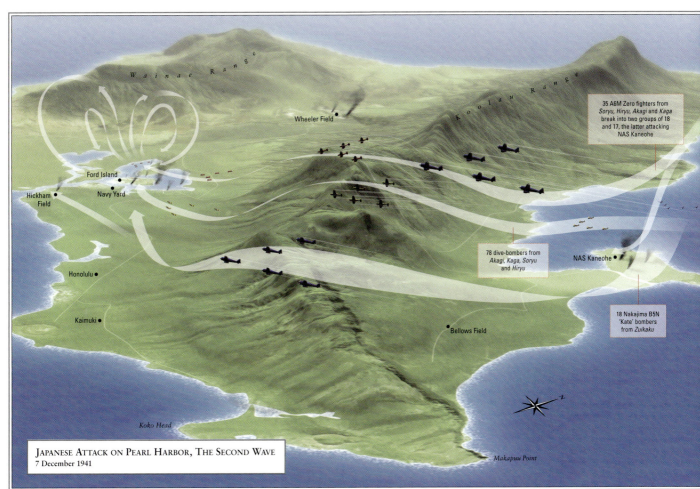

Japanese Attack on Pearl Harbor, The Second Wave
7 December 1941

Pearl Harbor: December 1941

Pearl Harbor: December 1941

action; these were assumed to be a flight of Boeing B-17s expected to be flying in from the mainland. The strike force was again unintentionally aided when they listened in to a US radio broadcast that helped them to close in on the target.

Deliberate timing

Sunday morning was specifically chosen as the day of the attack because many navy personnel would be on shore leave. The dive-bombers plunged on their targets just before 0800 hours, followed shortly by the torpedoes of the Kates on battleship row. All the while the accompanying Zero fighters strafed the nearby airfields, with no opposition; the US aircraft were conveniently lined up and easily picked off by the well-trained pilots. With few US interceptors and little anti-aircraft fire (the men had to smash the padlocks off ammunition lockers, as the keys could not be found), the Japanese pilots methodically lined up on their targets and loosed their deadly cargo.

USS *Arizona* was hit by an armour-piercing bomb in the magazine, immediately exploding and sinking, taking 1200 sailors down with her. She was followed by USS *West Virginia* and *California*, both victims of torpedoes. USS *Nevada* began a dash for the relative safety of the open sea, but was set upon and beached short of the harbour entrance. The first wave, ammunition, bombs and torpedoes expended, returned to their carriers victorious.

Pearl Harbor did not have long to recover before the second wave swung around the mountains of Oahu. By now the survivors had pulled themselves together and were beginning to open up all they could on the incoming aircraft. With heavy smoke now pouring from many of the first wave's victims, the second wave did not have as much success as its predecessors, but it still inflicted a hefty amount of damage. By lunchtime all the Japanese aircraft had landed back on their carriers and were en route back to Japan. In Pearl Harbor, there were 2335 dead service and civilian personnel, four battleships sunk with a further four severely damaged, three destroyers sunk and two cruisers heavily damaged, and 188 aircraft that were destroyed either on the ground or in the air. All this was for the loss of just 29 Japanese aircraft and their crew.

It was an astonishing victory, albeit a hollow one, because now the United States was irrevocably in the war. In addition, the attack's main target, the US carriers, were out of port that day, delivering aircraft to Midway or in repair on the mainland. None of the harbour's installations had been destroyed either, allowing Pearl Harbor to return to its primary purpose almost immediately.

(1) Tender *Whitney* and destroyers *Tucker, Conyngham, Reid, Case* and *Selfridge*
(2) Destroyer *Blue*
(3) Light cruiser *Phoenix*
(4) Destroyers *Aylwin, Farragut, Dale* and *Monaghan*
(5) Destroyers *Patterson, Ralph Talbot* and *Henry*
(6) Tender *Dobbin*, and destroyers *Worden, Hull, Dewey, Phelps* and *Macdough*
(7) Hospital ship *Solace*
(8) Destroyer *Allen*
(9) Destroyer *Chew*
(10) Destroyer-minesweepers *Gamble, Montgomery* and light-minelayer *Ramsey*
(11) Destroyer-minesweepers *Trever, Breese, Zane, Perry* and *Wasmuth*
(12) Repair vessel *Medusa*
(13) Seaplane tender *Curtiss*
(14) Light cruiser *Detroit*
(15) Light cruiser *Raleigh*
(16) Target battleship *Utah*
(17) Seaplane tender *Tangier*
(18) Battleship *Nevada*
(19) Battleship *Arizona*
(20) Repair vessel *Vestal*
(21) Battleship *Tennessee*
(22) Battleship *West Virginia*
(23) Battleship *Maryland*
(24) Battleship *Oklahoma*
(25) Oiler *Neosho*
(26) Battleship *California*
(27) Seaplane tender *Avocet*
(28) Destroyer *Shaw*
(29) Destroyer *Downes*
(30) Destroyer *Cassin*
(31) Battleship *Pennsylvania*
(32) Submarine *Cachalot*
(33) Minelayer *Oglala*
(34) Light cruiser *Helena*
(35) Auxiliary vessel *Argonne*
(36) Gunboat *Sacramento*
(37) Destroyer *Jarvis*
(38) Destroyer *Mugford*
(39) Auxiliary vessel *Argonne*
(40) Repair vessel *Rigel*
(41) Oiler *Ramapo*
(42) Heavy cruiser *New Orleans*
(43) Destroyer *Cummings* and light-minelayers *Preble* and *Tracy*
(44) Heavy cruiser *San Francisco*
(45) Destroyer-minesweeper *Grebe*, destroyer *Schley* and light-minelayers *Pruitt* and *Sicard*
(46) Light cruiser *Honolulu*
(47) Light cruiser *St. Louis*
(48) Destroyer *Bagley*
(49) Submarines *Narwhal, Dolphin* and *Tautog* and tenders *Thornton* and *Hulbert*
(50) Submarine tender *Pelias*
(51) Auxiliary vessel *Sumner*
(52) Auxiliary vessel *Castor*

CHAOS ON FORD ISLAND
Sailors and ground crew struggle to repair damage and put out fires on Ford Island, Pearl Harbor, while smoke still pours from the Arizona.

127

FALL OF SOUTHEAST ASIA: 1942

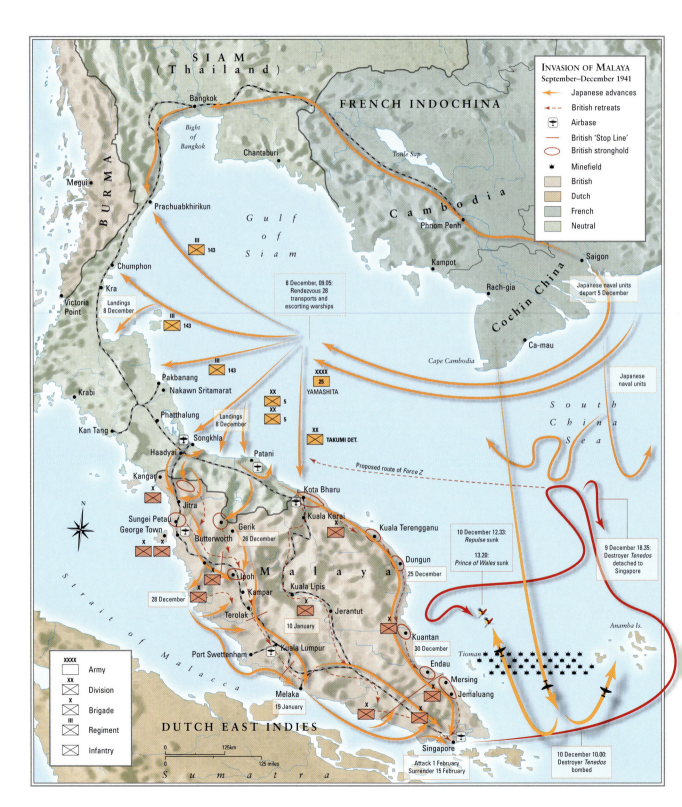

Fall of Southeast Asia: 1942

On 8 December 1941, General Tomoyuki Yamashita's 24th Army landed in southern Siam (Thailand) and northern Malaya. The region's raw materials had to be seized quickly to feed Japan's war industries. The air, land and sea units engaged in this massive operation had been tried and tested in savage fighting in China. Facing them were inexperienced Allied forces new to the region.

The fall of Singapore

The largest and most prestigious Alllied base was Singapore. Here, the British Empire concentrated the bulk of its forces. The main fighter defence rested on four squadrons of the outdated Brewster Buffalo. The Bomber Force was made up of four squadrons of early model Bristol Blenheims, two squadrons of Lockheed Hudsons and two squadrons of ancient Vickers Wildebeest torpedo-carrying biplanes. Together with a handful of other aircraft, these totalled some 362 aircraft available for the defence of Malaya and Singapore; only around 60 per cent were serviceable and ready for operations.

The land forces numbered around 60,000 men, with reinforcements arriving from Britain, India, Australia and New Zealand on a weekly basis. At sea, two British capital ships were Singapore-based, the battleship HMS *Prince of Wales* and the battlecruiser HMS *Repulse*. These operated with a small force of cruisers, destroyers and submarines. On 8 December, HMS *Prince of Wales* and HMS *Repulse* led a small force to locate and attack Japanese troopships supporting the invasion, but Japanese reconnaissance aircraft found them first. A force of 60 Mitsubishi G3M2 bombers (Allied code name 'Nell') and 26 G4M1 'Betty' bombers attacked with bombs and torpedoes, sinking both and illustrating the importance of air cover in naval engagements. This left just three US aircraft carriers as the only Allied capital ships facing the might of the Japanese fleet in the Pacific.

Experienced Japanese troops now fought their way down the Malay peninsula, outflanking and outfighting the untested Allied soldiers. Overhead, Japanese bombers flew support missions covered by the superb Mitsubishi A6M2 Zero fighter. Its speed, manoeuvrability and range came as a deep shock to the defenders. Some Allied reinforcements arrived, with 51 Hawker Hurricanes coming by sea.

INVASION OF MALAYA
In their invasion of Malaya, the Japanese had one big advantage: they treated the jungle as an ally, rather than an enemy, and could live off it if they had to. The Japanese army existed on rations which would have been quite unacceptable to western troops.

They were quickly uncrated, assembled and tested, and some were ready for action by 20 January 1942. On the same day, a group of Hurricanes caught 28 Japanese bombers bent on attacking Singapore. They shot down eight of the raiders. When the Japanese bombers returned, they were escorted by the fast Zero fighters; five Hurricanes were shot down. The Japanese forces continued to advance, their experience and determination telling on the raw British recruits, who were poorly trained and badly prepared. On 15 February 1942, Singapore fell. The road to the Dutch East Indies lay open.

Consolidating Japanese control

Within four months Japanese forces had achieved almost all of their aims. They drove into Burma, consolidated the Philippines and the Dutch East Indies, and moved down the Solomon Islands. In the Philippines, where the USAAF had stationed the largest formation outside of the mainland United States, swift Japanese air raids caught the US B-17 bomber force on the ground. Those stationed at Clark Field and surrounding areas were not sent on pre-emptive strikes to the Japanese air bases on Formosa. On the afternoon of 8 December, 12 B-17s were completely destroyed and three others damaged beyond repair. Curtiss P-40s were caught taxiing by strafing Zeros. In one fell swoop half of US air strength in the Philippines was destroyed, and the remainder would suffer the same fate over the next few days. Imperial Japan seemed unstoppable.

BRISTOL BLENHEIM
Three RAF squadrons in Malaya, Nos. 34, 60 and 62, were equipped with the Bristol Blenheim Mk I.

CAPTURE OF SINGAPORE
Heavy Japanese air attacks created a huge collapse of morale among the civilian population of Singapore. The island defences had always anticipated an attack from the sea, rather than from the Malay Peninsula.

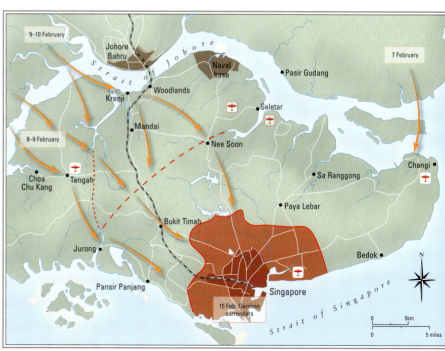

The Battle of the Coral Sea: 1942

THE BATTLE OF THE CORAL SEA: 1942

*BATTLE OF THE CORAL SEA
The Battle of the Coral Sea was the first naval engagement in history fought without opposing ships making contact. United States carrier forces prevented a Japanese attempt to land at Port Moresby, New Guinea, by turning back the enemy's covering carrier force.*

Japan's advance did not slow as its forces encroached further and further southwards. All that stood in the way of attacking and perhaps invading northern Australia was the dense, unforgiving jungle of Papua New Guinea. This island could then be used as a staging post for the invasion and a forward base for the Japanese medium bombers. The capture of Port Moresby, New Guinea's capital, was the linchpin of the campaign, and an invasion force was assembled in Rabaul and Kareing on New Britain.

Three Japanese convoys left the ports, the largest of these heading to Port Moresby. The other, smaller convoys headed to the island of Tulagi in the Lousiades to start the building of a seaplane base. Four heavy cruisers, one destroyer and the light carrier *Shoho*, all under the command of Rear Admiral Goto Aritano, provided protection. There was also a strike force comprising the two carriers *Shokaku* and *Zuikaku*, both veterans of the Pearl Harbor raid, and two heavy cruisers and several destroyers. This force was commanded by Vice Admiral Takagi Takeo, who was hoping to draw in any Allied forces with the convoys. His task force would then sweep around and attack first, destroying them.

Taking the attack to the Japanese

Japan's plan relied heavily on the element of surprise, but this was not to be. The Allies were fully aware of Japanese intentions because of the recent breaking of their JN-25 naval code by the US

The Battle of the Coral Sea: 1942

DOUGLAS SBD DAUNTLESS
During the Battle of Midway, SBD Dauntless dive-bombers from the carriers Enterprise, Hornet *and* Yorktown *scored a major success, sinking the Japanese carriers* Akagi, Kaga *and* Soryu *and damaging the* Hiryu *so badly that she had to be sunk by her own forces.*

code-breaking system known as 'MAGIC'; these decryptions proved invaluable. To counter Japan's moves, two task forces were created around the fleet carriers USS *Lexington* and USS *Yorktown*, under the command of Rear Admiral Frank Jack Fletcher. A third force under Australian Rear Admiral John Crace would be held in reserve.

On 3 May the first Japanese elements began landing on Tulagi without incident. Reconnaissance aircraft flying off the *Yorktown* spotted these forces the next day. They were duly attacked, and heavy casualties were inflicted, with the sinking of a destroyer and several transports. On 5 May the two US strike forces rendezvoused 670km (400 miles) south of Guadalcanal, where they began steaming northwestwards to intercept the main Japanese convoy bound for Port Moresby. As they sailed on this course, Takagi's force was entering the Coral Sea from the east. On 7 May Fletcher was informed that the Port Moresby invasion fleet had been spotted, and he immediately ordered an attack, making sure that the primary target was *Shoho*. US Navy Douglas TBD Devastator torpedo bombers and SBD Dauntless dive-bombers swooped down on the Japanese carrier; within minutes of the opening of the engagement, she began to sink. The invasion convoy was forced to pull back and began to return to bases on Truk and Rabaul. The two main opposing task forces were so close at this point that six returning Japanese reconnaissance aircraft attempted to land on *Yorktown* as night fell.

The following morning both the Japanese and US task forces launched search aircraft, with both sides spotting the other at almost the same time. The American and Japanese forces were separated by almost 340km (200 miles) as the simultaneous attacks went in. *Zuikaku* managed to evade the US dive- and torpedo-bombers as she sailed into a squall, while *Shokaku*, hit by three bombs on her deck and severely damaged, was forced to retire to Truk before gaining her returning aircraft.

Meanwhile, the Japanese strike approached the US task force with better aircraft and, more vitally, valuable experience. One bomb landed on the deck of the *Yorktown*, but she remained serviceable; USS *Lexington* took two direct hits from torpedoes that began numerous fires below decks, and she developed a list. She was later further damaged when fuel ignited and the resulting explosion tore her apart. She was scuttled after being evacuated.

Valuable lessons

There was no clear victor in the Battle of the Coral Sea, although the *Lexington*'s loss dealt more of a blow to the United States than that of the smaller carrier *Shoho* did to Japan. *Shokaku* was heavily damaged, though, and would not take part in the Battle of Midway. Japan also lost many of its experienced crew; the United States, although also suffering losses, learned some very important lessons. This was also the first naval engagement where the two belligerent fleets did not sight each other, highlighting the importance of carriers and the aircraft that flew from them. From now on, fleets would be built around this new weapon, bringing about the end of the battleship and her big guns.

THE BATTLE OF MIDWAY: 1942

ADMIRAL YAMAMOTO
Yamamoto's plan to destroy the United States Pacific Fleet in one major battle led to the confrontation at Midway. The resulting battle led to the loss of Japan's initiative at sea to the Americans.

MIDWAY ISLAND
Lying to the west of Pearl Harbor, Midway Island was a key outpost for US forces and a vital objective to be captured by Japan.

Shortly after the supposed Japanese victory over the US task force in the Coral Sea, Admiral Isoroku Yamamoto, the architect of the attack on Pearl Harbor the previous December, set about planning an invasion of the US outpost of Midway. This tiny atoll in the middle of the vast Pacific Ocean was the most westerly point now under US command, and all that stood in the way of the Japanese fleet steaming directly to the Hawaiian Islands.

An unsuccessful lure

For Yamamoto's plan to work, he would have to lure the US forces in the area to the Aleutian Islands. In order to ensure this, he would have to weaken his own force by sending two light carriers along with their escorts and troop transports to the area as a diversionary tactic. Yamamoto was also counting heavily on the belief that USS *Yorktown* had been lost in the previous month's engagement in the Coral Sea. This was not the case – the carrier was able to limp back to Pearl Harbor, where she was repaired in a staggeringly short 48 hours.

Yamamoto's plans for feinting north in the Aleutians while his main force headed for Midway came to no avail. The US commanders had access to the MAGIC decryptions breaking Japanese naval code, and prepared once again accordingly. The Pacific Commander in Chief, Admiral Chester W. Nimitz, a respected Texan, was able to deploy his forces to an advantageous position. He set about sending the carriers USS *Enterprise* and USS *Hornet*, under the command of Rear Admiral Raymond A. Spruance and heavily escorted, to sail north of Midway before the expected Japanese submarine screen was in position. This was to be joined by a second task force built around the now-repaired USS *Yorktown* and commanded by Rear Admiral Fletcher.

The Japanese force was separated into three main groups. The first comprised the invasion group supported by a powerful escort, under Yamamoto's command. The strike force was made up of four carriers: *Hiryu*, *Kaga*, *Akagi* and *Soryu*. There were also two battleships and other smaller craft, all under the command of Vice Admiral Chuichi Nagumo, veteran commander of the strike on Pearl Harbor, and the main group made up of three battleships and support craft. With all these vessels, the Japanese force heavily outweighed the US one facing them.

The invasion force was first sighted on the afternoon of 3 June and was attacked by B-17 Flying Fortresses based on Midway. The aircraft bombed the carriers with no result, clearly demonstrating the inherent shortcomings of high-level bombing against manoeuvrable naval targets. It was a job for

The Battle of Midway: 1942

CARRIER STRIKE
SBD Dauntless and TBD Devastator aircraft aboard a US carrier. The attrition rate of the Dauntless squadrons was the lowest of any US carrier aircraft in the Pacific, thanks to the SBD's ability to absorb an amazing amount of battle damage.

BATTLE OF MIDWAY
In addition to four aircraft carriers, the Japanese lost 258 aircraft and a large percentage of their most experienced carrier pilots in the Battle of Midway. Japan's decisive defeat put an end to their successful offensive and effectively turned the tide of the Pacific War.

The Battle of Midway: 1942

torpedo- and particularly dive-bombers. The attack did have the effect of occupying the Japanese carrier force, which engaged its Zero fighters. These had to be continually launched and recovered to fend off the four-engined bombers, giving the US carrier force time to reach a favourable position northeast of Midway without being spotted.

Launching the first strike

On the morning of 4 June, Yamamoto was ready to launch his first strike on the atoll. More than 100 aircraft, mostly Vals escorted by Zeros, flew to Midway, as strike aircraft from US bases on the island in turn flew to the now-located Japanese fleet. The US flyers had little success, with no hits on any targets for the loss of 17 torpedo bombers. The Japanese strike on Midway also had extremely limited success, but with a far lower loss rate.

As the aircraft returned to their carriers, Fletcher and Spruance were now northeast of Midway, in a position to strike into the flank of the approaching Japanese forces. The US carriers launched all they could muster – Douglas TBD Devastator torpedo bombers, Douglas SBD Dauntless dive-bombers and their Grumann F4F Wildcat escorts.

On board the Japanese carriers, following reports of a US carrier in the vicinity, Nagumo ordered the returning strike force be armed with armour-piercing bombs rather than the high-explosive ones that had been fitted. This bled precious minutes from Japanese readiness. As Devastators arrived on the scene – minus the SBDs, which had become lost while forming up, and more vitally the F4F escort – the Zeros covering the carriers pounced. Again no US torpedo found its mark, and all torpedo-bombers were lost to the Zeros' guns or anti-aircraft fire from the carriers and escorts. But the Zero fighters were now all at wavetop height – just as the SBDs arrived. They dived from 6100m (20,000ft), straight at the Japanese carriers, with their decks awash with ordnance and aviation fuel. *Hiryu* escaped the onslaught, as it was ahead of

THE BATTLE OF MIDWAY
4–6 June 1942

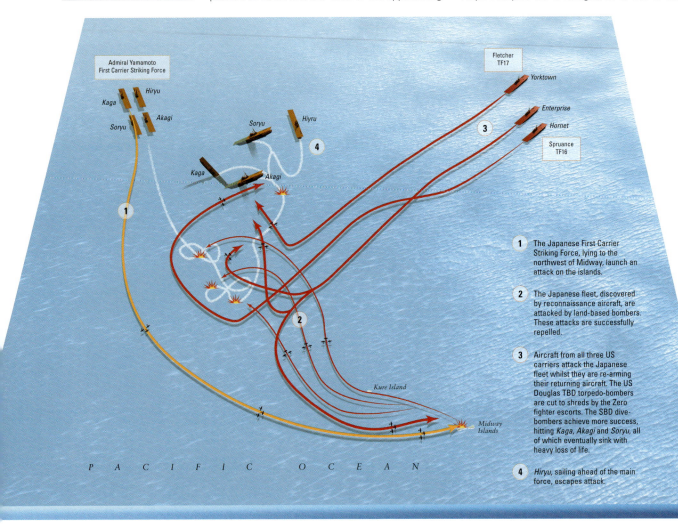

1. The Japanese First Carrier Striking Force, lying to the northwest of Midway, launch an attack on the islands.

2. The Japanese fleet, discovered by reconnaissance aircraft, are attacked by land-based bombers. These attacks are successfully repelled.

3. Aircraft from all three US carriers attack the Japanese fleet whilst they are re-arming their returning aircraft. The US Douglas TBD torpedo-bombers are cut to shreds by the Zero fighter escorts. The SBD dive-bombers achieve more success, hitting *Kaga, Akagi* and *Soryu*, all of which eventually sink with heavy loss of life.

4. *Hiryu*, sailing ahead of the main force, escapes attack.

The Battle of Midway: 1942

the formation at the time of the attack, but *Kaga*, *Akagi* and *Soryu* all took direct hits and began burning furiously. The latter two sank later that day, while *Kaga* blew up, taking much of her crew with her.

Hiryu, now alone, launched a strike against USS *Yorktown*. Three bombs and two torpedoes found their targets, and she sank some days later. As the attack went in, *Hiryu* herself was attacked by SBDs, and she received four direct hits along her deck.

With the loss of four carriers and their aircraft and crews, Yamamoto had no choice but to concede defeat and withdraw eastwards with what remained of the once-impressive strike force, harassed for much of the way by US bombers. The balance in the Pacific had now swung towards the United States, with air power once again proving decisive. From now on the United States would be on the offensive in the theatre, and Japan would be found severely lacking in naval air power with the loss of four of its best carriers, scores of aircraft and, most valuable of all, experienced pilots.

GRUMMAN F4F WILDCAT
Although very robust and capable of absorbing a tremendous amount of battle damage, the F4F Wildcat needed a highly experienced pilot at the controls to give it a fighting chance of survival in combat with Japanese fighters.

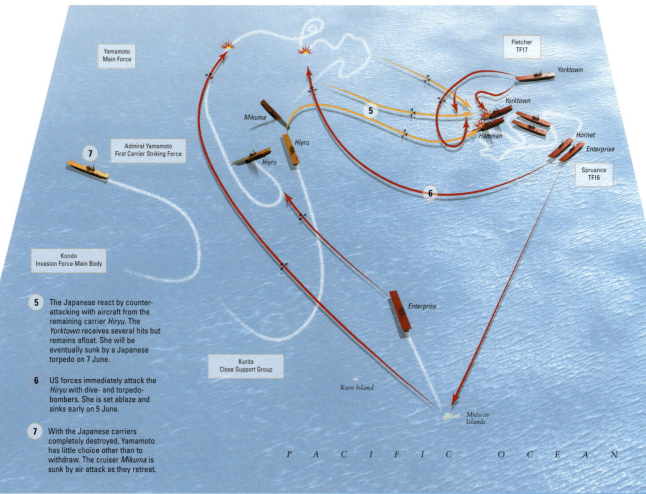

5. The Japanese react by counter-attacking with aircraft from the remaining carrier *Hiryu*. The *Yorktown* receives several hits but remains afloat. She will be eventually sunk by a Japanese torpedo on 7 June.

6. US forces immediately attack the *Hiryu* with dive- and torpedo-bombers. She is set ablaze and sinks early on 5 June.

7. With the Japanese carriers completely destroyed, Yamamoto has little choice other than to withdraw. The cruiser *Mikuma* is sunk by air attack as they retreat.

135

THE CAUCASUS AND SOUTHERN RUSSIA: 1942

With the arrival of spring 1942, German High Command planned to attack towards Moscow once again, driving back General Georgi Zhukov's gains of the previous winter and completing the capture of the Soviet capital. High Command was convinced that Moscow's capture would demoralize the Soviet war effort and bring a swift end to the war.

Hitler disagreed. He had a greater vision: the army would drive to Stalingrad and towards the Caucasus oilfields. With Field Marshal Erwin Rommel and the Afrika Korps driving the British back towards the Suez Canal, a link-up from the Caucasus into the Middle East could be effected, followed by a massive final sweep northwards behind Moscow and on to the Ural Mountains. Of the 2750 aircraft deployed on the Russian front, 1500 would be assigned to the new offensive. The plan – Operation Blue – was launched on 28 June. The Germans pushed forwards their usual combination of tanks supported by aircraft of Luftflotte IV, with infantry following along behind to clear up. They bypassed strongpoints and collected prisoners by the thousands.

By 9 July, German units reached Voronezh, then turned south to link up with armies moving from the Crimea through southern Ukraine. The Soviets abandoned Rostov-on-Don on 23 July almost without a fight. As in the summer of 1941, panic seemed to have spread throughout the Red Army. By the end of the month, Hitler was so confident of a massive victory that, instead of concentrating his forces on the capture of the oilfields, he split them into two parts. Army Group B, under the command of General Maximilian von Weichs, was sent eastwards with orders to capture the city of Stalingrad. Meanwhile, Army Group A and the 1st Panzer Army, under General Ewald von Kleist, continued on its mission to the oilfields.

Beginning the fightback

The setbacks suffered by the Red Army could not be hidden from the Soviet population, and rumours of failure and defeat soon spread. After Rostov-on-Don was lost, anger among the general population spread, especially in light of the sacrifices made before Moscow and Leningrad. The army was once again in headlong retreat, with troops abandoning equipment and ignoring the orders of their officers. Stalin, in some desperation, issued Order 227, *Ne Shagu Nazad!* ('Not a step back!').

The army ignored Stalin's orders and continued to fall back, but little by little resistance grew. The dreaded NKVD rounded up deserters, but many Soviet soldiers fought on for reasons other than terror and coercion. In the summer of 1942, Stalin called for the Soviet Union to become a single 'war camp', with the resources and people of the country focused on one agenda: defeating the invader and saving 'Mother Russia'. Religion was allowed to flourish once again in an atheist state, as it was what the people wanted, or perhaps needed, in order to survive. On 25 July Operation Edelweiss began, and for the first three weeks or so the

The Caucasus and Southern Russia: 1942

Germans advanced between 30 and 50km (20 and 30 miles) per day. But slowly the Soviets recovered, and German resources on the Caucasus Front were redirected to Stalingrad, especially Luftflotte IV, which was now ordered to send almost all of its aircraft to support the Stalingrad attacks.

As Army Group A drove further south, its progress slowed; by mid-August average progress was a little over a mile (1.6km) per day. On the Soviet side, fresh troops and new commanders arrived. Among these were the internal security NKVD division, sent to keep an eye on non-Russian nationalists and to stiffen resistance at the front.

The German 17th Army, with the Romanian 3rd Army, faced the Soviet Trans-Caucasus Front, struggling to gain control of the coast road running from Novorossiisk to Sukhumí. The 17th Army reached the outskirts of Novorossiisk on 6 September, but stubborn Soviet resistance prevented further progress. Attacks on the coast road also made little progress before winter set in, making any further meaningful advance impossible. The Luftwaffe, as in 1941, inflicted heavy losses on the Red Air Force with relatively small losses itself. Operating from primitive airstrips and at the end of an extended line of supply, however, created maintenance and availability problems. The Luftwaffe was losing around 120 bombers and the same number of fighters per month. Although German aircraft production began to rise in 1942, it could not match the Soviets' rising production levels. New Soviet models were being delivered to combat units and would be used to great effect from September 1942 onwards.

Meanwhile, to the east of the 17th Army, 1st Panzer Army advanced with apparent ease, skirting the northern foothills of the Caucasus Mountains. The river Terek was crossed at Mozdok on 2 September. In the face of Soviet counterattacks, the German advance faltered, finally coming to a halt in November on a front from Nalchik to Ordzhonikidze. Snowfalls prevented further advances, and the German line of supply was now long, thin and at its maximum extent.

Both sides dug in for the winter, making the best arrangements possible for defence. During the early winter, Soviet supplies of men and equipment strengthened the North Caucasus and Trans-Caucasus fronts.

Determined offensive

The Soviet winter offensive developed in Moscow, largely at Stalin's behest, was devised to trap Army Group A, and this needed cooperation between the Southern Front and Trans-Caucasus Front. Trans-Caucasus forces attacked along an axis from Tuapse to Krasnodar; unfortunately they made slow progress in freezing weather. Meanwhile, the 1st Panzer Army managed a fighting withdrawal. Soviet forces on the Southern Front, under General Andrei Yeremenko, failed to close the bottleneck. The German panzers escaped to rejoin General Erich von Manstein and the recently formed Army Group Don. The German 17th Army, with the Romanians, was left holding the Taman Peninsula.

For most of the summer attention focused on Rostov-on-Don and northwards; the Caucasus Front remained quiet. All this changed on 9 September, when a Soviet seaborne assault was launched on Novorossiisk, directly into the harbour area. Pressure from 58th, 9th, 56th and 18th armies, plus further landings along the coast, cleared the peninsula of German forces by 9 October. Liberation of the Caucasus ended Hitler's dream of capturing and exploiting the region's valuable oilfields.

NORTH CAUCASUS
January–April 1943

- German retreats
- Soviet advances
- German position at the beginning of January
- Soviet front lines 16 January
- Soviet front lines 24 January
- German front lines 4 February
- Soviet front lines 4 April
- Oilfields
- XXXXX Army group
- XXXX Army
- Armoured

STALINGRAD: 1942–43

HEINKEL HE 111
German bomber units flew operations against Soviet forces attempting to resupply Soviet enclaves on the west bank of the Volga. Later, as the fortunes of battle turned against the Germans, these same aircraft would be used in attempts to resupply the surrounded German Sixth Army.

In the autumn of 1942, Hitler ordered his armies in the east to concentrate on capture of the Caucasus oilfields, ensuring supply of the German war machine, while strangling that of Stalin. This thrust southwards meant that the majority of the Luftwaffe's strength was moved to Army Group South's front, and the rest of the Eastern Front ground to a halt and took up holding positions. But Hitler could not resist taking the city of Stalingrad on the river Volga, not only for strategic reasons, but also because of the propaganda coup that capturing his foe's namesake city would provide. This proved a grievous error in judgement.

Stalingrad at all costs

Hitler divided Army Group South into two units. Army Group A was to continue striking south; Army Group B, made up of the 6th Army under General Friedrich Paulus and supported by 4th Panzer Army, would capture Stalingrad. This would secure the left flank of the German advance and deny the Soviets the major transport route between the Caspian Sea and the north. The fact that capture of this city would entail heavy street fighting and close-quarter battles, making panzers virtually redundant, meant nothing to Hitler. He was confident of victory, believing the Soviets to be all but beaten.

In the last week of August, as Army Group B approached Stalingrad, General Wolfram von Richthofen's Luftflotte IV bombed the city relentlessly. It was hoped that the bombing would break the will of the defenders and the civilian population, who had been ordered not to evacuate by Stalin. The Luftwaffe's Stukas concentrated on shipping crossing the wide river Volga, bringing in supplies to the beleaguered defenders and evacuating the wounded. During the course of one week, 32 ships were sunk, and crossing the river under the constant barrage was a harrowing and dangerous experience. The city itself was reduced to rubble, and a vast firestorm was created in the streets, killing thousands of civilians in the process.

The Soviet air force attempted to put up fighters to counter the onslaught, but were shot down in droves, the result of a combination of inexperience and the Luftwaffe's professionalism. The Luftwaffe had complete control of the skies above Stalingrad and continued the constant annihilation of the great city on the Volga.

All the while, Soviet forces were building up a strategic reserve. As German forces entered the city, the Soviets prepared to unleash the true might of their manufacturing capacity. With the Russians holding on to a tiny strip on the west bank of the Volga, the German offensive began to lose steam. Luftwaffe strength was running at 60 per cent – more because of wear and tear, and landing accidents in the increasingly bad weather, than enemy action. This was further reduced with the Allied invasion of North Africa in Operation Torch, which stripped aircraft of all types from Luftflotte IV.

On the dawn of November 19, a massive Soviet counteroffensive, Operation Uranus, was launched. The brainchild of General Georgi Zhukov, leader of the successful defence of Moscow the previous winter, the plan was to break the German flanks to the north and south of Stalingrad, then sweep around and encircle the city, trapping Paulus's 6th Army within. These flanks, held by Romanian divisions, collapsed under the weight of the Soviet attack.

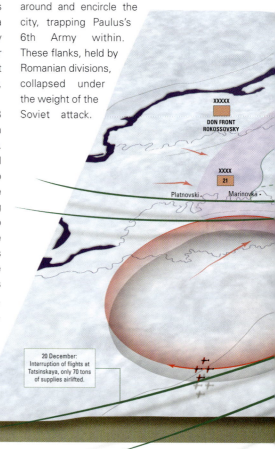

138

Stalingrad: 1942–43

The 22nd Panzer Division, held in reserve, was overwhelmed and began to fall back. The 6th Army's only chance for survival was a rapid withdrawal west before the claws of the pincer closed.

Denial in the face of certain defeat

Hitler, far away at his headquarters in Berchtesgarden, refused Paulus's request to withdraw. Five days after the start of the Soviet offensive, encirclement of Stalingrad was complete. Paulus again sought approval to break out from the pocket; again permission was denied – Göring assured Hitler that 6th Army could be supplied by air. This was a grave untruth. Meeting 6th Army's basic needs required 400–500 tons of supplies a day. The maximum an already depleted Luftflotte IV could deliver was 100 tons. Coupled with deteriorating weather conditions and the ever-constant threat of the Red Air Force, daily tonnage arriving was well under 100 tons.

Nonetheless, the pilots of Junkers Ju 52s and hastily converted Heinkel He 111s shuttled in supplies through a cordon of Soviet fighters and a storm of ground fire. On flights out, the transports brought with them wounded and non-essential personnel, successfully evacuating 42,000 troops from the 'Cauldron', as it was dubbed by those unfortunate enough to be left behind in the freezing rubble.

By the second half of January 1943, the airfields within the Stalingrad perimeter had been overrun, and the air bridge came to an end. In all, 266 Ju 52s had been destroyed in the effort, a third of the entire Luftwaffe fleet on the Eastern Front. A worse fate met the 91,000 German soldiers, as well as their commander, Paulus, who were captured in Stalingrad. They were marched to labour camps deep in the Russian interior, many perishing on the way. Most of the survivors would not return to Germany until the 1950s.

WINTER HELL
The Luftwaffe lost 266 Ju 52 transports in their efforts to resupply the 6th Army in Stalingrad. Total transport aircraft losses amounted to 490 aircraft, the equivalent of five Geschwader. Göring's boast that he could supply Stalingrad by air had proved empty.

STALINGRAD
In their attack on Stalingrad, the Germans relied on Hungarian and Romanian forces to protect their flanks. It was a fatal error, for these allies soon broke under relentless Soviet pressure, leading to the 6th Army's encirclement.

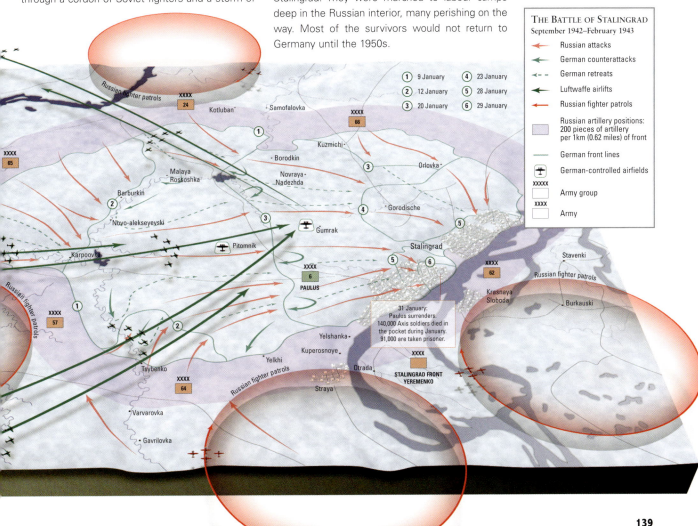

139

AVIATION INDUSTRIES AT WAR

SPITFIRE FIGHTER FUND
The Spitfire Fighter Fund was one of several British government drives to raise money specifically for aircraft production. Many organisations, and indeed towns, provinces and countries, raised funds to buy their 'own' Spitfire, which was then named in their honour.

World War II was won in the factories of the Allied nations. Germany had begun construction of its new air force in 1933–34, while the United Kingdom began rearming in 1935–36. It was the Soviet Union, however, who deployed the largest industrial effort in this period, producing an air force of some 20,000 aircraft by 1939.

Contrasting production capacity

In 1940, Germany, with a front-line force of about 4500 combat aircraft, conquered Norway, Denmark, the Low Countries and France, to some extent adding the industrial capabilities of those nations to its own. Germany had planned for a short war – its reserves to supply frontline units were therefore proportionately low. In the spring of 1940, German aircraft production was overtaken by that of the United Kingdom, which foresaw a long conflict with no apparent end in sight. If a British plan existed at all, it was first to survive, then hopefully to involve the United States as an active ally as soon as possible. This became imperative after the fall of France and the entry of Italy as Germany's ally.

While the United Kingdom could not match Germany's industrial capacity, it had mobilized its available industrial assets towards the war effort much earlier, working shifts around the clock. Even in 1941 Germany was still working only single eight-hour shifts, and had the capacity to expand relatively easily by bringing extra production on stream. The United Kingdom did enjoy one advantage: the friendly stance of the United States. In 1939, Britain and France placed orders with US manufacturers that effectively stimulated its aviation industry, allowing it to lay down new production lines and recruit and train new staff. They would all be needed in the following years.

After the German attack on the Soviet Union in June 1941, German industry began to increase production to meet the demands of this massive new campaign. Even then, German planners continued to assume that the campaign would last less than a year. Soviet aircraft plants, many located in vulnerable western provinces, would be destroyed in the onslaught. This, together with combat losses, would mean that any Soviet air threat would decline, while German industry would carry on producing aircraft largely unaffected, despite British bombing.

Germany, however, did not bargain for the utter commitment of Stalin and his government. Faced with the initial success of the German advance, Stalin ordered a complete transfer of more than a thousand industrial plants eastwards, beyond the reach of the invader. Aircraft plants, along with other wartime industries, were packed onto trains. Designers, draughtsmen, machine tool operators, and skilled workers of all kinds, together with their drawing boards, filing cabinets and millions of pieces of equipment, left towns and cities such as Minsk, Kiev and Kharkov, and were herded towards the foothills of the Ural Mountains and hundreds of other locations. In a miracle of organization, millions toiled – volunteers, forced labour, whatever it took to rebuild industry. On top of this, the Soviet Union found time to improve aircraft models already in production and come up with new designs.

The Soviet air force did not crumble, as German planners expected, but rather grew stronger. The Soviet Union's size, its vast population and the determination of its government pulled the country through its most desperate period from June 1941 to November–December 1942. In 1942, despite relocation, Soviet industry produced 15,735 aircraft; in the same year, Germany produced 11,776.

Rising to the challenge

In May 1940, US President Franklin D. Roosevelt issued an amazing challenge to US industry – to build 50,000 aircraft per year. In 1939 the aviation industry had received orders for fewer than 500 aircraft. As Britain's money ran short, the American policy of 'cash and carry' was eased. Churchill's pleading letters to Roosevelt stated that the United States' aircraft factories could 'lay the foundation of victory'. 'Give us the tools,' he said, 'and we'll finish the job.' Despite misgivings among many senior US adminstrators, Roosevelt came up with what became known as 'Lend-Lease'. The United States would provide loans to the United Kingdom and other Allies to purchase aircraft and other supplies, and undertook to deliver them in American ships. The Lend-Lease Act was passed on 11 March 1941.

In 1941, Britain's production began to reach its maximum capacity, with 23,672 aircraft produced, including an increasing number of four-engined heavy bombers. The majority of these aircraft were deployed in Britain's relentless night bombing of

Germany, a campaign that lasted until the final days of the war.

For the United States, 1942 was the first year of war. Spurred on by Roosevelt, the US automotive industry was mobilized for war production. In April 1941 Henry Ford began construction of a brand-new aircraft plant at Willow Run, not far from Detroit, with 28 hectares (70 acres) under one roof and a moving production line two-thirds of a mile (1km) long. This factory symbolized the US approach to wartime production – mass production. Across the United States, old plants were expanded, vast new ones built, and a huge recruiting and training drive was launched. Workers flocked to the new plants, eager to help their country – and earn a production bonus. In 1942 47,836 aircraft rolled off US assembly lines. Allied production for 1942, including small numbers built in Canada and Australia, was more than 97,000 aircraft; total Axis production was 27,235.

A losing battle

In 1943–44, German aircraft production began to rise. Nazi ideology discouraged women working in wartime industries; their job was tending the home and producing babies. This deficit was countered by deploying foreign workers, made up of a few volunteers but mostly from forced labour. Some of these were prisoners of war and, by 1944, inmates from concentration camps. By the end of 1944, about 400,000 camp inmates worked for Germany's industrial war effort. The Oranienburg camp supplied labour to a major Heinkel plant, and some 60,000 prisoners carved vast tunnels under the Harz Mountains to create production lines for V2 rockets.

Much of the Nazi Party's clumsy administration of Axis industry was reorganized by one remarkable man, Albert Speer. Productivity in arms factories grew under his management; waste and unwarranted complexity were reduced. By 1943, total aircraft produced reached 39,807.

WILLOW RUN PRODUCTION LINE Produced in a number of variants for a host of operational and training tasks, the Consolidated B-24 Liberator was built in larger numbers than any other US warplane of World War II, 18,431 being produced in total, and was delivered in greater quantities than any other bomber in aviation history.

On the other side of the world, Japan's relatively small aviation industry turned out 8861 aircraft during 1942. By 1943 this figure had almost doubled. Japan's problem was access to raw materials, impeded by the US submarine blockade. Despite this, Japan produced 28,180 aircraft in 1944, but was dwarfed by the US industry, which produced 96,318 in the same year.

By 1944 Soviet industry was in full gear, employing its peculiar combination of patriotism, persuasion and brutality. In this critical year, the Allies produced 163,025 aircraft; the Axis 68,760. Although many innovations came out of German industry, such as the Messerschmitt Me 262 jet fighter, and Japan produced the desperate Baka piloted bomb, it was too little, too late.

ANNUAL ALLIED AND AXIS MILITARY AIRCRAFT PRODUCTION 1939–45 (Units)

DATE	USA	USSR	UK	CANADA	EASTERN GROUP	TOTAL	GERMANY	ITALY	HUNGARY	ROMANIA	JAPAN	TOTAL
1939	5,856	10,382	7,940	n/a	n/a	24,178	8,295	1,692	–	n/a	4,467	14,454
1940	12,804	10,565	15,049	n/a	n/a	38,418	10,826	2,142	–	n/a	4,768	17,736
1941	26,277	15,735	20,094	n/a	n/a	62,106	11,776	3,503	–	n/a	5,088	20,367
1942	47,836	25,436	23,672	n/a	n/a	96,944	15,556	2,818	6	n/a	8,861	27,235
1943	85,898	34,845	26,263	n/a	n/a	147,006	25,527	967	267	n/a	16,693	43,454
1944	96,318	40,246	26,461	n/a	n/a	163,025	39,807	–	773	n/a	28,180	68,760
1945	49,761	20,052	12,070	n/a	n/a	81,883	7,544	–	n/a	–	8,263	15,807
TOTAL	324,750	157,261	131,549	16,431	3,081	633,072	189,307	11,122	1,046	c. 1,000	76,320	89,488

GUADALCANAL: 1943

The knowledge that Japan was building an airfield on Guadalcanal, one of the Solomon Islands, made it clear to the United States that capturing the island before the airfield was completed was of great strategic import. If Guadalcanal were not taken, the island and its airfield would afford Japan a base from which to attack convoy routes from the United States to Australia; Allied convoys would have to be diverted even further south to avoid interception.

The Guadalcanal operation would be the US forces' first offensive manoeuvre since the opening of hostilities between Japan and the United States, and heavily exploited the boost to US morale provided by victory at the Battle of Midway.

US landings on Guadalcanal

The US 1st Marine Division landed on Guadalcanal on 7 August 1943; smaller forces made landings on the islands of Florida and Tulagi, with the aim of capturing the seaplane base on the latter. Within two days the US Marines had captured the Lunga airfield on Guadalcanal and renamed it Henderson Field, after Major Lofton Henderson, the first Marine pilot to lose his life during the Battle of Midway.

After a Japanese night action sank four US cruisers that were covering the landing forces, Admiral Fletcher, who was in charge of the invasion force, ordered his carriers to pull out of range because he now lacked sufficient surface escorts to ensure their safety. This left the US Marines onshore with limited supplies and air cover. As they continued to build the half-finished airfield, utilizing bulldozers and equipment left behind by the retreating Japanese forces, they came under constant harassing fire from artillery and land-based Mitsubishi G4M Betty bombers, escorted by Mitsubishi A6M Zero fighters. On 19 August the first aircraft, Grumman F4F Wildcats and Douglas SBD Dauntlesses, landed on Henderson Field – although facilities were very limited. Fuel had to be pumped into aircraft from drums, and bombs slung under aircraft by hand, as there were no winches available on the island.

Japan attempted to retake full control of Guadalcanal by reinforcing the troops still on the island and attempting to puncture the ring around Henderson that was solidly held by the US Marines. Four transports were sent with a covering force made up of the carriers *Zuikaku* and *Shokaku*, three battleships, and cruisers and destroyers. A diversionary force built around the carrier *Ryujo* was also dispatched. Aircraft from USS *Saratoga* engaged and sunk the *Ryujo* on the 24 August, just as Japanese aircraft located and attacked the aircraft carrier USS *Enterprise*. She managed to dodge all torpedoes launched at her, but three bombs found their mark. Although badly damaged, she limped her way to Pearl Harbor for repairs. Land-based bombers flying from Henderson Field and Espiritu Santo in the New Hebrides found the Japanese invasion force and sank one transport, along with a destroyer. Japan decided to halt the operation and fall back.

Back on Henderson Field, the newly named 'Cactus Air Force' was slowly gaining strength, and the naval construction battalions, known as Sea Bees, completed 'Fighter 1' field about a mile from Henderson. F4F Wildcats flew high into the sky to meet oncoming Japanese Bettys flying from Rabaul. The fighters were warned of coming attacks by a series of 'coast watchers' based on the western side of the Solomon chain, who would radio in to base to inform it of any raids. On Henderson itself, a RADAR installation was built, aiding in the interception of Japanese aircraft.

F4F WILDCATS ABOARD USS WASP
Having served in the Atlantic and Mediterranean, USS Wasp *was torpedoed off Guadalcanal on 15 September 1942 and scuttled later that day.*

Guadalcanal: 1943

Attempting recapture

Towards the end of October, Japan sent a large carrier force to cover the Imperial Japanese Army's hopeful capture of Henderson Field. Admiral William Halsey, with the carriers USS *Hornet* and USS *Enterprise*, moved in to engage Admiral Chuichi Nagumo's *Shokaku*, *Zuikaku*, *Zuiho* and *Junyo*. US reconnaissance aircraft spotted *Zuiho* in the vanguard of the group and attacked, seriously damaging her with several bombs. Both sides then launched major attacks on the other. Japan concentrated its dive- and torpedo-bombers on the *Hornet*, scoring hits with both weapons; she later sank. The American riposte was to land three bombs on the *Shokaku*. A second Japanese raid then attacked the *Enterprise*; she was struck with several bombs, but managed to avoid all torpedoes and survived. Many of the Japanese planes were lost to effective US anti-aircraft fire. Both sides withdrew, bloodied and bruised.

The US Navy was now down to one carrier in the area, but Japan never again attacked in strength. The Cactus Air Force steadily grew and aided in the clearing Japanese forces from the island. By February 1943 Japan evacuated what remained of its troops from Guadalcanal, and the long campaign to push back Imperial Japanese aggression truly began.

MARINES ON GUADALCANAL
The successful defence of the vital airstrip at Henderson Field on Guadalcanal allowed US forces to maintain air superiority over the island.

OPERATION CARTWHEEL

The vast area of Southeast Asia and the Pacific controlled by the Japanese contained many of the natural resources deemed necessary for a prosperous future, but now it had to be defended. Two defeats dented Japanese confidence: Midway and Guadalcanal. Realizing the threat to their defensive perimeter, Japanese commanders began strengthening their base at Rabaul on New Britain and along the perimeter's southeastern sector, hoping to stall a forthcoming Allied offensive.

The Allied offensive plan, Operation Cartwheel, called for a two-pronged attack. Admiral William Halsey's US Third Fleet would sail northwards through the Solomon Islands, around the north of New Island. General Walter Krueger's US Sixth Army, with Australian forces, was to advance northwards through New Guinea, landing on New Britain and headed for Rabaul, to neutralize its major Japanese base. All of these forces now fell under the command of US Army General Douglas MacArthur.

Beginning the offensive

First moves began on 9 January 1943, when an entire brigade of Australian troops was airlifted to Wau, threatening Japanese coastal positions in New Guinea. As the campaign unfolded, air support was provided by both carrier-borne aircraft and the capably led US Fifth Air Force under Major General George C. Kenny. Its land-based aircraft became vital to the campaign, gaining air superiority over the battlefield and isolating Japanese units, denying them resupply and air support.

Pre-war policy dictated bombing the enemy from high altitude, out of reach of most anti-aircraft fire, but Kenny retrained his command to attack from low levels. This involved great risk, but meant far higher accuracy and increased enemy losses. Field modifications were carried out on North American B-25 Mitchell medium bombers; eight machine guns were fitted into the aircraft's nose, adding to its existing bombload. Even the larger Boeing B-17 Flying Fortress was ordered to bomb from lower altitudes.

These innovations proved decisive in the Battle of the Bismarck Sea. Here, the Japanese combined forces were involved in a major operation, moving their 51st Division from Rabaul to reinforce positions in New Guinea. Eight large transport ships escorted by eight destroyers moved cautiously along New Britain's coastline and out into the Solomon Sea, covered by up to 100 Japanese aircraft. The Allies, via MAGIC intelligence intercepts, were well aware of the operation. B-17s bombed the convoy, sinking two transports. As it passed through Dampier Straits, it was attacked by nearly 100 Allied aircraft. In the ensuing battles, the remaining transports and four destroyers were sunk. Japan's 51st Division lost almost all its staff and nearly 4000 soldiers.

Alarmed by Allied air power's growing efficiency, Admiral Isoroku Yamamoto ordered a counterstrike. A scratch force of 300 aircraft was raised from land and carrier-based units in the area, attacking Allied airfields in New Guinea and the Solomons in a huge

OPERATION CARTWHEEL
In their pursuit of conquest in the Pacific, the Japanese over-extended their area of operations, creating enormous supply problems. They were unable to prevent Allied landings in New Guinea, which secured Australia from the threat of Japanese invasion.

Operation Cartwheel

simultaneous strike. Substantial damage was inflicted, but at the expense of experienced pilots and crews. Newer aircraft then began arriving for the Allies – Lockheed P-38 Lightnings and Grumman F6F Hellcats. Air superiority over Japan continued.

On 18 April 1943, 16 long-range P-38 Lightnings of 339th Fighter Squadron were dispatched from Henderson Field to shoot down the Mitsubishi G4M Betty bomber carrying Yamamoto. Thanks to naval code intercepts, and Yamamoto being such a stickler for punctuality, the Americans knew exactly where his aircraft would be at any given time.

MITSIBISHI A6M5 ZERO
The A6M5 was a later variant of the Zero fighter. It was rushed into service in the autumn of 1943 to counter the US Navy's Grumman F6F Hellcat. The A6M5 had a modified wing featuring heavier-gauge skin.

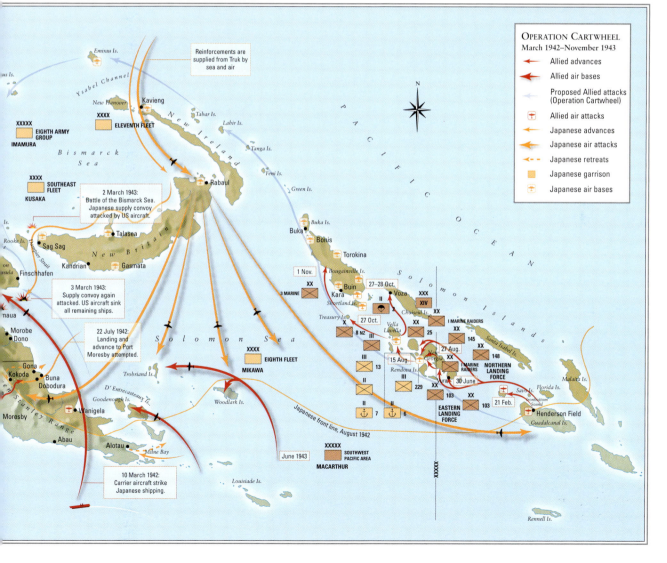

Bombing Germany: 1942–44

BOMBING GERMANY: 1942–44

AIR MARSHALL
SIR ARTHUR HARRIS
Air Marshal Sir Arthur Harris became commander in chief of RAF Bomber Command in February 1942. He reevaluated Bomber Command tactics and training, instigating new policies that led to the controversial area bombing of German cities.

SHORT STIRLING
The Stirling Mk I, the first of the RAF's four-engine heavy bombers, flew its first operational sortie on 10/11 February 1941. Stirlings flew their last bombing mission in September 1944, having equipped 15 squadrons of RAF Bomber Command. By this time the aircraft had found a new role as a transport and glider tug.

At the beginning of 1942, the campaign to bomb Germany into submission moved up a gear. Most squadrons of RAF Bomber Command were equipped with the Vickers Wellington at this time, and night operations had been flown since December 1939, when Bomber Command suffered heavy losses in daylight attacks on the northern German ports. But new and better aircraft were on the horizon, and RAF Bomber Command would also get a new commander, Air Chief Marshal Sir Arthur Harris. A true believer in the power of strategic area bombing, Harris pushed his men to breaking point to prove the theory drawn up in the inter-war years.

In 1942, USAAF Boeing B-17s Flying Fortresses and Consolidated B-24 Liberators and their crews were also beginning to arrive, bristling with up to 13 0.5-calibre machine guns. Time would be needed to bring these forces up to strength and experience. They would become the US Eighth Air Force, and 1942 to early 1943 saw them flying missions over occupied France and the Low Countries.

Improved technology and training
From 1942, better training, navigational aids and, most importantly, aircraft and crews started to appear on the aerodromes of East Anglia, Lincolnshire and Yorkshire, from where Bomber Command's sorties would be launched. Replacing the ageing Armstrong Whitworth Whitleys and Vickers Wellingtons were the big, four-engined bombers – the Short Stirling, Avro Lancaster and Handley Page Halifax. The Stirling's performance was disappointing, though, with its poor top speed and low ceiling height proving major disadvantages on what were to be long flights into the heart of the Reich.

Harris opened his campaign of night-time area bombing on Lubeck, during the night of 28/29 March

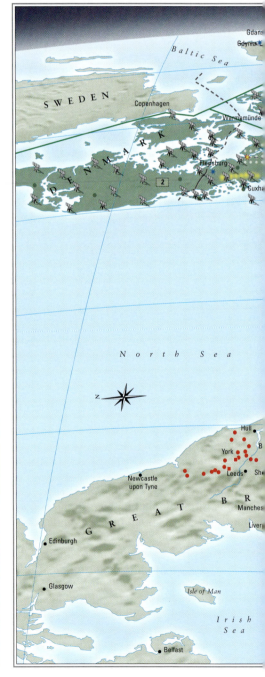

Bombing Germany: 1942–44

1942, followed by a raid on Rostock a month later. These attacks utilized about 250 bombers, flying in a 'stream' to overwhelm German radar defences. Large as they were, they would be just footnotes to Harris's first '1000' bomber raid, sent to Cologne on the night of 30/31 May in Operation Millennium. It was thought that the tonnage dropped on the city would not only destroy factories, but also displace or kill workers, crushing civilian morale. It would also be an extremely useful propaganda coup.

Harris acquired extra aircraft from training and conversion units, eventually making up some 1047 aircraft and crews for the mission; about 870 actually found and bombed their targets for the loss of 43 aircraft and crews. Very few military buildings or factories were hit, and the majority of damage was inflicted on civilian dwellings – although, thanks to the German fire service and, crucially, the width of Cologne's streets, no major conflagration erupted as a result of the bombing.

STRATEGIC BOMBING
1943

- Main Headquarters
- Group Headquarters
- Bomber Command airfields
- US 8th Air force airfields
- RAF-bombed target
- USAAF-bombed target
- RAF and USAAF target
- Fighter Division boundary
- Fighter Division
- German radar stations
- German night fighter stations
- Searchlight batteries
- Anti-aircraft batteries

Bombing Germany: 1942–44

AVRO LANCASTER
The Avro Lancaster entered service in early 1942 and soon proved to be the most effective of Britain's heavy bombers. 7,377 were built and flew 156,000 sorties, dropping 608,610 tons of bombs. 3,249 were lost in action.

DAMBUSTERS RAID
This map shows the routes, destinations and fate of the 19 aircraft that took part in the raid of 16-17 May 1943.

Two other raids of this magnitude were flown in June, to Essen on the night of 1/2 and Bremen on 25/26. Harris would then introduce the Pathfinder force, hand-picking the best crews from Bomber Command, usually ones that had survived 20 or more sorties, and using Oboe and H2S navigational aids. (Oboe, introduced in December 1941, was an aerial bombing targeting system that transmitted signals from two stations in the United Kingdom to de Havilland Mosquito bombers fitted with radio transponders; H2S, introduced in 1943 and in use until the 1990s, was a radar system that identified targets on the ground for night and all-weather bombing.) The Pathfinders would fly ahead of the main force, dropping flares as navigational aids, then dropping more to illuminate the target. 'Markers' would then drop incendiaries to set alight the target area for the main force to sight on.

Battle of the Ruhr and beyond

On the night of 5/6 March, 'Bomber' Harris launched one of his massive set-piece offensives – the Battle of the Ruhr. Largely industrial and well within range of Oboe's target designator radio beams, the Ruhr provided a host of targets. All were hit with great accuracy, even through the thick factory haze that coated the valley. Not all missions in the period between March and July were flown to the Ruhr. A fifth of missions were flown as far afield as Stettin on the Baltic coast and, of course, Berlin. This tactic meant that Germany could never place all its night-fighter force to cover an area in great numbers.

During this time, a squadron was created to hit pinpoint targets, the exact opposite of the Bomber Command dictum of area bombing. This squadron was commanded by Wing Commander Guy Gibson, an experienced bomber pilot, and was designated No. 617 Squadron, later to be famously nicknamed the 'Dam Busters'. Having trained in low-level flying for six weeks, 19 crews set out for the dams that supplied power and water to the Ruhr's industrial district. Armed with the Barnes Wallis-designed 'bouncing bomb', they were to make an extremely low approach and skip the bomb along the water's surface, avoiding the anti-torpedo nets. The bomb would then strike the dam, sink and explode at a fixed depth, hopefully breaching the dam. Before No. 617 Squadron arrived at its targets, one aircraft lost its bomb when flying so close to the sea that it was torn off; a further five were lost to flak and from flying into high-tension power lines.

Gibson attacked the Möhne dam with four of the aircraft, breaching it. Three other aircraft breached the Eder; the Sorpe and Schwelme dams were attacked with no results. The operation resulted in a high loss of life, particularly below the Möhne dam, but had a tangible effect on industrial production in the area. Many of the men flying the mission were highly decorated for gallantry, and Gibson received the Victoria Cross. He would later be killed in action in September 1944, flying his third tour.

From May 1942, the US Eighth Air Force began flying missions of relatively short range, flown in daylight with Supermarine Spitfire escorts. US airmen were confident that flying in mutually defending formations was enough to deter attacks. Spurred

Bombing Germany: 1942–44

on by relatively few losses, the Eighth Air Force flew further afield without escort, where it encountered Germany's solution to mass formations: head-on attacks aimed at the pilot and copilot's positions. The Americans added more guns in the nose and, in later Liberator and Fortress models, fitted specific turrets for the job. By January 1943, the Eighth was ready for an attack on Germany itself. The U-boat pens at Wilhelmshaven were chosen as the target. Only three aircraft were lost, but results were poor, even with the still top-secret Norden bomb sight.

Operation Pointblank

By June, Operation Pointblank, part of the Combined Bomber Offensive, was introduced. It focused on Germany's aviation production industry, targeting airframe factories, rubber plants and ball-bearing production. Raids were made on Kiel, Hamburg and Warmunde, all relatively successful and with few losses. The German forces needed time to adapt to new defensive tactics in daylight, but would soon be tearing the heart out of the mighty Eighth.

Regensburg, Bavaria, was a key manufacturing centre for the Luftwaffe's Messerschmitt Me 109, and Schweinfurt was thought to be where most of Germany's ball bearings were produced. A double-pronged raid was planned. One group would strike Regensburg, then fly on to North Africa. Another would hit Schweinfurt, hopefully splitting German defences. All did not go to plan. Cloud delayed the Schweinfurt group's departure, but the Regensburg force flew on to its target regardless. By the time it arrived at the Dutch coast, it was being continually attacked, until the German aircraft were forced to land to refuel and rearm. The group arrived over its target with little cloud cover and successfully hit all six Messerschmitt plants, putting some out of action for six months. It then flew south over the Alps, but some aircraft were forced to land in Switzerland, Italy and the Mediterranean Sea on the way to landing sites in Tunisia. Twenty-four bombers were lost in the raid; many more were left in Tunisia because of damage.

By the time the Regensburg force was flying south, the Schweinfurt force was crossing the Dutch border. By now, the entire Luftwaffe was prepared for an incoming raid. A total of 230 bombers from the Eighth Air Force headed for Schweinfurt, three hours behind the Regensburg force and escorted by relays of RAF Spitfires and Eighth Air Force Republic P-47s. This cover could fly only as far as Eupen, near the Belgo-German border; from here the bombers were on their own. They also had to fly lower than planned because of cloud, making them

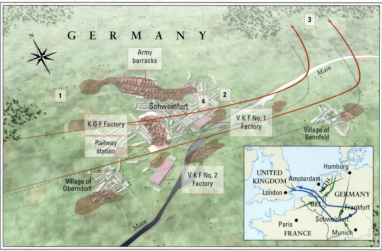

even more susceptible to fighter attacks. These soon came, with head-on strafing runs and rocket-firing Messerschmitt Me 110 and 410s. Casualties mounted but, just as the bombers turned onto their run-in on the target, the German fighters disengaged.

Accuracy was not great as the formations dropped their bombs, and smoke from the first loads impeded aim. After the bombers had flown over the target and through thick flak, the German fighters returned, this time concentrating on the rear of the formation. Allied fighter cover returned over the Netherlands, accounting for some German fighters, but the damage had been done. Sixty aircraft and crews had been shot down; a further 87 airframes were damaged beyond repair. The Eighth Air Force would not return to the Reich for months, illustrating the importance of an escort that could fly with the bombers all the way to the target and back. A second raid was flown to Schweinfurt on 14 October with 291 B-17s, but German defences had increased and losses were just as heavy. Raids to the Reich were suspended until February 1944, when long-range North American P-51 Mustangs were in large enough numbers to act as escorts.

BOMBING OF SCHWEINFURT
17 August 1943

- Bombed areas
- Ball-bearing factories
- Planned flight paths
- Bombers' route
- Major German interceptions

1. 198 bombers begin to arrive over the target area at 3.53 pm local time
2. By 4.11 pm, 265 tons of high explosive and 115 tons of incendiaries have been dropped
3. 36 aircraft are lost with 361 casualties
4. In the twelve-minute raid, most bombs fall wide of their target, killing approximately 275 people

B-17 FLYING FORTRESS
Boeing B-17G Flying Fortresses of the 532nd Bomb Squadron, 381st Bomb Group, Eighth Army Air Force. The 381st BG was based at Ridgewell, Essex, from June 1943 to June 1945.

149

TARGET BERLIN: 1944

BOMBER TACTICS
As the daylight bombing offensive progressed, the Americans modified their defensive tactics to counter increasingly ferocious enemy fighter attacks. In March 1943, three groups of 18 bombers were brought together to form a compact 54-aircraft combat wing, providing massive defensive firepower.

After the successes of the Ruhr and Hamburg, the RAF's Air Chief Marshal Sir Arthur Harris would launch his command at the primary target of Berlin, the 'Big City', as he called it. Harris thought that, if the city was totally destroyed, the German people's will to continue fighting would falter. Berlin lay on the eastern side of Germany, however, and would require Allied bomber crews to fly over enemy territory for a much longer period of time, exposed to even more more flak and night fighters. It was also out of range of the radio transponder technology of the targeting system Oboe. Add to this the fact that Berlin was probably the most heavily defended city in the world, and the prospect of flying there at night, with a full bombload, was a daunting one.

Offensive measures and countermeasures

By this time the radar countermeasure Window had been introduced in Britain. Window, or chaff, consisted of a mass of foil strips thrown from a bomber at regular intervals, as they flew in their streams; the falling strips were meant to confuse or overwhelm the German radar defences. Window worked well, but the Germans simply altered tactics. Rather than having a single night fighter directed onto a single target, fighters went up together and 'freelanced' once directed into the stream. 'Wilde Sau' (Wild Boar) missions also began. Utilizing the searchlights, single-engined fighters without radar would dive down from above on the silhouetted bombers below, often flying through their own heavy flak. To counter these new measures, Britain sent out Short Stirling bombers, pulled out from missions into Germany because of their poor ceiling and speed, on mining missions into the North Sea. It was hoped that this would draw the German defenders to an easy prey, but it rarely worked.

Before a raid, German forces could quite often estimate accurately how many aircraft would be sent against them on any given night by monitoring the RAF's radios as they were tested during the day before a raid. On the night 26/27 November, 443 bombers and seven Pathfinder Mosquitoes took off to bomb Berlin. To supplement this force, 157 Handley Page Halifaxes and 21 Avro Lancasters were ordered to bomb Stuttgart on a diversionary mission, hoping to at least split Germany's night fighters. To confuse the Germans further, a route was chosen that would take the stream as a whole south into France, before turning due east for Frankfurt, where the force would split for their individual targets. Having mostly evaded the night fighters, the main force arrived over Berlin, where the target was precisely marked on a rare clear night. Flak took its toll on the aircraft and crews, and in the melee Berlin's zoo was bombed. As the bombers made their way back to England, the night fighters pounced, shooting many down. Out of a total of 666 sorties flown that night, there were 34 losses – a rate of about 5 per cent.

Nuremberg disaster

This pattern continued for the entire winter of 1943–44, culminating in the worst night for the RAF on 30/31 March; the target was Nuremberg. Under a full moon, 795 aircraft set out in strong winds. German defences were waiting, shooting down 82 bombers before they even reached the target. Respite came only when the night fighters had to land to refuel and rearm, and a further 13 RAF aircraft were shot down on the outward leg. Many

B-17s FLYING IN STANDARD 'COMBAT BOX' FORMATION

Target Berlin: 1944

bombed Schweinfurt in the confusion, as the high winds ruined navigation. More than 10 per cent of the raiders were lost, the worst loss suffered by RAF Bomber Command in the entire war.

The hunter becomes the hunted

For the bomber crews, the chances of surviving the required 30 raids were minimal. The 100 (Bomber Support) Group was activated to improve prospects. It would fly missions in adapted bombers jammed with electronic equipment in an attempt to block radio signals between German ground controllers and the night fighters. The group also contained units of intruder and Serrate Mosquitoes and Beaufighters (Serrate was a radar detection and homing device used to track German night fighters equipped with Lichtenstein). On the night of a raid, the intruders orbited the night fighters' airfields, hoping to pounce as the aircraft took off or landed, when they were most vulnerable. The Serrate aircraft homed in on the radar on the German night fighters and exacted a similar punishment.

The USAAF also began missions to Berlin in the spring of 1944, with the arrival of long-range North American P-51 Mustang fighters, which could fly all the way to Berlin with the bombers. It was hoped to lure the Luftwaffe into fighting above Germany and wear it down as the bombers went on to their targets. By now, it struggled to replace lost aircraft, and numbers of trained pilots were ever diminishing. Its fighter defence basically died in that spring, and Allied aircraft could fly with ease above the Reich.

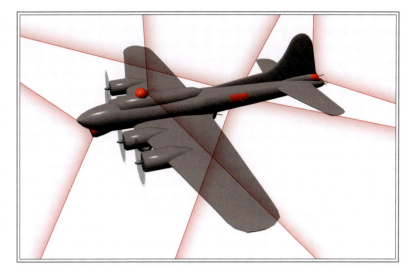

FORTRESS FIELD OF FIRE
The Flying Fortress had an excellent defensive field of fire, covering all aspects. Earlier B-17s had no chin turret, but one was quickly installed in the B-17G model to counter head-on attacks by enemy fighters, and retrofitted to most B-17Fs.

B-17 Flying Fortress
Crew: 10
Top Speed: 461kph (287mph)
Cruise Speed: 292kph (182mph)
Armament: Up to 13 x 0.5in machine guns
Bombload: 5805kg (12,800lb)

RAID CRASH LOCATIONS
This graphic charts the initial reports of crash locations given by RAF bomber crews bombing Berlin on the night of 24–25 March 1944. In actual fact losses were far worse, with 72 aircraft eventually being reported missing.

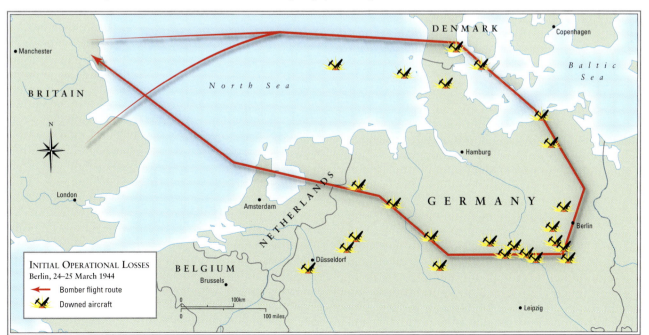

NORTH AFRICA AND THE MEDITERRANEAN

During June 1940, Italy's Regia Aeronautica was flying bombing raids over Malta. The only aircraft in place to defend the island were six antiquated Gloster Sea Gladiators, radial engined biplanes, outclassed by most aircraft in the theatre; these were quickly uncrated and flown into action, and managed to do just enough to hold off the Italian bombers before the arrival of 12 Hawker Hurricanes, rushed to Malta on board the carrier HMS *Argus*.

In North Africa, Marshal Rodolfo Graziani advanced into Egypt from Cyrenaica in Italian Libya, under orders from Mussolini, on 13 September. Graziani's overwhelming ground and air superiority could do little as the British forces launched a counterattack to drive them back out, pushing them all the way back to Tripoli in an audacious advance by British Army General Sir Richard Nugent O'Connor. Not being able to sail safely through the Mediterranean meant that aircraft had to be crated up and sent around the Cape of Good Hope, until the Tokaradi air route was opened. This entailed that aircraft be delivered to Africa's Gold Coast and flown across the breadth of the continent, where they would eventually arrive in Egypt, to be then flown on to a forward unit wherever required.

The tide turns in North Africa

Following Italy's disastrous attempts to capture the Canal Zone, 1941 saw Hitler send General Erwin Rommel and his Afrika Korps to take the initiative, to be supported by the Luftwaffe's Fliegerkorps X. The Allied Desert Air Force, having previously held

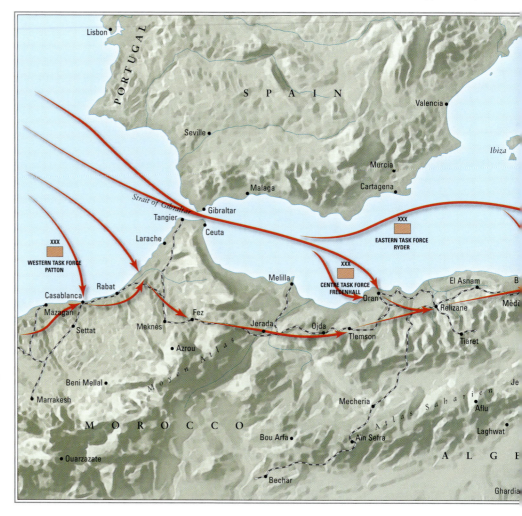

ALLIED ADVANCES
The Allied landings in North Africa, and the elimination of Axis forces in Tunisia in May 1943, provided an effective springboard for the invasion of Sicily only two months later. Italy quickly asked for an armistice, but bitter fighting was to continue in the theatre as powerful German reinforcements contested the Allied advance up the Italian peninsula.

North Africa and the Mediterranean

its own against a numerically superior force, now met experienced pilots flying modern aircraft above the vast desert of sand.

Malta also felt the pressure of the Luftwaffe's arrival. As raids on the beleaguered island intensified, more reinforcements were rushed in. Hurricanes were once again flown to the island and, although these managed to score victories, RAF casualties were heavy, and the aircraft were not able to fly a constant standing patrol because of the lack of fuel getting through to Malta. With RAF sorties falling in number, Fliegerkorps X concentrated its strength on the North Africa campaign and supporting Rommel's advance. In Malta, this allowed for the flying in of 15 Supermarine Spitfire Mk Vs to boost the defence. These were followed by over a hundred more, mostly flying off the USS *Wasp* on 9 May.

With Rommel's supply line under constant threat from the torpedo-bombers now based on Malta, the Afrika Korps advance ground to a halt. Following General Bernard Montgomery's victories at Al Halfa and El Alamein, it began its long retreat to Tunisia. Ground-to-air communication had been skillfully honed in the Allied pursuit, and ground forces could now call on the services of fighter-bombers almost whenever required, usually Hurricanes or Curtiss P-40s. This system would be successfully used much later in Normandy.

In November 1942, in Operation Torch, the Allies made landings in Morocco and Vichy-controlled Algeria. Paratroops were used to capture airfields in eastern Algeria. With these secure, RAF and USAAF bombers began to stream in, and air superiority was soon claimed. The Germans retreated into Tunisia, where supplies were flown in using the ubiquitous Junkers Ju 52 and the enormous six-engined Messerschmitt Me 323 transport plane. As these aircraft lumbered over the Sicilian Straits, they were easy pickings for Allied fighters constantly roaming the battle zone. The situation in Tunisia soon became untenable for the Axis powers – Italy and Germany's Afrika Korps surrendered on 12 May 1943.

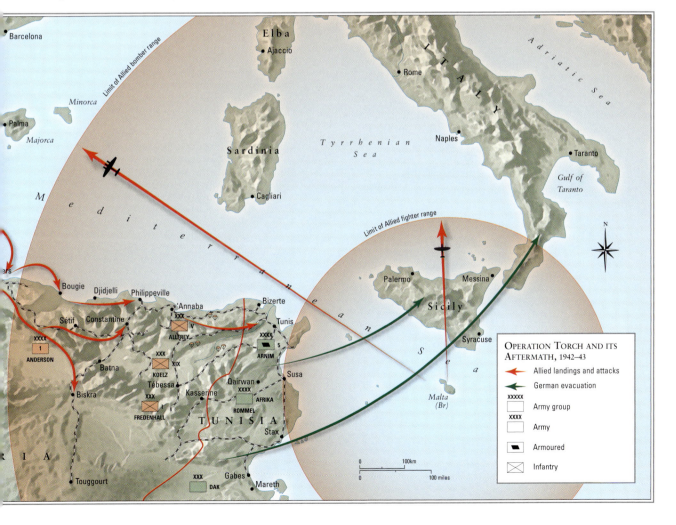

SICILY AND SOUTHERN ITALY

SICILY AND SOUTHERN ITALY
The Allied landings on Sicily, quickly followed by the invasion of southern Italy, were designed to strike a lethal blow at what was called the 'soft under-belly of Europe'. Instead, the campaign turned into a bitter slogging match, the problems compounded by terrible weather in the winter of 1943–44.

Planning for the Allied invasion of Sicily, known as Operation Husky, was hurried and confused. Each branch of the services pushed different plans for its differing requirements. Air Marshal Sir Arthur Tedder, in charge of the combined RAF and USAAF Mediterranean Air Force, was particularly keen that the airfields on the island be captured immediately, so that they would be available as soon as possible to host his fighters and bombers involved in the invasion. Compromise was reached, thanks to a confident Field Marshal Bernard Montgomery forcing his plan on the other commanders, doing nothing for interservice or international relations. The British and Canadians were to land on Sicily's eastern coast, near the port of Syracuse, utilizing airborne troops to capture airfields and strategic bridges required in securing the beachhead. The American contingent would land on the southwest coast between Licata and Scoglitti, again using airborne troops to capture the airfields situated behind the landing sites. The air commanders kept information very guarded in the planning stages, and did not liaise closely with the naval and ground commanders, wanting to remain independent of army and navy. This grew into further animosity between the three services, but more alarmingly meant that the naval and ground commanders had no idea of the number, type and timings of any of the Allied aircraft that would be flying above the beachhead – a lack of information that would lead to grave consequences.

Operation Husky begins

On the night of 9/10 July, Allied paratroops were dropped behind the beachhead from an assortment of aircraft, but mostly the Douglas C-47 Skytrain of the US Transport Command. The paratroops were scattered in the high winds, and worse befell the troops arriving by glider. Many of the glider pilots were inexperienced, and cast off early in poor weather; a large number of gliders crashed prematurely into the sea, drowning their occupants. Still, despite the fact that the troops landed on Sicily so far were so scattered, they succeeded in producing enough confusion and panic among the defenders that, when the seaborne element arrived, it met relatively little resistance.

The RAF and the USAAF under the steady hand of Tedder had reduced enemy aviation on the island to relatively few aircraft. These were soon forced to retire to the Italian mainland, where they were continually harassed by the medium and heavy bombers of US Fifteenth Air Force. Allied ground and naval commanders were pleasantly surprised by the lack of enemy air attacks. The only real resistance came in the shape of night bombers taking their chances on the invasion fleet. When these aircraft did appear, usually Heinkel He 111s or Junkers Ju 88s, they met a truly astonishing amount of flak put up by the fleet. Unfortunately when the 504th Parachute Infantry Regiment of the 82nd Airborne Division was flown in to reinforce the beachhead, they were fired upon by the fleet, who assumed them to be German raiders. In one of the worst 'friendly fire' incidents of the war, out of 144 C-47s, 33 were shot down and a further 37 were damaged, with a total of 318 casualties resulting. It was a prime example of the lack of communication between the commanders of all the services, a failing that would be promptly rectified to ensure that it never happened again.

Within a week, the Allied Air Force had fighters stationed on the island. The Luftwaffe and Regia Aeronautica were harried by day and stalked when they ventured out at night by radar-equipped de Havilland Mosquitoes based on Malta. These aircraft had already proved very successful over Britain in locating and destroying night bombers.

As the Allies worked their way northwards, the Axis doggedly held on to defensive lines as they were eventually pushed into Sicily's northeastern corner. The only route for escape was the Straits of Messina, from the port at Messina across to the toe of Italy. Allied air supremacy should have made this action impossible for Axis forces to execute. But somehow, under the noses of the combined air forces, 40,000 German and 60,000 Italian troops were evacuated by ferry, unmolested by air attack. This only strengthened the ground commanders misgivings towards the 'junior' service.

Taking the mainland

The first Allied landings on mainland Italy took place on 3 September, when the British Eighth Army crossed the Straits of Messina. The Allied medium and heavy bomber forces were ordered to make strong interdiction raids, to cripple German supply lines in central and northern Italy, and prevent any reinforcement. German forces had prepared a defensive line further north, however, and the Eighth Army faced light opposition. By the time of the Anglo-American landings at Salerno on 9 September, the Italians had overthrown Mussolini and surrendered to the Allies. Many pilots of the Regia Aeronautica immediately offered to fly for the Allies, with a few choosing to remain fighting for the Fascists. This significantly sapped Axis air strength in the region, and Germany was forced to transfer aircraft much needed on other fronts to bolster the defence.

The landings at Salerno were heavily contended, with the Luftwaffe employing Focke-Wulf Fw 190s in the role of fighter bombers to scream in over the landing beaches and terrorize the troops below. Germany also employed a new weapon for the first time: the Fritz X glide bomb. Dropped from its parent aircraft, usually a Dornier Do 217, this bomb ignited a flare behind the tail so it could then be easily guided via remote control from the bomb aimer in the nose of the Dornier. Its effectiveness was proved when a direct hit on HMS *Warspite* off Salerno resulted in the battleship being withdrawn for repair for six months.

The landings at Salerno were touch and go, as constant and vicious German counterattacks tried to split the landing forces in two. These were in turn countered by the dropping of two regiments of the 82nd Airborne Division over two nights. Together with the concerted efforts of the air forces strafing German columns, naval gunfire and the tenacity of soldiers on the ground, disaster was averted.

The Allied advance continued unabated after the breakout from the beachhead, until the Allies met the prepared defensive line between Naples and Rome. A particularly difficult region to navigate was the valleys around Monte Cassino, where a monastery on the mount dominated its surrounds. It was thought to be used by Germany as a spotting area for its artillery and, after failed attempts to take it, the monastery was heavily bombed by the Allies and reduced to rubble, despite it being inhabited only by monks and refugees at the time. The defending Fallschirmjager were more than happy to move into the easily defensible ruins after the raid, and held the position for even longer than intended.

A secondary landing was made at Anzio the following January with the hope of cutting German lines of communication. Instead, Germany managed to contain the beachhead, even in the face of Allied air supremacy. It was not until late May that the breakthrough in the south at Monte Cassino was made, followed by the breakout of the beachhead following a massive aerial bombardment. Rome was in Allied hands by 5 June, but German forces merely fell back on yet another prepared defensive line. The struggle for the peninsula continued while the eyes of the world turned to northwest Europe.

BRISTOL BEAUFIGHTER
The Beaufighter saw extensive service in North Africa and Italy and equipped four night-fighter squadrons of the USAAF in the same theatre.

EASTERN FRONT: 1943 Soviet Initiative

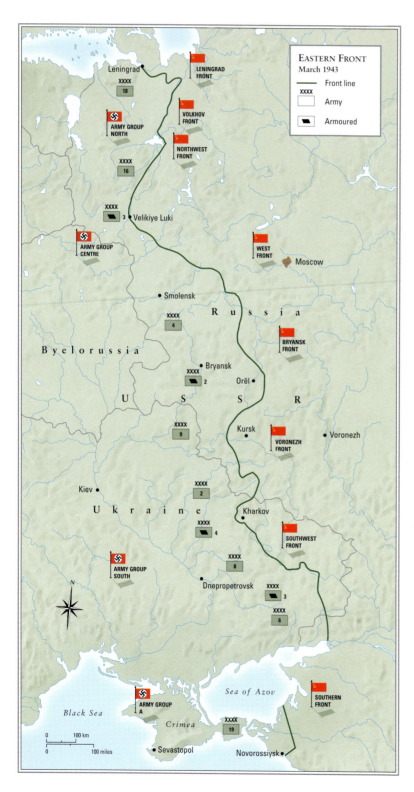

After the German defeat at Kursk, the Soviet counteroffensives began as a series of rolling attacks which took in the whole of the Eastern Front, except the far north. Stalin's ruthless policy was designed to allow the Germans no respite, no chance to reorganise and form a coherent defence. His first objective was the liberation of eastern Ukraine, most of the army groups (fronts) from Army Group Voronezh southwards would be involved. This massive drive was also focused on the destruction of Army Group South under the command of General Erich von Manstein, one of Germany's most able commanders. German forces available were 1,240,000 men, 12,600 guns, 2100 tanks and 2100 aircraft. Soviet forces massing against them totalled 2,633,000 men, 51,000 guns and heavy mortars, 2400 tanks (including increasing numbers of T-34s) and almost 3000 aircraft. The forthcoming titanic battles would take place on increasingly complex battlefields; behind German lines, large areas were under the control of partisans, all anti-German but by no means all pro-Soviet. In the chaos of war, nationalist groups had formed, particularly in Ukraine, with the objective of ridding themselves of Communist rule. Some had even chosen to fight with the German Army against Stalin's regime: Cossacks, Georgians, General Vlasov's Russian Liberation Army and the SS 'Galician 14th Division' – Ukranian Division. Despite Hitler's command not to give up any ground, German commanders had created the Wotan defensive line reaching from eastern Estonia in the north, southwards along the river Dnieper, to the Black Sea coast in the south.

Liberating Kharkov

In 1943 Soviet aircraft production comfortably surpassed the ouptut of German industry: 34,845 Soviet aircraft against 25,527 German left the factories. Increasing numbers of new Soviet designs were also reaching frontline units, and the sturdy and reliable Ilyushin Il-2 Sturmovik was prominent among these new aircraft.

STALEMATE IN THE EAST

With the coming of the spring thaw in 1943, large-scale operations along the whole Eastern front came to a standstill. As they had done a year earlier, both sides took the opportunity to strengthen their forces in preparation for a summer offensive.

As a series of gigantic attacks began, the city of Kharkov was liberated, retaken by the Germans, then liberated again. This series of massive operations was intended to liberate the eastern Ukraine with its crucial industrial areas of the Dombass, then advance to the Dnieper and liberate Kiev. The advance would take place along a 670km (400 mile) front, involving many separate operations. The distinctive feature of these would be numerous river crossings. Red Army commanders drove their soldiers hard. At river crossings, they were expected to improvise by utilizing anything that would float, lashing together timbers, oil drums or whatever came to hand to seize a bridgehead. Engineers immediately followed, bridging rivers to allow armoured vehicles and transport to move forwards in support.

Reaching the Dnieper

The Voronezh Front pushed forward a fast-moving mobile formation whose objective was to bypass German defences and to cause as much disruption and chaos in the enemy's rear areas as possible. This formation reached the river Dnieper north of Kiev on the night of 21 September. On 22–23 September, Soviet forces established exposed bridgeheads on the west bank. These were reinforced by airborne forces, the 1st, 3rd and 5th Guards Airborne Brigades, landed by parachute west of the river. Soviet air support was less than effective at this point, however, enjoying only a slight numerical superiorty on the battlefront that proved insufficient to protect the lightly armed paratroopers. Of the 4500 taking part, only half survived. These hardy souls fought on continuing offensive operations. This was the last Soviet airborne attack in the European war, but airborne soldiers would be used again successfully in Manchuria, against the Japanese, in 1945.

Soviet forces reached Zaporozhye early in October. Once there, they used abandoned river barges to cross the river. Two weeks later another bridgehead was established at Lyutezh. Kiev itself was finally liberated on 6 November after savage fighting, by which time numerous bridgeheads across the river Dnieper had been created despite a stubborn defence. In the north, Smolensk had been liberated, while to the south a massive group of Soviet forces attacked out of Zaporozhye, heading along the northern shore of the Sea of Azov, trapping the German 17th Army and elements of Army Group A in the Crimea.

By the end of 1943, Soviet forces on the southern front had consolidated their gains and were making ready for further offensive operations. Germany pinned its hopes on the winter slowing the Soviet offensives, allowing time for replacements and badly needed new equipment to arrive. Its hopes were to be dashed.

As pressure on German land forces grew during 1943, the Luftwaffe was increasingly used in the tactical 'fire brigade' role. Aircraft such as the Henschel Hs 129 tank buster were utilized to destroy Soviet armoured spearheads and frequently held long sectors of the front line by airpower alone. Gradually Soviet aircraft numbers began to tell, and the Luftwaffe's ability to deploy its aircraft at will to support overstretched ground forces was inevitably compromised. It was not just Soviet quantity but also quality of aircraft design and aircrew training that proved the difference. The Soviets had learned the lessons of German blitzkrieg tactics and reused and adapted them in their own inimitable style.

PETLYAKOV PE-2
The Pe-2 light bomber proved a versatile and capable aircraft from Kursk to the end of the war.

LUFTWAFFE VICTORIES
An Oberfeldwebel pilot adds victory number 12 to his score of enemy aircraft painted on the rudder of his Me 109.

157

KURSK: 1943

STUKA TANK-BUSTER
The last Stuka variant was the Junkers Ju 87G, a standard Ju 87D-5 converted to carry two BK 37 cannon (37mm Flak 18 guns) under the wing. No dive brakes were fitted, and the Ju 87G proved very adept at destroying Russian armour. Its chief exponent was Colonel Hans-Ulrich Rudel, who knocked out 500 tanks on the Eastern Front.

ILYUSHIN'S TANK-BUSTER
The Ilyushin Il-2 is best remembered for its part in the Battle of Kursk. Following a series of experiments, Il-2s were fitted with two long-barrelled anti-tank cannon, and these were used with devastating effect at Kursk on the latest German Tiger and Panther tanks. During 20 minutes of concentrated attacks on the 9th Panzer Division, Il-2 pilots claimed to have destroyed 70 tanks.

The battle of the Kursk salient was one of epic proportions, employing millions of men and women, thousands of armoured fighting vehicles and aircraft of all types. The front line between the Soviet and German forces ran from Leningrad in the north to Rostov-on-Don in the south, with a salient 200km (120 miles) wide and protruding 125km (75 miles) into the German sector between Orel and Kharkov. The Germans desperately needed to take back the initiative after the massive setback at Stalingrad the previous winter, where an entire German army had been killed or captured, and a third of the Eastern Front transport fleet destroyed. The plan was to launch attacks to the north and south of the Kursk pocket, and pinch out the salient, hopefully capturing a large number of Red Army troops in the process, as in the campaigns of 1941.

Preparing for the offensive

The Soviet commanders were well aware of Germany's intentions and set about creating a massive defensive perimeter in great depth, under the steady hand of General Georgi Zhukov, the victor of Stalingrad. If the German attack broke one line of defence, the army could simply fall back in good order onto another prepared defence. Once this had occurred a few times, the attacking force would be worn down, and Zhukov could release his reserves to push back the Germans and gain more ground in the process. Everyone, from Red Army engineers to civilians, was drawn into helping with the construction of defences, building blockhouses, digging anti-tank ditches or working on production lines building thousands of tanks and aircraft.

Soviet aviation had greatly improved since the catastrophic days of 1941, and the Polikarpov I-16 had been replaced with Mikoyan-Gurevich Mig 3s and 7s, and the Lavochkin La-5, which was a match for the Luftwaffe's Messerschmitt Me 109s and Focke-Wulf Fw 190s. Also starting to appear above the battlefield was the Ilyushin Il-2m3, a sturdy ground-attack platform heavily armoured around the engine and the pilot. This improved survivability as it flew low over the war zone, strafing with its 23mm cannon. Unfortunately the rear gunners had no armour and only a 12.7mm machine gun for protection. In all, the Soviet Union had 4000 frontline aircraft ready for the oncoming assault.

The Luftwaffe's strength was much smaller, about 2000 frontline aircraft, but what it lacked in numbers it more than made up for in skilled pilots. The Soviet Union lagged behind in this, expecting its pilots to fly into combat after an average of 15 hours in the air. The Luftwaffe still utilized the Heinkel He 111 and Me 109 as mainstays of its bomber and fighter forces, and had started to adapt the Junkers Ju 87 with additional armour and a 37mm anti-tank cannon fitted under each wing, although these were provided with only six rounds each. These aircraft were supplemented by the Fw 190 fighter-bombers and the specially designed Henschel Hs 129 fitted with an enormous PaK 40 cannon down its centreline, firing tungsten-tipped anti-armour rounds.

The attack begins

The Red Air Force set about annoyance raids as Germany worked on building up its forces, during which numerous Luftwaffe reconnaissance aircraft were destroyed on the ground. This deprived the German forces of much-needed aerial photography of the Russian ground works and defences.

On the morning of 5 July the German attack went in. Russian bombers sent in to disrupt the start of the attack were met by swarms of Luftwaffe interceptors. A massive air combat soon ensued, as the ground forces converged for the first contact between the new German Tiger and Panther tanks and the awaiting Russian cannon. As the two armies met with their massed armour, the Hs 129s and Ju 87s fell on the Soviet T-34 tanks and

Kursk: 1943

started to take a massive toll. The German forces, supported so well from the air, began making steady progress, and it looked as if their scheme may yet succeed, despite the sheer number of Soviet tanks that kept coming over the horizon. What they had not bargained for was Soviet production capability; as soon as 10 tanks were destroyed, they were replaced by 10 more, or repaired on the battlefield and thrust back in to the fray. The Red Air Force was beginning to make its presence felt more and more as the battle turned in favour of the Soviet Union. Zhukov ordered the counterattack as the Germans lost pace. An entirely new and fresh tank army was unleashed on the hapless German forces. Fearing that they would be overrun, they requested to fall back, but Hitler forbade any form of retreat.

The Soviet Il-2m3s flew low over the battlefield, winding along the columns of the German panzers and causing havoc. One squadron reported the destruction of 60 tanks, along with a further 30 vehicles, for no loss. Once the battlefield had been neutralized and the German forces were beginning to withdraw in disarray, the Soviet pilots flew into the German rear and caused even more damage in the supply chain, compounding German problems. This was the death knell for German offensive operations on the Eastern Front. Much of the Luftwaffe was pulled back to other fronts, especially after the Allied invasion of Sicily and Italy, and the Allied combined bomber offensive into the depths of the Reich now building up and being flown day and night required all available Luftwaffe fighters.

VAST NUMBERS
By the winter of 1943–44 vast numbers of Il-2m3s were in service (some sources put the total as high as 12,000), equipping units of the Soviet Naval Air Arm as well as the Soviet Air Force.

SOVIET GROUND-ATTACK TACTICS
Known as 'Nozhnitsi' (Scissors)

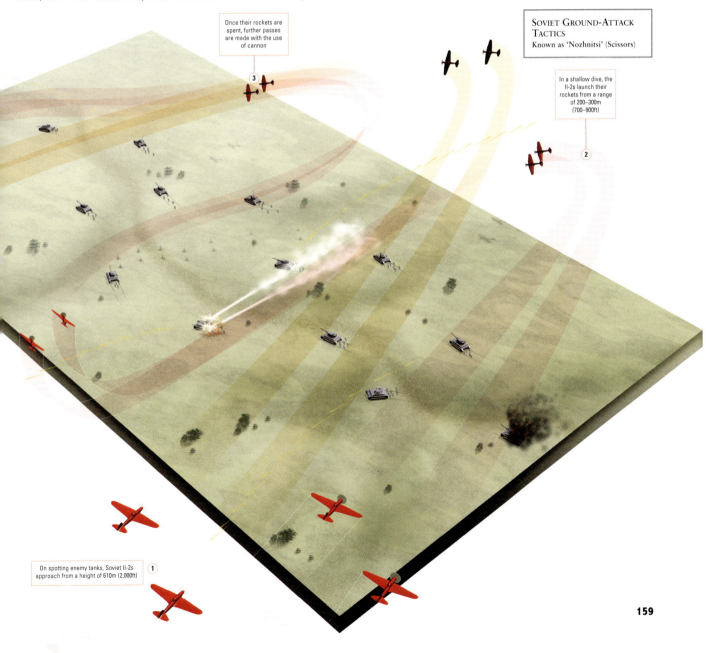

1. On spotting enemy tanks, Soviet Il-2s approach from a height of 610m (2,000ft)
2. In a shallow dive, the Il-2s launch their rockets from a range of 200–300m (700–900ft)
3. Once their rockets are spent, further passes are made with the use of cannon

159

UKRAINE AND THE CRIMEA

While Germany's Army Group Centre tried to cling on to its defence line along the headwaters of the river Dnieper, Army Group South fell back. It had been given permission by Hitler to give ground, and he also sent it four divisions taken from Army Group Centre. The three armies that made up Army Group South fought a fighting retreat, managing to keep an enemy superior in numbers and equipment at bay – but only just.

In a bold manoeuvre, Army Group Centre's three armies withdrew across the river Dnieper at just five crossing points. Here, the dwindling resources of the Luftwaffe were concentrated to provide a limited kind of air cover while the armies hurriedly crossed. The operation was a success, at least for a time, and none of the pursuing Soviet forces managed to trap significant German units east of the river. Later, however, Soviet forces managed to seize bridgeheads at Bukrin in a partly successful airborne operation, and at Rzhischer between 21 and 25 September.

From October to December battles developed around the steadily increasing number of bridgeheads. By December Soviet armies had established themselves west of the Dnieper and especially around Kiev. By now each of the Soviet Fronts had its own Air Army in support of operations. The total number of combat aircraft now facing the declining Luftwaffe and its Axis allies was around 5000 on the Ukrainian Front and approximately 9500-plus on the whole Eastern Front – and growing.

By 23 December 1943 Soviet forces had cut off the Crimea, trapping the German 17th Army and Romanian units. A new line had been established west of Kiev, and for a few hours the Axis forces licked their wounds. Then, on Christmas Eve, the Red Army launched a vast new offensive collectively known as 'Right Bank Ukraine'. Its objective was destruction of German Army Group A and Army Group South, numbering 10 operations in all, along a 1500 km (900 mile) front. The campaign would last until mid-April 1944.

Advancing westwards

The German salient west of Cherkassy attracted General Georgi Zhukov's attention, and he made it the focus of attacks by the 1st and 2nd Ukrainian Fronts. The positions were defended by 11 divisions of the German 8th Army and 1st Panzer Army. Facing them was a total of 27 Soviet divisions. The initial Soviet attacks, though well supported in the air, became bogged down in an early thaw. This gave the German forces time to plan their escape. On the night of 11/12 February the encircled German forces attempted to break out in a blizzard; only a few senior officers and a handful of infantry escaped. Of the 73,000 encircled, 18,000 were taken prisoner; the rest died in the snow. By 17 February it was all over, and the Soviet forces advanced westwards.

The Germans, however, clung on to the Crimea, now cut off by advancing Soviet forces to the north and subject to amphibious attacks from the Caucasus–Kuban area in the east. Full operations to clear the Crimea began on 8 April, with almost half a million Soviet troops deployed, backed by units of the Black Sea Fleet and approximately 800 combat aircraft. Facing this onslaught were 150,000 Germans and Romanians. German forces on the Crimea had virtually no air support. Various defence lines crumbled, and attempts to withdraw by sea were subject to heavy Soviet air attack, although a few key officers and men were flown out to bases in Romania. By 12 May the Soviets had recaptured the Crimea, eliminating the last major Axis stronghold east of the advancing Soviet forces.

FOCKE-WULF 190A-6
This rare colour image shows aircraft of JG 54 on a Russian airfield in the spring of 1943.

ADVANCE TO THE BLACK SEA
From February 1944, Soviet offensive operations by the 3rd and 4th Ukrainian Fronts were supported by the 8th and 17th Air Armies. During the initial phase of these operations, Il-2s and Pe-2s of the 9th Composite Air Corps were particularly active in attacking enemy rail communications. Operations continued throughout March and culminated in an advance on Odessa early in April.

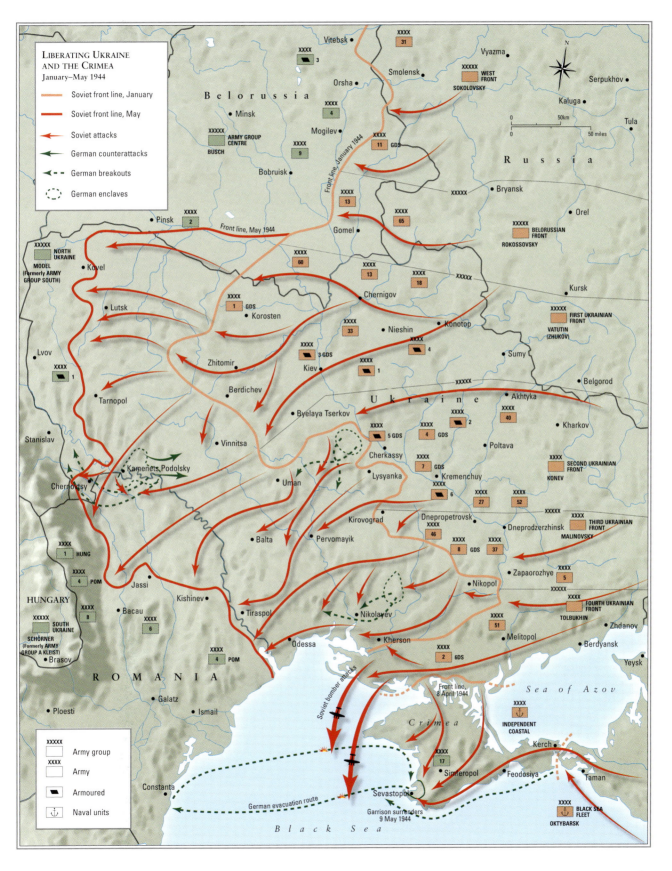

CARRIERS IN THE PACIFIC

Of the world's major navies during World War II, only four possessed aircraft carriers: the United States, Japan, the United Kingdom and France. Under the Washington Naval Treaty, Japan was prohibited from fortifying its Pacific territories and island possessions. Japan was therefore obliged to develop an aircraft-carrier force to protect its interests in the region.

The United States regarded Japan as its major threat in the Pacific and also decided to develop seaborne aviation. Capital ships' hulls, which were to be scrapped under the same treaty, were converted to aircraft carriers. Both the United States and Japan therefore acquired large carriers with well-equipped air groups, and by the late 1920s had quickly gained an understanding of their potential.

In 1941 the US Navy had seven fleet carriers and one escort carrier in service. With these ships, the vital battles of the Coral Sea and Midway were fought and won. As US industry got into gear, major new warships, especially the Essex-class carriers, were added to the US Navy. With the delivery of these new ships, the US fleet was able to attack Japanese island bases across the central Pacific, and this paved the way for the great seaborne offensives that followed. While the build-up of US Marine and Army forces was being made, US carrier task forces carried out several raids on important Japanese outposts and island bases. These were designed partly to take the war to Japan and keep it on its toes as to where the next landing was to take place, and partly to soften up any defences Japanese forces may have been building up or strengthening.

Carrier raids on Rabaul

With the US landing on Bougainville in the first days of November 1943, the US carriers USS *Saratoga* and USS *Princeton* approached the main Japanese base at Rabaul. Stationed at Rabaul were large warships that could be dispatched to cause major harm to US landing forces off Bougainville. The US carriers managed to get within range of Rabaul undetected, thanks to a squall providing ample cover. They then launched every aircraft possible, 97 in all – Douglas SBD Dauntless dive bombers and Grumman TBF Avenger torpedo bombers, plus fighter escorts. Surprise was complete, and six Japanese cruisers were damaged, four of them heavily, for the loss of just 10 US aircraft.

On 11 November the United States again attacked Rabaul. This time 185 planes flew off the carriers *Essex*, *Bunker Hill* and *Independence*. Again a Japanese cruiser was heavily damaged and a destroyer was sunk. A counterattack was launched by Japan, but was beaten off with great loss to the Japanese. After these attacks, Rabaul could no longer be used as a major Japanese naval base.

On 19 November, the United States attacked the Gilbert Islands. The main islands of defence out of the numerous tiny atolls that made up the group were Makin and Tarwa, the latter having a major airfield. The assault was supported by eight escort carriers with 216 aircraft at their disposal. They flew preliminary bombardment missions as well as close support, while the US Marine and Army forces struggled to clear incredibly stubborn Japanese resistance from bunkers constructed of tree trunks and coral that seemed impervious to naval gunfire.

Japan retaliated with a bomber attack on the US Task Force, with one torpedo hitting and damaging a light carrier. The escort carrier USS *Liscombe Bay* was sunk by a Japanese submarine. Lessons carried from the assault on these tiny islands resulted in heavier aerial bombardments of landing beaches, sometimes months ahead, in future operations.

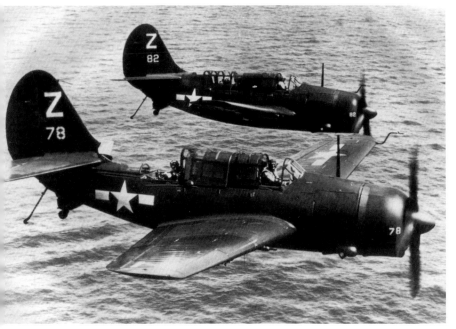

CURTISS SB-2C HELLDIVER
The Helldiver entered combat flying from USS Bunker Hill on 11 November 1943, when aircraft attacked the major Japanese base of Rabaul in the Solomon Islands.

Carriers in the Pacific

CRASH LANDING
Landing a carrier-borne aircraft was always a risky business. This F6F Hellcat crash-landed on the deck of the USS Enterprise and the catapult officer, Lt Walter Chewning, climbed up the side of the fuselage to drag the pilot, Ensign Byron Johnson, to safety.

CARRIER WAR IN THE PACIFIC
The aircraft carrier really came into its own during the Pacific offensives of 1944. The Japanese, their supply lines badly overstretched, never knew when and where an Allied carrier task force might appear to pound their island garrisons.

163

'The Marianas Turkey Shoot'

'THE MARIANAS TURKEY SHOOT'

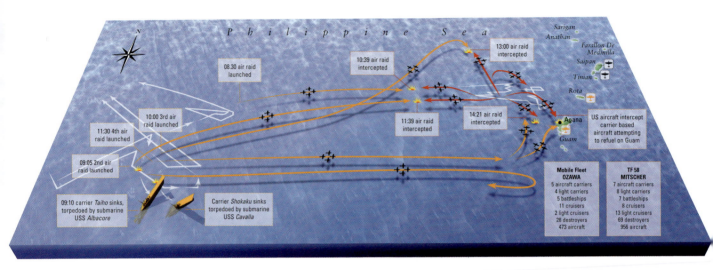

BATTLE OF THE PHILIPPINE SEA, FIRST PHASE
19 June 1944

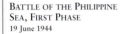 Japanese air movement
 US air movement
✈ Airfield

HELLCATS ON DECK
The Grumman F6F Hellcat accounted for 75 per cent of all victories recorded by the US Navy in the Pacific: 5,163 air victories at a cost of just 270 Hellcats, a kill-to-loss ration of 19 to 1.

Between 19 and 21 June 1944, the largest carrier engagement of World War II, the Battle of the Philippine Sea (known as 'The Marianas Turkey Shoot' for its one-sided nature), took place off the Mariana Islands. After making good losses incurred at Midway and Coral Sea at the hands of the United States, the Imperial Japanese Navy was once again ready to go on the offensive. Its Naval High Command came up with Operation A-Go, which involved a strike by carriers and land-based aircraft on the US fleet as it began the next phase of its island-hopping campaign.

Beginning the 'turkey shoot'

Commanding the Japanese strike force was Vice Admiral Jisaburo Ozawa. His fleet consisted of five fleet carriers, including the flagship *Taiho*, four light carriers and accompanying escort vessels. When the United States launched its invasion of Saipan on 15 June, Ozawa took the opportunity to strike and moved into the western Philippine Sea.

Ozawa's force was spotted by US submarines, and Admiral Marc Mitscher, in command of Task Force 58 covering the invasion fleet, wanted to engage immediately. He was ordered to fight a defensive battle by his superior, Admiral Raymond Spruance, and to block any attempt by Japanese forces to get through to the invasion area. Early on the morning of 19 June, the US carriers began launching patrols to search for the enemy fleet, as were the Japanese. A Japanese plane spotted TF 58 and immediately relayed its position to Ozawa, who ordered the land-based aircraft on Guam to attack. These aircraft were picked up on US radar and Grumman F6F Hellcats from the USS *Belleau Wood* launched to intercept. The Japanese pilots were caught still forming up, and lost 35 out of the 50 aircraft that took off from Guam.

The Hellcats were ordered back to the US fleet, as a larger force flying from the west was being picked up on radar – this was to be the first strike from the Japanese carriers. The US carriers immediately launched all available fighters to attack the approaching Japanese torpedo bombers and escorting Zero fighters, which were regrouping 120km (70 miles) short of US TF 58. Time spent forming up allowed the US aircraft to gain the height advantage, and they began engaging the Japanese well short of their target. It soon turned into a rout, with 41 of the 68 aircraft being shot down. Some Japanese aircraft did slip through, and engaged the

164

'The Marianas Turkey Shoot'

escort screen, causing damage to the USS *South Dakota*, but not putting her out of the action.

Later in the morning, Japan launched another strike, this time with 109 aircraft. Thanks to radar warnings, US fighters were able to respond with ample time and met the force 100km (60 miles) out from the task force. Seventy Japanese aircraft were shot down in the engagement, although some slipped through the net to attack USS *Enterprise*. Near misses were recorded, but the attackers succumbed to intense anti-aircraft fire. Eventually, 97 aircraft would be lost from the force of 109.

A third Japanese raid was launched comprising 47 aircraft, and this was again met by a strong force of Hellcat fighters. It was forced to return with few losses. A fourth raid was launched, but failed to locate the US task force because of incorrect coordinates, and decided to split and refuel at the strips on Rota and Guam. The force flying to Rota stumbled across the US carriers *Bunker Hill* and *Wasp*, and immediately attacked, but failed to cause any damage. The aircraft flying to Guam were spotted by patrolling Hellcats and torn apart as they began to land, further reducing Japanese strength. During these air battles the submarine USS *Albacore* sighted and torpedoed Ozawa's flagship *Taiho*. She eventually would sink after a massive explosion. Another submarine sighted the *Shokaku* and managed to launch three torpedoes into her side. She also exploded and sank.

The US task force then took the initiative and began to sail west in search of the remaining Japanese fleet. They were sighted mid-afternoon on 20 June, Mitscher immediately ordered a strike, even though his pilots would have to return in failing light. At 6.30 p.m., 216 aircraft left the task force and flew directly to the retreating Japanese. The Japanese carrier *Hiyo* was targeted, hit and eventually sunk. Three other carriers were hit and badly damaged, and with this the US aircraft turned back for their task force. Returning in almost pitch darkness, Mitscher ordered the task force to turn on all available light, even though they would be susceptible to Japanese submarines. Eighty aircraft were eventually lost, some from battle damage, some from heavy landings on the carriers' decks and others from overflying the deck and ditching in the sea. Japan began a hasty withdrawal. Mitscher wanted desperately to give chase. Spruance again overruled, assessing the battle as won, and ordered Mitscher back to guarding the Saipan invasion force.

HELLCAT PILOTS
The faces of this cheerful group of US Navy Hellcat pilots exude confidence and competence. By mid-1944 the Imperial Japanese Navy had lost the cream of its fighter pilots, and replacements were rushed into combat lacking anything like the standard of training enjoyed by their American adversaries.

BATTLE OF THE PHILIPPINE SEA, SECOND PHASE
20–21 June 1944
← US air movements
✢ Airfields

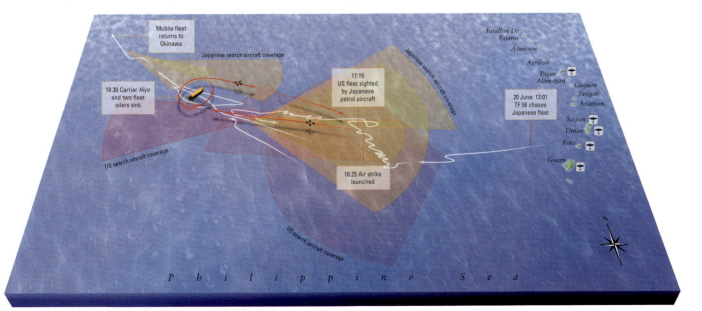

THE ISLAND-HOPPING CAMPAIGN

As air strikes were being flown to neutralize the Japanese base at Rabaul, the US Marines and US Army continued landings on the Pacific islands that had become Japanese outer defensive perimeter. First to be attacked were the Gilbert and Marshall islands, tiny atolls about halfway between Pearl Harbor in Hawaii and the northern shores of Papua New Guinea. Next would be the Marianas. The massive air combats that took place here were a tremendous boost to US flyers' confidence, but a harsh foretaste of what was to come for Japan. The island of Palau was next to be assaulted, then the Philippines, which saw the introduction of a new Japanese tactic, intentional crashing of aircraft into Allied shipping – the kamikaze. This method escalated in the battles off Iwo Jima as US Marines struggled across the volcanic island, and would come to an horrific climax off the coast of Okinawa.

The US Marines and Army assaulted Tarawa and Makin islands in November 1943, going ashore after bombardments from both sea and air. Carriers were also sent northwest of the islands to cover the threat of attack on the invasion fleet. The capture of the two islands was completed in a short time, with the only real loss to the air effort during the offensive being the sinking of the escort carrier USS *Liscombe Bay* by submarine on 23 November.

Striking at the heart of Japanese operations
Truk, part of the Caroline Islands in Micronesia, was Japan's major base in the region, with airfields and a large harbour. These were attacked by Admiral Raymond Spruance's task force of carriers. US Navy pilots strafed the enemy airfields and destroyed the majority of Japanese air power while it still languished on the ground. Japanese losses amounted to some 300 aircraft destroyed, for the loss of only 25 US aircraft.

General Douglas MacArthur then took the initiative to recapture the Philippines. Landings took place first on Leyte, then moved on to Luzon once a base for aircraft had been secured. As US troops were landing on Leyte, Japan launched operation A-Go. This involved using the remaining carriers in the Japanese fleet to lure the US carriers away from protecting the landing forces, thus allowing for two other large Japanese forces to engage with ease. One Japanese force was halted at the battle of Leyte Gulf, an enormous naval engagement of a scale never to be repeated. The Japanese carrier force was also intercepted by US naval aircraft, with US pilots sinking four carriers, including the *Zuikaku*, a survivor of the Pearl Harbor raid.

Meanwhile, a large Japanese battleship and cruiser force had sailed through the San Bernardino Strait and were fast approaching the invasion fleet. In its way stood three task groups of 'Taffies', each made up of light carriers and destroyers. The huge guns of the Japanese battleships and cruisers were capable of causing havoc among the lightly armoured escort carriers. The US destroyers engaged immediately and began desperately torpedoing the Japanese vessels, while the carriers launched what few bombers they had and even Grumman F6F Wildcat fighters to strafe the ships' decks. Faced with such a concerted onslaught, the Japanese forces assumed that they were facing much stronger opposition than was the reality, and decided to pull out. Thanks to the bravery of the US destroyer crews and the flyers relentlessly attacking the ships with what armament they could muster, what seemed inevitable destruction was averted.

Facing a terrifying new tactic
On 9 January 1945 the Allied assault on Luzon went in. It was marked by an increase of what at first seemed to be isolated incidents: intentional collision of Japanese aircraft into Allied warships. The cruiser HMAS *Australia* was struck five times by suicide aircraft and had to retire for extensive repair. This was to be one of many casualties of this menacing and unnerving new attack method.

Kamikaze attacks came to a climax off the coasts of Okinawa and Iwo Jima. Japan trained dedicated squadrons to fulfil this task, one that most Japanese flyers took on with great pride. The aircraft were escorted to the battle zone, then pilots carefully chose their targets. They then dove through thick anti-aircraft fire to attempt to hit a vessel. If successful, they could inflict horrific damage, with burning aviation fuel worsening the effects. At Okinawa, the kamikaze at first concentrated on the radar-equipped destroyer picket line set off from the fleet as an early warning. They then moved on to the fleet itself, sinking many ships and severely lowering Allied morale. This was a vital warning to Allied commanders that capture of the Japanese home islands would be a costly campaign.

The Island-hopping Campaign

CLOSING THE GAP: Patrolling the Atlantic

ANTI-SUBMARINE LIBERATOR
It was not until the deployment of very long range maritime aircraft in the shape of the Consolidated B-24 Liberator and the PBY Catalina, operating in concert with naval hunter-killer groups, that the tide of the Atlantic war began to turn in the Allies' favour.

Coastal Command was the RAF's least supplied arm of the force at the beginning of World War II, with the 'Bomber Barons' of Bomber Command jealously hoarding their long-range bombers for the strategic bombing of Germany when they were desperately required to fly cover missions over the Atlantic convoys. With the German army's advance through Europe and capture of ports with access to the Atlantic, in Norway and western France, Coastal Command had few assets to protect inbound convoys against the U-boat threat.

RAF Coastal Command did have the Short Sunderland, a massive, sturdy flying boat that could take a heroic amount of damage before succumbing to its wounds. It also had the obselescent Avro Anson, although this lacked any useful range, and the Lockheed Hudson, which did have an impressive range and a good weapons-carrying capability. The latter was the product of the Lend-Lease arrangement between Britain and the United States. These aircraft and their crews served with distinction during the first part of the war, but with limited resources could cover only a tiny portion of the vast Atlantic Ocean, and shipping losses started to mount, cutting off the United Kingdom from supply from the outside world.

Improving range capability
Range was an important factor in the losses suffered. With no RAF machine capable of flying to the mid-Atlantic to patrol for a sustained period, this is where the German U-boats now hunted without impunity. At last in 1941 the arrival of the Consolidated B-24 VLR (Very Long Range) Liberator from the United States began to expand Coastal Command's capability. Inroads were also made on weapons that could effectively counter the U-boat. Depth charges based on conventional bombs tended to 'skip' off the surface of the sea, often with disastrous results, as the bomb would often bounce and hit the aircraft that had launched it. Improvements were made so that the charges would enter the water more efficiently and explode at a shallow depth, in hopes of causing the greatest possible damage to a U-boat caught on the surface.

Also introduced was ASV (Air-to-Surface Vessel) Radar. This allowed an operator in the aircraft to 'see' any surfaced vessel in any weather conditions, day or night. When combined with the arrival of ex-RAF Bomber Command machines such as the Vickers Wellington and the Armstrong-Whitworth Whitley, as well as the Liberators, victories against the submarines started to mount, and shipping losses were down as the U-boat now became the hunted. The Leigh light, a powerful searchlight fitted to Coastal Command bomber, made attacking U-boats, which usually surfaced at night to recharge batteries, a possibility. This was especially true in the Bay of Biscay as the submarines left ports en route for mid-Atlantic hunting grounds. They now had to travel under the surface, in turn lowering their range and effectiveness.

Another aircraft in Coastal Command's expanding armoury was the Boeing B-17C Fortress. Experimented with by RAF Bomber Command as a daylight bomber, it was found wanting; most aircraft were then transferred to its sister command, but were soon replaced by the far more effective Fortress II (B-17E). With Portugal allowing the use of the Azores by the Allies, the B-17s, fitted with the latest ASV radar, operated from here, closing the mid-Atlantic gap still further.

As the war progressed, the advantage slowly tipped in the Allies' favour in the battles above the waves – so much so that Coastal Command started to fly more offensive missions with the acquisition of Bristol Beaufighters and de Havilland Mosquitoes. These aircraft were not only armed with cannon and machine guns, but could also carry eight rocket projectiles or one torpedo (Beaufighter only). These weapons proved to be extremely effective against U-boats unfortunate enough to be caught on the surface. Beaufighters and Mosquitoes were also a lot faster than any other types utilized by the Command, and the U-boats now had a very short time to bring their formidable anti-aircraft defences to bear on these swift machines. The strike aircraft were also used against surface vessels, particularly coastal transports. They would often fly in two groups. As one section suppressed any anti-aircraft fire by spraying the decks with automatic fire, the other section would line up for an accurate rocket or torpedo attack.

By the end of the war Coastal Command could be credited with the destruction of more than 200 U-boats and 500,000 tons of Axis surface vessels. The U-boat, once able to prowl in its 'Wolf Packs' almost at will, had been neutralized.

Closing the Gap: Patrolling the Atlantic

THE ATLANTIC GAP
In the early part of the war, the most serious losses to Allied shipping occurred in mid-Atlantic, where a large gap was created by the absence of air cover. By 1943 this gap had been filled, thanks to very long range maritime patrol aircraft like the Consolidated B-24 Liberator, and then it was the turn of the U-Boats to suffer unacceptable losses.

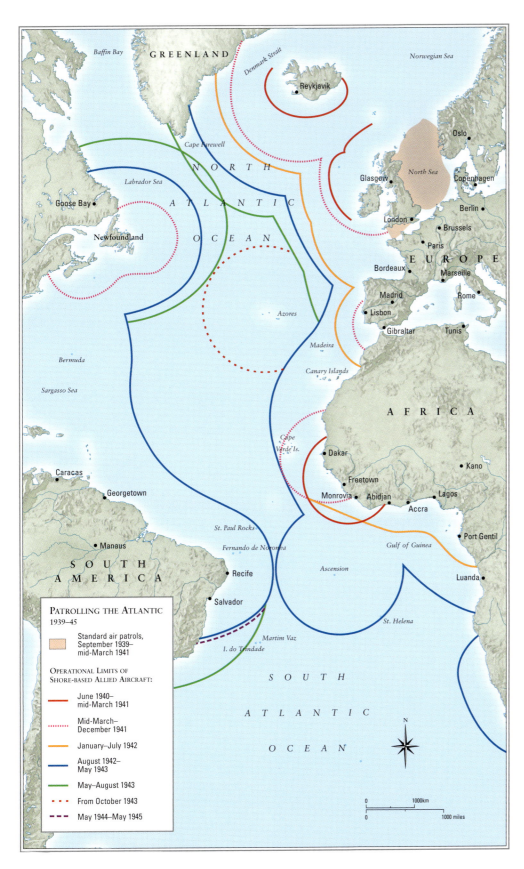

PATROLLING THE ATLANTIC 1939–45

- Standard air patrols, September 1939–mid-March 1941

OPERATIONAL LIMITS OF SHORE-BASED ALLIED AIRCRAFT:
- June 1940–mid-March 1941
- Mid-March–December 1941
- January–July 1942
- August 1942–May 1943
- May–August 1943
- From October 1943
- May 1944–May 1945

D-DAY: The Assault

SPITFIRE MK XVI
This Spitfire MK.XIV of No. 453 Sqn Royal Australian Air Force wears D-Day identification stripes. The photograph was taken on the eve of the Allied landings in Normandy.

HORSA GLIDER
The Airspeed AS.51 Horsa glider was key to the airborne invasion of Normandy. This example of the US IX Troop Carrier Command sits in a field in Normandy following the invasion.

Air power came of age in 1944, with the Allied invasion of northern France. It would be used as a means to cut the enemy's lines of reinforcement and communication, destroy defences, deliver paratroops and tow gliders, fly deception missions and halt any submarine attacks on the Allied invasion fleet. All this would be carried out while attempting to maintain total air superiority and continuing the Allied air forces' strategic and tactical bombing roles. The missions in their entirety would come under the command of the Allied Expeditionary Air Force, under the command of Air Chief Marshal Sir Trafford Leigh-Mallory.

In the spring of 1944 the RAF's Bomber Command and USAAF Eighth Air Force, much to the disdain of their respective commanders Sir Arthur Travers Harris and Carl Andrew Spaatz, were diverted from their role bombing the heartland of Germany and its industrial centres. They were now to take part in the 'Transportation Plan', devised by Professor Solly Zuckerman, which required attacks on German-occupied rail networks, marshalling yards and bridges, to isolate the invasion from German reinforcement. Attacks were made from western Germany across northern Europe to Brittany. To avoid any hint of where the invasion was to come, four times as many bombs were dropped outside the invasion zone as inside it. Heavy bombers targeted marshalling yards and rolling-stock repair depots, while medium and fighter-bombers of the Ninth Air Force and the 2nd Tactical Air Force made precision attacks on bridges and locomotives. By D-Day, out of 2000 locomotives available to Germany, 1500 were destroyed or undergoing repairs. Almost all the bridges over the river Seine, which would be the route of any main reinforcement, were destroyed.

In addition to these attacks, fighter-bombers, usually de Havilland Mosquitoes, Hawker Typhoons or Lockheed P-38 Lightnings, attacked German radar sites in northern France and Belgium. These targets were heavily defended, and many casualties fell to the heavy flak encountered, but again, by the time of D-Day, not one of the stations in the invasion area was operational.

On the eve of D-Day, 5 June, hundreds of transport planes took off, some towing gliders with the task of delivering the British 6th Airborne Division to protect the eastern flank of the invasion and the 82nd and 101st Airborne Divisions to the west, again to protect the flank and secure the routes off Utah Beach. Britain also landed a small coup de main force to capture bridges over the Orne river and canal. Transported in wooden Horsa gliders, the force landed in total darkness within yards of the target, just after midnight on 6 June; both bridges were captured with the minimum of casualties. Other paratroops in the eastern sector were widely scattered, however, resulting in many of the tasks being executed by very few men, Nonetheless they were all completed by the morning of the invasion.

D-Day: The Assault

To the west the US IXth Troop Transport Command, flying Douglas C-47s, were to fly in the US divisions. Approaching from the west and flying across the Contentin Peninsula, they hit low cloud and intense flak as soon as they made landfall. This caused the pilots, the vast majority having not seen combat before, to break from their tight formation as they desperately tried to evade enemy shells while not colliding with their compatriots. Again, this resulted in the two divisions being wildly scattered, but the paratroops' professionalism shone through on this occasion as well, with the majority of tasks being successfully carried out.

As the infantry on the ships clambered onto their assault craft, bombers of the Ninth Air Force flew along the beachheads to bomb the bunkers and strongpoints, and breach any wire defences. It was hoped that this would keep the defenders' heads down as the infantry approached and provide shelter on their arrival in the form of bomb craters on the beaches. Out of fear of their own men being hit, many of the Allied bombs fell well inland, not touching any of the defences and not providing the vital cover. This lack of preliminary bombardment from the air was felt particularly on Omaha beach, where the US 1st and 29th divisions encountered a ferocious and now fully aware defence.

As the troops on the ground struggled to claim a foothold on the coast of northern France, they were unhindered by air attack, as was the invasion fleet offshore. Constant air patrols meant that few Luftwaffe fighters could get through. What is more, submarines could not risk sailing into the Bai de la Seine for fear of attack. The Allies held complete air superiority, and this superiority would be maintained for the rest of the campaign.

D-DAY AIR COVER

During the 24 hours of D-Day, the Allied air forces flew 14,674 sorties for the loss of 113 aircraft. Combat Air Patrol sorties immediately over the invasion fleet were flown by the US Eighth Fighter Command's P-38 groups, the twin-tailed Lightnings being easily identifiable to naval gunners. Top cover over the beaches was provided by nine squadrons of Spitfires, while Typhoons and Mustangs of the 2nd Tactical Air Force, together with Mustangs, Thunderbolts and Lightnings of Ninth Tactical Air Command, flew armed reconnaissance missions inland.

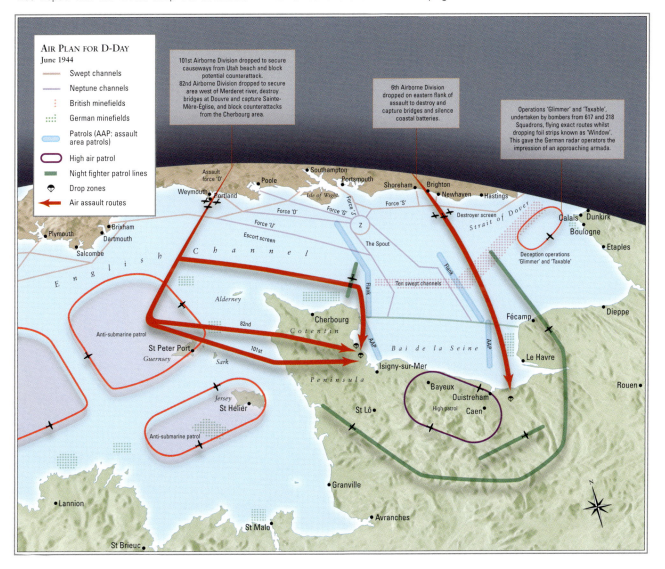

171

D-DAY: The Aftermath

ROCKET-ARMED TYPHOONS
Rocket armed Typhoons performed a critical role in the support of advancing ground troops, particularly in the destruction of enemy armoured units.

DISPERSED FORCES
Dispersal of forward operating bases at the Normandy beachhead allowed fighters and fighter-bombers to linger for longer periods of time above the battleground.

Now with a successful foothold in Normandy, the Allies needed to keep the initiative and increase the momentum of force against Germany. The fleet of ships that was ferrying supplies for the advance to continue required protection from both airborne and maritime attack, the troops required close air-support and the aircraft themselves needed protection from interception. All these tasks were ably fulfilled by the men and machines of the Allied Expeditionary Air Force, along with their brothers in the Eighth Air Force and Bomber Command.

Repelling Luftwaffe attack
From the first day of the invasion, the Luftwaffe attempted to attack the fleet laying off the Normandy coastline, disgorging troops and supplies. Very few of these attacks got through because of constant air patrols by Supermarine Spitfires and North American Mustangs. Those that did get through were met with an awesome barrage of anti-aircraft fire. Germany also attempted to use glide bombs, used with reasonable success in the Mediterranean, but none of these weapons found a target, and the launch aircraft were usually lost in the action.

Priority was given by the Allies to construction of advanced landing grounds, at first to aid damaged aircraft unable to make it back across the Channel. Eventually these became forward operating bases for several squadrons per field. Units were flying off these grounds by 13 June. These forward bases meant that Allied aircraft could react to intelligence and attack targets more quickly, without facing the haul over the English Channel, and they could linger over the battleground for longer periods of time.

The Transportation Plan continued with roaming patrols of fighter-bombers that attacked any enemy movement on the roads behind the front. Especially successful at this were the RAF's Hawker Typhoon and the USAAF's Republic Thunderbolt. Both carried bombs or rockets, and were feared by the Wehrmacht in the small lanes of the Norman bocage. Their tactics were to locate a column, and destroy the lead and tail vehicles, thus trapping the enemy and allowing them to be picked off at leisure. These aircraft could also be used in direct support of an Allied advance. With a forward air controller attached to the advancing infantry units and a direct radio link to the pilots, specific targets could be located and destroyed.

RAF Bomber Command and the Eighth Air Force were used for the first time in direct support of ground forces. During Operation Goodwood, the British and Canadians' advance into Caen, 2000 bombers blasted a path for the infantry. Although initially stunned and with many tanks destroyed, German forces were well dug in and soon able to fight again. The carnage also led to difficulty deploying Allied armour through the rubble and craters. This downside was highlighted even more at the start of Operation Cobra, the US breakout, when bombers of the Eighth Air Force dropped a stick of bombs short, inflicting many casualties on their own side.

Yet tactical support from the air utilizing fighter-bombers could not have been more exemplary. This was especially true during the last German counterattack at Mortain. US soldiers facing a massive panzer attack called on the services of the rocket-firing Typhoons, which destroyed more than 100 German tanks, thus blunting the attack. The same aircraft went on to inflict more damage as German forces retreated out of the Falaise Gap, destroying hundreds of tanks and thousands of other vehicles, and inflicting untold casualties.

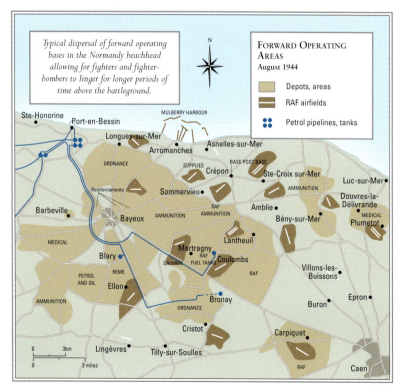

Typhoon attack on a German convoy

MARKET GARDEN AND VARSITY: 1944–45

MARKET GARDEN
In the weeks after D-Day, no fewer than 16 Allied airborne operations were hastily planned in northwest Europe, and were just as hastily cancelled. Market Garden was the seventeenth. Its objective was for the First Allied Airborne Army to lay an 'airborne carpet' ahead of XXX Corps to capture and control the main river and canal crossings. Market was the airborne operation; Garden the advance on the ground.

As the Allies raced across France to the German border, so their supply lines were stretched from the beaches of Normandy and the port of Cherbourg on the Contentin Peninsula. With supplies limited to one thrust on the wide frontage at any given time, Field Marshal Bernard Montgomery proposed a daring plan. Operation Market Garden, planned for mid-September 1944, would secure crossings over the many waterways of the Netherland's south. The mighty Rhine, gateway to Germany's industrial heartland, the Ruhr, would then be open.

The plan was to drop three airborne divisions to capture various water obstacles, with the final one, furthest away from the front line, being the bridge over the Rhine at Arnhem. Troops of the British 1st Airborne Division were told to hold the bridge, while an armoured column advanced up the road secured by the other two airborne divisions, the US 101st and 82nd. Ready to take in the veteran 101st and 82nd Airborne Divisions was the IX Troop Carrier Command, already blooded over Normandy a few months earlier. The British 1st Airborne Division, along with the 1st Polish Parachute Brigade, was to be flown in with RAF Transport Command. Both forces used the Douglas C-47 extensively, but the British also employed ex-bomber types, such as the Short Stirling, for glider towing purposes. Not enough aircraft were available to take the British contingent, however, and only half the force would be dropped on the first day. The remainder would arrive the next day, including the Polish brigade. This meant that, on landing, half the force would have to stay on the landing zone to secure it ready for the next day, leaving relatively few to advance to the main target of the bridge.

Heavy escort

On the day of the jump the troop transports were heavily escorted, with 1200 fighters flying. Supermarine Spitfires gave top cover, while de Havilland Mosquitoes and Hawker Typhoons strafing any flak positions en route. Casualties over

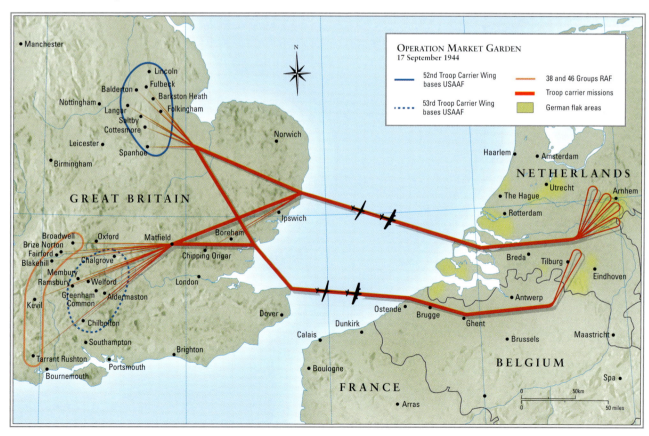

174

Market Garden and Varsity: 1944–45

AIRBORNE ATTACK
British parachute troops jump from C-47s while on the ground Horsa gliders unload heavier equipment on the outskirts of Arnhem during Operation Market Garden.

the drop zone were surprisingly light; most injuries were the result of awkward landings by paratroops or the violent 'crash' landings the glider men had to contend with. The 101st quickly secured its objectives bar one – the bridge over the Wilhelmina Canal was blown. This was solved by a Bailey bridge brought up by the advancing armoured column made up from XXX Corps. The majority of Nijmegen was captured by 82nd Airborne, but the two main spans remained in German hands when XXX Corps arrived, slowing the advance yet more.

In the British sector, the British had reached the northern edge of the bridge, but could not force a crossing. The Germans counterattacked successfully and soon overran many of the drop zones. A lack of working radios meant that the helpless paras could only watch in anger as supplies were dropped into what were now German positions. The lack of operational radios meant that the Hawker Typhoon ground-attack aircraft, so successful in the bocage of Normandy, could not be deployed effectively, severely blunting the paratroops' capability, especially in stopping armoured assaults. XXX Corps was stopped just after the crossings at Nijmegen – the assault on the Rhine had failed. Out of 10,000 men dropped in and around Arnhem, only 2500 escaped; 1500 men died, and the rest were captured.

Montgomery's second chance
Montgomery was again in charge of another major operation involving airborne troops with his set piece crossing of the Rhine at Wesel. This time there was a massive preparatory build-up. Thousands of troops swept across the Rhine in amphibious assault craft, after bombardment from artillery as well as Bomber Command. As the ground troops pushed forwards, the attack's airborne element, Operation Varsity, was launched. It utilized Britain's 6th Airborne Division, veterans of the Normandy campaign, and the US 17th Airborne Division on their first combat jump. All landed well, but the gliders bringing in heavy equipment such as anti-tank guns suffered badly. Over a quarter of all the glider pilots were casualties. But success was total, and the Allies were now firmly lodged on the eastern bank of the Rhine.

Southeast Asia: 1944–45

SOUTHEAST ASIA: 1944–45

In 1944, the tide was beginning to turn against Japanese aggression and success. The Allies' build-up of resources and acclimation to fighting such a ferocious enemy in a hostile environment meant that it was time to advance, pushing back the Japanese from what they had taken so easily two years previously. At Imphal and Kohima, Japanese forces made one last attempt to advance into northeastern India and secure their flank, while in China they were forced to make one final offensive to capture Allied air bases being built there. In the Philippines they were preparing for the relentless power of the US Navy's carrier force.

Defending northeastern India

Japan attacked Imphal and Kohima in northeastern India in March 1944, surrounding Indian and British troops garrisoned there. With the main supply route cut off, the troops were dependent on RAF supply aircraft, again usually the workhorse of World War II, the Douglas C-47. These aircraft brought in nearly 20,000 tons of supplies and 10,000 reinforcements while flying out thousands of casualties, until the siege was lifted in April. The RAF assisted in pushing Japanese forces from Kohima ridge by flying extensive ground-attack missions. As the Japanese forces fell back from their failed offensive, they were constantly harrassed by the vast assortment of aircraft flown by Allies, from Bristol Beaufighters and Hawker Hurricanes to North American P-51 Mustangs and Consolidated B-24 Liberators.

As Lieutenant-General William Slim's 14th Army advanced through Burma in pursuit of the retiring Japanese forces, the RAF strafed many of the river crossings strewn across Burma. Particularly good at this role was the Beaufighter, nicknamed 'Whispering Death' by the Japanese. Due to its relatively quiet engines, it could sneak up at low level and often take out targets with complete surprise, causing havoc with its cannon, machine guns and rockets.

As the Allies advanced across Burma in the second half of 1944 and into 1945, they had almost complete air superiorty. Hurricanes armed with cannon and bombs could be called upon to attack specific targets much like the Hawker Typhoons over the Normandy battlefield in Europe. By May 1945, Rangoon had been captured and the British forces were keen to reorganize and enter Malaya and retake Singapore.

China and the Philippines

In China, with the US Fourteenth Air Force a thorn in the side of its occupation army and the threat of the Boeing B-29's arrival, Japan launched Operation Ichi-Go to capture the airfields. Beginning in April 1944, quick advances were made, but the USAAF attempting to hamper every step. The Japanese advance soon ran out of steam at the end of the year, after horrific casualties had been incurred. The US airfields were never captured, but were of only limited use in the upcoming B-29 bombing campaign due to the difficulties of supply.

In the Philippines, the United States inflicted heavy casualties on the Imperial Japanese Navy in the battles following the landings on Leyte and Luzon. A tropical typhoon tore through the US Third Fleet off Luzon, and three destroyers were capsized and many crew lost, along with scores of aircraft that were blown overboard. While the landings went in, a task force was dispatched to the South China Sea to cover any possible counterattack. None came, but this allowed the US carrier aircraft to attack targets in French Indochina, Formosa and China. On its return, the task force had to face the new Japanese tactical method—the kamikaze. It did not matter that these pilots were only basically trained, often barely able to take off. Flying their fuel- and often bomb-laden aircraft into Allied warships proved highly effective off the Philippines and escalated at Iwo Jima and Okinawa.

ROYAL AIR FORCE P-47S
RAF P-47 Thunderbolts of No. 134 Squadron transferred to Burma from India in December 1944, in support of Lieutenant-General Slim's Fourteenth Army.

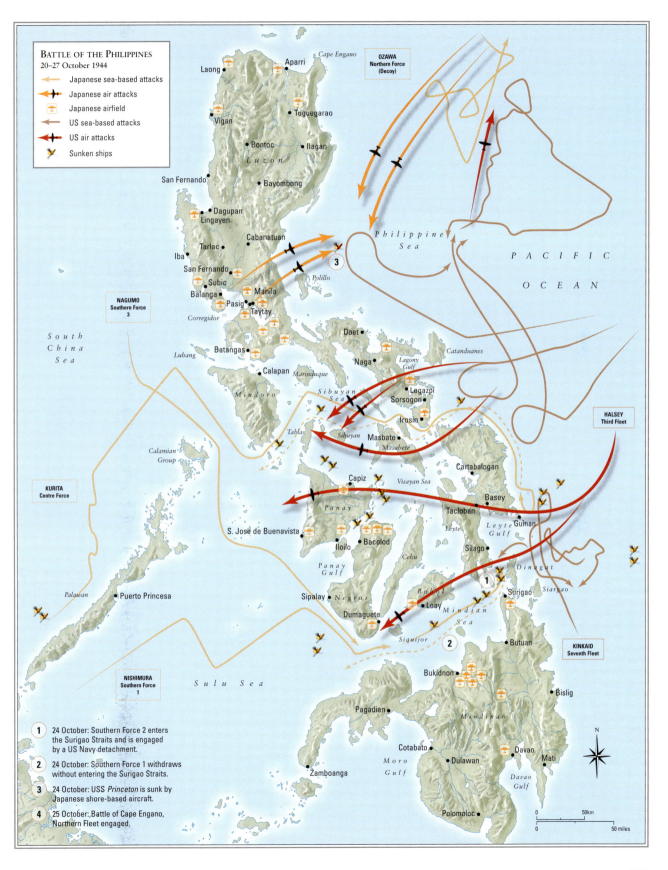

CHINA: 1941–45

CURTISS C-46 COMMANDO Although largely eclipsed by the celebrated C-47 Dakota, the Curtiss C-46 Commando, seen here flying over the Himalayas between India and China – known to aircrews as flying over 'The Hump' – was a true workhorse of the USAAF, especially in the Pacific theatre. The C-46 did not appear in Europe until March 1945, when it took part in the airborne assault on the Rhine.

Claire Lee Chennault was a retired USAAC major who was going slightly deaf when he was asked in 1937 by the Chinese government to help organize and implement a fighter defence system for the country. He wasted no time in securing as many aircraft as possible for the task. Among these was the improved Curtiss P-40 Warhawk, secured through the US Lend-Lease policy.

Along with the aircraft came a line of volunteer American pilots. Sixty of these were former US Marine or US Navy pilots, while the rest came from the USAAC – and most were looking for action and adventure. From this core of more than 80 pilots, plus more than 100 American ground crew, evolved the American Volunteer Group, or AVG, more commonly known as the 'Flying Tigers'. Based at Kunming in China, they intercepted Japanese bombers, immediately making an impact and scoring enormous victories. A squadron was also based further south, tasked with defending against Japanese advance into Burma, alongside the RAF's outclassed Brewster Buffalo fighters and a handful of Hawker Hurricanes. Here the unit was less successful, and casualties and losses soon stacked up against the Japan's relentless push for the resources of Southeast Asia.

Parts and fuel were at a premium because of the squadron's geographical isolation in central southern China. Fighters could be kept flying only by cannibalising other aircraft, further reducing the unit's strength and therefore its effectiveness.

A new role in the USAAF

After the fall of Burma, impressed by the Flying Tigers' impact, the US Government supplied more up-to-date versions of the P-40, as well as reinstating Chennault and giving him the rank of Major General, and officially incorporating the AVG into the USAAF as the 23rd Pursuit Group. This unit continued to fly from Chinese airfields for the rest

China: 1941–45

of World War II, intercepting or escorting bombers, strafing Japanese positions and supply lines, and generally making a nuisance of itself. Towards the end of the war, the 23rd's trusty P-40s were slowly replaced by the North American P-51 Mustang; many retained the unit's iconic shark's-mouth markings.

Flying over the 'Hump'

With Burma in Japanese hands, and the Burma Road, principal route for supplying Chinese Nationalist forces, cut off, the only route was over the Himalayas, via transport aircraft and converted bombers. Everything from ammunition and fuel to pack mules and Jeeps had to be flown over the vast mountain range. The route from bases in Assam, India, to Kunming was particularly hazardous, as the aircraft had to be flown over ranges that often peaked 4900m (16,000ft). This was exacerbated by the unpredictable weather that caused high turbulence, and while flying in the valleys could be disrupted by thick cloud, flying above this caused heavy icing, which could easily make an aircraft inoperable.

Casualties flying over what pilots christened the 'Hump' were high. All along the route lay scattered remains of lost aircraft, a grim reminder to pilots and crew of the mission's danger. Chinese landing strips were often attacked by Japanese bombers, and monsoon weather often led to the fields being unserviceable. Accidents occurred on take-off and landings because of the heavy loads the aircraft were carrying, and constant wear on the machines soon took its toll, as spares were practically impossible to attain. The USAAF and RAF combined to fly this dangerous, unglamorous mission, flying the Douglas C-47, although the Curtiss C-46 Commando, with its larger load-carrying ability, was the shining star of the campaign.

Towards the end of the conflict more than 600 aircraft were flying the torturous route every day. By war's end more than 600,000 tons of supplies had been delivered to all the forces fighting in the region: China's Nationalists, General Joseph Stilwell's US forces and the B-29s of XX Bomber Command.

P-51 MUSTANG IN CHINA
The North American P-51 Mustang replaced the P-40 with General Chennault's 'Flying Tigers' in China. The war-weary P-51B carried the traditilonal sharks' teeth insignia first adopted in 1940.

> **FLYING THE 'HUMP'**
> 1944–45
> ← Allied transportation routes

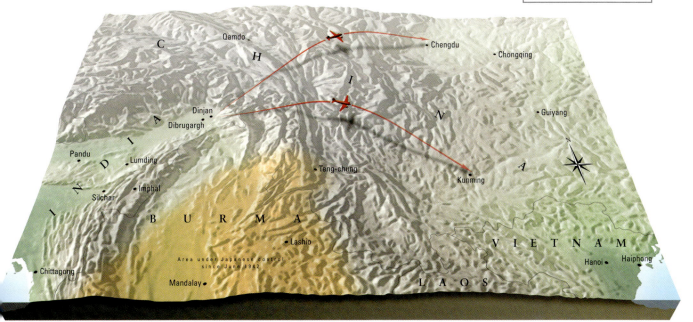

BAGRATION AND THE LIBERATION OF WEST USSR

Operation Bagration, the largest Soviet offensive yet planned, was named by Stalin after a famous field marshal and fellow Georgian who fell, mortally wounded, at the Battle of Borodino during Napoleon's invasion of Russia. It was designed to smash German Army Group Centre, which held the majority of Belorussia. Planning for this vast undertaking had been in hand since the spring of 1944, as Soviet armies continued their advance through Ukraine. Stalin had also been informed by his western Allies that the planned landings on the coast of western Europe would finally happen at the end of May. No doubt the suspicious Stalin would have confirmed this via his excellent Soviet intelligence service.

The Belorussian Balcony

Between mid-January and 1 April 1944 the siege of Leningrad had been lifted and Novgorod liberated. To the south, in April and May, the Crimea was freed, ending the threat to the flank of the Soviet advance into western Ukraine. The result left the massive German salient ranging around Vitebsk, the vital rail junction at Orsha and down to the area of Bobruysk. To both the German and Soviet armies, this became known as the 'Belorussian Balcony'.

German High Command expected the offensive to come to the south, continuing the success on the Ukrainian front – south of the vast Pripyat marshes and aimed at Moldavia and Romania, well south of the balcony. Meanwhile, the small Soviet team completed its plan, and at the final meetings the STAVKA (the Soviet forces' main headquarters) decided to attack north of the marshes, straight at Army Group North's heart, while managing a careful deception that it intended to attack in the south. Germany, led by its assumptions, was convinced.

After robust debate, it was decided that the Soviet attack would be based on two axes of attack, to maximize its superior numbers and minimize the options left to Germany in response. In the west, D-Day – the Allied landings in Normandy – got under way on 6 June. In keeping with the agreements of the Tehran conference, Stalin was ready to launch his massive offensive in the east. Germany was now truly fighting on two fronts.

The final formations of Soviet forces gathered at their frontline locations – 2.4 million men, 5300 aircraft, more than 36,000 guns and heavy mortars, and 5200 tanks. Facing them were 1.2 million German and Axis troops, with 1350 aircraft, 9500 guns and 900 tanks. On 20 June 1944, coordinated partisan attacks began on important rail junctions and supply routes behind German lines. On the first night alone almost 150 trains were derailed. Following the deception plan, Soviet forces sent a diversionary attack into the southern sector, and what few reserves Germany had hurried south.

On 22 June small attacks began along the front, supported by scattered air strikes. The main barrage and main attack began the following day. Following well-rehearsed routines, Soviet infantry attacked behind artillery barrages. When they cleared an opening in the German lines, tanks stormed forwards, while above flew waves of Il-2s destroying German anti-tank positions. Luftflotte 6, supporting Army Group Centre, was in a sad state, with only 40 to 60 serviceable fighters and not enough fuel. It could make little contribution to the battle, Soviet air superiority was total.

Hitler insisted that a number of 'fortified places' be held at all costs. As a result tens of thousands of German soldiers were killed or captured; usually killed. Mogilev fell on 28 June; Minsk on 3 July. On 5 July the second phase of this truly massive battle began. Heavy artillery forces moved south of the Pripyat marshes, and the offensive continued through Kovel, pushing on to reach Poland as the front to the north finally eliminated the balcony and with it almost all of Army Group Centre.

LAVOCHKIN LA-5
The Lavochkin La-5FN, seen here being refuelled at a forward airstrip, made its appearance at the front in March 1943, and soon began to make its presence felt in the hands of some very competent Soviet fighter pilots. Among them was Ivan Kozhedub, who went on to score 62 kills while flying Lavochkin fighters, making him the top-scoring Allied air ace.

SPECIAL OPERATIONS: Partisan Support

Aircraft flying singly, rather than in formation, made it possible to fly into enemy airspace, usually at night, relatively safe and undetected. Crews could then carry out various missions in support of resistance groups on the ground such as resupply or infiltrating operatives. Small groups of aircraft could also pinpoint specific targets, proven with the successful raid on the dams of the Ruhr Valley in May 1943 by No. 617 Squadron RAF. These specialist operations were carried out not only in occupied Europe, but also in the jungles of Burma, with the dropping of the Chindits, a small guerilla-type unit sent into the rear of Japanese lines to disrupt supply. These units were resupplied by air, and small Piper Cub aircraft also evacuated casualties from jungle clearings.

Aiding the resistance

Members of the resistance in occupied Europe, especially France, were hugely important in defeating the Axis armies. They supplied information on troop numbers and movements, sabotaged transport and communications links, and aided in the plight of downed Allied airmen, helping them to return to Britain and continue the fight. Special Duties Squadrons of the RAF were tasked with helping to carry out these roles. Based in Britain, North Africa and, after 1944, Italy, these units flew in massive amounts of weapons, ammunition and radio equipment to be used by resistance groups.

At the beginning of World War II, the RAF's Special Operations Squadrons used aircraft passed on to them from Bomber Command. The Armstrong Whitworth Whitley found a new lease of life as a clandestine supply transport, painted entirely in black. Another aircraft associated with these operations was the Westland Lysander. Originally designed as an army cooperation aircraft, it had remarkable short take-off and landing capabilities, making it the perfect platform for delivering operatives and rescuing downed airmen, as it could land on any reasonably open field. From the end of 1942, the mainstay of the RAF's long-range special duties operations was the Handley

SPECIAL DUTIES
Special Duties operations cost the Allies many aircraft and crews, especially on supply drops to the Netherlands. Between January 1942 and March 1945, for example, No. 138 (SD) Squadron lost over 80 aircraft in operations over Europe.

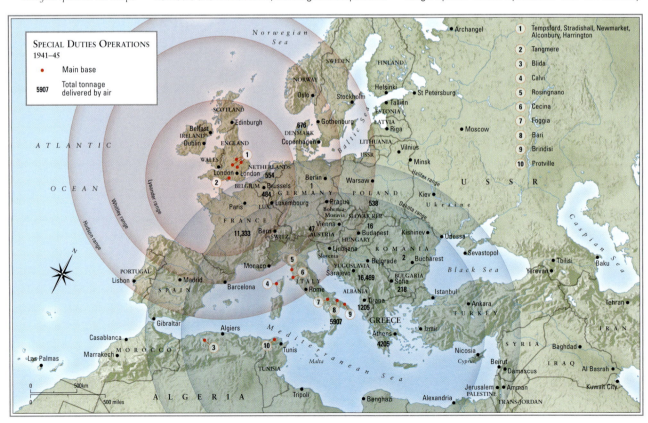

Special Operations: Partisan Support

Page Halifax, which replaced the Whitley. It remained the standard long-range type in service with Nos 138, 148, 161 and 624 Squadrons, and the Polish 1586 Flight, until mid-1944, when it was replaced by the Short Stirling.

During the Warsaw Uprising of August 1944, the western Allies attempted to supply beleaguered Polish fighters with weapons and medical supplies. This involved flying enormous distances and having to ask permission from the Soviet Union to land in its sphere of influence. Several missions were flown totalling more than 200 sorties, but many of the supplies dropped fell into German hands or were not plentiful enough. In Yugoslavia, the partisans under Tito were plentifully supplied by the Allies, as their operations tied down German troops to garrison the area that could have been used on other fronts. The Yugoslavs were supplied with the greatest tonnage of supplies during the war, with RAF Douglas C-47 Dakotas and Halifaxes flying from bases in North Africa and Italy.

Resistance in Southeast Asia

In Southeast Asia the Chindits, under the command of Brigadier Orde Wingate, established themselves as a long-range penetration group. Their task was to disrupt Japanese lines of communication and generally spread fear and uncertainty in Japanese rear areas. The group's only source of supply was by air, and after its first mission ended with the loss of many men a stop was put operations.

The United States saw the merits of such forces and created its own, named 'Merrill's Marauders', after its commander General Frank Merrill. These units would have a whole USAAF group to aid in supply and infiltration, as well as counterparts in the RAF. In 1944 units were flown into landing zones deep in the Burmese jungle. These were then fortified and units sent out on raiding duties. Dakotas flew more than 9000 troops to these landing grounds. Fighting was immediately heavy, as Japan recognized the importance of putting the landing sites out of action as soon as possible, effectively leaving the Allied soldiers stranded. After nearly two months of fighting and limited success, the Allied soldiers were withdrawn.

Missions were also carried out by RAF squadrons of de Havilland Mosquitos, including an attack on Amiens prison, which held resistance operatives about to be executed by the Gestapo. The Mosquitos flew at extemely low level and bombed the prison's walls and buildings. Unfortunately some prisoners were killed in the attack, but many more managed to escape.

WESTLAND LYSANDER
The Westland Lysander found fame flying clandestine operations. This large aircraft could be fitted with long-range fuel tanks and a ladder to aid the rapid entry or exit of an agent.

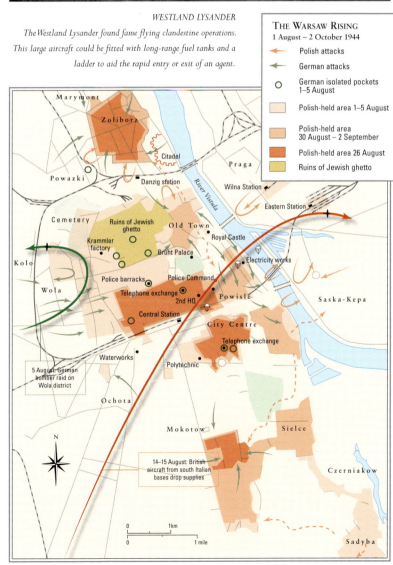

183

The End of the Reich

THE END OF THE REICH

LAST DEFENCE
Designed by Alexander Lippisch, the Me 163 was powered by a liquid-fuel rocket motor. It had an incredible climb rate and could reach speeds in excess of 900kph (550mph). Messerschmitt also designed the Me 262, the first turbojet-powered aircraft to enter combat service.

By the beginning of 1945, Germany was on the brink of defeat. Its aircraft and tanks were thirsty for fuel after Allied bombardment of oil and synthetic oil facilities, and transportation and communication links obliterated. Manufacturing, though damaged, was still churning out weapons of war, but these were redundant without fuel to power them.

Yet the German High Command had still been able to launch its last major ground offensive: the Battle of the Bulge. This was to be the last desperate attempt to split the advancing Allies, with the aim of reaching Antwerp; however, the gamble relied on capturing Allied fuel reserves. It almost worked, with Allied air power being stymied by bad weather over the Christmas period. Operation Bodenplatte was to be carried out in conjunction with this attack, but it, too, had to be cancelled because of the same bad weather affecting the Allies. Instead it was launched on January 1 1945 and entailed a surprise attack on 17 Allied airfields in Belgium, the Netherlands and France, with the aim of destroying as many Allied aircraft as possible while they were still on the ground. Every Luftwaffe fighter and fighter-bomber unit that could be spared was moved west for the operation.

Fatal flaw
The German attack was led by pathfinders from night-fighter units, their main force being made up of Focke-Wulf Fw 190 and Messerschmitt Bf 109 fighters. They were meant to arrive over their targets at nine in the morning, before many Allied aircraft were airborne, flying at treetop height to avoid radar detection. The routes flown by the fighters took them over heavily defended German ground positions, particularly around the V1 and V2 launch sites. Knowledge of the attack had not filtered down to the flak units, and the men on the ground, used to Allied air superiority, unwittingly opened up on their comrades. This was compounded by the fact that many of the pilots, straight out of training, were flying higher and slower than more experienced fellow airmen. They made easy pickings for the well-practised anti-aircraft gunners of both sides.

The Luftwaffe found many of the bases easily, and managed to put in numerous strafing and bomb runs. Again the newer pilots showed their inexperience, this time with poor marksmanship. Still, nearly 500 Allied aircraft were destroyed on the ground, for the loss of some 280 aircraft out of 1000 employed during the mission. The operation was a tactical success, but many pilots were killed or forced to bail out over Allied-held territory. The loss of these pilots was far worse than any loss of machines. The Allies replaced their lost aircraft within weeks; the Luftwaffe, although showing extreme daring, had achieved little and lost a great deal.

The bombing of Dresden
The bombing of Dresden proved to be another controversial decision made by Allied bomber commanders. With the Allied advance in the west slowing as it approached the river Elbe, the RAF and USAAF opted to attack the previously untouched city. A major cultural landmark, it was estimated that the city held more than 100 factories and was a major transport and communications hub for shifting German troops from the west to the east to meet the ever-approaching Soviet Red Army.

The first attack was to be flown by the Eighth Air Force, but bad weather over the target meant that the first mission fell to Bomber Command on the night of 13 February 1945. Pathfinders marked the old town around the marshalling yards, a heavily built-up area constructed mostly of timber. The main force following dropped high explosives, including 1800kg (4000lb) 'Cookie' bombs that blew the roofs off buildings, allowing incendiaries to fall among the exposed roof beams. By the time the second wave arrived, the fires could be seen burning hundreds of miles away. The intensity did not let up on 14 February with the Eighth Air Force's arrival. More than 300 Boeing B-17s dropped their load on the already shattered city. The next day the Eighth was to bomb a synthetic oil plant near Leipzig, but it was obscured by cloud. It attacked Dresden again instead, causing even more damage.

On 3 February, nearly 1000 B-17s were sent on a daylight raid to Berlin, aiming to destroy the city's rail links. Like Dresden, Berlin was thought to be a hub for sending troops to the Eastern Front. The city was attacked again two weeks later. The bombings were reinforced by nuisance raids from RAF de Havilland Mosquitos for a full month until Soviet forces were on the capital's outskirts. By the end of April, Hitler was dead; a little more than a week later, the war in Europe would be over.

The End of the Reich

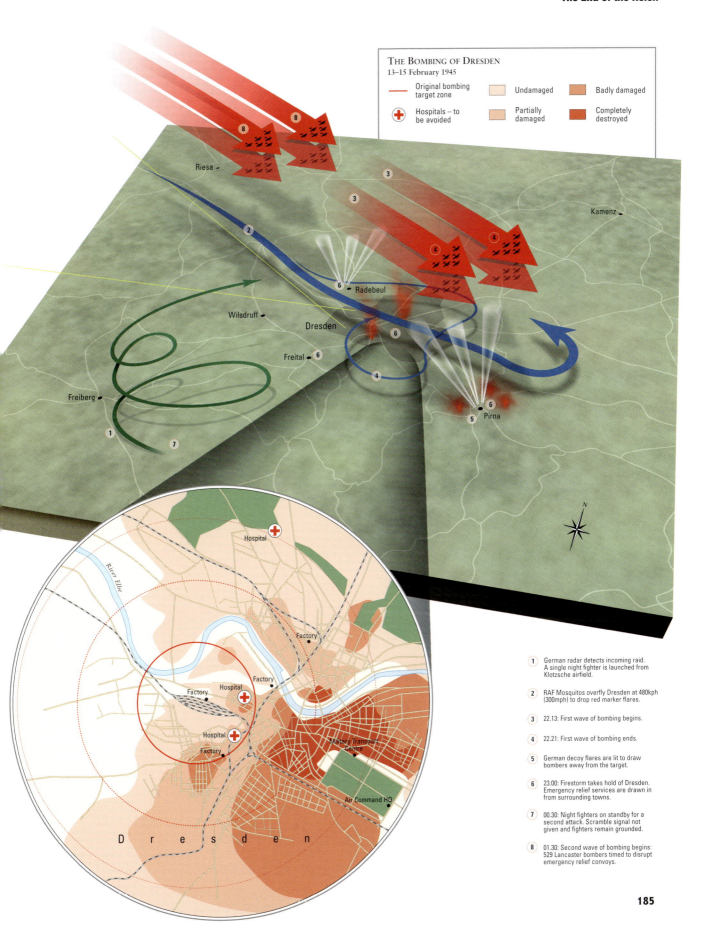

B-29: Development and Deployment

In the summer of 1940, the Government of the United States sent a letter to all major aircraft manufacturers requiring a radical new type of bomber. It was looking for a machine that could transport a large bombload over a range of 8400km (5000 miles) at an average speed of 500kph (300mph). Boeing immediately took the lead, having worked on improving the already operational B-17 Flying Fortress. Boeing envisioned everything that the government required, as well as the aircraft being completely pressurized, a feature it had proven in the pre-war Stratoliner commercial transport plane. Another innovation was the aircraft's central fire control system, which utilized an early analogue computer that gunners could operate in order to figure out variables such as airspeed and angle of attack so that their guns would hit their targets. These were then translated to the remotely operated turrets situated two above the fuselage and two below. Any gunner, bar the tail gunner, could take control of one or all turrets in order to concentrate fire when engaging an enemy.

Problems with pressurization arose with the need to open the bomb bay, which in a traditional aircraft would have resulted in total depressurization at altitude. This was resolved by incorporating a tubular catwalk between the aircraft's fore and aft sections.

Flying the prototype

The first prototype of the B-29 Superfortress flew on 21 September 1942. Initial impressions were good, particularly for an aircraft with such a large airframe, but disaster struck on 18 February 1943, when the second prototype crashed due to a double engine failure, killing all the crew. The engine used on the B-29 was the Wright R-3350, rushed into production specifically for the project. It was notoriously prone to overheating, a problem that was never completely remedied during its career.

B-29 production was spread out across the United States, resulting in manufacturing problems. As the aircraft was so advanced and designs were being changed all the time, as soon as one rolled off the line it would have to go to another line to have additional improvements fitted.

Bringing the B-29 into service

Major General H.H. 'Hap' Arnold, Chief of the USAAF, put General Kenneth Bonner Wolfe in charge of overseeing all aspects of B-29 production and introduction to service, implementing intense training programmes. Initially impeded by the lack of aircraft, men trained on war-weary Consolidated B-24 Liberators, as B-29 pilots were usually drawn from returning crew of this type. Although they were used to flying a large aircraft, they were not used to the aircraft's vastly improved speed.

On the B-29 would be a crew of 11: commander, pilot, bombardier, navigator, flight engineer, radio operator, radar operator, central fire control gunner and three more gunners. Men trained separately for these roles and were often not formed into crews until departure to forward operating bases.

The B-29's arrival with its units meant that the Allies now had a weapons platform that could deliver a payload to the Japanese home islands and put Japan's war production and population under increasing pressure. The one place where these attacks could be launched from was central southern China, already used as a base for Claire Chennault's Flying Tigers and Chiang Kai Shek's Chinese nationalist forces. This required the first bomb wing to deploy by flying via Marrakech, Cairo, Karachi and Calcutta, before reaching the final staging posts in eastern India, then flying over the 'Hump' of the Himalayas. Flying to its new bases around Chengdu, the newly activated XX Bomber Command began building up its supplies before launching its first attack on Japan. This was complicated by the amount of fuel required to be flown in from India; flying in 1 gallon of fuel for the B-29 used up 2–3 gallons flying over the 'Hump' to get it there. Stockpiling it was both time-consuming and extremely uneconomical.

BOEING B-29 SUPERFORTRESS
The establishment of five operational bases in the Marianas in March 1945 brought the B-29s much closer to Japan, and four bombardment wings, the 73rd, 313th, 314th and 315th, were quickly redeployed there from their bases in India and China, being followed a little later by the 58th BW. All the B-29 wings came under the control of XXI Bomber Command, with its HQ on Guam.

B-29: Development and Deployment

After the airstrips had been completed by Chinese labourers, and enough supplies had arrived, XX Bomber Command was ready to launch the first raid of what became Operation Matterhorn. Some cursory build-up raids were carried out on targets in Thailand with disappointing results, and an alarming rate of planes aborted even before they had reached the target due to the inevitable engine failures. Then, on 14 June 1944, 68 B-29s took off to bomb the Imperial Steel and Iron Works on the southern Japanese island of Kyushu. In all, 47 aircraft made it to the target just as darkness fell. The target was not hit, and XX Bomber Command lost one aircraft to enemy action and half a dozen to accidents. It was an inauspicious start to the B-29's career. The next raid could not be launched for another three weeks, again highlighting supply problems. B-29s returned

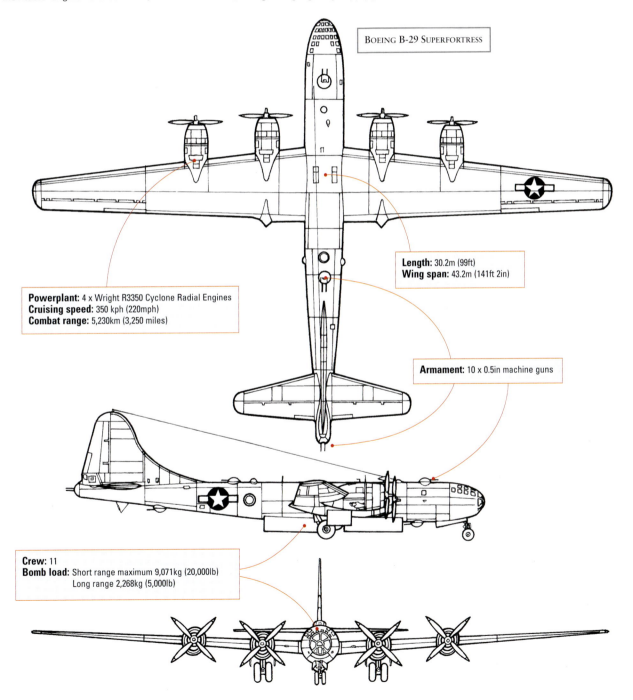

BOEING B-29 SUPERFORTRESS

Length: 30.2m (99ft)
Wing span: 43.2m (141ft 2in)

Powerplant: 4 x Wright R3350 Cyclone Radial Engines
Cruising speed: 350 kph (220mph)
Combat range: 5,230km (3,250 miles)

Armament: 10 x 0.5in machine guns

Crew: 11
Bomb load: Short range maximum 9,071kg (20,000lb)
Long range 2,268kg (5,000lb)

B-29: Development and Deployment

to southern Japan on 7 and 9 July, but caused little damage and accumulated yet more casualties.

General Wolfe, commander of XX Bomber Command, was recalled to Washington and replaced by Major General Curtis LeMay, fresh from commanding a bombardment division of the Eighth Air Force in Europe. He immediately made his presence felt by implementing formation changes he had developed in the European theatre of operations, which improved accuracy results on targets. Despite this, XX Bomber Command was still averaging only a mission a month. Another important weapon that LeMay introduced was the incendiary bomb, particularly potent in Asia's predominantly timber cities. A raid by 84 B-29s on Hankow in China left the city burning for three days.

Moving the base of operations

After Japan launched Operation Ichi-Go, which thrust into the interior of China with the aim of capturing Allied airfields, and faced with a prohibitively high attrition rate to enemy action and accidents, the United States began winding down operations flying B-29s from China. With the capture of the Marianas chain, the USAAF now had airstrips within range of Tokyo. More importantly, these could be easily supplied by ships sailing directly from the United States or Australia, in contrast to the limited supply route over the 'Hump'.

The Marianas were made up of the principal islands of Saipan, Tinian and Guam. Vast bases had been constructed there in record time, with most of the work being carried out by Naval Construction Battalions, or Seabees. The first B-29 touched down in October 1944; by late November 100 B-29s were stationed at the newly named Isley Field on Saipan.

Missions were flown against Japanese positions on Truk and Iwo Jima, but the problems of engine failure and poor accuracy still prevailed. On 24 November, 111 B-29s were dispatched to Tokyo, the first bombers to overfly the Japanese capital since the infamous Doolittle raid of 1942. As the bombers flew up to formation at 8200m (27,000ft) they hit the jet stream over Japan, a weather phenomenon yet to be identified. This made holding formation extremely difficult, and a minimum of ordnance found the target; the rest was wildly scattered by the high winds and cloud banks.

Missions continued over the next few weeks. All were effected by flying high to avoid the worst of the Japanese anti-aircraft fire and fighters. The B-29 crews were taking more casualties than they were inflicting on the ground. Change had to be wrought if the B-29, after all its expense and effort, was to prove its worth.

Arnold, dismayed by the B-29's lack of impact, assigned LeMay to assume command of XXI Bomber Command in the Marianas. Having noted the impact of the fire-bombing of Hankow, he wanted to repeat the success on Japanese cities. Raids with incendiaries were carried out on Tokyo in February 1945, but these were still being flown from 8200m (27,000ft) or more, to escape the worst of the Japanese defences. The raids caused more damage than previous ones, but LeMay still thought more could be done. He decided on a similar approach to that of the RAF in Europe: night-time incendiary raids, led by a pathfinder force. The first of these night raids went in on 9/10 March against Tokyo. It caused a massive firestorm and killed an estimated 84,000 people. The B-29 was starting to make an horrific impact.

By June, 60 per cent of Japan's six major cities lay in ashes. Japan's industry was all but crippled. Along with the naval mines the B-29s were now dropping on Japanese home waters, preventing the movement of mercantile shipping essential to Japan's survival, the B-29 greatly assisted in shortening of the Pacific conflict. But there was still one more task for the giant aircraft to perform.

THE MARIANAS BASE
The move to the Marianas was followed by a complete revision of tactics, the B-29s now carrying out large-scale night incendiary area attacks on Japan's principal cities, with devastating results.

B-29: Development and Deployment

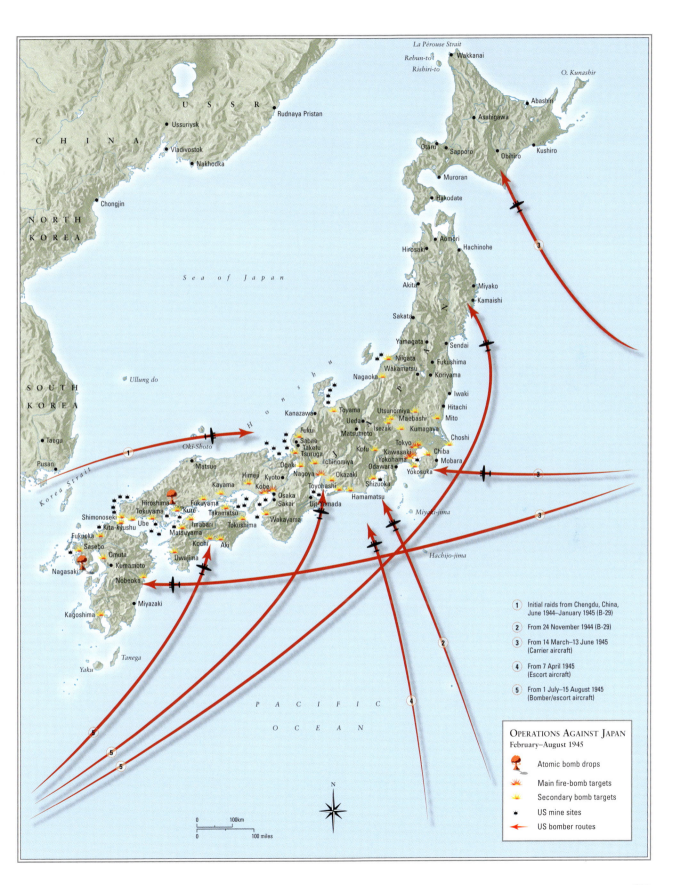

NUCLEAR WAR

BOMBING OF NAGASAKI
This vast mushroom cloud was created by 'Fat Man' exploding about 550m (1,800ft) above Nagasaki on 9 August 1945.

On 6 August 1945, the first atomic weapon to be used in war, 'Little Boy', was dropped on the Japanese city of Hiroshima, killing an estimated 70,000 people almost instantly. Three days later another atomic bomb, 'Fat Man', was dropped on Nagasaki, exacting a similar death toll. Much debate has gone into the question of whether the Allies needed to use such a destructive weapon. Many felt that Japan was already beaten, especially with the Soviet Union's entry into the conflict, when it declared war on Japan and invaded Manchuria on 9 August. Japan's civilian administration was already pursuing a peace policy, and it was only the military hierarchy that wanted to continue the fight to its bloody conclusion.

With scientific assistance from the United Kingdom and Canada, the US Government had set up the Manhattan Project in pursuit of building the first atomic weapon, a device so destructive that whoever had it in their possession held the strategic initiative. The Allies chose a policy of strategic bombing involving the bombing of civilian targets to break the enemy's industrial infrastructure and lower morale. The atomic bomb would take destruction to a new, horrific level.

Hammering the message home

Many of Japan's major cities had been hit in raids carried out by the new Boeing B-29 Stratofortress bomber, using incendiaries that decimated cities. The vast majority of housing in Japanese cities was constructed of wood. This, combined with the traditionally narrow streets, meant that bombing caused huge civilian casualties; 100,000 civilian lives were claimed in Tokyo alone. During the invasion of Okinawa and Iwo Jima, the US forces suffered appalling losses, leading to speculation of even greater losses of US servicemen in the planned invasion of mainland Japan itself. It was estimated that casualties there could be in the hundreds of thousands. The atomic bomb offered great force and the least amount of US casualties.

At Potsdam US President Harry S. Truman gave Japan the ultimatum to surrender or the 'alternative for Japan is prompt and utter destruction'. Japan declined, and Truman gave the order for the bomb to be dropped. The target of Hiroshima was chosen not for military reasons, or for its factories and installations, but because of its high population – the pyschological impact created by its bombing would be huge. Hiroshima had remained more or less untouched by the bombing campaign, and other than its central area was made up largely of wooden buildings, lending itself to utter destruction from this new weapon.

Enola Gay, the B-29 bomber piloted by the commander of the 509th Composite Bomb Group, Colonel Paul Tibbets, was accompanied on its mission by two other B-29s to record the event. At 8.15 a.m. the bomb was released, then detonated 580m (1900ft) above Hiroshima. Almost the entire city was affected by the blast, and an estimated 70,000 people were killed immediately. The blast radius was 1.6 km (1 mile), and the resultant fires destroyed everything within a further 7km (4 miles).

Nuclear War

Three days later *Bockscar*, flown by Major Charles W. Sweeny, dropped 'Fat Man' on the city of Nagasaki, a large port in the south of Japan that was home to several large factories; again its buildings were constructed mostly of wood. Cloud over the primary target of Kokura led *Bockscar* to overfly Nagasaki as a secondary option, The bomb was released at 11.01 a.m. and killed an estimated 70,000 people. This second display of ultimate power led Japan to accept unconditional surrender.

Use of these weapons and their destructive power has been the centre of much controversy,. Many believe that use of the atomic bomb should not have been authorized and that invasion of the Japanese home islands was the only viable option. Others argue that it was a necessary show of strength to the Soviet Union, which was at the time invading Manchuria and already in possession of large parts of central and eastern Europe. The bomb's after effects and the suffering it caused to tens of thousands for many years after the event highlights why this horrific weapon has not been used again – and hopefully never will be.

CREW OF ENOLA GAY
Colonel Paul Tibbets (with pipe) is flanked by some of the crew of Enola Gay, *the B-29 that dropped the first atomic bomb.*

BOMBING OF HIROSHIMA
Extent of Fire and Limits of Blast Damage

THE POST-WAR WORLD

By the end of 1945 the vast armed forces assembled by the Allies had utterly defeated their Axis enemies. Much of Europe and large areas of Asia lay in ruins and faced starvation. The average soldier, sailor and airman yearned to go home, get back to the farm, factory floor or office, and resume 'normal' life. Their political masters faced a new reality, however, something akin to the old great power rivalry, but with a difference: ideology. The communist regime of the Soviet Union, with its huge, seemingly all-powerful Red Army, controlled a vast area of Eurasia reaching from central Germany in the west to Vladivostok in the east. In China the Communist Party was gaining influence and control. In the west, the United States and its allies regarded this new entity with a mix of enthusiasm for a wartime ally and nervousness at its potential power, communism representing as it did an ideological alternative to captalism, which had been less than successful during the Great Depression.

Britain's wartime leader Winston Churchill, now out of office after an election defeat, spoke in Fulton, Missouri, in March 1946. He warned: 'From Stettin in the Baltic to Trieste in the Adriatic, an Iron Curtain has descended across the continent.' His speech shocked many, but did highlight a new dynamic in the relationships between erstwhile allies. Most pinned their hopes for a peaceful post-war world on the newly formed United Nations, a world forum for solving international problems after the devastation of global war.

A new world order

For many people living in the war-ravaged regions, communism offered attractive solutions. It became clear to many western leaders that this trend and its ramifications for the balance of world power must in some way be confronted. In August 1947, when US President Harry Truman announced a doctrine of containment of totalitarianism, he meant communism. It became a critical task of western policy-makers to generate economic recovery in western Europe. This would offer the 'free' way of life more appeal when facing communist propaganda. The result was the Marshall Plan, named after the US Secretary of State, which pumped billions of dollars into reconstructing Europe, including Germany. This alarmed Stalin, who wanted the former enemy state kept as weak as possible. He decided on an all-out propaganda war, which in turn focused on the increasing divide in European politics.

The United Kingdom had ended the war in dire economic condition and benefited significantly from the Marshall Plan. The plan in part allowed it to maintain an army of occupation in Germany, together with significant air forces, deployed alongside its US allies. Air and sea power were where the western allies had a clear advantage over the Soviet 'threat'. On the European battlefield it was hoped that the available land forces would at least hold the line, the Rhine–Alps–Piave, when facing the Red Army, while air power would destroy its spearhead lines of supply. This emphasis on the use of air power was formalized by the US Department of Defense plan developed in 1949 under the code name Operation Dropshot.

Both the United States and the United Kingdom had ended the war with air forces that included large fleets of long-range heavy bombers, while the Soviet Air Force had been largely designed for tactical air support. During the period 1944–46 the Soviet Union had increased its emphasis on developing a long-range bomber force. Ironically,

ILYUSHIN IL-28
Designed as a tactical light bomber to replace the piston-engined Tupolev Tu-2, Ilyushin's Il-28 formed the mainstay of the Soviet Bloc's tactical striking forces during the 1950s and was widely exported to countries within the Soviet sphere of influence.

The Post-War World

the first manifestation was the Tupolev Tu-4, a reverse-engineered copy of the Boeing B-29 Superfortress. By 1948 this aircraft was being issued to long-range bomber squadrons.

Long-range enemies

News of this development threw the US Air Force into a state closely resembling panic. For the first time continental United States was within range of long-range enemy bombers operating from their home bases. As if to emphasize this threat, the Soviet Union exploded its first atomic bomb in 1949. A new balance of terror had begun to develop that gave impetus to the expansion and modernization of the US Strategic Air Command, which had been founded three years earlier. Alongside B-29s (later models were redesignated B-50) came the gigantic Convair B-36 Peacemaker from 1948.

If Operation Dropshot had been initiated, it would have deployed the bulk of Strategic Air Command's bombers, together with squadrons of Avro Lincolns and B-29s from RAF Bomber Command. These aircraft would have headed out on missions to obliterate 200 precisely designated targets within Soviet territory. Plans were also in place for the allied bomber force to deliver on target some 300 nuclear bombs, included among the thousands of bombs intended to wipe out 85 per cent of Soviet industrial potential in a single stroke. Between a quarter and one-third of bombloads were to be used to destroy Soviet aircraft on the ground. As the Allied bombers headed eastwards towards their targets they would have witnessed Tu-4s heading westwards on Soviet counterstrikes.

CONVAIR B-36
The huge Convair B-36 gave the USAF Strategic Air Command the ability to deliver nuclear weapons to any target anywhere in the world.

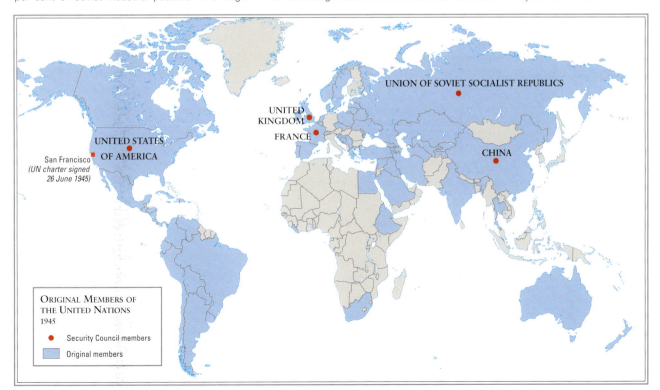

BERLIN AIRLIFT

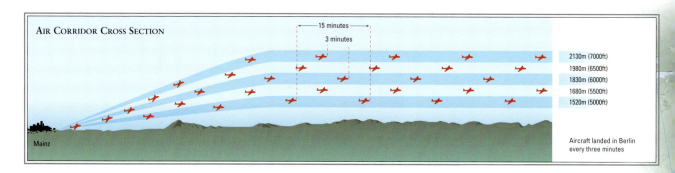

After the end of World War II, the United States, United Kingdom and France began to regard their occupied zones of Germany as one entity – what would become West Germany. The western Allies also occupied the western half of Berlin. On 21 June 1948, Germany's western half adopted a single currency. The Soviet Union saw this as a provocative act and immediately closed all surface traffic into Berlin, isolating its citizens. The Allies were unwilling to abandon west Berlin, but decided not to force through armed convoys to supply the city. They chose to fly in all the necessities of daily life, and so began the greatest air supply operation in aviation history.

Supplying the necessary

To hold out, the western-occupied half of Berlin needed around 4500 tons of supplies per day. The US Air Force had just over 100 Douglas C-47s stationed permanently in Europe; the RAF had a similar number of aircraft, Avro Yorks and more C-47s. Long-range maritime patrol flying boats, Short Sunderlands, were pressed into service, landing on the Havel lakes on the western outskirts of Berlin.

The airlift began on 26 June. As the operation gathered pace, so the concentration of transport aircraft increased, arriving on West German airfields from all over the world. Among these aircraft was the new Douglas C-54 Skymaster four-engined transport, capable of lifting a 10-ton load.

The Soviet Union expected the airlift to fail, recalling German attempts, on a smaller scale, to supply the surrounded Sixth Army at Stalingrad. To its astonishment, the airlift grew in capacity almost daily. By the end of the first month of operations, the airlift was delivering enough to keep the city going. The Soviet Union responded by flying fighter aircraft through the flight paths, guns occasionally firing, but not directly at the cargo aircraft. Hundreds of incidents were recorded by western aircrews, but none of the Soviet measures proved sufficient to disrupt the flow of supplies. As the airlift dragged on into winter, efforts were made to increase capacity at Berlin's airports. Extra runways were laid at Tempelhof, and Gatow and Tegel were rebuilt and extended. Ex-Luftwaffe ground crews were hired to shift cargo.

On Easter Sunday, 15/16 April 1949, a special attempt was made to boost the morale of Berliners. Aircrews worked around the clock and ran a total of 1383 flights carrying some 12,941 tonnes of fuel without loss. It was clear to the Soviet Union that the airlift was a major propoganda success, and it grudgingly agreed to lift the blockade. On 12 May the first land convoy reached Berlin. The airlift officially continued until 30 September 1949. On 278,288 flights it delivered 2,326,406 tonnes of supplies; the USAF contributed 76.7 per cent, the RAF 17 per cent and British civil aircraft 7.6 per cent.

TRAFFIC AT TEMPELHOF
USAF Military Air Transport Service unload their cargoes at Berlin's Tempelhof Airport. The C-47, known as the Dakota in RAF service, was the backbone of the Berlin Airlift.

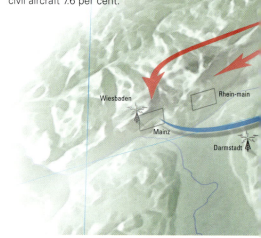

Berlin Airlift

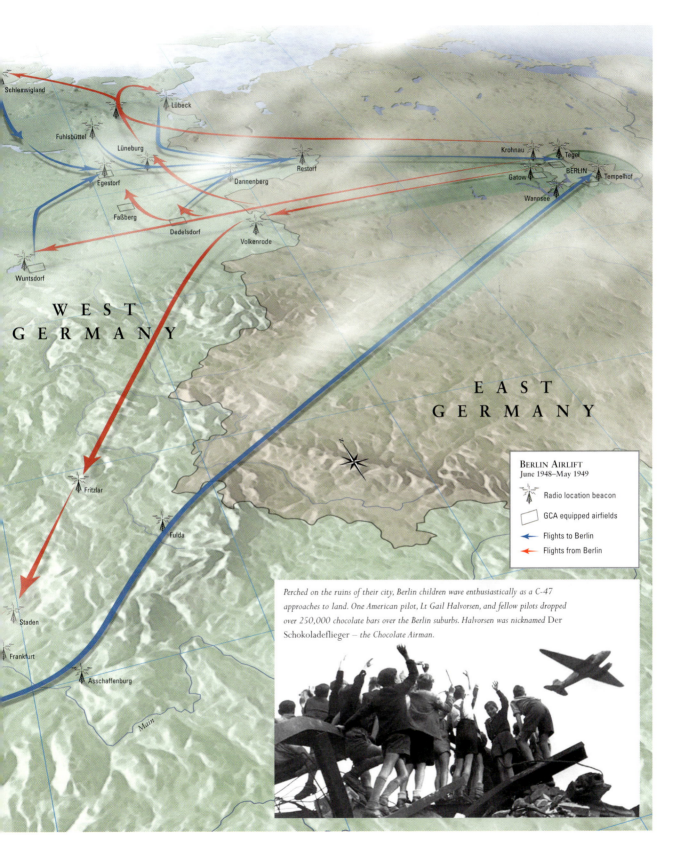

Perched on the ruins of their city, Berlin children wave enthusiastically as a C-47 approaches to land. One American pilot, Lt Gail Halvorsen, and fellow pilots dropped over 250,000 chocolate bars over the Berlin suburbs. Halvorsen was nicknamed Der Schokoladeflieger – the Chocolate Airman.

KOREA: 1950–53

On 25 June 1950, eight divisions of the North Korean Army surged over the 38th Parallel, a line separating the communist-controlled north from the United Nations-backed south. Supporting the ground units were Russian-manufactured aircraft of World War II vintage, such as Yakovlev Yak-9 and Lavochkin La-9 fighters and the Iluyshin Il-10, an improved version of the tried-and-tested Il-2 ground-attack aircraft.

The South Korean air force had no offensive aircraft, only trainers, and was of little help in stemming the relentless communist advance. South Korean forces were pushed back until they held a fragile perimeter around the port city of Pusan in the country's southeast. The nearest United Nations aircraft were stationed in Japan, on occupation duty. These aircraft included the North American F-82 Twin Mustang night-fighter and the Douglas B-26 Invader attack bomber. The Twin Mustangs, which had good endurance and were able to fly over the battlefield for extended periods of time, were used effectively to cover the advance. The B-26 also proved its worth by bombing, rocketing and strafing the extended North Korean supply lines, allowing the United Nations, led by the United States, to build up its forces and retaliate.

Enter the MiG

The United Nations forces, including contingents sent from Belgium, Australia, South Africa and the United Kingdom, would be led by the legendary General Douglas MacArthur, who immediately put down plans to make a landing at Inchon, at the rear of the North Korean forces. This would enable the capture of Seoul and the cutting of the communist supply line. As the Marines stormed ashore to face a completely surprised enemy, a vast variety of prop-driven aircraft supported them – an odd sight in the jet age. Chance Vought F4U Corsairs, North American F-51 Mustangs and Hawker Sea Furies all flew ground-support missions, allowing for capture of Seoul within a few days of the landings. With these successes and the communists being pushed back behind the 38th Parallel, MacArthur wanted to continue pursuit of the enemy and capture the entirety of Korea. It was at this point that China began to build up its forces behind the Yalu.

China not only a huge army to call upon, but also had been supplied with the latest jet fighter from Soviet Russia, the MiG-15. At the time of its introduction, nothing on the United Nations' side could compete with the MiG's speed and armament. The UN pilots, some flying jets such as the Grumman F9F Panther and others in piston-engined aircraft, did manage to score victories over the MiG. But the real saviour of the UN campaign in Korea in the early months was the Lockheed F-80, which bore the brunt of ground-

THE KOREAN WAR
In the early weeks of the Korean War, the North Korean offensive came close to succeeding, forcing the Allies to make a last stand inside a perimeter around the port of Pusan. It was air power, operating initially from bases in Japan, that brought the enemy to a standstill and bought time for reinforcements to arrive.

attack operations alongside the US Navy's aircraft until being supplanted by the Republic F-84 Thunderjet in 1952.

To counter the threat of the MiGs, the US Air Force's latest jet fighter, the North American F-86 Sabre, was posted to the war zone. Although it initially arrived in small numbers, soon the force was considerable. These aircraft, in the hands of experienced pilots, soon achieved air superiority. The only thing holding them back from decimating the MiG force was the order that they could not fly over the Yalu River into Chinese airspace, infuriatingly allowing many MiGs to escape out of 'MiG Alley'.

Another veteran of World War II to fly in the Korean conflict was the huge Boeing B-29 Superfortress. It was used in the strategic bombing role, bombing industrial and transport targets in the north, as well as occasionally flying tactical missions bombing troop concentrations or bridges. These aircraft, despite their heavy defensive armament, were very susceptible to the MiG-15, and after substantial losses B-29s were relegated to flying night operations only.

A role for helicopters

Although employed in small numbers towards the end of World War II, the helicopter received its baptism of fire in Korea. It was ideal as a medical evacuation platform, flying casualties that may have otherwise succumbed to their wounds back to aid stations in the rear. It was also used to rescue downed airmen. At the forefront of this new type of aviation was the Bell H-13, recognizable by its large Plexiglass cockpit and scaffold-like tail section. It could carry two casualties, held in special litters attached to the helicopter's sides. By the end of the conflict larger helicopters such as the Sikorsky H-19 were in use. As well as flying medevac missions, they were now used as troop and supply transport.

Over the course of the three-year conflict a stalemate prevailed; no real advances were made after the initial offensives of 1950. Towards the end of July 1953 a ceasefire was agreed, halting any military action. No peace has been settled officially, however, effectively meaning that North and South Korea are still at war. The conflict was a transitional period for combat aircraft. Piston-engined aircraft, although still to be utilized in specialist roles, were replaced by the incredible speeds of the jet.

MIGS ON THE FLIGHTLINE
Soviet-built MiG-15 jet fighters sit on the flight line at Antung, Manchuria. The MiG-15 proved a formidable adversary, especially in the hands of the Soviet fighter pilots who flew most of the communist combat missions over Korea.

F-86A SABRE
United Nations pilots flying F-86 Sabres claimed to have destroyed ten MiGs for every Sabre lost in combat, but later research caused this figure to be drastically revised. Nevertheless, the Sabre established air superiority over north-western Korea.

World Realignment

WORLD REALIGNMENT

During the testing time of the Berlin Airlift the world crystallized into ideological blocks of communism and capitalism led respectively by the Soviet Union and the United States. The west viewed the immense power of the Soviet war machine controlling a vast portion of the Eurasian landmass with considerable anxiety. What was later dubbed as the Cold War may have had its origins in the political confrontation in Europe, but it soon spread around the world. In 1949 the United States and its allies formed the North Atlantic Treaty Organization (NATO), followed by the Southeast Asia Treaty Organization (SEATO) in 1954 and the Central Treaty Organization (CENTO) in 1955. In 1955 the Soviet Union and its satellites answered by forming the Warsaw Pact.

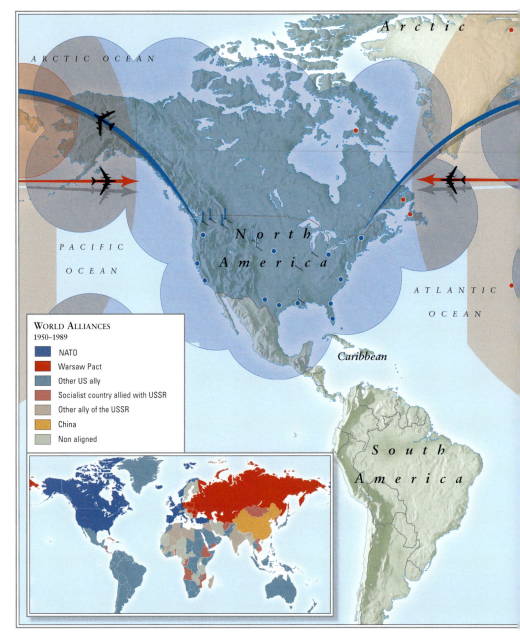

A NEW THREAT
At the end of World War II the new threat would come from air-delivered atomic weapons. The United States and the Soviet Union both developed long-range bombers capable of carrying an atomic bomb thousands of miles. To counter this, a vast defensive array of fighter cover was introduced. However, this would all become redundant with the introduction of the intercontinental ballistic missile at the end of the 1950s.

198

World Realignment

The Soviet Union based its military posture on vast conscript armies backed by a largely tactical air force. The West, unable to deploy conventional ground forces on the same scale, increasingly relied on nuclear weapons to create a convincing deterrent force. After the Soviet Union exploded its first nuclear weapon in 1949, a new climate of fear began to prevail. The West possessed far greater numbers of long-range bombers capable of hitting targets deep within Warsaw Pact territory. The Soviet Union also had long-range bomber forces, but never quite reached the numbers deployed by the United States and it allies. From the late 1950s ICBMs (Intercontinental Ballistic Missiles) began to replace bombers as the nuclear weapon's chosen delivery system.

For more than 50 years the great power blocks prepared themselves for war. Strategists devoted a great deal of time, energy and investment in the methodology of nuclear war and, importantly, how to avoid it. Theories developed varying from tactical nuclear wars to Mutual Assured Destruction – the MAD theory. On the periphery, the great powers tested each other's resolve in Korea and Vietnam, and for decades the world faced the possible – and sometimes likely – threat of nuclear war.

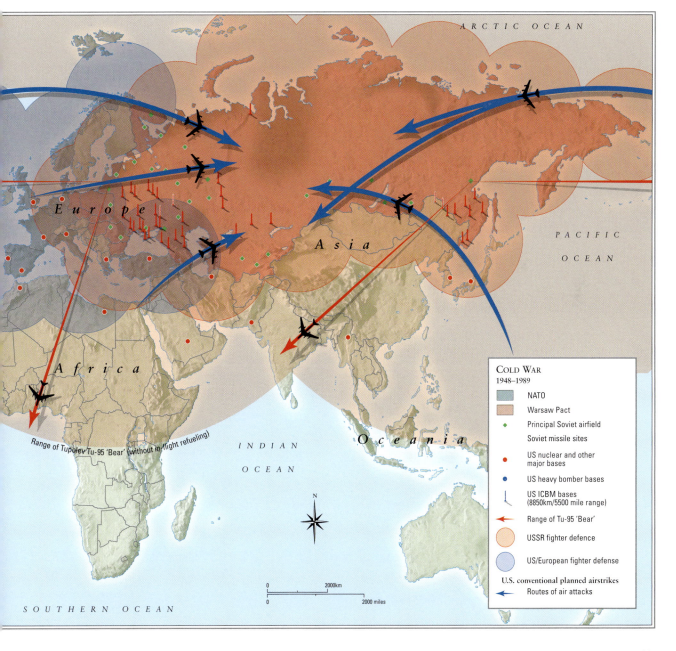

THE CUBAN MISSILE CRISIS

After Cuba endured a guerrilla war that destroyed the pro-American dictatorial regime of Fulgencio Batista, one of his most determined opponents, Fidel Castro, emerged as the new head of state. Castro's new government was gravely concerned with the probability of US intervention in the early days of his regime, but this did not prevent Castro from nationalizing American-owned businesses on the island. US President Dwight Eisenhower responded by declaring economic sanctions on Cuba and set about attempts to destabilize the regime of Castro and his eventual transformation of Cuba into a one-party socialist state.

Moscow kept a careful eye on these new developments in Cuba. By the time of US President John F. Kennedy's inauguration in January 1961, diplomatic relations between the United States and Cuba had finally been broken. Among the ruling elite surrounding Castro was a number of communists who urged a closer relationship with Moscow. Castro, eager to circumvent economic sanctions imposed by the United States, found a new trade and defence partner in the Soviet Union.

Meanwhile, President Kennedy had inherited a plan devised by the Central Intelligence Agency to use disaffected Cubans to mount an invasion and

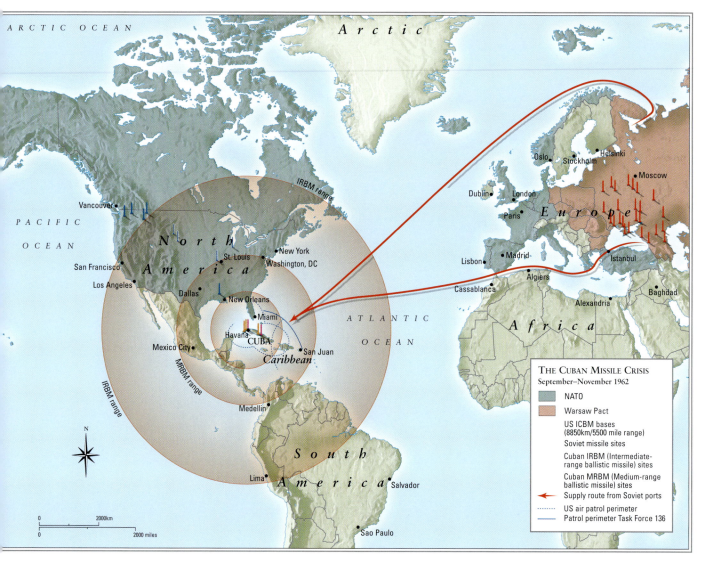

The Cuban Missile Crisis

raise an anti-Castro revolt. This attempt was finally launched in April 1961 when 1400 Cuban rebels landed in the Bay of Pigs. The invasion collapsed because of bad planning and a total lack of air support. It was not the plan envisaged by the CIA; nor did it deliver the popular uprising Kennedy desired.

The Bay of Pigs disaster and the subsequent Operation Mongoose, a secret plan approved by President Kennedy aimed at stimulating a US-supported uprising in Cuba, had the opposite effect, serving only to push Castro further into the Soviet fold. Soviet President Nikita Khrushchev pounced on the opportunity, persuading Castro to grant permission to establish missile bases on Cuba as an act of socialist solidarity. This move would allow the Soviet Union to close the missile gap. In the early 1960s the United States could deploy more ISBMs and IRBMs than the Soviet Union, It had also successfully deployed 15 Jupiter IRBMs at Izmir, Turkey, bringing Moscow to within just 15 minutes' flight time of the missiles – much to the annoyance of the Soviets.

Secret spy flights

Covert deployment of Soviet missiles and their supporting units in Cuba went ahead. A key role in revealing the Soviet Union's plans to base missiles in Cuba was now played by the Lockheed U-2 high-altitude reconnaissance aircraft, whose clandestine 'spy flights' over the Soviet Union had begun in 1956 and continued for four years, until one was shot down near Sverdlovsk on 1 May 1960 amid much publicity. On 14 October a U-2 reconnaissance flight photographed evidence of Soviet missile bases under construction in Cuba. Within a week the United States responded by imposing a limited quarantine on shipments of military supplies to Cuba and also ordered preparations for a major war. US strategic nuclear forces were placed on full alert. Within US Government circles there was discussion regarding immediate air strikes to destroy the missile bases. This was rejected as too serious an escalation, and there was also possibility that some Soviet missiles could launch, leading to full-scale war. It was hoped that the quarantine would allow time for a diplomatic solution.

President Kennedy made a television address to the nation on 22 October outlining the US position. Channels of communication were developed with the Soviet Union over the next few days, but initial exchanges produced very little. Soviet ships held their positions, reluctant to test the quarantine line. On 26 October, Khruschev sent a letter outlining a possible settlement, indicating a willingness to withdraw Soviet missiles from Cuba in return for a US promise not to invade. This letter was to some extent contradicted by an official statement from the collective Soviet leadership on the following day. This linked US missiles in Turkey with Soviet missiles in Cuba. On that same day, a U-2 reconnaissance flight was shot down while operating over Cuba. After some deliberation Kennedy decided to answer Khrushchev's letter and for the time being ignore the formal communique. The US Attorney General, Robert Kennedy, met with the Soviet Ambassador in Washington and assured him that there would be no invasion of Cuba, and offered an unofficial promise that US missiles in Turkey would be removed. He also gave a clear and unofficial warning that things were reaching a point of no return. Khrushchev, by now deeply worried, almost immediately accepted Kennedy's terms. The crisis had been averted.

LOW-LEVEL VOODOO
Low-level reconnaissance missions over Cuba were flown by McDonnell RF-101 Voodoos of the 363rd Tactical Reconnaissance Wing from Shaw Air Force Base, South Carolina, and by RF-8A Crusaders of the US Navy's Light Photographic Squadron 26.

RECONNAISSANCE PHOTO
As the Cuban missile crisis developed, US intelligence agencies identified 24 IRBM launchers on the island, of which 20 were fully operational. A further 33 SS-4s were stored at San Cristobal and Sagua la Grande, and more advanced SS-5 missiles were on the way.

Indochina and Vietnam

INDOCHINA AND VIETNAM

UH-1 IROQUOIS 'HUEY'
A soldier uses a smoke grenade as a marker as he waves a UH-1 'Huey' down onto a landing zone in Vietnam.

After World War II's end, the European powers attempted to retake control of their Far Eastern colonies previously lost to the Japanese onslaught. In French Indochina, the Communist Party was growing and wanted Vietnam free of the imperial yoke. Communists based in the country's north were backed by the newly formed Communist People's Republic of China, which supplied weapons and training to the Viet Minh. The French were backed by the United States, set on not allowing the further spread of communism. But the French were finally decisively beaten at the Battle of Dien Bien Phu, when an attempt to hold an air base deep in North Vietnam failed; the surrounded French paratroops, supplied only from the air, were eventually overrun by superior numbers. The French pulled out out of Vietnam after this defeat, but the United States continued to assist pro-western forces in the south of Vietnam, sending in military advisers and masses of equipment.

Among equipment send were Piasecki CH-21 'Flying Banana' and Bell UH-I 'Iroquois' helicopters, to aid the mobility of the Army of the Republic of Vietnam (ARVN). These machines entered battle under testing circumstances at the battle of Ap Bac. The Viet Cong, in good defensive positions and armed only with light weapons, managed to defeat a vastly superior and technologically advanced foe. US advisers saw first hand the susceptibility of helicopters in a 'hot' landing zone.

> **THE BATTLE OF AP BAC**
> 2 January 1963
>
> (1) American advisor to AVRN Lt. Col. John Paul Vann orbits the battlefield.
>
> (2) 1st Civil Guard Battalion approaching Ap Bac is pinned down by Viet Cong positions hidden in the treeline and forced to dig in.
>
> (3) CH-21s bringing in the 7th Infantry Battalion land 180m (600ft) from the western treeline. Taking small arms fire, two CH-21s are downed with a further two are heavily damaged while attempting to rescue the crew.
>
> (4) Supporting UH-1 Hueys make strafing runs. One Huey lands to rescue downed CH-21 pilots and is also lost.
>
> (5) M113 APCs are ordered in to protect the heli-troops, but are beaten off by stubborn VC defence.
>
> (6) Vann orders an AVRN parachute drop east of the village to block any VC escape route. The parachutes drop further west and come under heavy machine gun fire while descending.
>
> (7) A-1 Skyraiders drop napalm in order to destroy defenders but hit open areas and an empty hamlet instead.
>
> (8) Viet Cong withdraw having inflicted heavy casualties on the AVRN.

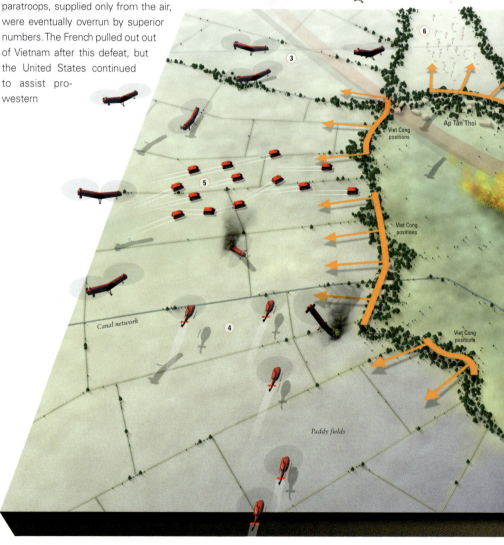

Indochina and Vietnam

Full-blown conflict

The Vietnam War escalated into full conflict in 1964, when the United States officially entered the struggle. What it had learned was that, if troops were to be flown into a landing zone in hostile territory, they must first of all suppress the enemy. This was achieved by fixing machine guns and rockets to the side of UH-I helicopters, at first with rudimentary mounts, then with properly fixed and sighted weapons stations. The helicopter gunship was born.

Fighting in the jungle with no definitive front line presented great problems for the US war machine. Fire bases were established, and from these patrols could be sent out to make contact with the enemy and destroy him. Locating an enemy operating in small numbers, who knew the terrain well and could melt back into the civilian population, was going to be difficult. Troops had to be moved great distances and rapidly, and again this is where the helicopter came in to its own. The distinctive 'whup whup' of the 'Huey's' rotor blades became the soundtrack to the Vietnam conflict.

As in the Korea, the helicopter was extensively used in the medevac role, saving many lives. This evolved into a highly successful combat rescue role. Flying with an escort of helicopter gunships or Douglas A-1 Skyraiders, helicopters searched the vast jungle for downed US airmen, and flew down to rescue them, often under fire. The Skyraiders and gunships gave covering fire during the rescue.

Ground support was another important aspect in the Vietnam War, but in the dense jungle it was difficult to recognize where the enemy was placed and where friendly forces were, especially flying in a 'fast mover' such as the North American F-100 Super Sabre or Republic F-105 Thunderchief. This is where the forward air controller, or FAC, came into his own. Flying in a small Cessna O-1 'Birddog', an FAC could loiter over the battle zone, marking enemy positions with smoke rockets and directing the final attack for the jet bombers flying in fast and low. Ground-attack aircraft often used an assortment of ordnance, napalm being particularly effective in the dense jungle.

CESSNA O-1 'BIRD DOG'
The Cessna O-1 was used extensively by forward air controllers in Vietnam, using smoke rockets to mark enemy positions for the 'fast movers' to come in and strike.

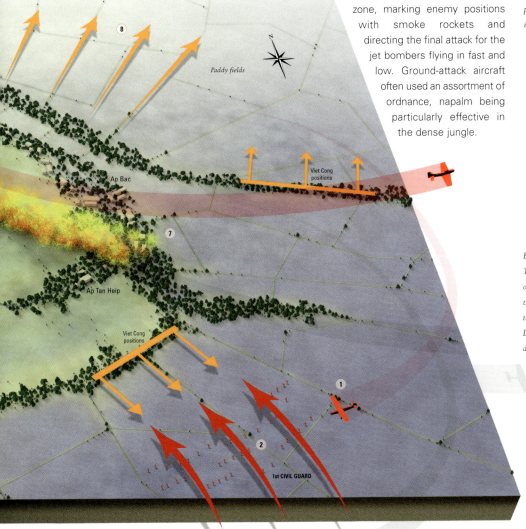

BATTLE OF AP BAC
The battle of Ap Bac started as an operation to seize a Viet Cong radio transmitter near the village, but a plan to land troops of the ARVN 7th Division in the area by helicopter went disastrously wrong when the South Vietnamese forces ran into an ambush. To add to the general confusion, Vietnamese Forward Air Controllers proved incapable of directing air strikes accurately. The battle was a clear victory for the Viet Cong, with 65 ARVN troops and 3 US advisors killed. The Viet Cong slipped away during the night while confused ARVN troops engaged each other in firefights.

Indochina and Vietnam

ROLLING THUNDER
In three years and nine months of Rolling Thunder operations, US fighter-bombers flew 304,000 missions, while B-52 bombers flew 2380, dropping a combined total of 643,000 tons of bombs on North Vietnam's war industry, transportation network and air defence complex.

From March 1965, air strikes on North Vietnam by USAF and US Navy aircraft were coordinated under the code name Rolling Thunder. The principal facets of this campaign would be to strangle the flow of men and arms to the fighting in the south, the lowering of North Vietnamese morale and destruction of industrial bases. North Vietnam was split up into 'packages', each with specific targets. The most important was VI, with its inclusion of Hanoi and North Vietnam's principal port, Haiphong. Incredibly, decisions regarding the targeting of enemy positions was not made by commanders in theatre, but often by politicians back in Washington, leading to targets being hit but not destroyed, and events moving on before the task was complete.

Flying these missions were F-105 Thunderchiefs and F-100 Super Sabres. The Thunderchief, or 'Thud', was capable of carrying an impressive load, and would have to be refuelled in flight before making the final run into North Vietnam, as vast amounts of fuel were burned as it struggled to heave its combat load to operational height. These aircraft were led in by a type of pathfinder force, flying Douglas EB-66s that were packed with navigational aids. On their mark the flight would loose their bombs and make a hasty retreat.

North Vietnamese air defence was at first made up of a few surface-to-air missiles (SAMs), but was mostly anti-aircraft artillery. US bombing operations had to be flown with more and more escorts against the highly manoeuvrable MiG-17. More sophisticated SAM systems were also supplied by the Soviet Union and China, forcing the United States to think of more and more effective countermeasures. Missions were flown using newly arrived McDonnell F-4 Phantom IIs. Tricking the enemy into believing they were on a usual bombing run to the north, they were laden with air-to-air missiles, and vast dogfights would break out above the city of Hanoi.

'Wild Weasel'

SAMs were becoming an increasing problem. Soviet SA-2 'Guideline' missiles were introduced into the North Vietnamese air defence system in 1965. These claimed their first US aircraft, an F-4C Phantom, on 23 July of that year. The United States quickly introduced defence suppression aircraft known as 'Wild Weasels' – first F-100F Super Sabres, then F-105s, and later F-4 Phantoms. These aircraft flew in ahead of the bombing flight of aircraft and attempted to suppress SAM defences. They carried electronic countermeasures and 'Shrike' anti-radar missiles that could home in on the radar emissions of the SAM sites. The missions were successful, but SAMs were so prevalent that aircraft still fell to them. In 1968 the operation against the North was wound down. Poor command structure meant that no real damage had been done, and North Vietnam continued to fight. It would be nearly another four years before a concerted attempt was made to bomb the North out of the war.

US Air Force bombers based in Thailand and the US Navy aircraft on 'Yankee Station' in the Gulf of Tonkin continued to fly missions in support of the ground war in this interim period, as well as flying

MIKOYAN-GUREVICH MIG-21 By September 1966 The North Vietnamese Air Force had received some numbers of the MiG-21, armed with Atoll infra-red AAMs and operating from five bases in the Hanoi area. The tactics employed by the MiG pilots involved flying low and then zooming up to attack the heavily-laden fighter-bombers, mainly F-105 Thunderchiefs, forcing them to jettison their bomb loads as a matter of survival.

missions against the Ho Chi Minh Trail. This often led to them dropping their ordnance in neighbouring Laos and Cambodia, as the trail flowed out of North Vietnam into these countries, then back into South Vietnam. (The Ho Chi Minh Trail was a vital communication artery for the North Vietnamese, enabling them to infiltrate supplies and indeed entire NVA army regiments into the south.) The Boeing B-52 Stratofortress was often used in the tactical role, bombing large areas of jungle where the enemy was suspected to be hiding. The enormous bombloads could be devastating, but often fell on empty forest and did very little real damage.

In April 1972 bombing of North Vietnam began again with Operation Linebacker I. NVA troops had surged into the south, and US ground troops were pulled out of the front line. It was now up to US air power and the ARVN to prevent the communists taking control. The port of Haiphong was mined, strangling incoming supplies. It was then hoped to destroy stockpiled munitions and supplies. On 18 December 1972, after another breakdown in peace talks, President Richard Nixon ordered resumption of air strikes above the 20th Parallel (Linebacker II). This developed into the heaviest bombing offensive of the war, with round-the-clock attacks on targets. North Vietnam responded to the 11-day campaign by using up almost all of its missile stocks, but electronic countermeasures helped to keep US losses to a minimum. Of 26 aircraft lost, 15 were B-52s shot down by SAMs. Deprived of most of its air bases, the NVAF could launch only 32 aircraft; eight were shot down. On 15 January 1953, with peace talks again in progress, the United States announced an end to all offensive operations against North Vietnam. A ceasefire came into effect on 28 January.

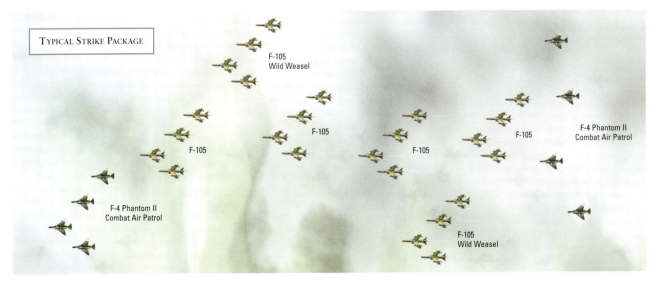

ARAB-ISRAELI WARS

In May 1948 the UK Mandate in Palestine ceased to exist and the state of Israel came into being. An influx of Jewish immigrants from all over Europe and Soviet Russia displaced many Arab Palestinians into the neighbouring Arab countries of Egypt, Syria, Jordan and Iraq. This caused significant discord in the region, and conflict was almost inevitable.

Equipping a new air force
Egypt immediately began strikes against Israel by converting Douglas C-47 transports into makeshift bombers, as well as using Supermarine Spitfires in the ground-attack role. Israel was poorly equipped and scoured Europe for an effective deterrent. It eventually acquired a number of Avia S.199s, a Czech derivative of the Messerschmitt Me 109. These were immediately pressed into service. By October of 1948 the new Israeli Air Force (IAF) was far better equipped, with more than 40 Spitfire IXs and a small number of Boeing B-17s for strategic bombing, as well as a mix of many other World War II types. Ever increasing in strength, Israel had faced down its first test of conflict. It would be nearly a decade before it entered its next confrontation.

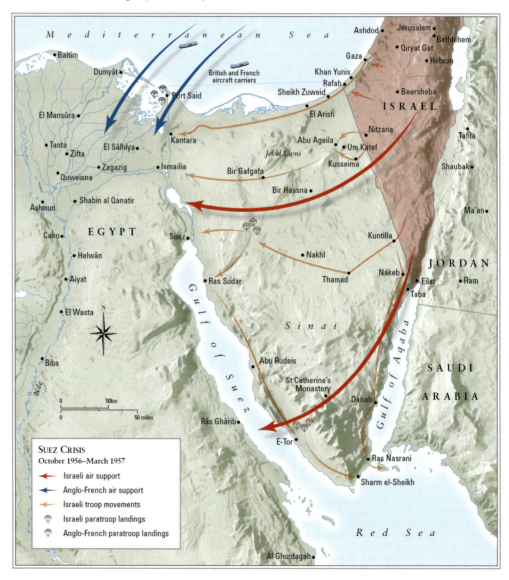

SUEZ CRISIS
The Anglo-French invasion of the Suez Canal Zone in October 1956 involved joint air operations by Israeli and French fighter-bombers, operating from bases in Israel, and British and French naval strike aircraft and RAF bombers operating from Cyprus and Malta.

Arab-Israeli Wars

In 1956 Gamal Abdel Nasser, President of Egypt, nationalized the Suez Canal zone, much to the consternation of the UK and French governments, who saw the canal as a link to their colonies in the Far East. Planning to retake control of the canal zone started immediately, with Israel offering assistance and wanting retaliation for terrorist attacks on its nation believed to have originated in Egypt.

Egypt's Air Force had substantial numbers of interceptors, made up mostly of de Havilland Vampires and Gloster Meteors, although these were almost obsolete. Backed up by a number of Soviet-supplied Mikoyan-Gurevich MiG-15s, as well as Ilyushin Il-28 attack bombers, they were ranged against British Hawker Hunters, French Republic F-84 Thunderstreaks and Israeli Dassault Mystère IVs. The United Kingdom, France and Israel had numbers on their side. The RAF deployed 10 squadrons of English Electric Canberra medium bombers, along with escorts and supply aircraft, to Cyprus alone. Four squadrons of Vickers Valiants of the RAF's Medium Bomber Force also deployed to RAF Luqa, Malta. Five carriers were deployed in the Mediterranean. The Royal Navy's HMS *Albion*, HMS *Bulwark* and HMS *Eagle* flew off de Havilland Sea Venoms and Hawker Sea Hawks in the ground-attack role; the French carriers *Arromanches* and *La Fayette* flew Vought F4U Corsairs in a similar role.

Suez confrontation

On 29 October the Suez confrontation opened with the dropping of 1600 Israeli paratroops east of the the Mitla Pass in the western Sinai desert. These troops came under almost immediate air attack from Egyptian Vampires and MiG-15s. This led to the UK and French governments issuing their 'Ultimatum'. This entailed withdrawal of Egyptian troops from the canal zone and control ceding back to the European powers. Egypt naturally refused, and continued to attack and successfully hold off the Israeli paratroops. Air battles above the Sinai were common, with Israeli Mystères usually getting the better of the Egyptian machines.

Egyptian airfields were targeted by the French and British, first at night to little effect, then by day, destroying many aircraft on the ground. The two countries then dropped paratroops on Port Said and Port Fuad on 5 November. Heavy street fighting was met and the advance stumbled. El Kap was captured before international pressure brought the venture to a halt. Very little had been achieved apart from the cementing of Arab distrust for the United Kingdom and France, and a deeper resentment of Israel.

By 1967, tensions in the Middle East had risen once again and conflict was on the horizon. Egypt, Syria and Jordan signed an agreement that would unify their cause and ally their forces, forces that had been greatly improved with the purchase of the latest Soviet aircraft such as the Mikoyan-Gurevich MiG-21 interceptor and Sukhoi Su-7 ground-attack aircraft. Likewise Israel had been improving its air arm with the purchase of mostly French types such as the Super Mystère fighter-bomber and Mirage III, both from Dassault. The impressive Mirage, with its delta wing design, was exceptionally fast.

Six Day War

On the morning of 5 June 1967, the IAF sent most of its attack force on a mission that became known as Operation Focus. The force took off as usual and

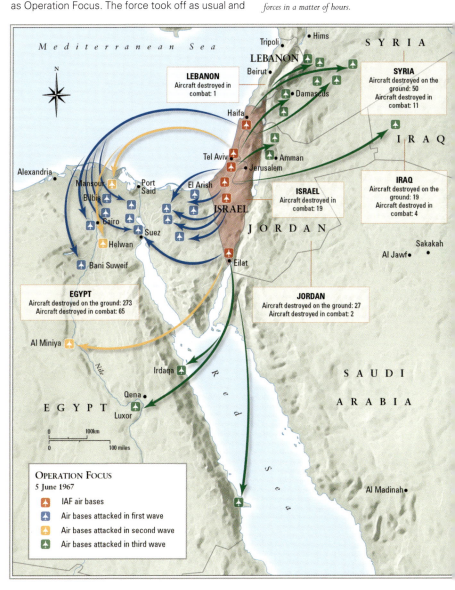

SIX-DAY WAR
The Six-Day War of June 1967 began with massive attacks by the Israeli Air Force on Egypt, Jordan and Syria, effectively neutralising the Arab air forces in a matter of hours.

207

Arab-Israeli Wars

flew out into the Mediterranean. As this had been done for many of the previous months, it did not arouse the suspicions of Egyptian radar controllers. The IAF jets then dipped below radar coverage and turned south towards Egypt itself. Making landfall, they split and flew to their respective targets: Egyptian air bases.

Taking Egypt by complete surprise, the Israeli pilots began to bomb and strafe the neatly parked aircraft, paying particular attention to the Egyptian bomber force of Tupolev Tu-16s, as these carried the most risk of attacking Israeli infrastructure. Their munitions depleted, the aicraft returned to their bases, where they were refuelled and rearmed in a rapid turnaround before heading back to Egypt for more attacks. This time targets included radar and anti-aircraft sites, as well as air bases. Some Egyptian Air Force fighters managed to scramble into the air, and dogfights erupted above their bases, but the advantage was squarely with Israel. Israel also employed French Durandel bombs, designed to heavily crater the runways of

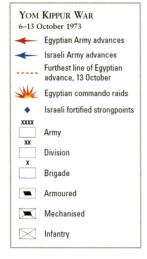

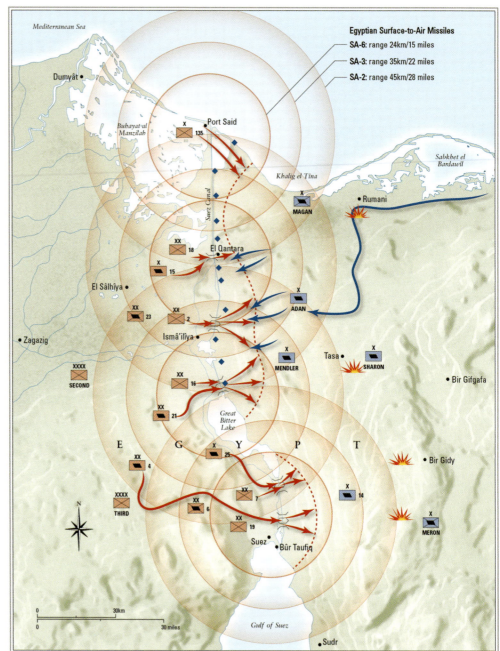

YOM KIPPUR WAR
The Yom Kippur War of October 1973 took Israel by surprise. Subsequent operations by the Israeli Air Force were hampered by strong Egyptian surface-to-air missile defences on the west bank of the Suez Canal.

Arab-Israeli Wars

the Egyptian air bases, again limiting the Egyptian Air Force's response. It had been an awesome display of air power. In one morning Egypt's air fighting capability had been all but crippled.

The IAF then turned its attention east, attacking Jordanian air bases and destroying all but four of the RJAF's Hunters on the ground or in air combat. Syria responded by attacking Israeli air bases with MiG-21s. This was followed by retaliatory attacks on Syrian air bases, as well as strikes on Iraq's H-3 base. These brought little damage, as Syria, Jordan and Iraq were now fully aware of Israeli intentions.

The following day the IAF was able to fly above the Sinai desert with relative impunity, attacking Egyptian positions along the border to allow Israeli ground forces to break through easily. After raids by paratroops flown in by helicopter to the rear of the Egyptian positions, a general withdrawal from the Sinai peninsula began, with the Israeli forces in hot pursuit. As the Egyptian columns fell back, they were strafed from the air by IAF aircraft. Egypt attempted to put up a token force of MiG-21s and Su-7s, easy prey for the high-patrolling IAF warplanes.

Israeli victory in the Sinai assured, Egypt signed a ceasefire on 9 June. Clashes continued in the east, with a prime target being further attacks on the H-3 airbase in Iraq. Air battles were a common sight above the air base, with both sides claiming massively inflated victories. Israel wanted to capture the Golan Heights on the border between Israel and Syria, thus creating a buffer zone much as the Sinai did. This achieved, a UN ceasefire was brought into effect on 10 June. For Israel it had been a resounding victory, destroying nearly 300 Egyptian aircraft and nearly 80 Jordanian, Syrian and Iraqi machines. However, peace would not last in this turbulent region.

Yom Kippur War

As the decade ended, the Arab nations and Israel made good their losses. France now refused to supply updated versions of the Mirage, however, so Israel now looked to the United States and purchased the McDonnell F-4 Phantom II and Douglas A-4 Skyhawk. The Egyptians would carry on being supplied yet more MiG-21s and Tupolev Tu-16s by the Soviet Union, as well as helicopters and, most importantly, surface-to-air missiles (SAMs).

On the afternoon of 6 October 1973, Egypt and Syria exacted revenge for the one-sided conflict of 1967. Choosing the date of Yom Kippur, the Jewish Day of Atonement, was to their advantage. Much

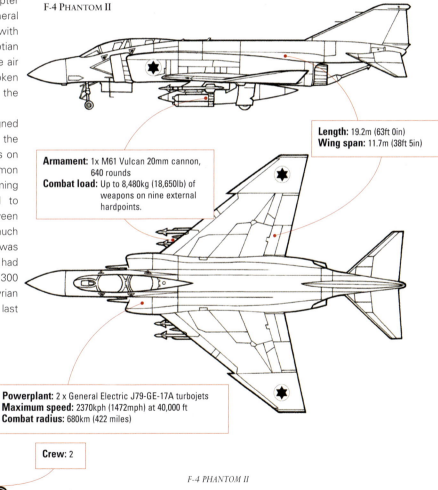

F-4 PHANTOM II

Length: 19.2m (63ft 0in)
Wing span: 11.7m (38ft 5in)

Armament: 1x M61 Vulcan 20mm cannon, 640 rounds
Combat load: Up to 8,480kg (18,650lb) of weapons on nine external hardpoints.

Radar: AN/APQ-59 radar with 81cm (32in) dish and AWG-10 pulse-Doppler fire control system, permitting the detection of high and low altitude targets.

Powerplant: 2 x General Electric J79-GE-17A turbojets
Maximum speed: 2370kph (1472mph) at 40,000 ft
Combat radius: 680km (422 miles)

Crew: 2

F-4 PHANTOM II
The Israeli Air Force was the largest foreign user of the F-4 Phantom II. The IAF received over 200 F-4Es between 1969 and 1976, these aircraft seeing considerable action during the Yom Kippur war of 1973.

Arab-Israeli Wars

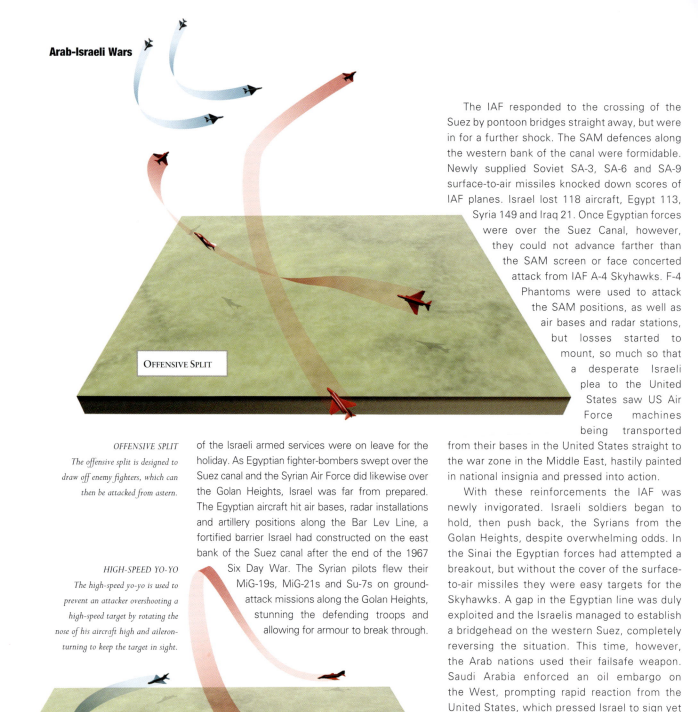

OFFENSIVE SPLIT

HIGH-SPEED YO-YO

OFFENSIVE SPLIT
The offensive split is designed to draw off enemy fighters, which can then be attacked from astern.

HIGH-SPEED YO-YO
The high-speed yo-yo is used to prevent an attacker overshooting a high-speed target by rotating the nose of his aircraft high and aileron-turning to keep the target in sight.

The IAF responded to the crossing of the Suez by pontoon bridges straight away, but were in for a further shock. The SAM defences along the western bank of the canal were formidable. Newly supplied Soviet SA-3, SA-6 and SA-9 surface-to-air missiles knocked down scores of IAF planes. Israel lost 118 aircraft, Egypt 113, Syria 149 and Iraq 21. Once Egyptian forces were over the Suez Canal, however, they could not advance farther than the SAM screen or face concerted attack from IAF A-4 Skyhawks. F-4 Phantoms were used to attack the SAM positions, as well as air bases and radar stations, but losses started to mount, so much so that a desperate Israeli plea to the United States saw US Air Force machines being transported from their bases in the United States straight to the war zone in the Middle East, hastily painted in national insignia and pressed into action.

of the Israeli armed services were on leave for the holiday. As Egyptian fighter-bombers swept over the Suez canal and the Syrian Air Force did likewise over the Golan Heights, Israel was far from prepared. The Egyptian aircraft hit air bases, radar installations and artillery positions along the Bar Lev Line, a fortified barrier Israel had constructed on the east bank of the Suez canal after the end of the 1967 Six Day War. The Syrian pilots flew their MiG-19s, MiG-21s and Su-7s on ground-attack missions along the Golan Heights, stunning the defending troops and allowing for armour to break through.

With these reinforcements the IAF was newly invigorated. Israeli soldiers began to hold, then push back, the Syrians from the Golan Heights, despite overwhelming odds. In the Sinai the Egyptian forces had attempted a breakout, but without the cover of the surface-to-air missiles they were easy targets for the Skyhawks. A gap in the Egyptian line was duly exploited and the Israelis managed to establish a bridgehead on the western Suez, completely reversing the situation. This time, however, the Arab nations used their failsafe weapon. Saudi Arabia enforced an oil embargo on the West, prompting rapid reaction from the United States, which pressed Israel to sign yet another ceasefire. This came into effect on the evening of 22 October.

During the conflict and following encounters, Israeli pilots, flying mostly western types, proved themselves exceptional fighter pilots. Stories of a pair of Phantoms taking on 20 or so enemy aircraft in the Yom Kippur War and coming out victors are commonplace. Israel continues to be supplied by the United States, including obtaining the superb McDonnell Douglas (now Boeing) F-15 Eagle fighter; Israeli pilots are the

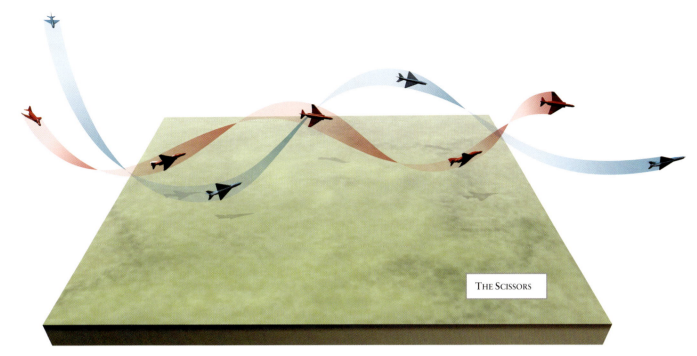

highest-scoring aces in the type. Israel has also produced home-grown aircraft, such as the IAI Nesher (Eagle), which is an unauthorized copy of the Dassault Mirage V.

Superior air fighting tactics

Israeli and Arab pilots, having met on such a regular basis, fast evolved the best air fighting tactics to hande these encounters. Flying at twice the speed or more of their contemporaries who flew in the massed air battles of World War II, they retained elements of what had been learned in that conflict, such as flying in pairs so that a leader always had a wingman for mutual protection. The pair could also operate in an offensive way, flying such manoevres as the 'offensive split', which involved the leader drawing the enemy fighters towards him, while the wingman, hopefully unseen, would fly below and swoop up to the turning enemy, to engage the vulnerable belly of their aircraft with either missiles or cannon.

In all manoeuvres the most important element was always to engage from the rear of the enemy, as the hot exhaust was required for the missiles to 'lock on'. If this failed, it was also the best position from which to use cannon.

Israeli pilots went on to prove their worth again in smaller-scale conflicts such as the 1982 Lebanon War, where the Israeli Air Force took out Lebanon's entire air defence network without loss of a single aircraft. It has flown exceptionally long-range bombing missions, such as the attack on the Iraqi nuclear facility at Osiraq using Lockheed Martin F-16 Flying Falcon, multirole jet fighters, This mission required the pilots to fly low and fast, all the while watching the fuel consumption in their aircraft, as well as attack a nuclear facility. This was done with great success, and all aircraft returned to base.

Carrying and using a big stick

Israel has continued to use its extensive air force to protect or project its strength, often on targets that have no anti-aircraft defences. This was evident with the Israeli invasion of Lebanon in 2006, where it was engaged in the destruction of Hezbollah rocket-launching sites. These were taken out with extreme accuracy, using laser-guided munitions. It is still important to have sound intelligence on the ground, however, as these same munitions were responsible for the death of many Lebanese civilians when they were dropped on 'suspected' hideouts of members of the Hezbollah militia.

THE SCISSORS
In the scissors manoeuvre, each pilot flies as slowly as he can, constantly reversing his turn in an attempt to make his opponent overshoot.

BARREL-ROLL ATTACK
In the barrel-roll attack, the attacking aircraft flies across the target's turning circle with an anticlockwise roll, pulling up out of the turn and dropping into position astern of the target.

THE FALKLANDS WAR

FALKLANDS HARRIERS
A Royal Navy Sea Harrier recovers to the carrier HMS Hermes *during the Falklands war. In the foreground is one of the RAF's Harrier GR.3s, which took over the ground support task from the Sea Harriers, releasing the latter for combat air patrol (CAP) duty.*

On 2 April 1982 an Argentinian invasion force landed on the British territory of the Falkland Islands in the South Atlantic. Argentina had long claimed them as Argentine territory. After brief resistance by a single company of Royal Marines garrisoned there, the islands, along with South Georgia, were in Argentinian hands. Plans were immediately put into action by the UK government, at the time making extensive military cutbacks, to create a task force to retake the islands.

The task force gets under way
As the task force of Royal Navy ships, including the carriers HMS *Hermes* and HMS *Invincible*, were prepared for action, a force of Hawker Siddeley Nimrod maritime patrol aircraft stationed on Ascension Island in the mid-Atlantic began to fly extensive reconnaissance flights to gain as much intelligence as possible for the upcoming battle. Ascension would also welcome a flight of five Avro Vulcan bombers. This giant delta-winged aircraft was originally designed as a nuclear bomber. In the Falklands it reverted to a more conventional role, flying long-range missions to the island's main town, Stanley, bombing the airport there and attacking anti-aircraft defences.

Argentina had stationed FMA IA 58 Pucará ground-attack aircraft at the airport, as well as an assortment of helicopters. On the first mission of Operation Black Buck, a single Vulcan flew from Ascension, refuelled along the route by Handley Page Victor tankers. It flew on to Stanley, where it released its 21 bombs in a diagonal pattern across the runway. Damage was minimal. Only one bomb hit the runway itself, and repairs were easily made. It did prove, however, that the RAF had the strike capability to hit targets on mainland Argentina. Argentina consequently chose not to deploy its fighter squadrons on the islands themselves, instead preferring to keep them on the mainland for home defence.

On 1 May, the same day as the first Black Buck mission, the British task force had approached near enough to the islands to launch Hawker Siddeley Harrier missions, attacking targets in Darwin, Goose Green and Stanley. The Argentine response was swift. Retaliatory strikes were launched, but four aircraft were lost to Fleet Air Arm Sea Harriers now flying combat air patrols above the task force.

On 4 May two Argentine Dassault Super Etendards, equipped with the new Exocet anti-shipping missile, approached the line of British destroyers at extreme low level. HMS *Sheffield* was hit and would eventually sink. The Argentine pilots used the tactic of flying in low to their targets so that they could use the rugged coastline to keep as low a profile as possible so that they were not picked up on radar. On 21 May Royal Marines and paratroops began an amphibious landing at San Carlos Water, a large sheltered cove on the west coast of East Falkland. As the forces came in on landing craft, they were supplemented by Sikorsky Sea King, Westland Wessex and smaller Westland Scout helicopters flying in supplies.

Low-flying tactics
The British task force laying at anchor on San Carlos Water offered an outstanding target for the pilots of the Argentinian Air Force. Flying IAI Daggers and Douglas A-4 Skyhawks, they employed standard 'iron' bombs on the ships of the Royal Navy. Many of these found their mark, despite the Sea Harriers flying round-the-clock combat air patrols, which amounted to some 1000 patrols flown by the end of the conflict. The Sea Harriers also had AIM-9 Sidewinder missiles, which claimed many of the shot-down Argentine pilots.

Despite this, some Argentine aircraft always got through. On 21 May, HMS *Ardent* was hit with no fewer than nine bombs, three exploding on the helicopter deck towards the rear of the ship. Badly mauled, she attempted to sail into San Carlos, but was attacked again, this time with no hits being recorded. But the damage had been done; fires burned throughout the night and the ship was lost the next day. A similar fate befell HMS *Antelope* on 23 May. She was hit by two time-delayed bombs and sank, with minimal loss of life.

At one minute to midnight on 14 June, surrender documents were signed. The United Kingdom had reclaimed the Falklands. Casualties were relatively few, but the fleet's air defence had proven extremely susceptible to concerted attack from the low-flying tactics of the Argentine pilots.

The Falklands War

THE FALKLANDS WAR
2 April–15 June 1982

1. 21 May, HMS *Ardent* is attacked by four A-4 Skyhawks and struck by nine bombs. Three explode on the helicopter deck.
2. Crippled, *Ardent* attempts to sail for San Carlos Water. She is attacked again but no hits are recorded. Fires burn out of control and she sinks the next day in Grantham Sound.
3. HMS *Antelope*, guarding the entrance to San Carlos Water, is attacked by Skyhawks on 23 May. Two time-delayed bombs tear her apart. Fires continue through the night before she is abandoned the following morning.
4. Royal Navy Sea Harriers fly almost constant Combat Air Patrols, downing many Argentine aircraft.

THE FALKLANDS WAR
The Falklands War showed that surface vessels are extremely vulnerable to determined air attack, especially to sea-skimming missiles such as the Exocet.

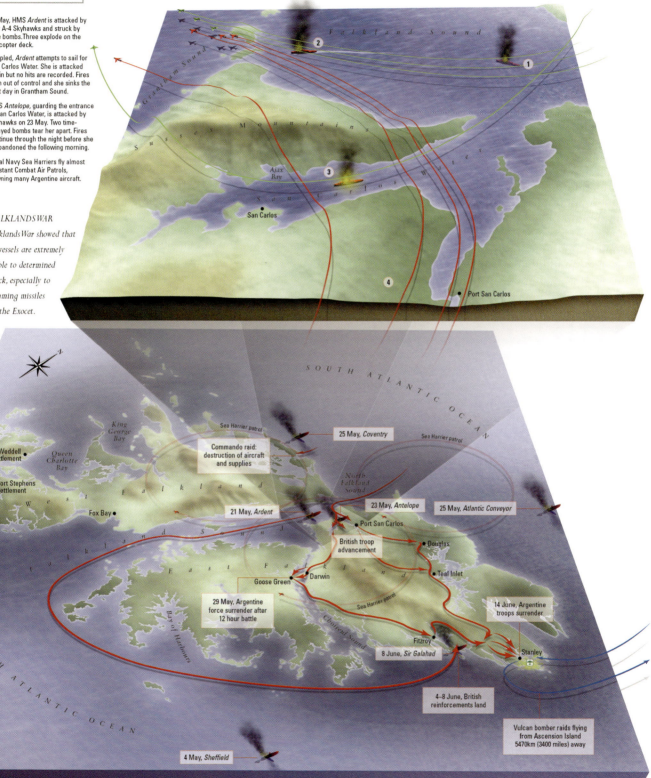

CRISIS IN THE GULF

Iraq's invasion of the neighbouring Arab state of Kuwait triggered a massive build-up of air power on a scale that had not seen since the end of World War II. With the economically important oilfields of Kuwait captured, and the oilfields of Saudi Arabia under threat, the West, and particularly the United States, was quick to respond.

Preparing for battle

Saddam Hussein commanded the fourth-largest army in the world. Battle-hardened from conflict with Iran the previous decade, Iraqi forces easily took control of Kuwait in August 1990. Some of the Kuwaiti Air Force did manage to escape to Saudi Arabia in their Douglas A-4 Skyhawks. Operation Desert Shield was put into effect to contain the Iraqi army and prevent its advance into Saudi Arabia. This involved the rapid dispatch of USAF McDonnell Douglas (Boeing) F-15 Eagle air superiority fighters to the region to supplement the Royal Saudi Air Force's Panavia Tornado fighters. With these aircraft flying constant combat air patrols and keeping a vigil on Iraqi movements, the military build-up of hundreds of thousands of troops, vehicles and naval power could mass, while politicians attempted to find a diplomatic solution. As this took place, US Navy carriers, along with their massive air groups, flying McDonnell Douglas (Boeing) FA-18 Hornets, Grumman F-14 Tomcats and Grumman E-2 Hawkeyes, sailed into the Red Sea, ready to engage if Iraqi forces crossed the border. Six carriers along with their escorts and support vessels were stationed in the Red Sea by the start of the conflict.

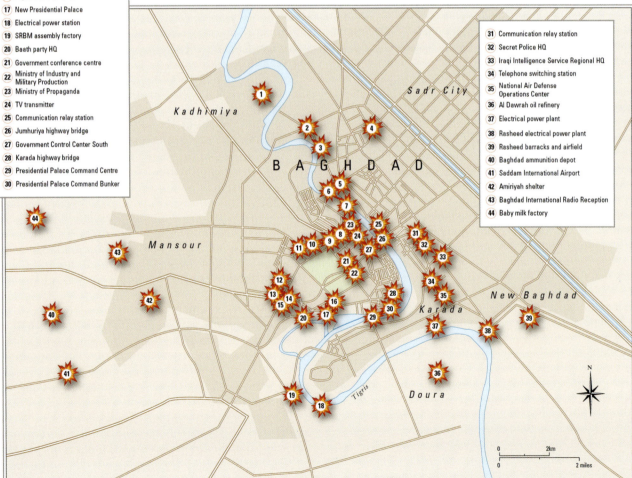

Gulf War Baghdad Air Strikes 17 January–28 February 1991

1. Directorate of Military Intelligence
2. Telephone switching station
3. Ministry of Defence National Computer Complex
4. Electrical transfer station
5. Telephone switching station
6. Ministry of Defence HQ
7. Ashudad highway bridge
8. Telephone switching station
9. Railroad yard
10. Muthena airfield (Military section)
11. New Iraq Air Force HQ
12. Iraqi Intelligence Service HQ
13. Telephone switching station
14. Secret Police complex
15. Army storage depot
16. Republican Guard HQ
17. New Presidential Palace
18. Electrical power station
19. SRBM assembly factory
20. Baath party HQ
21. Government conference centre
22. Ministry of Industry and Military Production
23. Ministry of Propaganda
24. TV transmitter
25. Communication relay station
26. Jumhuriya highway bridge
27. Government Control Center South
28. Karada highway bridge
29. Presidential Palace Command Centre
30. Presidential Palace Command Bunker
31. Communication relay station
32. Secret Police HQ
33. Iraqi Intelligence Service Regional HQ
34. Telephone switching station
35. National Air Defense Operations Center
36. Al Dawrah oil refinery
37. Electrical power plant
38. Rasheed electrical power plant
39. Rasheed barracks and airfield
40. Baghdad ammunition depot
41. Saddam International Airport
42. Amiriyah shelter
43. Baghdad International Radio Reception
44. Baby milk factory

Crisis in the Gulf

From the United Kingdom arrived Tornados, both in the strike and interceptor roles, plus SEPECAT Jaguars, transport helicopters such as the Boeing CH-47 Chinook and elderly Blackburn Buccaneers. These machines, although outmoded, carried sophisticated target designation devices; they would keep station with Tornados and assist in their bomb runs. Dassault Mirage 2000s and F1s arrived from France, while Italy deployed Tornados as well as the Skyhawks from the escaped Kuwaiti Air Force. The build-up was epic in scale.

To organize all these aircraft and where and when they would fly, the Coalition had Boeing Joint Stars and E-3 Sentry Airborne Early Warning and Control (AWACS) aircraft flying above the battle zone at all times. These aircraft, packed with avionics, radar and listening devices, kept constant control over the Coalition forces' air movements, directing them to their targets or helping them to engage enemy aircraft.

Plan of attack

A plan of attack was drawn up. First on the agenda would be knocking out any Iraqi early warning capability, then destroying any air defence systems and the Iraqi Air Force. The command and control structure of the Iraqi regime could then be destroyed, the army would lose cohesion and the supply lines would be cut. Targets would also include power stations, water supplies and communications links, bringing the entirety of Iraq to a virtual standstill. With all these elements destroyed or made void, Coalition air forces could concentrate on effective support of the ground troops as they moved in to retake Kuwait and push the Iraqi army back into Iraq.

In the early hours of 17 January 1991, eight AH-64 Apache attack helicopters, supported by Sikorksy MH-53 Pave Low helicopters, flew over the Saudi-Iraqi border and attacked two early warning radar stations. The air war had begun. This strike force kicked open the doors for Coalition bombers to begin. Lockheed F-117 Nighthawks flew on to Baghdad, Iraq's capital, and commenced precision bombing of the Iraqi government and infrastructure. These attacks were supplemented by Tomahawk missiles, launched from US Navy ships anchored in the Persian Gulf. The F-117 was a remarkable aircraft. Able to fly at subsonic speeds, its shape and the materials from which meant that it could absorb and deflect any radar beams aimed at it, making it almost 'invisible' to the radar operator. The Iraqi defenders knew that an aircraft was in the vicinity, but the radar returns were so small or nonexistent that the surface-to-air missiles could not make a lock-on. This meant that the F-117 pilots did not have to be so concerned with evasive manoeuvres and could concentrate on locating and hitting the target accurately.

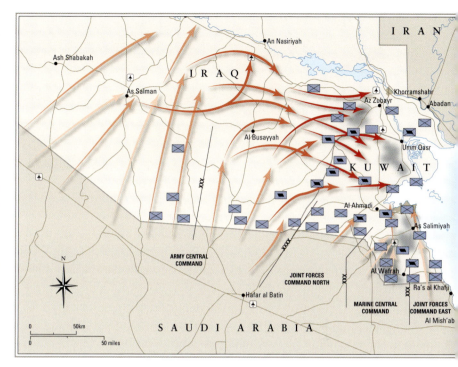

As the Nighthawks attacked Baghdad, Coalition strike aircraft, escorted by F-15 Eagles and supported by McDonnell Douglas F4 Phantom II 'Wild Weasels' armed with anti-radar missiles, were ready to hit any SAM sites that might engage the strike 'packages'. The targets were air defence systems and Iraqi air bases, where the aims were to destroy aircraft on the ground and drop guided munitions into the reinforced concrete shelters. Nothing was safe. Power stations, pumping stations and dams were destroyed, leaving Iraq with a tiny fraction of the power it had prior to the conflict.

RAF Tornados, flying at low level, attacked Iraqi runways, using JP233 runway-cratering munitions. With this level of intensity the Iraqi Air Force rarely intercepted raids. Some were shot down without ever seeing their enemy, while the rest fled to Iran after a week of fighting. This surprised the Coalition. Although it had anticipated a retreat by the Iraqi Air Force, it had expected it to to be to Jordan, rather than Iran.

With the death knell of the Iraqi Air Force sounded and many of the priority targets hit, the air forces could now concentrate on effective assistance to the ground troops, which began moving into Iraq on 24 January. If the troops faced a concerted defence, they could call upon USAF

215

Crisis in the Gulf

A-10 THUNDERBOLT II
With its nose-mounted 30mm rotary cannon and an array of air-to-ground missiles and bombs, the 'Warthog' is a formidable ground-attack platform.

Fairchild-Republic A-10 Thunderbolt IIs or Marine Corps McDonnell Douglas AV-8 Harriers to clear a path. The A-10 'Warthog' was designed from day one to be a ground-attack platform. The pilot sat in a 'tub' of armour, and the engines were spread far apart so that if one was damaged the other could be relied apon to get the machine home. Although slow-flying it could linger over the battle zone for long periods and absorb a great amount of damage. It carried the formidable 30mm GAU-8 Gatling type cannon, firing depleted uranium rounds that could defeat most types of armour. Alongside these operated AH-64 Apaches. As the Iraqi army went into full retreat, these two ground-attack aircraft laid waste to the vast jams of army traffic. After only five days of the ground offensive the war was over, the Iraqis in full retreat and Kuwait liberated.

The invasion of Iraq

In 2003 the US administration under George W. Bush decided that Iraq was harbouring weapons of mass destruction and was allied to terrorist causes. In the context of the ongoing 'War on Terror', it was an opportune time for the Bush administration to topple Saddam's regime, even if under spurious circumstances. Without UN backing, US and UK forces would lead the assault, with the support of Spanish, Australian, Polish and Danish forces.

On 20 March 2003 the Second Gulf War commenced under the title 'Operation Iraqi Freedom'. The plan differed from the previous war's in that the air bombardment and ground campaign commenced on the same day – in tactics dubbed as 'shock and awe'. This was so as little as possible of the Iraqi infrastructure was incapacitated and the Coalition could wrest control of the country, then then let it continue as usual. Targets in Baghdad were again struck with pinpoint accuracy by cruise missiles and F-117s, although some of the 'precision' weapons did not find their targets.

Paratroops were used in the north of Iraq to quickly secure Kurdish areas, then pursue the Iraqi army as it fell back on Baghdad. By early April Baghdad was captured and relatively few Coalition aircraft had been lost in the venture. As the forces prepared themselves for occupation duty, the helicopter became the principal machine in the country, along with the Humvee. As the troops began to fight an increasing insurgencey, the use of fast jets became moot; the small nimble gunship came into its own. The Marine Corps Bell AH-1 Cobra gunships could be called upon to take out relatively small targets and support troops moving through the city streets.

Increasingly, unmanned aerial vehicles (UAVs) were used for reconnaissance and could be fitted with Hellfire missiles. Using a live feed, operators could locate a target, make the decision to engage and destroy that target as they sat in operations rooms halfway around the world. A new type of air power had evolved, allowing for a combat aircraft to fly into hostile skies and attack the enemy, but at no risk to the life of the operator, or 'pilot'.

AFGHANISTAN

Following the attacks on the World Trade Center and Pentagon in the United States on 11 September 2001, the war on terror began. Al Qaeda members, under the command of Osama Bin Laden, hijacked commercial airliners and used them as guided 'bombs' to attack the two targets.

Locating the enemy

The next month the United States connected the extremist Taliban government of Afghanistan with harbouring the al Qaeda terrorist group, allowing it to open training centres in the vastness of the country. The United States set about overthrowing the government and destroying these training camps. Utilizing almost every type of aircraft and weapon in its arsenal, it launched strikes using the heavy bomber force of B-1 Lancer and B-2 Spirit 'stealth bombers', alongside the old warhorse the Boeing B-52 Stratofortress. These aircraft, flying from the US air base on Diego Garcia in the Indian Ocean, flew missions carpet-bombing vast swathes of Afghanistan, forcing many Taliban and al Qaeda fighters to retreat to mountain strongholds. The extensive cave systems found there were impervious to the vast amount of ordnance dropped on them, but the entrances could be blocked by bombing and the enemy entombed. The Taliban had no real means to counter these attacks as it had no anti-aircraft defences.

Taliban targets within the Afghan capital, Kabul, were targeted by precision weapons dropped from McDonnell Douglas (Boeing) F-15 Strike Eagles and carrier-launched McDonnell Douglas F/A-18 Hornets. French Dassault Mirage 2000s were also deployed to Afghanistan, again making precision drops using laser-guided bombs. All this pushed the Taliban government into hiding and allowed the allied Afghan Northern Alliance to enter the city and take control of the government, giving freedom to the people.

Out in the countryside, wherever the Taliban set up positions, the USAF flew missions with special Lockheed C-130s, dropping 6800kg (15,000lb) 'Daisy Cutter' ordnance. These hefty weapons were primed to explode above the ground to maximize damage outwards, literally clearing paths through enemy positions and demoralizing them in the process.

Unmanned aerial vehicles (UAVs) also proved invaluable. Commanders were fed real-time pictures of the battle zone by remote operators, so that they could strike targets utilizing their Hellfire missiles. UAVs were responsible for locating and attacking al Qaeda convoys and targetting the organization's senior leaders.

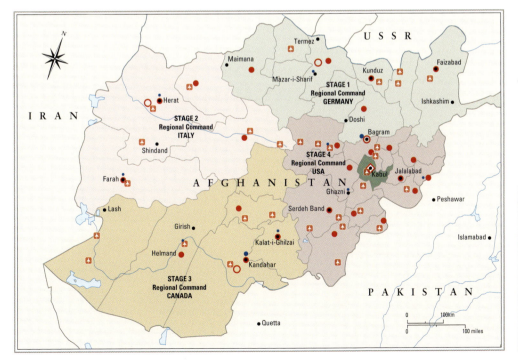

AFGHANISTAN
The conflict in Afghanistan, where NATO forces often met with fanatical resistance, has demonstrated the need for swift and effective close air support on numerous occasions.

RUSSIA–UKRAINE WAR

On 24 February 2022 Russian ground forces invaded Ukraine, advancing along four axes, heading south and southwest toward the capital Kiev; southwest toward Kharkiv; northwest, west and southwest through the Donbas from the pro-Russian insurgent-held Donetsk region; and northwest from the Crimea toward Odessa and Kherson.

Air force strength
The Russian Air and Space Forces (VKS) on paper had at its disposal 4,090 operational aircraft, including 1,091 MiG-29, MiG-31, Su-27, Su-31, Su-34 and Su-35 fighters; 465 Su-24 and Su-25 ground-attack aircraft; 123 Tupolev bombers; and 752 attack helicopters. In addition, the Russian Army also fielded 512 strategic 'kamikaze' strike drones. Many of these aircraft were based far from European Russia, others were non-operational, but nonetheless 1,050 platforms were committed to the Ukrainian war.

The defending Ukrainian ground forces were supported by their air force (PS-ZSU) and army aviation wing, which between them fielded 306 platforms. This included 72 MiG-29 and Su-27 fighters, 18 Su-24 and Su-25 attack aircraft, 61 attack helicopters and 72 other helicopters. In addition, the Ukrainian air defence forces fielded 48 mobile S-300 and 9K37 Buk surface-to-air missile (SAM) batteries, plus 38 fixed S-135 ones. The Ukrainians also had 3,900 man-portable anti-air missiles (MANPADs), including 9K32 Strela-2, 9K38 Igla and NATO-supplied FIM-92 Stinger weapons.

Ukrainian SAM systems
During 24–27 February, the Russians conducted hundreds of missions to secure air superiority by destroying or suppressing Ukrainian air defence systems. Alongside ground- and sea-launched long-range missiles, Russian aircraft and attack helicopters – plus Tupolev bomber-launched Kh-101 and Kh-555 cruise missiles – struck numerous Ukrainian targets, including command HQs, airfields, radars and particularly surface-to-air (SAM) batteries.

Although Russian strikes destroyed 14 static S-125 missile batteries, the Russians failed to spot that the Ukrainians had redeployed 24 mobile batteries into forest areas during 22–23 February, which remained unscathed. By constantly redeploying these batteries, the Ukrainians managed to preserve many of them, despite repeated Russian strikes. Despite the grievous threat posed by numerically superior Russian

LONG-RANGE CRUISE MISSILE STRIKE
Some 350km (220 miles) from its target, a Russian HQ bunker, a Ukrainian Sukhoi Su-24M aircraft releases its British-supplied Storm Shadow cruise missile. Flying low over the ground, the contour-following missile navigates itself toward the target. As it approaches the enemy's radars and SAMs that protect the bunker, the missile flies upward until it is beyond enemy radar range. Finally, it plunges vertically at Mach 0.95 into the target, setting off its 450kg (990lb) multi-stage BROACH warhead, which can penetrate up to 4.6 metres (15 feet) of reinforced concrete.

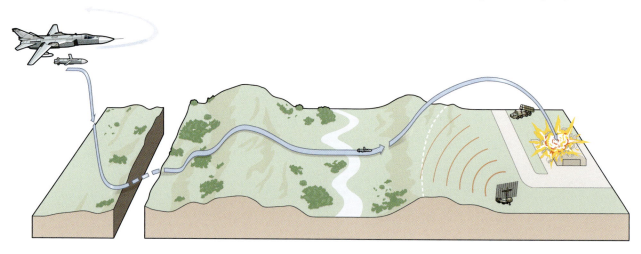

F-16 FIGHTING FALCONS
For many months the Ukrainians had pinned their hopes of gaining an advantage in the air war on the arrival of NATO-supplied General Dynamics F-16 multi-role fighter aircraft. Capable of a top speed of Mach 2.05, the F-16 can carry many combinations of weapons, including Sidewinder and AMRAAM missiles, three types of rockets, and M61A1 Vulcan 6-barelled 20mm cannon.

fighters, Ukrainian aircraft continued to contest the skies, disrupting Russian sorties; 28 Ukrainian platforms were lost in that bitter first week of fighting, however.

In addition, on 24 February 32 low-flying Russian Mil Mi-8 transport and Kamov Ka-52 attack helicopters, carrying 250 VDV airborne troops, attempted to seize Hostomel Airport, close to Kiev. A further 1,050 VDV troops, embussed on 18 Ilyushin Il-76 transport planes, waited to land at the airport and charge into Kiev to 'decapitate' the government.

The 300 Ukrainian defenders' Igla MANPADs and ZU-23-2 twin-barrelled anti-aircraft guns downed three Russian helicopters, but could not prevent the landing. The ensuing fierce Ukrainian resistance, however, led to the abandonment of the second-wave Russian landing, and thus the 'decapitation' charge into Kiev did not occur. Although southward-advancing Russian ground forces reached Hostomel the next day, by then Kiev was firmly defended.

NATO donations

From March 2022 the Ukrainian air defence system gradually recovered, meaning that Russia only fleetingly enjoyed local air superiorities in eastern Ukraine. The continuing Ukrainian threat to Russian aircraft owed much to NATO's deliveries of air defence weaponry, including 1,450 Stinger MANPADs and 72 SAM batteries (including six US Patriot and four German IRIS-T systems). This contribution has been crucial, because since 2023 Russia has launched an average of 3,000 long-range missiles or drone strikes into Ukraine each month.

NATO donations have also helped the Ukrainians slow the decline in their aircraft strength. Up to August 2024, Ukraine had lost 376 platforms, including 68 fighters, 62 attack aircraft, 24 other aircraft, 83 helicopters and 139 drones. In contrast, Russian forces had lost 311 platforms, including 47 fighters and 102 helicopters.

Meanwhile, NATO has supplied Ukraine with 63 aircraft (including 27 MiG-29 fighters) and 71 helicopters. Repeated Ukrainian requests that NATO provide them with F-16 Fighting Falcon air-defence fighters led to their pilots being trained on the type in neighbouring Romania. Finally, in summer 2024 NATO pledged to dispatch 95 F-16s, the first deliveries of which arrived in late July.

In August 2024 Ukraine still fielded 302 aerial platforms, including 72 fighter and 31 attack aircraft, plus 33 attack helicopters. In contrast, the VKS still fields on paper 4,055 platforms, including 809 fighters and 730 attack aircraft, plus 559 attack helicopters; many of these, however, are deployed far from Ukraine, while some aircraft remain barely operational. The desperate struggle above beleaguered Ukraine's skies looks set to continue, with neither side gaining a decisive advantage for the foreseeable future.

INDEX

Entries in *italics* refer to photographs, illustrations or maps

Ader, Clement 10
Aero Club of Milan 16
Aero Club of Paris 31, *31*
Aéronautique Militaire 18, *46*, *57*, 68
Aéronavale 104
Afghanistan 217
AGM-114 Hellfire air-to-ground missile *217*
A-Go, Operation, 1944 164, 166
AH-64 Apache attack helicopter 215
ailerons 12, 43
AIM-9 Sidewinder missile 212
air forces, early, 1914-1918 18, *19*, 20–9
  see also under individual air force name
air routes, pioneering:
  1921–30 70–3, *71*, *72*, *73*
  1934–39 90–1, *91*
Airborne Early Warning and Control System (AWACS) 215
Airco:
  DH.2 *41*, 44, 47, 48, 49, *49*, 50, 51
  DH.4 37, 62, 64
aircraft carriers:
  carrier raids in the Pacific, 1943 162, *162*, *163*
  first 78–9, *79*
  see also under individual carrier name
Aircraft Transport and Travel Limited 70
airships 17, 28, 29, 30–9, *31*, *32*, *33*, *34*, *35*, *36*, *37*, *38*, *39* *see also under individual airship name*
Airspeed Horsa glider *170*, 170
air-to-air combat *see* fighter aircraft
Ajax 115
Akagi 79, 124, 125, *125*, *131*, 132, *133*, *134*
al Qaeda 217
Alam Al Halfa, Battle of, 1942 153
Albacore, USS 165
Albania 118
Albatros:
  C.III 51
  D.I 48, 49, 50
  D.II 44, *50*, 51–2
  D.III 50, *50*, 54, 55
Albion, HMS 115
Alcock, Captain John *72*, 73–4, *73*
Algeria 114–15, 153
Allies (World War I & II) *see under individual nation state*
Allied Air Force 155, *174*
Allied Desert Air Force 152
Allied Expeditionary Air Force 170, 172
Alps, first crossing of 16–17
American Volunteer Group (AVG) 178
Anglo-American rearmament, inter-war 92–3, *92*, *93*
Antelope, HMS 212, *213*
Antoinette IV 14
ANZAC troops 119 *see also under individual nation state*
Anzani engine 14
Ap Bac, Battle of, 1963 202, *202–3*
Arab-Israeli wars 206–11, *206*, *207*, *208*, *209*, *210*, *211*
Arbruzzi 115
Ardent, HMS 212, 213
Arethusa, HMS 29
Argentinian Air Force 212
Argus, HMS 78, 152
Aritano, Rear Admiral Goto 130
Arizona, USS 127
Ark Royal, HMS 78
Armée de l'Air 92, 93, 94, 104 *see also* France
Armor Company of Chicago 16
Armstrong Whitworth:
  Argosy 77
  Whitley 93, *93*, 111, 146, 168, 183
Army of the Republic of Vietnam (ARVN) 202, *202–3*, 205
Arnold, Major General H.H. 'Hap' 186
Arromanches 207
Astra-Torres 32
ASV (Air-to-Surface Vessel) radar 168
Atlantic Conveyor, HMS 213
Atlantic Ocean:
  battle of, 1939-40 112–13, *112*, *113*
  first crossings of 70–4
  patrolling, 1939-45 168, *168*, *169*
Atoll infra-red AAMs 205
Australia, HMAS 166
Australia 71, 90, 115, 144, 166, *170*

Austria-Hungary 10–11, 18, *19*, 36, 54, 55, 56, 66
Avia S.199 206
Aviation Corporation of America 90
Avro:
  Anson 168
  Lancaster 146, *148*, 150
  Lincoln 192
  Vulcan 212, *213*

BAe Sea Harrier 212, *212*, 213, *213*
Bacon, Gertrude 15
Bagration, Operation, 1944 180, *180*, *181*
Baka piloted bomb 141
Balbo, Italo 75
Balkans 17, 118–19, *118–19*, 120
balloons 10–11, *10*, *11*, *19*, 26, 30, 32, 49, 60, *63*, 64, 68
Barbarossa, Operation 1941 119, 120–3, *120*, *121*, *122*, *123*
Barham, HMS 115
barrel-roll attack manoeuvre *211*, 211
Batista, Fulgencio 200
Bavarian Aircraft Company 81
Bay of Pigs, 1961 200–1
Bell:
  H-13 197
  UH-1 'Iroquois', 'Huey' 202, *202*, 203
Belleau Wood, USS 164
Bennett, Gordon 15, 16
Berlin Airlift, 1948-49 194, *194*, *195*, 198
Berlin, bombing of, 1944 150–1, *150*, *151*
Beta 32
Bin Laden, Osama 217
Black Buck, Operation, 1982 212
Blackburn:
  Buccaneer 215
  Skua 101
Blériot:
  V 14
  XI 14, 17, 18
  XII 14, 15
Blériot, Louis 14–15, *14*
blitzkrieg 68, 86, 96–7, *96*, *97*, 102, 157
Blücher 100
Bock, General Fedor von 102–3
Böcker, Kapitänleutnant 37
Bockscar 191
Bodenplatte, Operation, 1945 184
Boeing:
  247 90
  314 91
  B-17 Flying Fortress 95, 127, 129, 132, 144, 146, 149, *149*, *150*, *151*, 168, 184, 186, 206
  B-29 Superfortress 95, 176, 186–7, *186*, *187*, 188, 190, 193, 197
  B-52 Stratofortress *204*, 205, 217
  E-8 Joint Stars 215
Boelcke, Oswald 41, 43, 50, 52
Boelcke's 'Dicta' 43–4, 52
Böhme, Erwin 44
bombers:
  airships and 30, 36, 39
  blitzkrieg *96*, 97
  Britain and Germany, bombing of, 1940-41 110–11, *110*, *111*
  early 10–11, 15, 31
  Germany, bombing of, 1942-44 146–51, *146–7*, *148*, *149*, *150*, *151*
  long-range post-war 193, *193*
  Moscow, bombing of, 1941 120, *121*, 122–3, *122*, *123*
  1916-18 56–63, *56*, *57*, *58*, *59*, *60*, *61*, *62*, *63*, 85–6
  nuclear 150–1, *150*, *151*
  Spanish Civil War 84, 85, *85*, 86, 87, *87* *see also under individual aircraft, area, nation and operation name*
Bonaparte, Napoleon 10
Borodino, Battle of, 1812 180
Boulton-Paul Defiant 108
Brand, Flight Lieutenant Quintin 71
Brandenburg, Hauptmann Ernst 58, 59, 80, 79
Breese, Lieutenant J.W. 72
Breguet Br XIV 27, *53*, 60, *68*
Breguet, Corporal Louis 22
Brest-Litovsk, Treaty of, 1918 *55*, 66, 67
Bretagne 115
Brewster Buffalo 129, 178
Brindisi 115
Bristol:
  Beaufighter 151, *155*, 168, 176
  Blenheim 99, 103, 111, 118, 129, *129*

Bulldog 99
F2B Fighter *43*
Britain:
  air force *see* RAF
  aircraft production, World War II 140–1, *141*
  airships raids on, 1914-17 28, 29, 32–9, *33*, *34*, *35*, *36*, *37*, *38*, *39*
  Balkans, 1941, role in 118–19, *118–19*
  Battle of Britain, 1940 83, 85, 106–9, *106*, *107*, *108*, *109*
  bombing of ('blitz') 1940-41 110–11, *110*, *111*
  D-Day, role in 170–2, *170*, *171*
  Empire of the air *76*, 77, *77*
  Falklands War, 1982 212, *213*
  first bomber force 61–2, *62*
  France, Battle of, involvement in, 1940, 102, 103, 104
  Germany, bombing of, 1940-44 111, *111*, 146–9, *146–7*, *148*, 149, 150–1, *151*
  Gulf Wars, role in 216, 217
  maritime patrols, 1940-41 112, *112*, 113, *113*
  Market Garden and Varsity, role in Operations 174–5, *174*
  Mediterranean, 1940-42, role in 114–17, *114*, *116–17*
  North Africa, 1943, role in 152, 153, *152–3*
  post-war 192, 193, 194
  rearmament, inter-war 92–3, *92*, *93*
  seaborne aviation, early 78
  Sicily and Southern Italy, role in invasion of, 1943 154, 155
  strategic bombing offensive, 1918 63, *63*
  under aerial bombardment 1914-17 28, 29, 32–9, *33*, *34*, *35*, 38, *39*, 57–63, *58*, *59*, *60*, *61*, *62*, *63*
  World War I 18, *19*, 21, 22, 26, 27–8, 29, 32–9, *33*, *34*, *35*, *38*, *39*, 44, 49–51, 53, 57–63, *58*, *59*, *60*, *61*, *62*, *63*, 66–8
British Army units:
  1st Airborne Division 174
  3rd Army 67
  4th Army 68
  5th Army 67
  8th Army 155
  Afrika Korps 152, 153
  Airship Section 32
  Balloon Section 32
  military aeronautical branch, birth of 12 *see also under individual battle, war and operation name*
British Expeditionary Force (BEF) 21, 22, 100–1, 102
Brown, Captain Roy *50*, 68
Brown, Lieutenant Arthur Whitten *72*, 73, 73, 74
Brumowski, Godwin 55
Brusilov Offensive, 1916 54, 66
Bulge, Battle of the, 1944-45 184
Bulwark, HMS 207
Bunker Hill, USS 162, *162*, 165
Burma 129, 176, 178–9, *178*, *182*, 183
Bush, George W. 217

California, USS 127
Camm, Sydney 92
Canada 113, 141, 154
Cape Matapan, Battle of, 1941 115, *115*
Caproni 36, *57*, 58
  Ca.3 *55*, 56, *56*
Caproni, Gianni 56
Cartwheel, Operation, 1942-43 144–5, *144–5*
Castro, Fidel 200
Caucasus 118, 136–7, *136*, *137*
Cayley, Sir George 10
Celeste 10
Central Intelligence Agency (CIA) 200–1
Central Powers *see under individual nation state*
Central Treaty Organisation (CENTO) 198
Cessna O-1 'Bird Dog'
Chamberlin, Clarence 72
Chance Vought F4U Corsair 196
Chávez, Jorge 16, 17
Chennault, Major Claire Lee 178, *179*, 186
Chewning, Lieutenant Walter 163
China 10, 70, 88, *89*, 95, *128*, 129, 176, 178–9, *178*, *179*, 188, 202
China Clipper 91
Churchill, Winston 32, 104, 106, 109, 140,

192
Clément-Bayard 31, 32
clippers 90, *90*, *91*
Cobra, Operation 172
Cockburn, George 15
Codbury, Major Egbert *37*
Cold War 191, 192–201
Colt machine guns 92
combat air control (CAP) 212, 213, *213*
Command of the Air, The (Douhet) 57
commercial air travel, birth of 90–1, *90*, *91*
Commission des Communications Aériennes 11
Compagnie d'Aérostiers 10
Condor Legion 83, 86
Consolidated:
  B-24 Liberator 113, 141, *141*, 146, 149, 168, *168*, *169*, 176, 186
  PBY Catalina 113, *168*
Conté, N.J. 10
Convair B-36 Peacemaker *193*, *193*
Coral Sea, Battle of, 1942 130–1, *130*, *131*, 132, 162
Corpo Aeronautico Militare 55, 56
Cot, Pierre 92
Coutelle, Charles 10
Courageous, HMS 101
Coventry, HMS 213
Crace, Rear Admiral John 131
Cranborne, Lord 88
Crete 115, 116, 118–19, *118*, *119*
Crimea 160, *160*, *161*
Crocco-Ricaldi N1 31
Croix, Félix du Temple de la 10
Cruise missile strike 218
Cuban Missile Crisis, 1962 200–1, *200*, *201*
Cunningham, Admiral Sir Andrew Browne 115, 116
Curtiss:
  C-46 Commando *178*, 179
  Hawk 75A 99, *99*
  Jenny 70
  NC-1/NC-2/NC-3/NC-4 70, 71–2, *72*
  P-40 Warhawk 95, 129, 153, 178, 179
  SB-2C Helldiver *162*
Curtiss, Glenn 13, 15, *15*, 70
Custis, G.W. Parke *10*
Cuxhaven Raid, 1914 28–9, *29*, 32

d'Arlandes, François Laurant 10
Daily Mail 14, 15, 16, 70, 73, 74
Dambusters Raid, 1943 148, *148*
Dassault:
  Mirage III 207
  Mystère IV 207
  Super Etendard 212
  Super Mystère 207
D-Day, 1944 170–3, *170*, *171*, *172*, *173*, 180
de Havilland:
  Comet racer 90
  DH 17 62
  Mosquito 148, 150, 151, 155, 168, 170, 174, 183, 184
  Sea Venom 207
de Havilland, Geoffrey 44
de Rozier, François Pilâtre 10
Delta (airship) 32
'Demoiselle' monoplane aircraft 12
Denmark 100–1, *100*, *101*
Desert Shield, Operation 214
Desert Storm, Operation 214–15, *214*, *215*
Deutsch de la Meurthe Prize 31
Deutsche Luft Hansa 81
Deutsche Luftschiffahrt-AG (DELAG) 11, 30, 70
Deutscher Luftsportverband (German Air Sports Association) 81
Dewoitine D.520 *102*
Dien Bien Phu, Battle of, 1963 202
Doolittle raid, 1942 188
Dornier:
  Do 17 83, 97
  Do 18 113
  Do 19 83
  Do 217 155
Douglas:
  A-1 Skyraider 203
  A-4 Skyhawk 209, 212, *213*, 214
  B-26 Invader 196
  C-47 Dakota/Skytrain 154, 155, 171, 174, *175*, 178, 179, 183, 194, *195*, 206
  C-54 Skymaster 194
  DC-1 90
  DC-2 90, *90*

220

Index

DC-3 90
EB-66 204
SBD Dauntless 131, *131*, *133*, 135, 142, 162
TBD Devastator *94*, 131, *133*, *134*
Douglas, Lieutenant William Sholto 26
Douhet, General Giulio 55, 56–7, 59
Dowding system 106
Dowding, Air Chief Marshal Sir Hugh 106, 109
Dropshot, Operation 192–3
Dunkerque 114, *115*
Dunning, Commander E.H. *78*, 79
Durouf, Jules 11
Duthuil & Charmers engine 12
Dyle Plan 103

Eagle (balloon) 11
Eagle, HMS 207
Eastern Front, World War II, 1943 156–61, *156*, *157*, *158*, *159*, *160*, *161*
Edelweiss, Operation 136–7
Egyptian Air Force 207, 209
Eisenhower, Dwight D. 200
El Alamein, Battle of, 1942 153
Empress 28, *29*
Engadine 28
engines 12, 14, 16, 17, 21, 44, 53, 64, 70, 73, 90, 92, 110, 186 *see also under individual engine company name*
England *see* Britain
England to Australia:
 air race, 1934 90
 first flights *71*, 71
English Channel, first flight over 14–15, *14*
English Electric Canberra 207
Enola Gay 190, *191*
Enterprise, USS *131*, 132, *134*, *135*, 142, 143, *163*, 165
Essex, USS 162
Eta 32
Everett, Lieutenant R.W.H. 113
Exocet anti-shipping missile 212

Fairchild Republic A-10 Thunderbolt II 'Warthog' *216*
Fairey:
 Battle 93, 103, *104*
 Swordfish *114*, 115
Falkenhayn, General Erich von 46, *46*, 54
Farman F.20 *21*
Farman, Henri 15, 16, *21*
Ferdinand, Archduke Franz 18
Fiat:
 CR.32 86, *87*
 G.50 99
fighter aircraft:
 early 26
 fighter squadron, birth of 48
 1914–18 40–55, *40*, *41*, 42, 43, 44, 45, *46*, *47*, 48, *49*, 50, 51, *52*, 53, 54, 55
 tactics 68, 86, 96–7, *96*, 97, 102, 157, 166, 210–11, *210*, *211*
 see also under individual aircraft, conflict, nation and operation name
Finland 78, 98–9, *98*, *99*, 100
Finnish Air Force 79, 99
Fitzmaurice, James 74
Fiume 114, *115*, 116
Fleet Air Arm, UK 101, 115, 212
Fletcher, Rear Admiral Frank Jack 131, 132, *133*, *134*, *134*, 142
Fleurus, Battle of, 1794 10
flying boats 70–2, *72*, 74–5, *75*, 91, *91*, 112, 113, *113*, 115, 168, *194*
'Flying Tigers' 178, *179*, *179*
FMA IA 58 Pucará 212
Foch, Ferdinand 70
Focke-Wulf:
 Fw 190 155, 158, *160*, 184
 Fw 200 *113*, *113*
Focus, Operation, 1967 207
Fokker 88
 D.VII 67, 68
 D.XXI 99
 DR.1 Triplane 44, 52, *52*, 53–4
 E.1 41, *43*, 51
 E.111 monoplane *41*, 44
 Eindekker 41, 43
 F.VIIB-3m 70, *70*
 FE.2D *44*
Fokker, Anthony 41
Ford, Henry 141
Forlanini, Enrico 17
Formidable, HMS 115, *115*
France:
 1st Army 68
 Aéronautique Militaire (French Army Air Force) *18*, 46, *57*, 58
 Aéronavale (French Fleet Air Arm) 92, 104

aircraft production, World War II 140
airships 31, *31*, 32
Battle of, 1940 94, 102–3, *102*, *103*, 104, *105*, 106
early air force 18, *18*, *19*, 24
early aviation 10, 11, 12, 14–15, *14*, 16–17
Escadrille Layfayette 64
fighters 1914–1918 44, 46–7, *46–7*
fighters, early 40, *40*
navy 92, 104, 112, 115
rearmament, inter-war 92, 93, 94, *95*
Vichy 102, *105*
World War I 20, *20*, 21, 22, *22*, 23, 24, *25*, 26, 40–1, *40*, 52, 54, 66, 68
Franco, Francisco 83, 84, 85, 87, 95
Franco-Prussian War, 1870-71 11, 18
Freycinet, Charles Louis de Saulces de 11
Fritz X glide bomb 155
Fumas, Charlie 13
Furious, HMS *78*, 79, 117

Gallard, Adolf 85
Galliéni, General Joseph-Simon 22
Gambetta, Leon 11
Gamelin, General Maurice 103
Gamma 32
Garibaldi 115
Garros, Roland 12, 40, *40*, 41
GAU-8 Gatling-type cannon 217
Gaulle, General Charles de 104
Gavotti, Lieutenant Guilio 17
Geisse, Oberstleutnant Hans 113
Geneva Disarmament Conference, 1932 82
George V, King 36
George, David Lloyd 15, 60
General Dynamics F-16 Fighting Falcon 219
German Army units:
 1st Panzer Army 104, 137, 160
 2nd Panzer Army 104
 3rd Armoured Division 104
 4th Armoured Division 103
 4th Panzer Army 138
 6th Army *138*, 138, 139
 8th Army 160
 9th Panzer Division 103, *103*, *158*
 10th Mountain Division 119
 17th Army 137, 157, 160
 22nd Panzer Division 139
 Army Group A 103, 136, 137, 138, 157, 160
 Army Group B 102–3, 136, 138
 Army Group South 138, 156, 160, 180
 Fallschirmjäger ('parachute troops') 100, 103, 119, 155
 Panzerwaffe 103
 Russian Liberation Army 156
 SS Galician 14th Division – Ukranian Division 156
 Wehrmacht 97, 100, 104, 122
Germany:
 aircraft production, World War II 140, 141
 air forces, early 18–29, *19*, 24
 airships 11, 30–9, *31*, *32*, *33*, *34*, *35*, *36*, *37*, *38*, *39*
 Amerikaprogramm 66
 Atlantic war, 1940-44 112–13, *112*, *113*, 168, *169*
 aviation industry, early *11*, *11*
 aviation industry during World War II 140, 141, *141*
 Bagration and the liberation of West USSR, involvement in 180, *181*
 Balkans, 1941, role in 118–19, *118*, *119*
 Barbarossa and the bombing of Moscow, 1941 120–3, *121*, *122*, *123*
 Battle of Britain, 1940 106, *106*, *107*, 108–9, *108*, *109*
 Berlin airlift, 1948-49 194, *195*
 bombers 1916–18 57–63, *57*, *58*, 59, *60*, *61*, *63*
 British and Allied bombing of, 1940-4 108, 110–11, 111, *111*, 146–51, *146–7*, *148*, *149*, 150, *151*, 170–2, *171*
 Caucasus, 1942 134–5, *134*, *135*
 D-Day, role in 170–2, *171*
 Eastern Front, 1943 156–7, *156*, *157*
 fighters 1914-18 41, *41*, 42, 43, 44, *44*, 45, 46–55, 46–7, 48–9, 50, *51*, 52, 53, 54, 55
 Imperial German Air Service 19, *19*, 24, 67–8, *67*
 inter-war years 70, 77, 80–3
 Kursk, 1943 158–9, *158*, *159*
 Luftwaffe *see* Luftwaffe
 Mediterranean 1940-42 114–17, *114*, *115*, *116–17*
 North Africa and the Mediterranean,

1943 152–3, *152*, *153*
Poland, 1939 96–7, *96*, *97*
rearmament, inter-war 92, 94, 95
Reich, end of 184, *184*, *185*
Scandinavia, 1939-40 98–101, *98*, *99*, *100*, *101*
Sicily and Southern Italy 154–5, *154*
Spanish Civil War, role in 84–7, *87*, 94
Stalingrad 1942-43 138–9, *138*, *139*
Ukraine and the Crimea, 1943 160, *160*, *161*
World War I 18–69
Zeppelins and *see* Germany: airships
Gibson, Wing Commander Guy 148
Giffard, Henri 11
gliders 10, 12, 81, 103, 118, 119, 146, 154, 170, 174, 175
Glorious, HMS 101
Gloster Gladiator 92, 99, 100, *100*, 101, 117, 118, 152
Gloucester, HMS *115*
Gneisenau 101
Gnome Engine Company 16, 17, 44
Gnys, Wladyslaw 97
Goodwood, Operation 172
Gordon Bennett prize 16
Göring, Hermann 81, *82*, 104, 106, 108, 109, 139
Gort, General Lord 104
Gotha 58–60:
 G.IV bomber 58–9, *59*, 60
 G.V 59, *59*, 60
Grahame-White, Claude 16
Grand Prix de la Champagne 15
Grande Semaine d'Aviation de la Champagne 15
Graziani, Marshal Rodolfo 152
Greece 115, *115*, 118, *118–19*, 119
Grey, Spencer 34
Grumman:
 E-2 Hawkeye 214
 F-14 Tomcat 214
 F4F Wildcat 134, *135*, 142, *142*, 166
 F6F Hellcat 145, *163*, 164, *164*, 165
 F9F Panther 196
 TBF Avenger 166
Guadalcanal, 1943 142–4, *142*, *143*
Guderian, General Heinz 103, *103*
Guernica, bombing of 1937 86–7
Guise, Battle of, 1914 21
Gulf War, First, 1991 214–17, *214*, *215*, *216*
Gulf War, Second, 2003 217

Haakon, VII, King 100
Haegan, Oberleutnant von der 34
Haig, Field Marshal 54
Halsey, Field Admiral William 142, 144
Halvorsen, Lt Col Gail 195
Handley Page:
 Halifax 146, 150, 182–3
 Hampden 111
 HP.42 77
 O/100 60, *63*
 O/400 62, *62*, *63*, 70
 V/1500 62, 70
 Victor 212
 W8F 77
Harris, Air Marshal Sir Arthur 'Bomber' 146, *146*, 147, 148, 150, 170
Hawker Aircraft 92
 Fury 92
 Hunter 207
 Hurricane *92*, 93, 101, 106, 108, 110, 117, 118, 129, 152, 176, 178
 Sea Fury 196
 Sea Hawk 207
 Sea Hurricane 113
 Typhoon 170, *171*, 172, *172*, *173*, 174, 176
Hawker Siddeley:
 Harrier 212
 Nimrod 212
Hawker, Major Lance 44, 49–50, *49*, 50–1
Hearst, William Randolph 16
Heinkel 80, 141
 He 51 84, 87
 He 111 83, 87, *138*, 139, 154, 158
 He 115 113
Heldsen, Lieutenant von 21
helicopters 196, 197, 202, *202*, 203, 215
Henderson, Major Lofton 142
Henschel:
 Hs 123 97
 Hs 129 157, 158
 Henshaw, Alex 93
Hercule (balloon) 10
Hermes, HMS 28, 212, *212*
Hezbollah 211
high-speed yo-yo manoeuvre 210, *210*
Hindenberg, General Paul von 24, 82

Hinton, Lieutenant W. 72
Hiroshima, bombing of, 1945 190, *191*
Hiryu 124, 125, *125*, *131*, 132, *133*, 134–5, *134*, *135*
Hispano-Suiza engines 53, 92
Hitler, Adolf 81, 82, 83, 84, 100, 102, 104, 106, 109, 113, 116, 118, 119, 120, 136, 137, 138, 139, 152, 156, 159, 160, 180, 184
Hiyo 165
Ho Chi Minh Trail 205
Hoeppner, General Ernst von 58
Hornet, USS *131*, 132, *134*, *135*, 143
Hosho (carrier) 79
Hughes, Howard 61
Hughes H-4 Hercules 'Spruce Goose' *61*
Hünefeld, Gunther von 74
Huntziger, General Charles 104
Husky, Operation, 1943 154–5, *154*
Hussein, Saddam 214

Iachino, Admiral Angelo 115
IAI Dagger 212
ICBMs (Intercontinental Ballistic Missiles) 199
Ichi-Go, Operation 176, 188
Illustrious, HMS 115
Ilyushin:
 Il-2 Sturmovik 156, 158, *158*, 159, *159*, *160*, 196
 Il-10 196
 Il-28 192, 207
Immelmann turn *42*, 43
Immelmann, Max 41, *42*, 43, *43*
Imperial Airways 70, 77, *77*
Independence, USS 162
India 71, 77, 129, 176, 179, 186
Indochina 89, 176, 202–5, *202*, *203*, *204*, *205*
inter-war years 70–5
Intrepide (balloon) 10
Invincible, HMS 212
Iran 216
Iraq 77, 209, 214–17, *214*, *215*, *216*
Iraqi Air Force 215, 216
Iraqi Freedom, Operation 216
IRBMs 200, 201, *201*
island-hopping campaign, 1943-45 166, *167*
Israeli Air Force (IAF) 206, 207, *207*, 208, *208*, 209, *209*, 210–11, *210*, *211*
Italy 17, 31, 56–7, 66
 airships 31
 Fleet in the Mediterranean, 1940–41 112, 115–16
 Italian-Turkish war, 1911 17, *17*, 31, 56
 Sicily and Southern Italy, Allied invasion of, World War II 154–5, *154*, *155*
 Spanish Civil War, 1936–39, role in 85–6
 Trans-Oceanic flights, 1927–33 74–5, *75*
 World War I, role in 36, 54, 55, 56, *57*, 58
Iwo Jima 166, 176, 188, 190

James, Archibald 26
Japan 11, 88, 95
 aircraft production, World War II 94, 95, 141
 Army Air Service 95
 Cartwheel, Operation, 1942-43 144–5, *144*, *145*
 China, war in, 1937-45 88, *88*, *89*, 178–9, *178*, *179*
 Coral Sea, Battle of, 1942 130–1, *130*, *131*, 162
 Guadalcanal 142–4, *142*, *143*
 island-hopping campaign and, US, 1943-45 166, *167*
 Marianas, 1944 164–5, *164*, *165*
 Midway, Battle of, 1942 132–5, *132*, *133*, *134*, *135*, 142, 144, 162
 Naval Air Service 95
 navy 78, 79, 95, 124, *125*, 132, *132*, *133*, 162, *163*, 164 *see also under individual area, battle and operation name*
 nuclear bombing of, 1945 190–1, *190*, *191*
 Pearl Harbor 124–7, *124*, *125*, *126*
 seaplane carriers 78, 79, 162, *163 see also under individual battle and carrier name*
 Southeast Asia, 1942-44 *128*, 129, *129*, 176, *177*
 US bombing of, 1945 186–8, *186*, *187*, *188*, 190–1, *190*, *191*
Jatho, Karl 11
JN-25 naval code 130–1
Joffre, General 22, 46–7, 52
'Joffre's Wall' 22, *23*

221

Index

Johnson, Amy 74
Johnson, Ensign Byron *163*
Jordan 209
Junkers 80
    Ju 52 *82*, 83, 84, 87, *87*, 100, 119, *119*, 139, *139*, 153
    Ju 87 'Stuka' 80, *80*, 83, *83*, *95*, *96*, 97, 103–4, 108, *121*, 138, 158, *158*
    Ju 88 109, 154
    Ju 89 83
    W.33 'Bremen' 74
Junyo 143

Kai-shek, Chiang 186
Kaga 79, *124*, 125, *131*, 132, *133*, *134*, 135
kamikaze attacks 166
Kawasaki 88
Kazakov, Aleksandr 54–5
Kennedy, John F. 200, 201
Kenny, Major General George C. 144
Kensington Court 113
Kesselring, Albert 83
Khrushchev, Nikita 201
Kleist, General Ewald von 136
KLM 90
Kluck, General Alexander von 22
Knickebein beams 110, *110*
Köhl, Hermann 74
Königsberg 101
Korean War, 1950–53 196–7, *196*, *197*
Kozhedub, Ivan *180*
Krebs, Arthur 12
Kriegsmarine 106
Krueger, General Walter 144
Kursk, Battle of, 1943 156, 158–9, *158*, *159*
Kuwait 214–15
Kuwaiti Air Force 214, 215, *215*

L 3 (airship) 32, 33, *33*
L 4 (airship) 32, 33, *33*
L 5 (airship) 29, 32
L 6 (airship) 29, 32, 33
L 9 (airship) 33, *33*
L 10 (airship) 33, *33*
L 11 (airship) 35
L 13 (airship) 35
L 14 (airship) 35
L 16 (airship) 35
L 17 (airship) 37
L 21 (airship) 35
L 22 (airship) 35
L 23 (airship) 35
L 24 (airship) 35
L 30 (airship) 35
L 32 (airship) 35
L 33 (airship) *36*, 37
L 41 (airship) 38
L 44–50 (airships) *38*
L 52–5 (airships) 38
L 59 (airship) 39, *39*
L 70 (airship) *37*, 39
L'Entreprenant (balloon) 10
La France 10, 11, 12
La Neptune (balloon) 11
La Patrie 31
La République 31
Lambert, Charles de 14
Langley, Samuel P. 10, 13
Lanrezac, General Charles 21
Latham, Hubert 14, 15
Lavochkin:
    La-5 *180*
    La-9 196
Le Matin 15
League of Nations 82
Lebanon, invasion of, 2006 211
Lebaudy brothers 31
Leckie, Captain Robert *37*
Leeb, General Wilhelm Ritter von 103
Leigh-Mallory, Air Chief Marshal Sir Trafford 109, 110
LeMay, Major General Curtis 186
Lend-Lease 140, 168, 178
Lewis gun 47
Lexington, USS 78, *79*, 131
Leyte 166, 176
Liberty engine 64, 70
Lilienthal, Otto 10
Lindbergh, Charles A. *72*, 74, *74*, 90
Linebacker I & II, Operations 205
Lippisch, Alexander *184*
Liscombe Bay, USS 162
Littorio 114, 115
Lockheed:
    C-130 217
    F-80 196–7
    F-117 Nighthawk 215, *216*
    Hudson 129, 168
    P-38 Lightning 145, 170, *171*
    U-2 201

Lockheed Martin F-16 Flying Falcon 211
London to Manchester air race, 1910 16
long-range air transport, 1934–39 90–1, *90*, *91*
Lowe, Professor Thaddeus 11
Ludendorff, General Erich 24, 67, 68
Luftschiff Zeppelin see LZ 1
Luftschiffbau Zeppelin 30
Luftwaffe:
    birth of 80–3, *80*, *81*, *82*, *83*
    Condor Legion 83, 86
    Fliegerkorps IV 108, *108*
    Fliegerkorps X 117, 152–3
    Luftflotte I *96*
    Luftflotte IV *96*, 119, 136, 137, 138
    Luftflotte V *108*
    Operational Areas of Command, 1939 *81*
    Operational Chain of Command, World War II *83*
    see also under individual aircraft, area of operation and conflict name
Luke, Frank 68
Lusitania 64
Luzon 166, 176
LZ 1 (airship) 11, *11*, 30
LZ 2 (airship) 11, 30
LZ 3 (airship) 11, 30
LZ 4 (airship) 30
LZ 18 (airship) *32*
LZ 37 (airship) 33, *33*, 34
LZ 38 (airship) 33, *33*, 34
LZ 90 (airship) 35
LZ 97 (airship) 37
LZ 99 (airship) 35

MacArthur, General Douglas 144, 166, 196
Magdeburg 28–9
MAGIC (code-breaking system) 130–1, 132, 144
Maginot Line 94, 102, 103
Maison Clément-Bayard 32
Makin 166
Malaya *128*, 129, *129*, 176
Malta 115, 116–17, *116–17*, 152, 152, 155, 207
Manchuria 82, 88, 94, 157, 160, 190, 191
Manhattan Project 190
Mannerheim Line 99
Mannerheim, Marshal Carl Gustaf von 98
man-portable anti-air missiles (MANPADs) 218, 219
Manstein, General Erich von 102, 137, 156
Maplin 113
Marianas islands 164–5, *164*, *165*, 186, 187, *187*
maritime air patrols 1940-41 112–13, *112*, 113
Market Garden and Varsity, 1944-45 174–5, *174*, *175*
Marne, Battle of the, 1914 22, *22*, 24
Marshall Plan 192
Martin:
    M-130 91
    Maryland 117
Masurian Lakes 24, *24*
Matterhorn, Operation 187
Mayfly (airship) 32
McClellan, George B. 10
McDonnell Douglas:
    FA-18 Hornet 214
    F-4 Phantom 204
    F-4 Phantom II 'Wild Weasel' 209, *209*, 215
    F-15 Eagle 211, 214
    RF-101 Voodoo *201*
Mediterranean 114–17, *114*, *115*, *116*, *117*, 152–3, *152–3*
Medwecki, Captain Mieczysław 97
Merkur, Operation 119, *119*
Merrill, General Frank 183
Mers-el-Kébir 114–15
Messerschmitt:
    Bf 109 *81*, 83, 86, 97, 108, 109, *109*, 119, 149, 158, 184, 206
    Bf 110 97, 100, 119, 149
    Me 262 141, *184*
    Me 323 153
    Me 410 149
Messerschmitt, Willi 81
Messines Ridge 54
MG 17 machine gun 81, *81*
Midway, Battle of, 1942 132–5, *132*, *133*, *134*, *135*, 142, 144, 162
Mikoyan-Gurevich:
    MiG-3 *123*, 158
    MiG-7 158
    MiG-15 196, 197, *197*, 207
    MiG-17 204
    MiG-19 210
    MiG-21 *205*, 205, 207, 209, 210
    MiG-29 219
Mikuma 135

Milch, Erhard 81, 82
Millennium, Operation 147
Mitchell, General W.L. 'Billy' *78*, 79
Mitchell, Reginald 92, 93
Mitsubishi 88
    A5M 88
    A6M2 Reisen (Zero Fighter) *124*, 125, *125*, 127, 129, 134, 142
    A6M5 Zero *145*
    G3M2 129
    G4M1 'Betty' *129*, 142, 145
Modena Military Academy 56
Mölders, Werner 85
Mollison, Jim 74
Moltke, Helmuth von 21, 30
Mongoose, Operation 201
monoplane, first successful 14
Monosoupape Gnome engine 44
Montgomery, General Bernard 153, 154, 174, 175
Morane-Saulnier 34, 40, 47, 54, 92
    MS.406 99
    Type 'N' *40*, 41
Morlot, General 10
Morning Post 31
Mussolini, Benito 83, 118, 155
Mutual Assured Destruction (MAD) 199

Nagasaki, bombing of, 1945 190–1, *190*, 191
Nagumo, Vice Admiral Chuichi 132, *133*, 134, 143
Nakajima 88
    B5N 'Kate' *124*, 125, *125*, 127
    Ki-27 95
Nasser, Gamal Abdel 207
Nazi Party 82, 141 see also Germany
Nevada, USS 127
Nieuport 51
    II 'Bebe' 44
    X *47*
    XI 47
    28 64
Nimitz, Admiral Chester W. 132
9/11 217
Nivelle, Robert Georges 52, *53*, 54, 66
Nixon, Richard 205
NKVD 136, 137
North Africa 152–3, *152–3*
North American:
    B-25 144
    P-51 Mustang 149, 151, 171, 172, 176, 179, *179*, 196
    F-82 Twin Mustang 196
    F-86 Sabre 197, *197*
    F-100 Super Sabre 203, 204
North Atlantic Treaty Organisation (NATO) 198, *217*, 219
North Vietnamese Air Force 205, *205*
Northcliffe, Lord 70, 74
Northrop Grumman B-2 Spirit 217
Norway 100–1, 112
nuclear warfare/bombing 190–1, *190*, *191*
Nulli Secundus 32

O'Connor, General Sir Richard Nugent 152
Oberkommando des Heeres (OKH) 102a
Oboe targeting system 150
offensive split manoeuvre 210, *210*
Oiseau Canari 72
Okinawa 166, 176, 188, 190
'ornithopter' 14
Orion 115
Ostfriesland 78, 79
Ozawa, Admiral Jisaburo 164, 165

P.2 (airship) 17
P.3 (airship) 17
Pacific Ocean:
    commercial air routes over, first 91, *91*
    first complete crossing of 70–1, *70*
    World War II conflict in 94, 124–7, *124*, *125*, *126*, 127, 130–5, *130*, *131*, *132*, *133*, *134*, 135, 142, *142*, 143, 144, 145, 162–7, *162*, *163*, *164*, *165*, *167*, 186–91, *186*, *187*, *188*, *189*, *190*, *191*
PaK cannon 158
Palestine 206
Pan Am 90, 91
Panavia Tornado 214, 215
parachutes, first *68*
Park, Keith 109
Patrick, Major General Mason 64
Paulhan, Louis 16, 139
Paulus, General Friedrich 138
Pearl Harbor 78, 88, 115, 124–8, *124*, *125*, *126*, *127*, *128*, 132, 142, 166
Pearse, Richard 11
Pedestal, Operation 1942 117
Peltier, Thérèse 15
Perth, HMAS 115, *115*

Petlyakov Pe-2 157, *160*
Peuty, Jean du 51
Philippine Sea, Battle of, 1944 164–5, *164*, 165
photography, aerial 11, 26, *54*, *54*, 68, 158, 201, *201*
Piasecki CH-21 'Flying Banana' 202
pilot-training schools, first 12
Pinedo, Francesco de 75
pioneering air routes:
    1921–30 70–3, *71*, *72*, *73*
    1934–39 90–1, *91*
Piper Cub 182
'Plan 17' 20
Plan Yellow 103
Pohl, Admiral Hugo von 32
Pointblank, Operation, 1943 149
Pokryshkin, Aleksandr *123*
Pola 115, *116*
Poland 96–7, *96*, *97*, 102, 111, 174, 183
Polikarpov:
    I-15 *84*, 95, 99
    I-16 'Rata' 86, *95*, 99, *120*
Popular Mechanics 12
Pour le Mérite 43
powered flights, first successful 12–13, *12*, *13*
Pratt & Whitney engines 90
Pridham-Wippell, Admiral Sir Henry 115
Prince of Wales, HMS 129
Prince, Norman 64
Princeton, USS 162
Princip, Gavrilo 18
Prodhommeaux, Corporal *18*
PZL P11 97

R34 (airship) 74
radar 93, 106, 107–9, *109*, 110, 111, 112, 125, 142, 147, 148, 150, 151, 155, 164, 165, 166, 168, 170, 184, 188, 204, 208, *209*, 210, 212, 215
Ramsay, Vice Admiral Bertram 104
Read, Lieutenant Commander A.C. 72, *72*
Regia Aeronautica 85–6, *85*, 95, 117, 152, 155
Renard, Charles 12
Renault engines 21
Rennenkampf, General Paul von 24
Republic:
    F-84 Thunderjet 197
    F-84 Thunderstreak 207
    F-105 Thunderchief 202, 204, 205
    P-47 Thunderbolt *171*, 172, *176*
Repulse, HMS 129
Rhoads, E.S. 72
Rice, Bernard 52
Richards, Wesley 49
Richthofen, Baron Manfred von *44*, 50, *50*, 51, *52*, 54, 55, 68
Richthofen, General Wolfram von 138
Rickenbacker, Captain Eddie 64
Riviera 28
Robertson, Sir William 60
Robinson, Lieutenant Leefe 37
Rodd, Ensign H.C. 72
Rodgers, Calbraith Perry 16
Rolling Thunder operations, 1965–68 204, 204
Rolls-Royce:
    Eagle VIII engine 73
    Merlin engines 92, 110
Romania 118, 137, 138, *139*, 160
Rommel, Field Marshal Erwin 136, 152, 153
Roosevelt, Franklin D. 75, 111, 140, 141
Roosevelt, Teddy 15
Royal Aircraft Factory:
    BE.2c 37, 41, *66*
    Re. 8 *66*
    S.E.5a 53, 64, 70
Royal Air Force (RAF) 62, 70, 77, 78, 92, 97
    41st Wing 62
    Advanced Air Striking Force *103*
    AFGB (Air Defence of Great Britain) 93
    'Big Wing' 109
    Bomber Command 111, 112, 146, 148, 151, 168, 170, 172, 184, 187, 193
    Coastal Command *95*, 109, 168
    Empire, role throughout 77
    Fighter Command 26, *95*, 106, *106*, 107, *171*
    inter-war expansion of 94–5
    Medium Bomber Force 207
    No. 4 Group 111
    No. 10 Squadron *93*
    No. 11 Group 108, 109
    No. 12 Group 109
    No. 34 Squadron 129
    No. 46 Squadron 101
    No. 60 Squadron 129
    No. 62 Squadron 129
    No. 138 Squadron 183

Index

No. 148 Squadron 183
No. 161 Squadron 183
No. 203 Squadron 113
No. 218 Squadron 104, *171*
No. 230 Squadron *113*
No. 263 Squadron 101
No. 617 Squadron 148, *171, 182*
No. 624 Squadron 183
Observer Corps 106
Sector Command 106
Special Operations Squadrons 182–3, *182, 183*
see also under individual aircraft, area of operation and conflict name
Royal Australian Air Force *170*
Royal Australian Navy 115
Royal Canadian Navy 113
Royal Flying Corps (RFC) 18, 26, 34, 37, 40, 41, 43, 44, 48–9, *50*, 51, *60*, 62, *66*, 68
Royal Jordanian Air Force (RJAF) 209
Royal Marines 212
Royal Naval Air Service (RNAS) 26, 28, 29, 34, 52, *60, 62*
Royal Navy 28, 29, 32, 78, 92, 101, *101*, 106, 114–16, *114, 115*, 118–19, 119, 212
Fleet Air Arm 101, 115, 212
Royal Saudi Air Force 214
Ruge, Major General Otto 100
Ruhr, Battle of, 1942 148
Rumpler Taube 21, 24, *24*
Rundstedt, General Gerd von 103
Russia:
  aeronautical training school, first 11
  World War I 18, 19, 20, 24, 54–5, 56, 66
  war in Ukraine 218–9
  see also Soviet Union
Russian Air and Space Forces 218
Russia Imperial Air Service *19*
Russian Liberation Army 156
Russia–Ukraine War 218–9
Ryan Monoplane 74, *74*
Ryneveld, Lt Col Pierre von *71*

SA-2 'Guideline' missile 204
Salmson 2 64
Salon de l'Automobile et de l'Aéronautique, Paris 14
Samsonov, General 24
Santa Maria 75
Santa Maria II 75
Santos-Dumont, Alberto 12, 31, *31*
Saratoga, USS 78, *79*, 142, 162
Sarvanto, Lieutenant Jorma 99
Saudi Arabia 214
Saulnier, Raymond 40
Savoia-Marchetti:
  S-55 75, *75*, *75*
  S.M.81 *85*, 85–6
Scharnhorst 101
scheduled air services, birth of 70
Schlieffen Plan 18, *20*, *20*, 21
Schlieffen, Field Marshal Alfred von *20*, *20*, 21
Schramm, Wilhelm 37
Schütte-Lanz 30
Schwarms 85
Schwartz, David 30
Schweinfurt, bombing of, 1943 149, *149*
scissors manoeuvre 211, *211*
seaborne aviation 78–9, *78, 79*
Seeckt, General Hans von 80, 81, 82
Selfridge, Thomas 13
SEPECAT Jaguar 215
Sheffield, HMS 212
shipping, patrolling in World War II 112–13, *112, 113*
Shoho 130, 131
Shokaku 124, 125, *125*, 142, 143, 165
Short:
  Seaplane No.74 *29*
  Stirling 146, *146*, 150, 174, 183
  Sunderland 112, *113*, 168, 194
'Shrike' anti-radar missile 204
Sicily 154–5, *154, 155*
Sickle Stroke 102
Siegert, Major Wilhelm 57–8
Sikorsky:
  H-19 197
  Ilya Muromets 54, 56, *57*, 58, 183
  MH-53 Pave Low helicopter 215
  S-42 91
  Sea King 212
Sikorsky, Igor 56
'Silent Raid', 1917 *38*, 39
Singapore 113, 128, 129, *129*, 176
Sir Galahad, HMS 213
Six-Day War, 1967 207–9, *207*
SL 8 (airship) *35*
SL 11 (airship) 35, *35*, 37
Slim, Lieutenant-General William *176*
Smith, Charles Kingsford 70, *72*

Smith, Herbert *51*
Smith, Keith *71*
Smith, Ross *71*
Smuts, General Jan 60, 62
Société Astra des Constructions Aéronautiques 32
Somme, Battle of, 1916 *48*–9, 51, 67
Sopwith:
  1½ Strutter 48
  Camel *51*
  Pup 50, *78*, 79
  Snipe 92
  Triplane *51*, 52
Soryu 124, 125, *125*, 130, *131*, 132, *133, 134*, 135
South Dakota, USS 164
Southeast Asia Treaty Organisation (SEATO) 198
Southeast Asia:
  fall of, 1942 128–9, *129, 129*
  1944–45 174, 176, *176, 177*
Southern Cross 70
Soviet Union 137, 158, 159, 184
  1st/3rd/5th Guards Airborne Brigades 157
  6th Fighter Air Corps 123, *123*
  8th Air Army *160*
  9th Composite Air Corps 160
  17th Air Army 160, *160*
  air force strength, 1939 94
  aircraft production, World War II 140, 141, 156
  anti-aircraft defences, World War II 122, *122*, 123
  Army Group Voronezh 156
  Bagration, Operation 180, *181*
  Barbarossa, Operation, defence against, 1941 113, 118, 119, 120–3, *120, 121, 122, 123*
  Caucasus and Southern Russia, 1942 136–7, *136, 137*
  Cold War 191, 192, 194
  inter-war commercial air routes 77, 81
  liberation of, World War II 180, *180, 181*
  Moscow, bombing of, 1941 119, 120–3, *120, 121, 122, 123*
  Moscow, Treaty of, 1940 99
  Russian Liberation Army 156
  Spanish Civil War, role in 84, 86, 87, 94
  Stalingrad, 1942–43 138–9, *138*–9, 158
  Winter War, 1939–40 98–9
  see also Russia
Spaatz, Carl Andrew 170
SPAD XIII 53, 64
Spanish Civil War, 1936-39 83, 84–8, *84, 85, 86, 87, 88*, 94, 95
Spanish Republican Air Force 84–5, *84, 85*
special operations, World War II 182–3, *182, 183*
Sperrle, General Major Hugo 83
Spirit of St Louis 74
Spruance, Rear Admiral Raymond A. 132, *134, 134, 135*, 164, 166
Spuy, Kenneth van der 40
Stalin, Joseph 94, 136, 138, 140, 156, 180
Stalingrad, 1942–43 138–9, *138*–9, 158
Stilwell, General Joseph 179
Stone, Lieutenant E. 72
Strasbourg 101
Strasser, Korvettenkapitan Peter 32, 33, 36, 37, 39
Stumpff, Jürgen 108
Suez Canal 114, 152, 206, *206*, 207, 210
Suez Crisis, 1956 206, *206*, 207
Sukhoi Su-7 207, 210, 218, 219
Super Zeppelins 36
Supermarine Spitfire 92–3, *93*, 106, 108, 110, 117, 140, 148, 149, 153, *170*, 172, 174, 204
surface-to-air missile (SAMs) 204, 205, 209, 215, 218–219
Sweden 100
Sweeney, Major Charles W. 191
Syria 209

Taiho 164, 165
Takeo, Vice Admiral Takagi 130
Taliban 217
Tannenberg, Battle of, 1914 24, *25*, 54
Taranto, Battle of, 1940 *114*, 115, 124
Taube, Etrich 24
Tedder, Air Marshal Sir Arthur 154
Tempelhof Airport 194
Templer, Colonel James 32
Tibbets, Colonel Paul 190, *191*
Tomahawk missile 215
Tonkin, Gulf of 204
Torch, Operation, 1942 138, 153, *152*–3
Transcontinental and Western Air Inc (TWA) *90*, 90

Treaty of Versailles, 1919 68, 70, 80
Trenchard, Sir Hugh 51, 52, 57, 59, 62, 77, *77*, 92
Trento 115
Trieste 115
Trippe, Juan 90, 91
Truman, Harry S. 190, 192
Tupolev:
  SB-2 99
  Tu-4 193
  Tu-16 208, 209
U-boats 29, 60, 64, 112–13, *112, 113*, 149, 168, *169*
Ukraine 118, 120, 122, 136, 156, *156*, 157, 160, *161*, 180, 218–219
ULTRA intelligence 115, *115*
Undaunted, HMS 29
Union Army Balloon Corps 10, *10*, 11, 30
United Airlines 90
United Nations 196, 217
United States 113
  aircraft production, World War II 140, 141, *141*
  American Ambulance Field Service 64
  Americans in French air force, World War I 64
  Atlantic, patrolling the, 1939-45 168, *168, 169*
  Aviation Act, 1917 64
  balloons, early 10, *10*
  Berlin airlift, 1948-49 194, *194, 195*
  carrier raids in the Pacific, 1943 162, *162, 163*
  Cartwheel, Operation, 1942–43 144–5, *144, 145*
  China, 1941-45 178–9, *178, 179*
  Civil War, 1861-65 *10*, 11, 30
  coast-to-coast flight, first 16
  Cold War 192–3, *192*, 193, 198–9, *198*–9
  commercial air travel, birth of 90–1, *90, 91*
  Coral Sea, Battle of, 1942 130–1, *130, 131*
  Cuban missile crisis 200–1, *200, 201*
  D-Day 170–3, *170, 171, 172, 173*
  early aviation 10, *10*, 12–13, *12, 13*, 15, *15, 16, 17*
  Germany, bombing of, 1944 150–1, *150, 151*
  Guadalcanal, 1943 142–3, *142, 143*
  Gulf wars 214–17, *214, 215, 216, 217*
  inter-war years 70–2, *72, 74, 74, 75*
  island-hopping campaign, 1943-45 166, *167*
  Korea 1950–53 196–7, *196, 197*
  'Marianas Turkey Shoot', 1944 164–5, *164, 165*
  Market Garden and Varsity, 1944-45 174–5, *174, 175*
  Midway, Battle of, 1942 132–5, *133, 134, 135*
  mobilizes, 1917 64, *65*, 66–7
  nuclear bombing of Japan, 1945 190–1, *190, 191*
  Pearl Harbor 124–7, *124, 125, 126, 127*
  seaplane aviation 78–9, *79*
  Sicily and Southern Italy, invasion of, 1943 154–5, *154, 155*
  Southeast Asia, 1944-45 176, *176, 177*
  Torch, Operation, 1942 152–3, *152, 153*
  Vietnam War, 1959-75 202–5, *202, 203, 204, 205*
  unmanned aerial vehicle (UAVs) 217
Uranus, Operation, 1942 138
US Air Service 64, 68
US Army units 162
  1st Army 68
  1st Division 171
  6th Airborne Division 171, 175
  6th Army 144
  8th Fighter Command 171
  14th Army *176*
  17th Airborne Division 175
  29th Division 171
  51st Division 144
  82nd Airborne Division 155, 170, *171*, 174
  101st Airborne Division 170, *171*, 174, 175
  504th Parachute Infantry Regiment 155
  Aviation Section 64
  Signal Corps 12
  Transport Command 154, *170*, 171, 174
  see also United States and under individual area of operation, battle and conflict name
USAAF/USAF 129, 146, 151, 153, 154, *155*, 172, 176, 178–9, 184, 194, 204
  2nd Tactical Air Force 170, *171*
  5th Air Force 144

8th Air Force 146, 148, 149, 170, *171*, 172, 184, 188
9th Air Force 170, *171*
10th Bomber Command 179, 186, 187, 188
11th Bomber Command 188
15th Air Force 154
23rd Pursuit Group 178–9
52nd Troop Carrier Wing *174*
58th Bomb Wing 186
73rd Bomb Wing 186
313th Bomb Wing 186
314th Bomb Wing 186
315th Bomb Wing 186
363rd Tactical Reconnaissance Wing *201*
509th Composite Bomb Group 190
532nd Bomb Squadron, 381st Bomb Group 149
AVG and 178–9
'Cactus Air Force' 142, 143
Strategic Air Command 192
see also United States and under individual area of operation, battle and conflict name
US Marine Corps 78, 142, *143*, 144, 162, 166, 178, 216
US Navy 131, 143, 145, 197, 201, 204, 214, 215
  Bureau of Aeronautics 71
  carriers 72, 78, 143, 144, 162, 164, 166, *167*, 176, 214, 215
  Fast Carrier Task Force 167
  inter-war years 71
  Light Photographic Squadron *201*
  Pacific Fleet *79*, 115, 124, 132
  Seaplane Division One 72
  Southeast Asia 178
  Third Fleet 176
  see also United States and under individual area of operation, battle and conflict name
US Postal Department 90
USSR see Soviet Union

V1 rocket 184
V2 rocket 141, 184
Valiant, HMS 115
Varsity, Operation, 1945 175
Verdun, Battle for, 1916 *46*–7, 51, 54
Vickers:
  FB5 44
  Vimy 71, 73, *73*
  Wellington 93, 111, *111*, 117, 146, 168
  Wildebeest 129
Vietnam War, 1959-75 202–5, *202*–3, 204, 205
Vimy 71, 73, *73*
Vittorio Veneto 114, 115, *115*, 116
Vlasov, General 156
Voisin Pusher 26
Voss, Werner 52
Vought:
  F4U Corsair 207
  RF-8 Crusader *201*

Wakamiya 78
Wallis, Barnes 111, 148
war from the air, birth of 10–11
War on Terror 217
Warneford, Flight Sub-Lieutenant R.A.J. 34, *34*, 36
Warsaw Pact 198, 199
Warsaw Uprising, 1944 183, *183*
Warspite, HMS 115, *115*, 155
Washington (balloon) *10*
Washington Naval Treaty 162
Wasp, USS *142*, 153, 165
Weichs, General Maximilian von 136
Wells, H.G. 15, 28
Wenham, Francis 10
West Virginia, USS 127
Westland:
  Lysander 182
  Scout 212
  Wessex 212
Wever, General 82–3
Wicker 97
Wilcockson, Bennett and Carter transatlantic crossing *72*
'Wilde Sau' ('Wild Boar') missions 150
Wilson, Lieutenant J.P. 34
Wilson, Woodrow 64
Window (radar countermeasure) 150
wing warping 43
Wingate, Brigadier Orde 183
Winter War, 1939-40 98–9, *98, 99*, 120
Winterbotham, Frederick 18
Wolfe, General 188
world realignment, Cold War 198–9, *198*–9
World War I 18–29, 32–69, 94, 112
  airships in 32–9
  America mobilizes 64, *65*

223

Index

bombers in 56–63
early air forces in 18–29
fighters in 40–55
final battles, 1918 66–9
see also under individual battle and operation name
World War II 11, 81
air force strengths, 1939 94–5, *94, 95*
Atlantic, patrolling the 168, *168, 169*
aviation industries in 140–1, *140, 141*
Bagration, Operation 180, *180, 181*
Balkans 118–19, *118–19*
Barbarossa and the bombing of Moscow 119, 120–3, *120, 121, 122, 123*
Berlin, bombing of, 1944 150–1, *150, 151*
bombing of Britain and Germany, 1940–41 110–11, *110, 111,* 150–1, *150, 151*
Britain, Battle of, 1940 106–9, *106, 107, 108, 109*
Cartwheel, Operation, 1942-43 144–5, *144–5*
Caucasus and Southern Russia, 1942 136–7, *136, 137*
China, 1941-45 178–9, *178, 179*
Coral Sea, Battle of, 1942 130–1, *130, 131,* 132, 162
D-Day 170–3, *170, 171, 172, 173,* 180
Denmark and Norway, 1940 100–1, *100, 101*
Eastern Front, 1943 156–61, *156, 157, 158, 159, 160, 161*
Finland, 1939-40 98–9, *98, 99,* 100
France, Battle of, 1940 102–3, *102, 103, 104, 105,* 106
Germany, bombing, 1942-44 146-51, *146–7, 148, 149, 150, 151*
Guadalcanal, 1943 142–4, *142, 143*
island-hopping campaign, 1943-45 166, *167*
Kursk, Battle of, 1943 156, 158–9, *158, 159*
Maginot Line 94, 102, 103
'Marianas Turkey Shoot', 1944 164–5, *164, 165*
maritime air patrol, 1940-41 112–13, *112, 113*
Market Garden and Varsity, 1944-45 174–5, *174, 175*
Mediterranean 114–17, *114, 115, 116, 117,* 152–3, *152–3*
Midway, Battle of, 1942 132–5, *132, 133, 134, 135,* 142, 144, 162
North Africa 152–3, *152–3*
Pacific War *94,* 162-7, *162, 163, 164, 165, 167*
Pearl Harbor, 1941 124-8, *124, 125, 126, 127, 128,* 132, 166
Phoney War, 1939-40 102
Poland, 1939 96–7, *96, 97,* 102
Reich, end of 184, *184, 185*
Sicily and Southern Italy 154–5, *154, 155*
Southeast Asia, fall of, 1942 128–9, *129, 129*
Southeast Asia, 1944–45 176, *176, 177*
Soviet Union, Germany attacks 119, 120–3, *120, 121, 122, 123,* 138–9, *138–9*
Soviet Union, liberation of 180, *180, 181*
special operations 182–3, *182, 183*
Stalingrad, 1942-43 138–9, *138–9,* 158
Ukraine and the Crimea 160, *160, 161*
Winter War, 1939-40 98–9, *98, 99,* 120
Wright:
'Flyer' 10, 12, *12,* 13, *13,* 16
'Flyer III' 12
'Flyer, Military' 13
R-3350 engine 186
Whirlwind engine 74
Wright, Orville 10, 12–13, *12,* 15
Wright, Wilbur 10, 12–13, *12,* 15

Yakovlev Yak-9 196
Yamamoto, Admiral Isoroku 124, 132, *132, 133,* 134, *134,* 135, 144
Yamashita, General Tomoyuki 129
Yankee Clipper 91, *91*
Yom Kippur War, 1973 208-11, *208*
Yorktown, USS 131, 132, *134,* 135, *135*
Ypres, Third Battle of, 1917 54
Yugoslavia *69,* 118, 183

Z9 (zeppelin) 28, 32
Zara 114, *115,* 116
Zeppelin, Count Ferdinand Adolf August Heinrich Graf von 11, 30
Zeppelins 11, 27, 28, 29, 30–9, *30, 31, 32, 33, 34, 35, 36, 37, 38, 39*
Zeppelin-Staaken R-Type bomber 58, 60, *61*

INDEX OF MAPS

Admiral Yamamoto's Plan to Seize Midway, May–June 1942 132–3
Afghanistan Under NATO, 2006 217
Air Defence of the United Kingdom, 1918 60
Air Plan for D-Day, June 1944 171
Air Transport in the Spanish Civil War, 1936 85
Aircraft Deployed at the Western Front, 1917–18 65

Balkans, April 1941 118
Battle of Ap Bac, January 1963 202–3
Battle of Britain, June–October 1940 107
Battle of Cape Matapan, March 1941 115
Battle of Midway, June 1942 134–5
Battle of Stalingrad, 1942-3 138–9
Battle of the Atlantic, 1939–40 112
Battle of the Coral Sea, April–May 1942 130
Battle of the Philippine Sea, First Phase, June 1944 164
Battle of the Philippine Sea, Second Phase, June 1944 165
Battle of the Philippines, October 1944 177
Battle of the Somme, July–November 1916 48–9
Battle of Verdun, February–June 1916 46–7
Berlin Airlift, 1948–9 194–5
Blériot's Cross-Channel Flight, July 1909 14
Blitz, The, 1940–41 110
Bombing Moscow, September–December 1941 123
Bombing of Dresden, February 1945 185
Bombing of Hiroshima, August 1945 191
Bombing of Nazi Europe, 1940–42 111
Bombing of Schweinfurt, 1943 149
Britain Under Aerial Bombardment, 1914–17 58
British Strategic Bombing Offensive, 1918 63

Capturing Singapore, February 1942 129
Carrier Raids in the Central Pacific, October 1944 163
Caucasus, June–November 1942 136
Cold War, 1948–89 198–9
Cuban Missile Crisis, September–November 1962 200
Cuxhaven Raid, 1914 29

Dambusters Raid, May 1943 148
Daylight Gotha Raids, 1917 59
Denmark and Norway, April–June 1940 101

Early Tyneside Raids, April–June 1915 33
Eastern Front, March 1943 156

Empire of the Air 76
Europe, 1920 69
European Military Strengths, August 1914 19

Falklands War, April–June 1982 213
Fall of France and The Rise of Vichy, June–July 1940 104–5
Fighter Command and Control, 1940 106
First Airship Raid on Norfolk, January 1915 33
First Humber Raid, June 1915 33
First Successful Powered Flights, December 1903 13
First Zeppelin Raid on London, May–June 1915 33
Flight of the L 59, November 1917 39
Flying the 'Hump', 1944–5 179
Forward Operating Areas, August 1944 172

German Airship Construction Plants and Bases, 1918 36
German Invasion, August–September 1914 20
Guadalcanal, August–October 1942 143
Gulf War Baghdad Air Strikes, January–February 1991 214

Initial Operational Losses, March 1944 151
Invasion of Iraq, March–April 2003 216
Invasion of Malaya, September–December 1941 128
Invasion of Poland, September 1939 96
Island-Hopping Campaign, 1943–5 167
Italian Front, 1917–18 57
Italian Trans-Oceanic Flights, 1927–33 75
Italian–Turkish War, 1911 17

Japanese Attack on Pearl Harbor, The First Wave, December 1941 124
Japanese Attack on Pearl Harbor, The Second Wave, December 1941 125
Japanese War in China, 1937–41 89
Joffre's Wall', 1914–1915 23

Korean War, 1950–51 196

Largest German Airship Raid, September 1916 35
Largest Luftwaffe Raid, August 1940 108
Liberating Ukraine and the Crimea, January–May 1944 161
Long-Range Transport, 1934–9 91
Mediterranean, late 1942 116–7
Miracle of the Marne, August–September 1914 22
Moscow Anti-Aircraft Defences, September–December 1941 122

Nivelle's Plan for Victory, 1916–17 53
North Caucasus, January–April 1943 137

Operation Bagration, June–August 1944 181
Operation Barbarossa, June–October 1941 121
Operation Cartwheel, 1942-3 144–5
Operation Desert Storm, February 1991 215
Operation Focus, June 1967 207
Operation Market Garden, September 1944 174
Operation Merkur, May–June 1941 118–9
Operation Torch and its Aftermath, 1942–3 152–3
Operations Against Japan, February–August 1945 189

Panzer Strike Through the Ardennes, May 1940 103
Patrolling the Atlantic, 1939–45 169
Pearl Harbor, Battleship Positions, December 1941 126
Pioneering Routes, 1921–30 71

Rolling Thunder, 1965–8 204

Schlieffen Plan, 1914 20
Sicily and Southern Italy, July–December 1943 154
Silent Raid', October 1917 38
Spanish Civil War, 1936–38 86
Special Duties Operations, 1941–5 182
Strategic Bombing, 1943 146–7
Suez Crisis, 1956–7 206

Tannenberg and the Masurian Lakes, August–September 1914 25
Taranto Attack, November 1940 114
Transatlantic Crossing Routes, 1919–38 72–3
Treaty of Brest-Litovsk, March 1918 55

Warsaw Uprising, August–October 1944 183
Winter War, 1939–40 98
World Alliances, 1950–89 198

Yom Kippur War, October 1973 208

BIBLIOGRAPHY

Birkers, Richard Townshend, *The Battle of Britain*, Guild Publishing, 1990.
Budiansky, Stephen, *Air Power*, Viking, 2003.
Braithwaite, Rodric, *Moscow 1941*, Profile Books, 2006.
Dear, I.C.B. (Gen. Ed.), *Oxford Companion to the Second World War*, O.U.P., 1995.
Deighton, Len, *Blood, Tears and Folly*, Vintage, 2007.
Deighton, Len, *Fighter*, Vintage, 2008.
Dorr, Robert F., *Air War Hanoi*, Blandford Press, 1988.
Everitt, Chris and Middlebrook, Martin, *Bomber Command War Diaries*, Viking, 1985.
Freeman, Roger A., *The Mighty Eighth*, Weidenfeld Military, 2000.

Hastings, Max, *Korean War*, Pan Books, 1987.
Hastings, Max, *Nemesis, the Battle for Japan*, Harpor Perennial, 2008.
Hastings, Max, *Bomber Command*, Book Club Associates, 1979.
Isaacs, Jeremy and Downing, Taylor, *Cold War*, Bantam Press, 1998.
Layman, R.D., *Cuxhaven Raid*, Conway Maritime Press, 1985.
Levine, Joshua, *On a Wing and a Prayer*, Collins, 2008.
Macksey, Kenneth, *Technology of War*, Guild Publishing, 1986.
Myers, Richard B. and Boyne, Walter J., *Beyond the Wild Blue*, Thomas Dunne Books, 2007.
Pimlott, John, *Luftwaffe*, Aurum Press, 1998.